International Poli

International Police Cooperation
Emerging issues, theory and practice

Edited by

Frédéric Lemieux

WILLAN
PUBLISHING

Published by

Willan Publishing
Culmcott House
Mill Street, Uffculme
Cullompton, Devon
EX15 3AT, UK
Tel: +44(0)1884 840337
Fax: +44(0)1884 840251
e-mail: info@willanpublishing.co.uk
website: www.willanpublishing.co.uk

Published simultaneously in the USA and Canada by

Willan Publishing
c/o ISBS, 920 NE 58th Ave, Suite 300,
Portland, Oregon 97213-3786, USA
Tel: +001(0)503 287 3093
Fax: +001(0)503 280 8832
e-mail: info@isbs.com
website: www.isbs.com

First published 2010

ISBN   978-1-84392-760-0 paperback
        978-1-84392-761-7 hardback

British Library Cataloguing-in-Publication Data

A catalogue record for this book is available from the British Library

FSC
Mixed Sources
Product group from well-managed
forests and other controlled sources

Cert no. SGS-COC-2482
www.fsc.org
© 1996 Forest Stewardship Council

Project managed by Deer Park Productions, Tavistock, Devon
Typeset by GCS, Leighton Buzzard, Bedfordshire
Printed and bound by T.J. International, Padstow, Cornwall

"Genuine tragedies in the world are not conflicts
between right and wrong.
They are conflicts between two rights."

Georg Wilhelm Friedrich Hegel

Contents

Part II   Applied police cooperation: initiatives and limitations

Part III   Special issues on international police cooperation

Part IV Accountability and effectiveness in police cooperation

Acknowledgements

First of all, I would like to express my deepest gratitude to all contributors who made this project possible. I want to thank all of the authors for the originality and the high quality of the work they produced. This book represents a major contribution to the field of international police cooperation and achieving this objective in a short period of time was a heavy demand.

I want to thank the Social Sciences and Humanities Research Council of Canada as well as The George Washington Institute of Public Policy for their financial support. Research grants were crucial to conduct several interviews with police investigators working in Canada, Colombia, France, the Netherlands, the United States and Venezuela. Also, I was delighted to work with Brian Willan and his team. The confidence they had in the project and their judicious advice were instrumental to the realization of the book.

I am deeply indebted to my special assistant, Melinda Hull, who worked hard on the revision and editing of the chapters. Thank you Melinda for having been flexible and reliable and for offering excellent suggestions throughout the editing process. Finally, I am grateful to have few life-long friends who always supported me in the good times as well as in the bad. Thank you to Bernard L'Host, Nathalie Pageau and Mathieu Vaillancourt … *Merci pour votre écoute et surtout pour votre amitié!*

Frédéric Lemieux

List of abbreviations

ACCORD	African Centre for the Constructive Resolution of Disputes
ADF	Australian Defence Force
AFP	Australian Federal Police
AMIS	African Union Mission in Sudan
APSTA	The African Support Trainers Association
ARATS	Association for Relations Across the Taiwan Strait
ASF	African Standby Force
AWF	Analysis Work Files
CAF	Civilians Accompanying Military Forces
CCIP	Cross Channel Intelligence Conference
CEPOL	European College of Police
CPCC	Centres for Police and Custom Cooperation
CSIS	Canadian Security Intelligence Service
CT	Counter Terrorism
DEA	Drug Enforcement Administration (US)
EAW	European Arrest Warrant
ECIM	European Criminal Intelligence Model
ECOWAS	Economic Community of West African States
ECRIS	European Criminal Records System
EDU	European Drugs Unit
EIE	Europol Information Exchange
EIS	Europol Information System
EJN	European Judicial Network
ELO	Europol Liaison Officer
ELU	European Liaison Unit
ENJ	Europol National Units
EPDP	Executive Police Development Programme
EPICC	Euro-regional Police Information and Cooperation Centre
ESTA	Electronic System for Travel
EURODAC	European Fingerprint Database

EUROSUR	European Border Surveillance System
GNR	Guarda Nacional Republicana
GPOI	Global Police Operations Initiative
ICPO	International Criminal Police Organization
IDG	International Deployment Group
ILEA	International Law Enforcement Academies
IHL	International Human Rights
INSET	Integrated National Security Enforcement Team
IO	International Organization
IPCO	International Police Cooperation Organization
ISS	Institute for Security Studies
JHT	Joint Hit Team
JIT	Joint Investigation Team
JTTF	Joint Terrorism Task Forces
MACP	Military Aid to the Civil Power
MEJA	Military Extraterritorial Jurisdiction Act
NCIS	National Criminal Intelligence Service
NSB	National Security Branch
OCTA	Organized Crime Threat Assessment
OLAF	The European Anti-Fraud Office
PCC	Police Contributing Countries
PCCC	Police and Customs Cooperation Centre
PNR	Passenger Name Record
PSC	Peace and Security Council
PTAP	Police Training Assistance Programme
PWGOT	Police Working Group on Terrorism
RCMP	Royal Canadian Mounted Police
RECAMO	Reinforcement of African Peacekeeping Capabilities
RECs	Regional Economic Communities
RIS	Regional Integrated Squad
RLAU	Regional Legal Assistance Unit
SCCOPOL	Central Section for Operational Police Cooperation
SEF	Straits Exchange Foundation
SIS	Schengen Information System
SOCA	Serious Organized Crime Agency
TC	Transnational Crime
TCS	Transnational Commercial Security
UAV	Uninhabited Aerial Vehicle
UCMJUS	Code of Military Justice
VIS	Visa Information System

List of tables and figures

Notes on contributors

Stéphane Birrer is a PhD candidate at the Ecole des Sciences Criminelles, Lausanne University, Switzerland.

Monica den Boer is Academic Dean at the Police Academy of the Netherlands and holds the Police Academy Chair on Comparative Public Administration, in particular the Internationalization of the Police Function, VU University, the Netherlands.

Cyrille Fijnaut is Professor of International and Comparative Criminal Law at the Law School, Tilburg University, the Netherlands.

Andrew Goldsmith is Executive Director and Professor of Law at the Centre for Transnational Crime Prevention, University of Wollongong, Australia.

Nadia Gerspacher is Program Officer at the United States Institute of Peace in Washington, DC, the United States.

Laure Guille is a lecturer of Criminology at the University of Leicester, the United Kingdom.

Vandra Harris is a research fellow at the Flinders University Law School, Adelaide, Australia.

Les Johnston is a Professor of Criminology at the Institute of Criminal Justice Studies, University of Portsmouth, the United Kingdom.

Frédéric Lemieux is an Associate Professor and Director of Police Science and Security & Safety Leadership programs, The George Washington University, Washington DC, the United States.

John D. Occhipinti is Professor and Chair of the Department of Political Science and Director of European Studies at Canisius College, Buffalo, the United States.

Chantal Perras is a researcher and PhD candidate at the School of Criminology, University of Montreal, Canada.

Véronique Pujas (in memoriam) was a Primary Researcher at CNRS, Institut d'Études Politiques Grenoble (Science-PO Grenoble), France.

Olivier Ribaux is an Associate Professor at the Institut de Police Scientifique, University of Lausanne, Switzerland.

James Sheptycki is Professor and Chair of the Department of Criminology at York University, Toronto, Canada.

Philip C. Stenning is Professor at the Institute for Law, Politics and Justice, Keele University, the United Kingdom.

Toine Spapens is a senior research fellow at the Department of Criminal Law, Tilburg University, the Netherlands.

Elrena van der Spuy is an Associate Professor and is attached to the Centre of Criminology and Department of Public Law, University of Cape Town, South Africa.

Yungnane Yang is currently Professor and Associate Vice President for Research and Development, National Cheng Kung University (NCKU), Taiwan. He serves at the Department of Political Science and Institute of Political Economy. He is also a research fellow at the Center for Humanity and Social Sciences and the Sustainable Environment Research Center in NCKU.

Chapter 1

The nature and structure of international police cooperation: an introduction

Frédéric Lemieux

Generally, police cooperation refers to the intentional or unintentional interaction between two or more police entities (including private and public agencies) for the purposes of sharing criminal intelligence, conducting investigations, and ultimately apprehending suspects. International police cooperation is one dynamic by which criminal intelligence is shared across national and geo-political borders (Robertson 1994). It allows police services to tap information sources made available to them in other countries in order to better understand the *modus operandi* of their suspects. When information collected during an investigation is made available to foreign police agencies, it enables those organizations to identify the specific criminal activities of specific criminal groups and to develop a knowledge base about actual or potential criminal activity that occurs beyond their jurisdiction. Exchanging information gathered during criminal investigations not only establishes networks and links between police professionals (Bigo 1996), it also goes a long way in building trust based on the principles of reciprocity and communication (Anderson 2002). In addition, sharing information provides opportunities to develop crime-fighting strategies and determine the resources needed to conduct multilayered operations which often require the establishment of a team of interested foreign police officers.

International police cooperation allows investigators to organize their plan of attack more accurately since they gain more of a 'big picture' perspective and knowledge of the activities of the group/perpetrator being investigated. Since transnational crime displays a complete disregard for national boundaries, police services must be able to counter this behaviour with a relaxation of the concept of national jurisdiction. International police cooperation allows police operations to mirror this disregard by operating on an international scale and more accurately assessing the priorities of criminal groups (e.g. both vulnerabilities and threats). Finally, international police cooperation allows for the type of networking that is often credited with many successes.

In essence, effective police cooperation addresses inter-agency competition and investigation overlap. In reality, collaboration between law enforcement agencies is plagued by competing agendas, limited resources, and nationalistic/discretionary information-sharing. Furthermore, powerful national agencies tend to asymmetrically influence operational decisions without regard to the sovereignty principle. Indeed, national political preoccupations dictate police cooperation in terms of dynamics, management models, and structures. Inevitably, cultural and social norms, along with individual experiences, impact on inter-agency relations. Most studies focus on the reasons for the desirability of police cooperation as an approach to transnational crime, on the interactions between national police services, or on the challenges of keeping the collaborative process democratic and respectful of human rights.

In the first section of this introduction, I shall briefly expose the main theoretical perspectives on international police cooperation that have been developed by scholars over the past 30 years. The second section of this chapter outlines past and current international police cooperation structures deployed to address transnational crime. The third section presents an overview of existing training programmes related to international police cooperation. Finally, the fourth section introduces the contents of this book and underlines its originality in terms of approaches and applications.

Conceptual frameworks on international police cooperation

The growing literature on the issue of international police cooperation offers a variety of explanations as to how a multilateral fight against international criminal activity can provide significant support and guidance to national police authorities. It should be noted that the term *national* is used for a global level of analysis perspective. Thus, the term is meant to encompass all police authorities that make up the law enforcement institutions of a given country. We have an increasing awareness of the complexities inherent in law enforcement practices which aim to disregard national borders. We must keep in mind that the criminalization of specific acts is the premise for launching international crime control strategies, structures and procedures (Andreas and Nadelmann 2006). As only compatible laws can create the international enforcement mechanisms capable of addressing the problem of transnational crime, a criminal act standardization process has been initiated within certain political and operational circles. One can argue that there is a certain degree of Western hegemony in the criminalization of various activities, largely based on global prohibitions, whereas developing countries formulate or reformulate their criminal justice systems along the lines of those of Western countries (Andreas and Nadelmann 2006) or with the guidance of the legal departments of international police organizations (Gerspacher 2005).

Bigo (1996) offers a horizontal model which aims to redirect the perception that international police cooperation involves a common will or a specific project. Instead, international police cooperation takes place as a result of individual strategies, bureaucracy priorities, and/or particular interests pursued at specific moments in specific issue areas. This strategic pursuit leads to the construction of the required elements of police cooperation. These cooperative elements can be visualized as concentric circles that surround and impact on each other. There are three essential elements that foster police cooperation. The first is a geo-political consideration needed to create an international environment ripe for the exchange of information that has traditionally been secured along nationalist interests. Thus, cooperation rests on the ability of nation-states to create that environment through the negotiation of bilateral agreements, regional accords, and intergovernmental and/or supranational organizations.

A range of material criteria is the second element needed, as efforts to cooperate will be successful depending on the resources and competencies that are mobilized. These material considerations have been addressed in the creation of sophisticated technical forums such as Interpol, Europol, and the 'Club de Berne'. These data and analysis centres provide a framework which is built on the pooling of resources and expertise. A judicial environment that either recognizes the procedures of other states or is standardized is another important material criterion. In addition, diplomatic and political actors are also part of the material criteria, as they pave the way for the necessary legal conditions to encourage and facilitate cooperation.

Finally, the model includes an organizational element. The level of organizational institutionalization and the legitimacy of a multilateral agreements are also key variables; there are working groups (tripartite working groups), a non-institutionalized agreement (TREVI), and Interpol and Europol which are at the highest level of institutionalization of police cooperative efforts. Therefore, effective police cooperation depends on structural factors that nation-states must develop through compromise, standardization, and a mindset that embraces the internationalization of policing.

As with transnational crime, international police cooperation takes place under difficult and even hostile environmental conditions. The national agency that participates in a system of police cooperation faces numerous obstacles due to the incompatible nature of various structures, cultures, technologies, judicial procedures, policies, and politics which limit the impact of the cooperative behaviour. The asymmetry of the various structures of national police organizations (centralized and decentralized) results in a proliferation of agencies involved in the cooperation process and thus encourages the convergence of the communication channels (formal and informal) and the explosion of information sources (Den Boer 2002c). Furthermore, the cultural heterogeneity inherent in international cooperation introduces the potential to aggravate the ever-present lack of trust in police subcultures (Skolnick 1996). There are also myriad problems linked to the integration of information technology, as incompatibilities in systems can considerably complicate the establishment of informational bridges between police services (Sheptycki 2004). This phenomenon is particularly noticeable in northern hemisphere/ southern hemisphere cooperation efforts when the use of technology is often disproportionate.

Opportunities to exchange information between foreign police colleagues are present within the multi-layered framework in which cooperation occurs. Benyon (1996) offers a vertical model to demonstrate that police cooperation takes place at three interrelated levels of participation. These interrelated levels represent the various sets of actors that are involved in making the process work. There is a macro level which includes constitutional issues; a compliance with agreements; a coordination of legislation and national laws; rights; and ethical issues of policing. The actors at this level formulate policies and negotiate agreements, while safeguarding their respective places in the national supremacy. The meso level includes the operational structures, practices, and procedures of police and law enforcement agencies. The actors in this intermediary level serve as a buffer between the political and purely operational sets of actors and their interests. Liaison officers are a sophisticated but small group of police professionals who link policy makers with investigators and law enforcement practices and function at this level (Bigo 2002). Influences at the micro level include the investigation of specific offences and prevention and the control of particular forms of crime. These tasks are performed by police officials and police administrators whose duty is to enforce the laws unilaterally or in conjunction with foreign police institutions.

The coordination of police activities at the international level has been explained as a four-step model in which each phase furthers the capacity of police institutions to participate in an information exchange system, among other activities (Kube and Kuckuck 1992). First, an information exchange structure has to be established in order to provide appropriate channels between foreign police entities. Thus, the creation of a centralized location for computerized data exchange offers an opportunity for the sending and receiving of information. Next, collaboration is organized around common projects with a view toward the standardization of methods, instruments and procedures in order to render these compatible and thereby circumvent one of the most cited obstacles to effective cooperation. A third step is to establish working groups that receive information, analysis (finished intelligence), and the coordination of joint operations and/ or investigations from a centralized location or entity. Finally, the creation of a formal organization allows the coordination to become standardized, streamlined and practised. This formal organization can provide participating police institutions with assistance, guidance, and the competent coordination of joint projects using sophisticated analysis, threat assessment, and the strategy development tools that are much needed by these police institutions. Ultimately, international crime control initiatives require the collection of evidence that is admissible in the courts in the jurisdiction in which a case is being prosecuted. Much of the evidence in these types of cases comes from foreign sources and has to be collected in a manner that the relevant legal systems are designed to process and/or accept.

According to Deflem's (2004) model that is based on the bureaucratic nature of police structures, international police work is often justified by the ability to identify the centrality and commonality of international crime. Some states will put enormous pressure on the yield of their police activities, which in turn requires any other concerned states to be more actively involved in an investigation that they otherwise may not have prioritized. In other words, an international police organization with true international representation 'could only be formed when police institutions were sufficiently autonomous from the political centers of their respective national states to function as relatively independent bureaucracies' (Deflem 2000: 2). Only when relative autonomy from the respective national apparatus is achieved can foreign police colleagues begin to exchange on an operational level.

Structures of international police cooperation

It is increasingly rare for states and their police agencies to engage in the struggle against transnational crime unilaterally. Whether they opt to deploy their own networks of liaison officers to another's national police agencies or whether their policy is to participate in an international forum to facilitate police cooperation, states have already recognized that protecting their own territories from threats posed by transnational criminal activity forces them into interdependence. This interdependence specifically relates to the sharing of information, the exchange of expertise, and the standardization of criminal codes and investigation procedures. Multinational efforts aim for successes against the largest criminal groups by establishing political and operational channels to enhance the ability of the police to initiate and carry out investigations that will span two or more borders.

Effective international police cooperation requires that national police agencies restructure certain procedural conditions so they may operate beyond the constraints of their national jurisdiction. Once national police institutions are structured in such a manner that information can flow more easily, the police agencies must manage a shared system of practical knowledge, in terms of data and expertise on international crime. Specifically, national police institutions must have achieved a relatively autonomous relationship with other bureaucratic and political centres within their respective states. Inherent is a commitment to professional policing practices based on standards and the efficient use of resources, resulting in the transcendence of physical and legal national boundaries (Deflem 2002: 19–20).

The core function of such cooperation activity – the exchange of information – is set apart from traditional operational policing. We no longer distinguish only between the political elite and the operational policing, but depend instead on the contributions of the intermediary stratum of policing, the 'meso level' (Benyon et al. 1993). The liaison officer and other institutions, such as international information systems (Europol's EIS, Interpol's 24/7), facilitate and promote a collaboration that goes beyond national jurisdictions. These relatively new actors, whose position is marginal to the overall law enforcement mission of their respective police institutions, have become a sort of elite unit of police officers whose arena is international. Their stature as non-operational, sophisticated, and well-connected and experienced police professionals allow them to have a twofold mission. They codify and institutionalize operational policing at the international level and they legitimize institutionalized approaches by persuading the political actors in their respective states to make the resulting practices into laws (Bigo 1996, 2002). A handful of states, including the US, the UK, France, Germany, the Netherlands, and Australia, have established sophisticated investigative branches whose international duties include the enforcement of violations (such as drug trafficking) that have international implications. These states deploy a small, but powerful, system of liaison officers abroad and administer international police training programmes. However, most states are light years away from establishing such sophisticated networks that would allow them to protect their interests and participate in international law enforcement initiatives.

Treaties and agreements

The political arena provides a conundrum of policies that shape the environment in which law enforcement takes place. We must distinguish between the formal and informal environments which are both at play in international police cooperation. These policies can originate from an external, global context as part of international conventions designed to address drug control as part of larger trade treaties, as in the case of the EU's interest in controlling the exchange of drug precursors and manufacturing equipment, along with the drug substances themselves. In Europe, the building blocks of external drug control policies include the establishment of TREVI (1975); the Schengen Treaty (1985) and the Schengen Convention (1990); and the Maastricht Treaty recommendation to create Europol (1992) (Busch 1988; Fijnaut 1987; Le Jeune 1992). Alternatively, there are sectorial external policies that are specifically formulated in the areas of security, development, and enlargement (EU), or in the context of free trade agreements (Dorn 1996).

The formal environment has been organized on both global and regional levels to facilitate the exchange of information in a more homogeneous setting. The variety of treaties that have been drafted to facilitate and promote international police cooperation has influenced policy, practice, and processes. European-US cooperation, for example, did not take shape until the formation of Interpol in 1923, suggesting the role of formal agreements to induce a rapprochement in terms of policy and practice between states that are worlds apart in geographic terms. All in all, however, international police practices mostly include the enforcement of the law of the land in each respective country (Deflem 2003). The standardization of rules of law, judicial procedures, and rules of prosecution and admissibility of evidence still remains largely problematic, even though it is widely recognized that incompatible legal and justice systems represent a huge set of obstacles in the development and structuring of international police cooperation initiatives.

Regional initiatives have also encountered formative successes and challenges. In some instances, collaboration emanating from bilateral treaties proves difficult to achieve due to political conditions in one or both of the concerned states, as has been the case between the US and Mexico (Deflem 2001: 72). While the challenges to international police cooperation are numerous, one reality that is grounded in the multi-jurisdictional nature of most national law enforcement infrastructures stands out. In most cases, international policing efforts are little more than local law enforcement initiatives that are joined together with those of national agencies, whether specialized or not (Andreas and Nadelmann 2006).

International police cooperation structures

One of the approaches to ensure smooth information sharing between sovereign states and their respective police institutions is the adopting of international cooperation agreements that can translate into the creation of intergovernmental organizations based on international treaties. The European Police Office is the intergovernmental organization whose mission is to facilitate police cooperation among its membership of 25 EU states with regard to a list of transnational crimes that now spans 18 forms of crime. Europol has enjoyed a rapid development and substantial support at the political level (namely from EU ministers), evolving from the European Drugs Unit (EDU) in 1995 into a large secretariat that now employs over 300 people: Europol has enlarged its mandate from the inside out.

Today, Europol has an extensive array of products including analysis and assessment, along with a sophisticated communication system using state-of-the-art technology and highly skilled police professionals who man the system and promote its use and accuracy.

As a result, this international body has become a knowledge broker whose ability to initiate, lead, and support has surpassed the confines of its own mandate that was drafted just a decade ago. Participation in the information-sharing system has increased dramatically, even by those countries that were initially very reluctant to do so. Further, Europol represents a regional initiative that responded to the limitations that heterogeneity and size place on the ability to foster international police cooperation. Europol has enlarged its intelligence-sharing capacity through informal entrepreneurship and initiatives that promote the development of national information flow systems, knowledge, and expertise in fighting transnational crime from a strategic perspective. Its developmental curve has not reached a plateau yet, as it has encountered challenges to its organization and structure, including its lack of built-in accountability (Bruggeman 2002; Den Boer 2008).

Another multilateral forum is the International Criminal Police Organization (ICPO-Interpol). Interpol is an apolitical organization whose contributions to the fight against transnational crime include a secure intranet to facilitate communication between foreign police colleagues; the diffusion of arrest warrants; the standardized criminalization of certain offences; and the negotiation of cooperation agreements, guidance which is especially attractive to developing or transitioning countries (Bressler 1992; Fooner 1989). Since international police structures and mechanisms rely on institutional interdependence among police institutions, professional expertise and the efficiency of structures (Deflem 2002), Interpol emphasizes the coordination and networking benefits inherent in the global rule of law enforcement (Deflem 2006). The Interpol secretariat, with its network of liaison officers dispersed in several regions of the world, and the National Central Bureaus together represent the most important global police cooperation structure.

Institutionalized regional initiatives also exist. In Europe, Joint Investigation Teams (JITs) have been established by mutual agreement between two or more member states of the EU. A JIT consists of a team of national experts who can provide rapid technical and operational assistance to member states on a bilateral or multilateral basis. Despite its existence on paper since 2002, experience in the member states regarding the use of Joint Investigation Teams is still limited. According to Brady (2008), EU national police agencies have only set up a few teams and none involves more than two countries. The author suggests that setting up JITs is overly bureaucratic and operating them is complicated. Since major improvements are needed, police investigators prefer to use traditional procedures or informal agreements.

Another example, though less recent this time, is the Police and Custom Cooperation Centre (PCCC). Several PCCCs have been established in the past two decades to ensure that law enforcement forces on both sides of national borders can work together. This bilateral form of cooperation involves exchanges of information, joint operations and controls, and the planning of coordinated security actions. However, several issues have been raised regarding the expansion of PCCC's activities addressing security matters far from transborder regions, and the lack of information exchanges between PCCCs.

More recently, the European Union Justice Ministers have discussed the content of the Stockholm Programme and tried to set up the first 'domestic security strategy for the EU'. The paper presented by the Commission calls for stricter border controls, a better exchange of information on criminal and security issues between the member states, and an increased police cooperation both with Europe and with non-member states. The forthcoming agenda will clearly emphasize the creation of new (or a significant improvement of existing) securization structures and tools which have already triggered a wide range of critics. The case of Frontex as a new security structure constitutes a good example.[1] Frontex was created mainly to integrate the national border security systems of member states against all kind of threats that could happen at or through an external border of member states of the European Union. This agency promotes a pan-European model of 'integrated border security' based on: 1) information and cooperation between Member States on immigration and repatriation; 2) surveillance, border checks and risk analysis; 3) cooperation with border guards, customs, and police authorities in non EU neighbouring countries; and 4) cooperation with third countries such as the United States and its Department of Homeland Security[2] (Frontex 2008).

International police cooperation systems

Currently, the European authorities are completing the implementation of a revised version of the Schengen Information System (SIS-II), a inter-governmental database system used by several European countries for the purpose of maintaining and distributing information related to border security and law enforcement (Schengen Agreement 1985).

In addition to this, few other information systems have been recently modified or incepted: examples here are the Passenger Name Record (PNR) and the Visa Information System (VIS).[3]

In the near future, Frontex and EU member states' police authorities will have access to a new and upcoming information system to enforce and improve border controls: the European border surveillance system (EUROSUR). This system will aim to improve the detection of cross-border movements by using a technical framework required for synchronous cooperation and will enable an information-sharing environment among national and European systems. Other securization tools have already been or will be implemented in Europe. For example, EURODAC (a European fingerprint database), has been in operation since 2003 and is designed to identify asylum seekers. The member states of EURODAC transmit fingerprints on three categories of persons over 14 years old: 1) individuals who apply for asylum; 2) third country nationals apprehended while illegally crossing a member state's border; and 3) third country nationals found illegally residing in a country within a member state.

In addition, in 2008, the European Data Protection Supervisor (EDPS) published a positive opinion toward the creation of an electronic European Criminal Records Information System (ECRIS). ECRIS would be a criminal record database available to member states, that would include citizens' criminal convictions. ECRIS will be based on a *decentralized* information technology system consisting of three elements: 1) a criminal records database in each member state; 2) a common communication infrastructure; and 3) interconnection software. The EU Commission will be the provider of the communication network. The S-TESTA[4] system will be the common communication infrastructure and the Commission will also be qualified as the controller for data protection purposes (European Data Protection Supervisor 2009). In fact, the main mission of the European Data Protection Supervisor is to make sure that the fundamental right regarding the protection of personal data is respected by the European Union's institutions and bodies.

Finally, the Europol Information System (EIS) is made up of three components: the IT information system, work files, and an index system. The data concern persons who, under the national law of a member state, are suspected of having committed or having taken part in a criminal offence for which Europol has jurisdiction or who have already been convicted of such an offence (Europol 2008). Figure 1.1 shows the progression of criminal intelligence-sharing (information exchanges) since the inception of the European Police Office.

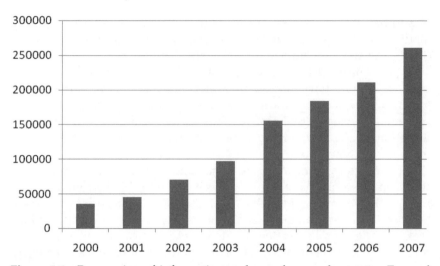

Figure 1.1 Progression of information exchange by member states, Europol units, non-European Union states and international organizations, from 2000 until 2007.

Unfortunately there are currently no common or shared information systems in North America that are comparable with European databases. In North America, multilateral police cooperation between Canada, Mexico, and the US is not very well developed (Deflem 2001). The US authorities have preferred to cooperate in a bilateral mode setting, using Integrated Investigation Teams as well as a Fusion Centre dedicated to conducting joint investigations and exchanging intelligence in the monitoring of trans-border regions. Also, large national police agencies like the US Federal Bureau of Investigation (FBI), the US Drug Enforcement Administration (DEA), and the Royal Canadian Mounted Police (RCMP) rely on extensive liaison officer networks with a global reach.

Indeed, formal organizations have contributed significantly to police cooperation in intended and unintended ways. While the training and development of a national information flow system and other such capacity-building functions were not included in the original mandate of these organizations, they have initiated programmes that assist in these areas in order to facilitate cooperation internationally in matters of justice. These international structures have been described as strategic agents of change that pursue their interests based on relevance and resources (Barnett and Coleman 2005). However, institutionalized police cooperation relies on high degrees of institutional dependence and heavy bureaucratic mechanisms and processes among police institutions. This situation continues to deter several police officers and investigators from using formal cooperation structures, as they prefer instead to utilize informal professional networks to exchange information with their foreign counterparts (Lemieux 2006).

Training: preparing the next generation of global police officers

Police cooperation training is an area that still remains little explored by scholars. During the past two decades, several formative programmes have been created to address the lack of 'practical knowledge' on international crime trends and investigation procedures (e.g. legal frameworks, variations in judicial system components). Actually, a review of past and current training initiatives shows that programmes related to police cooperation can take many forms, be offered in several formats, and delivered by a variety of institutions. This section examines selected training programmes from the following four perspectives: 1) procedural; 2) analytical; 3) offered by a national entity; 4) offered by an international entity. Procedural training is usually centred on organizational or governmental IT systems, information-sharing procedures, and any specialized investigative process (criminal analysis, joint investigation, etc.). Analytical training focuses on specific domestic, regional, or worldwide security issues and crime trends, especially the jurisdiction level of a given institution providing nationally- or internationally-oriented police cooperation training. The European College of Police (CEPOL) represents an excellent example of an international institution within the European Union that provides analytical training on the security issues that police cooperation initiatives often attempt to address. CEPOL was established in 2005 and its governing board is constituted mainly of directors from national police training colleges. This network of colleges has developed a diverse array of seminars that can be offered to senior police officers in order to address the common security problems encountered by European police forces. According to a recent report published by CEPOL (2008), a total of 85 courses and seminars were delivered by 28 member states and associated countries last year alone, representing a sharp increase of 50 per cent since its inception. The actual number of participants attending a CEPOL activity was estimated at 1900, with an average attendance of 23 participants per activity. A total of 762 instructors[5] contributed to CEPOL training activities (CEPOL 2008). Other international institutions, such as Europol, the European Anti-Fraud Office (OLAF), the Chiefs of Police Task Force, Eurojust, Interpol, the European Commission, and the Council of the European Union, have also participated in these programmes. The core curriculum of CEPOL courses and seminars mainly covers international security issues related to serious crime[6] and these are delivered in more than ten languages. CEPOL has also developed an e-library, international discussion forums, and an electronic journal (the *European Police Science and Research Bulletin*) covering a variety of topics related to international policing.

In contrast to CEPOL, the primary mission of Interpol is not to offer training programmes, but rather to facilitate cross-border police cooperation worldwide. Even though it is not its primary mission, Interpol delivered a total of 83 police training programmes[7] to 2,722 participants coming from 169 countries in 2008 (Interpol 2009). More importantly, Interpol generally trains participants on its own systems and services through seminars and hands-on experience at the General Secretariat which is located in France. By offering such training, Interpol aims to reinforce the capacity of national police agencies to contribute and more effectively use Interpol's resources. The international police organization also offers an Executive Police Development Programme (EPDP) which provides training to African law-enforcement officers at senior management level. The agency is currently developing a distance-learning capacity, a web-based learning platform via its Global Learning Centre. Similarly, Europol offers procedural as well as analytical training. From a procedural standpoint, the agency delivers training on its internal systems and services, covering topics such as data protection, new IT technologies, computer skills, project management, intercultural management, languages, media relations, and administrative specialization. On its own initiative or by request, Europol will provide analytical training regarding its priority crime areas to member states, non-European Union states, and international organizations. The agency also provides regular courses in operational and strategic intelligence analysis (Europol 2008: 36–37).

Examples of police cooperation training at a national level are undoubtedly more frequent than on an international level, and are exceptionally diversified. A first example comes from the Police Staff College in the United Kingdom, where a European Senior Detectives' Course was offered in the late 1990s. This training aimed to develop the knowledge and skills of senior detectives coming primarily from other European countries. More precisely, the goal was to improve the officers' English language skills, enhance their cultural understanding of the United Kingdom and its policing structure, disseminate information on problems facing policing in the United Kingdom, and compare policing issues in the United Kingdom with those of the participants' home countries (Frost 1996).

Government institutions, such as the German Ministry of the Interior, offer comprehensive briefings, training measures and consultancy, fact-finding trips, and internships to promote judicial cooperation with foreign countries. At a domestic level, the Ministry grants police training and equipment assistance as an integral part of international cooperation. The main goal pursued by this training is the standardization of police cooperation procedures within Germany and to foster the establishment and consolidation of democratic structures in those countries that generate security problems which then spill over into Germany.[8] Another example of procedural training delivered by a government entity is found in the case of the Australian government which has also initiated a procedural and cooperative initiative with other regional countries to strengthen their capacity to fight terrorism. In the aftermath of the Bali bombing, the Regional Legal Assistance Unit (RLAU) provides training, legislative assistance, and legal advice to Southeast Asian countries. The RLAU delivers workshops and training on legal concepts and international responsibilities in order to improve the capacity of domestic legal regimes to counter terrorism.[9] Finally, some governments will also sponsor analytical training on specific criminal problems in other countries. In 2008 for example, the Ghana Police Service, in collaboration with the French government, organized a one-week training session on procedures to fight money laundering and corruption generated by organized crime. This training initiative was funded by the French Embassy in Ghana.

Several large national police agencies are also involved in police cooperation training at the international level. In addition to internal training for their own workforce, these national agencies provide training on a consulting basis. For example, the DEA has conducted international counter-narcotics training since 1969. The DEA provides advanced training in specialized investigative techniques by focusing on drug trafficking in a specific region. In fact, the DEA acts as an international consultant to law enforcement agencies and foreign governments seeking to develop narcotics law enforcement programmes, organizational infrastructure, and judicial reforms.[10] The FBI also offers international training to foreign national police agencies via its International Law Enforcement Academies (ILEA), which deliver courses on leadership and investigative techniques, as well as specialized seminars on several security issues. The FBI heads facilities in Hungary, and offers seminars at national police academies located in Thailand, Botswana, and San Salvador.[11] Finally, we should also mention that the RCMP administers a Police Training Assistance Program (PTAP), providing learning activities to personnel working within the international police community. The aim of this programme is to increase foreign police officers' skills and knowledge in operational and administrative matters. The RCMP delivers its programme in more than 20 countries worldwide, especially where police apparatuses are being rebuilt or reformed.[12]

Despite the growing popularity of so-called police cooperation training, constructive criticism can be offered on both the curriculum contents and learning approaches. First, international police cooperation is highly politicized and the training often reflects nationalistic or organizational agendas. Some seminars, workshops, and courses do attempt to define a specific crime issue as a common priority target, enlarge the scope of information systems and data gathering, harmonize investigative methods and procedures, and promote specialized analytical services. In fact, police cooperation training can constitute a perfect political forum for influencing global or regional law-enforcement practices (see the chapter by Gerspacher and Lemieux in this book). This is especially the case when training is designed by Western countries and delivered to national police forces from developing countries (see Lemieux in this book). Second, the focus of regional cooperation in police training should go beyond the scope of the modular operational training issues. It should also emphasize the politics of leadership and management at the senior and middle levels by sharing best practices and transferring knowledge from relevant industrial and business management models. Third, the police cooperation training curriculum must include learning objectives oriented toward the development of essential competencies and skills to improve police officers' social abilities and networking capacities, intercultural communication and political etiquette, and knowledge of diplomatic concerns related to crime trends and security problems. Finally, a police cooperation training approach should go beyond informative and practical knowledge and address conceptual thinking related to transnational crime, criminal groups and legal frameworks, especially for key actors like legal advisers, prosecutors, criminal analysts, and lead investigators. Enhancing the conceptualization capacity at the investigative, legal and analytical levels can improve the capacity of national and international police agencies to develop innovative practices, novel legal strategies that foster civil liberties, and security programmes adapted to regional or domestic realities.

Yet, enhancing the effectiveness of international police cooperation cannot be accomplished solely by relying on adequate training programmes. Police officers and law enforcement agencies work under specific frameworks. Their actions are shaped by certain patterns or drivers in order to successfully conduct international investigations. The next section highlights the differences in police cooperation between Europe and the United States by examining how political drivers and leadership patterns influence cooperative modes.

Emerging issues in police cooperation

As the border disputes and debates that rage between the US and Mexico or Turkey and the EU indicate, international law enforcement largely remains the function of local and national police agencies. While the political actors of most states in the international community have acknowledged the desirability of international police cooperation as suggested by the various bilateral and multilateral agreements that now exist, implementing this on an operational level has suffered from a lack of support. The resulting lack of capacity at an operational level translates into countless missed opportunities to gain access to information gathered on foreign soil, but which is pertinent to a domestic investigation. States have attempted to address the problem from a variety of angles, including the creation of formal intergovernmental structures (Europol and Schengen); the setting up of UN agencies (UNDCP and UNOCCP); the adoption of informally-created instruments as internationally legitimized forums (Interpol); the negotiation of bilateral agreements based on the needs of police professionals as their investigations require them to go overseas (Cross Channel Intelligence Conference – CCIC); and the networks of liaison officers that wealthy states have strategically deployed across the globe.

Nevertheless, recent trends have emerged that attempt to address the recurrent obstacles in international police cooperation. New initiatives transcend traditional cooperation structures and systems and unconventional collaborations between private and public security sectors are being formed as well (Gerspacher and Dupont 2007). These recent trends are occurring worldwide, possessing their own particularities and requiring a review of current conceptual frameworks and practicalities.

This book presents a compilation of original research conducted by established academics and rising researchers who study the most recent trends in police cooperation. More specifically, this book examines cooperation opportunities and initiatives (practices and processes) undertaken by agencies themselves and those resulting from external changes (legal, political and economic realities). By using an extended and recent empirical corpus, contributors explore emerging initiatives and new challenges in several contexts at both national and international levels. Authors adopt a diversity of approaches and theoretical frameworks to reach a broader understanding of current and future issues in police cooperation. Forms of police cooperation and trends in transnational crime control are examined in relation to concepts drawn from the following disciplines: criminology, ethics, organizational science, political science, and sociology. Theoretical and practical approaches are proposed to understand police cooperation evolution and provide multidisciplinary examination of trends around the globe. This book will help policy makers, law enforcement leaders and students to understand the current changes and issues in police cooperation. The purpose of this book is also to highlight the outcomes of police cooperation.

This book is divided into four sections. The first section addresses current conceptual issues in police cooperation. More precisely, *Laure Guille* scrutinizes the differences and similarities between multilateral and bilateral cooperation in criminal matters at the European level. Relying on data gathered from four different countries (France, Spain, the United Kingdom, and Luxembourg), the author examines if Europol and Eurojust add more value to police cooperation actions than do the traditional bilateral relations, or whether bilateral cooperation actually works better than multilateral cooperation, and what the reasons are for such a situation. In the same section, *Monica den Boer* analyses the development of European police cooperation from an evolutionary governance point of view. The chapter applies four theoretical governance perspectives to the development of international policing, namely neo-functionalism, liberal inter-governmentalism, multi-level governance, and network governance. These perspectives predict different outcomes as to how police cooperation in Europe is organized and governed. A leading question in this chapter is whether nation-states will transfer power if and when policing continues to develop itself along a networked style of governance. Finally, *Nadia Gerspacher* and *Frédéric Lemieux* examine how Europol operates in an environment of overlapping information exchange systems with several technological means at its disposal aimed specifically at enhancing cooperation. The authors demonstrate how Europol is increasingly mobilizing its informal networks to influence the way member states exchange information, engage in joint activities, and contribute to the harmonization of the legal framework of international police cooperation and the standardization of information exchange processes.

The second section addresses some recent initiatives and limitations related to specific and applied forms of police cooperation. In this section, *Olivier Ribaux* and *Stéphane Birrer* look at the specific development and evolution of a regional analysis centre in Switzerland. Having a particularly scattered security system, Switzerland possesses all types of cooperation problems between all types of organizations, from a local to an international level. Relying on this background, the authors describe how difficult it is to recognize intractable difficulties within cooperative systems that are in need of rational frameworks. Ribaux and Birrer show there is a movement toward more iterative and adaptive methods when police cooperation initiatives have to cope with a complex and continuously changing environment. In Chapter 6, *Cyrille Fijnaut* and *Toine Spapens* address the developments of cross-border crime and safety issues in the Meuse-Rhine Euroregion. More precisely, they scrutinize the practical solutions that have already been devised to enhance law enforcement cooperation. Fijnaut and Spapens also outline recent developments related to the legal framework for police and judicial cooperation in the broad context of the European Union and, more specifically, of the Netherlands, Belgium and Germany. Thirdly, *Chantal Perras* and *Frédéric Lemieux* examine the convergence of police cooperation by comparing police investigations of organized crime and terrorism in Canada. The authors suggest that cooperation models applied to organized crime investigations have been replicated to other forms of serious crime such as terrorism. Perras and Lemieux examine whether there is evidence of a diffusion of innovations between fields of criminal investigation and a national security operation. The primary focus of this chapter is the interaction between social learning and knowledge transfer that perhaps explains the structural adaptations of multi-jurisdictional structures committed to fighting terrorism. Finally, *Nadia Gerspacher* identifies and analyses the sources of changes in cooperative behaviour in the relationship between France and Europol. Gerspacher examines recent figures showing that France's participation in the Europol information system has increased significantly in recent years. This chapter retraces the factors explaining why a French utilization of Europol services has rotated amongst the top three positions out of 25 member states of Europol and does better than the most traditionally cooperative European countries in terms of information exchange.

The third section addresses special cooperation issues occurring in different regions of the world and outlines current and future challenges related to international police cooperation. In this section, *John D. Occhipinti* explores recent developments related to police cooperation between the United States and the European Union in counter-terrorism matters. The author analyses legal and institutional changes in both the US and the EU, and compares them by focusing on three areas of common goals, namely information-sharing, leadership and coordination. This chapter also examines US cooperation with Europol because of the emphasis placed on judicial cooperation, container security, airline security and travel documents. Afterward, *Yungnane Yang* and *Frédéric Lemieux* examine the incentives and problems of cross-strait police cooperation between China and Taiwan. The chapter analyses the political and institutional considerations that compelled Chinese police to cooperate with Taiwan authorities. The authors scrutinize several judicial cases which demonstrate just how complex police cooperation can be in a highly politicized environment. Thirdly, *Elrena van der Spuy* explores recent debates and developments relating to the role of the police in peacekeeping efforts in Africa, set against the background of international developments on the continent. In this chapter, the level of policy engagement and issues relating to the politics and logistics of implementation are considered with a view to understanding the challenges likely to confront the integration and deployment of police contingents in future peace interventions. Finally, *Andrew Goldsmith* and *Vandra Harris* look at how Australian police deployed in Timor-Leste and the Solomon Islands between 2003 and 2008 have dealt with the military forces of Australia and outside military entities (mainly UN missions). The chapter examines how stability operations worked, or didn't work, in particular cases, including the challenges of dealing with looting and arson in urban areas. The authors draw upon a unique data set of interviews with Australian policing personnel involved in joint police/military missions that outline the innovations as well as the limitations related to 'inter-operability' issues.

The last section of the book addresses several concerns related to police cooperation accountability and effectiveness. Firstly, *Nadia Gerspacher* and *Véronique Pujas* examine the origins and developments of two IPCOs, Interpol and Europol, in order to better understand what prevents states and their national law enforcement agencies from benefiting from the IPCO they formed. This chapter shows that IPCOs have developed, at different rates, as 'informal entrepreneurs' by introducing capacity-building initiatives in order to fulfill their mandates and establish their legitimacy in the expanding security market. Secondly, *Frédéric Lemieux* assesses the outcomes of major international investigations initiated by the US's DEA. An assessment of police cooperation gives an opportunity to measure the effectiveness of the DEA's international joint investigations and helps to gauge indirectly the fundamental nature of international police cooperation: criminal intelligence sharing. This chapter offers an original assessment approach of international police cooperation and criminal intelligence sharing outcomes. In the following chapter, *Les Johnston* and *Philip C. Stenning* explore the challenges of policing accountability in a cooperative globalized environment. More precisely, they examine the growing diversity of policing provisions, and the new 'policing family' that includes an increasing diversity of 'public' (state-sponsored) policing providers, as well as a host of 'private' and civil society providers. Collectively, these providers have posed major challenges for effective and coherent regimes of governance and public accountability. The authors scrutinize these developments at the international level, explore the challenges for effective governance and accountability that they pose, and consider some of the possibilities for meeting these challenges. Finally, *James Sheptycki* presents a chapter that applies the notion of a 'constabulary ethic' to transnational policing by proposing a reflection on what William Ker Muir (1972) identified as the four paradoxes of coercion and contextualizing the issues for a world that has gone global. The aim of the chapter is to take the insights Muir developed about the ethics of 'street corner politicians' and then to elaborate on the general philosophical lessons that are applicable to policing the global polity.

Notes

1 Frontex is composed of operational heads of national border guard services and representatives of the European Commisson.
2 Currently, Frontex and the DHS have set up a working arrangement on the establishment of operational cooperation which includes the exchange of strategic information, training, capacity building and collaboration on technology interoperability.

3 VIS will be supported by two computer centres connecting 3,500 consular posts worldwide and 12,000 users in 30 participating countries. More information is available at http://europa.eu/legislation_summaries/justice_freedom_security/free_movement_of_persons_asylum_immigration/l14517_en.htm

4 According to *European eGovernment Services*: 'STESTA offers a telecommunications interconnection platform that responds to the growing need for secure information exchange between European public administrations. It is a European IP network, similar to the Internet in its universal reach, but dedicated to inter-administrative requirements and providing guaranteed performance levels.' For more information consult http://ec.europa.eu/idabc/en/document/2097/5644

5 The majority of instructors came from Portugal (73), France (61), Germany (60), Italy (53), the United Kingdom (40), Spain (39), the Netherlands (34) and Austria (31).

6 Curriculum topics covered several security issues such as Domestic Violence; Money Laundering and Trafficking in Human Beings; Counter Terrorism Civilian Crisis Management; Drug Trafficking; and the Management of Diversity.

7 Training programmes covered topics such as bioterrorism; criminal intelligence analysis; crisis and major events; DNA and fingerprints; drugs; forensics; high tech crime; intellectual property rights; organized crime; stolen motor vehicles; trafficking in cultural property; and human trafficking.

8 Source: http://www.en.bmi.bund.de/cln_028/nn_1159784/Internet/Content/Themen/Police/DataAndFacts/International__police__co__operation__training__and__equipment__aid.html

9 Source: http://www.ag.gov.au/www/agd/agd.nsf/Page/International DevelopmentAssistance_RegionalLegalAssistanceUnit

10 Source: http://www.usdoj.gov/dea/programs/training/part18.html

11 Source: http://www.fbi.gov/hq/td/academy/itp/itp.htm

12 Source: http://www.rcmp-grc.gc.ca/fs-fd/ipt-fpi-eng.htm

Part I

Current conceptual issues in police cooperation

Chapter 2

Police and judicial cooperation in Europe: bilateral versus multilateral cooperation

Laure Guille

The Single European Market, the dismantling of frontier controls within the European Union, and the free movement of persons and capital require a closer coordination and cooperation between national law enforcement agencies, as in such a European area criminality is changing and moving very fast. Indeed it seems to be moving faster than police and judicial/prosecutorial action, as criminal justice personnel are often restricted to national boundaries. The sphere of police and judicial cooperation in Europe has experienced huge growth in the last 20 years. There has been considerable research looking at structures for transnational cooperation and the legal dimension of the instruments involved in this domain, as well as many speculations on how it would work in the future. However, very little research has been undertaken on what happens in practice and showing how the instruments are working at present. Moreover, almost nothing has been written from the perspective of the practitioners who have to use these instruments. Most research has taken the perspective of legislators or policy makers, with rare exceptions being, for example, Gallagher (1998) and Sheptycki (2002), who have undertaken work on the Anglo-French border, and Maguer (2004) who has looked at the French-German border.

The findings presented in this chapter are part of more comprehensive research[1] which has explored shifts in police and judicial cooperation in Europe, analysing the current levels of efficiency and the limitations of European instruments of cooperation and looking at transnational law enforcement action nationally and bilaterally to allow each of the pieces of the puzzle to fit together into a European picture. It particularly focuses on how practitioners experience and view the different methods of cooperation. In order to complete the picture as fully as possible, the research also included work on understanding and the use of the developments, changes, functioning and evolution of strategies, agencies and structures at a multilateral level, including Schengen and the European Judicial Network, with Europol and Eurojust being the main focus points.

As there are different legal systems in Europe which vary considerably, it is important to consider transnational cooperation from the point of view of a variety of countries. This research therefore specifically investigated four different European countries, namely France, Luxembourg, Spain and the UK, to compare their level of involvement in matters of cooperation, explore how practitioners work in practice, and see what means are made available for them to undertake their duties. Indeed, if practitioners lack information on the various instruments available for cooperation and if governments do not provide translation in the field of the initiatives adopted at the macro level, cooperation cannot be fully achieved. In addition to these four countries, two borders were also examined – the French-Spanish Catalonian border and the Anglo-French border at Folkestone – so that the European picture could be complemented.

As the cornerstone of the research was to look at inter-country police, prosecution and judicial assistance on criminal matters in practice, the investigation was, hence, based on an empirical model, with face-to-face interviews[2] conducted in various countries with police officers, civil servants, prosecutors, customs, diplomatic representatives at the Council of the European Union, liaison officers, liaison magistrates and members of the judiciary, as well as members of Europol and Eurojust, and combined with periods of observation – such as at border zones and in centres for police and customs cooperation – and internships[3] undertaken in relevant institutions – such as Europol.

The major question is whether bilateral cooperation works more effectively than multilateral police and judicial cooperation for practitioners, such as the police, and what the reasons are for such a situation. Whereas bilateral and informal cooperation are the oldest forms of cooperation (Anderson *et al.* 1995; Bigo 1994, 1996; Deflem 2002; Elsen 2007), having existed for years, Europol, Eurojust and the European Judicial Network (EJN) are relatively new instruments. In the European context, and with an increasing trend towards transnational crime, is bilateral cooperation being left aside and taken over by multilateral cooperation at a supra-national level?

Bilateral cooperation

Until now, informal and bilateral levels of cooperation have prevailed, and still do, over the formal and European level, as all the interviewees from the empirical research admitted preferring to work on a bilateral basis despite the clear tendency towards a globalization of crime. The fundamental elements necessary for cooperation are based on trust and communication. In Robertson's terms (1994: 112), 'Where cooperation exists, there is trust and where there is trust, there is cooperation'. This statement has definitely been confirmed by the research. According to the literature (Anderson 2002; Gallagher 1998; Sheptycki 1998a, 2002), the interviewees and all the findings from the study, for efficient cooperation amongst practitioners there is no doubt that personal and informal contacts and the good will of the people involved in the process are key elements in terms of trust and speed. An example would be the case of an Iranian driver stopped by the British officers in the English control zone (located in France) at the Eurotunnel terminal. His documentation was checked and a stamp on his passport forbidding him entry into Denmark was found. As a consequence, the European Liaison Unit (ELU)[4] officers immediately checked with the Danish authorities to determine the reason for the ban as they have direct contact with the forces of that country. The Danish database and the Security Danish team in charge of terrorism matters checked the details but the driver had only been recorded for 'normal' criminality. The point to make here is that all the checks were done using a coordination of both countries' forces and that the most important information, particularly that regarding any potential terrorism links, was received in ten minutes and the complete information in two hours. The police forces in charge of the case explained that if the same case had gone through the Europol network, a delay of several days would have been necessary to receive the same details. The authorities cannot handle such a long time-scale as they have a person who is being physically held at the border. This shows that phoning a colleague is a much faster solution, on which one can really rely, than going through a centralized European organization, which would take much longer to find a solution.

A similar comment was also made by several liaison officers based in Europol when admitting that they would prefer to phone a colleague as it speeds up the investigation and because less bureaucracy is involved in the process, a point also raised when several interviewees referred to the need to create direct contacts abroad in order to avoid going through the UK Central Authority (UK CA) which in their view has too many layers of bureaucracy.[5] The effectiveness of just picking up the phone in order to create a network of personal contacts also appears in the 2005 Evaluation Report of the European Judicial Network[6] and is mentioned in Nelken (1991, 1994) and Sheptycki (2002). The key to successful cooperation is to trust each other so that processes of mutual legal assistance can be speeded up and also in order that any type of information can be received more easily. Unfortunately, most of the time this 'trust-giving' feature cannot be developed in formal and institutionalized organizations.

Police cooperation at the individual case and practitioner level is driven by efficiency rather than by formal methods of cooperation, which is why personal contacts – and therefore trust – play such a major role in efficient cooperation. Many examples can again be cited in this context, such as the successful outcome of a large-scale potential fraud which criminals were believed to be committing in the UK. An international *commission rogatoire* (letter of request)[7] was issued by the German authorities to the UK to visit premises and locate, detain and extradite the people involved in the fraud. They also wanted to interrogate neighbours and check telephone numbers. German officers came to the UK to execute the commission rogatoire and the case ended successfully. It was a very complex file but was dealt with more quickly than some much easier files. A key element here was the good relations the English forces had with the German authorities. Another point of interest is the informal networking that occurs between the various Centres for Police and Customs Cooperation (CPCC) and between the CPCCs and the European Liaison Unit (ELU). CPCCs are often in contact with each other. For example, if the Spanish authorities need to check some information with German counterparts, they would request the information of the French officers in the French-Spanish CPCC who would in turn contact their colleagues in the French-German CPCC. According to all the officers such a network ensures rapidity and avoids linguistic problems. However, a senior officer at central level in Paris explained that this situation should not be permitted as CPCCs should only support border areas. Yet due to real needs in the field, an extensive network of interlaced CPCCs has started to appear. In the same context, the ELU does not have any official agreement with the CPCCs but is often in contact with these and has made many contacts. Whether this network of communication is allowed or not remains an open question. But a police officer from the ELU did comment that the CPCCs in France have developed a whole network which works very well and that there are no texts to regulate such a network. A last example that illustrates well the need for real-time information using informal contacts occurred in the ELU office. They received a phone call from a local French police station, with which they had very good contacts, asking to check an English car's number-plate. This situation is also not officially authorized but they chose to cooperate for reasons of efficiency. As has already been described by Gallagher (1998) and Sheptycki (2002), the success of the cooperation in the Channel Tunnel area is based on the wide network of direct and informal contacts, which is also a point that can be applied beyond the Channel Tunnel area to any country.

Even though bilateral contacts are seen as the very essence of cooperation activities, informal cooperation also has some drawbacks, amongst which we can cite difficulties in making contacts due to language problems with some countries, the breaking of contacts (deceased persons, retirement, changes in posts, etc.), the duplication of efforts through informal cooperation and a lack of proper coordination, a limited scope for strategic intelligence, the lack of a legal basis and also the lack of accountability and transparency (Anderson et al. 1995; Santiago 2000). At first sight the linguistic factor within the cooperation process would appear to be a complementary aspect to other main issues of the process. However, this research parallels the findings of Gallagher (1998) and Maguer (2004) who both argue that it has to be considered as the first and major step to surmount. Common languages for communication are even more important than understanding the other country's national legislation (Maguer 2004). And the language issue is a central issue,[8] as police officers are usually not multilingual. Cooperation with Southern countries, Spain and Italy for example, has been mentioned as being very difficult in that context. Even if practitioners can deal with border languages, the communication link can easily be broken by other linguistic combinations (such as Greek-Finnish), which is a point where organizations created at a European level could demonstrate their unique contribution if approached in the right way.

Furthermore, efficient transnational cooperation is logically based on good cooperation existing between law enforcement authorities at a national level first, which unfortunately does not always exist. Luxembourg seems to be best placed for cooperation at the transnational level since there is a single police force and also the size of the country allows practitioners (i.e. police, prosecutors and the judiciary) to become acquainted with each other more easily. However, in France, the UK and Spain, the study has shown that there is a different story and that competition nationally between forces and institutions is very strong. A recurrent issue that has been raised throughout the research is the reluctance of police forces to share information, which can in some cases be even worse at a national level than at a bilateral level, one example being a Spanish national police officer who would rather give information to the French authorities than to the *Mossos d'Esquadra*.[9] As Spain is composed of multiple police forces, it is a very complex system of cohabitation which involves strong competition at two levels: first of all, rivalry between the two national police forces, the *policía nacional* and the *guardia civil*, and secondly, between the national forces and the autonomous police forces, as we have just explained. Indeed, traditionally and according to the written legislation *Ley Organica de Fuerzas y Cuerpos de Seguridad* of 1968, the national police are the main force that has competences in international remits, though the *guardia civil* has competence to a certain level as well as they deal with border controls especially in relation to drug-smuggling; the autonomous police have no powers officially in relation to international matters but they are fighting to have their remit increased in this context and therefore the national forces see themselves as being diminished. Rivalry can therefore translate into a lack of cooperation, with forces refusing to help one another and give information to another force and also an overlapping and duplication of work and inefficiencies as each force wants to be 'in charge' of a situation. It is important to stress that this difficulty is not particular to Spain and does exist in other countries. Competition definitely seems to be stronger in centralized models of policing; however, it has been demonstrated in the study that such rivalry is also present in a decentralized structure such as exists in the UK between the various agencies involved with international matters.

To further illustrate this strong competition at a national level, we can also mention the well-known example of the rivalry between the national police and the *gendarmerie* in France. These examples show the lack of unity that a country can present to the outside world and that a situation which is generally acknowledged to have been established for a long time, such as in the case of national cooperation, can still disappear within a relatively new situation with, for example, cooperation at a bilateral or European level. Many interviewees specified that while daily cooperation in the field was mostly smooth, the main problems started when one force had to give or share information at an investigative level, which is an issue probably related, among other factors, to the glory a force receives when a case is solved and the frustration another force will feel when this happens. They also stressed that cooperation depended totally on the good will of the people involved, personal contacts, and often the hierarchy's dynamics. The personal element is again a major point. This kind of situation shows how difficult it is to gain trust and how fragile this can be. The rivalry between police forces obviously results in a lack of cooperation, leading to an overlapping of work and inefficiencies, which is one of the reasons why in France inter-ministerial actions have been taken that have created, among other initiatives, the Central Section for Operational Cooperation (SCCOPOL). The SCCOPOL is an inter-ministerial pivotal unit created in July 2000 and based in the headquarters of the Judicial Police in Paris where officers from the national police, the *gendarmerie* and the customs dealing with Schengen, Interpol and Europol matters work alongside each other in the same offices. This therefore facilitates the work of the officers and provides them with fast and effective support, acting as a national operational clearing house.

More importantly, with the different agencies involved in the law enforcement system in France, such a central section gives the police/*gendarmerie*/customs officers and magistrates the advantage of contacting one single interface, without having to worry about which channel to use. Furthermore, in order to improve national contacts between police and prosecutors/judges in France, which are very difficult, liaison magistrates have also been posted within the SCCOPOL. This situation allows magistrates to contact the SCCOPOL through the liaison magistrates and has proved to be a successful initiative in order to smooth out cooperation between the judiciary and the police in France.[10]

Another example of competition at national level is the tension that exists between the ELU and the National Criminal Intelligence Service (NCIS),[11] as the NCIS from time to time sends a liaison officer to the ELU offices. Concerns have been expressed that this attitude might result from the NCIS wanting to monopolize the role of 'international contact' and therefore there is suspicion that the ELU would not provide them with all the information it had received from abroad or with enough information about their activities. Tensions seem to be fostered by the fact that the ELU not only deals with matters and contacts in the region but also with other European countries, for which the NCIS had seemed to feel it should be the key contact point. The liaison officer sent to the ELU could be seen as a form of rivalry by which means the NCIS was reminding the ELU that they were there to supervise and 'check up' on them. The NCIS was 'frustrated' to a certain extent by the wide network of international contacts the ELU had managed to create.

This can also be related to the choice of communication channel used by each force in each country, linked in turn to the practical action provided. Both channels of communication are available: the NCIS and the ELU. So, why does one of the channels prevail over the other as, here, the ELU channel definitely prevails? In this case, it could be that the NCIS might at that point have been seen as political with its activities linked to MI5 and investigating terrorism, and therefore not corresponding to the needs perceived by the police to be required on a daily basis at a practical level. Between, on the one hand, practitioners at field level with a high level of language skills and good awareness of European judicial systems emphasizing cooperation through strong personal contacts, and on the other hand, practitioners seen as bureaucrats with whom contact is more impersonal and with longer delays in replying, we have seen that the decision of foreign officers to contact one or the other 'agency' is clear and focused on operational needs with personal contacts – the ELU. The ultimate interests of the ELU and of the NCIS were probably different as Reuss-Ianni and Ianni (1983) have also explained, citing the gap that exists between street level and management level. Moreover, the Europol national unit in the UK (ENU) was located within the NCIS which might also further explain the 'frustration' that the NCIS showed by sending a liaison officer to the ELU, as officially Europol could only be contacted through the national unit and therefore not directly by the ELU as was the case.[12] It looks as though this is a struggle for power. At the time of the fieldwork, Europol could not provide real time information and had not given proof of its efficiency to become accepted as being of 'added value'.

Bilateral instruments of cooperation

The secure computerised data-exchange system, known as the Schengen Information System (SIS), was established by the Schengen Implementation Convention signed in 1990 and facilitates police and judicial cooperation in criminal matters for the signatory states. It was created as a *mesure compensatoire* for the freedom of movement created by the abolition of frontiers to ensure that borders become as open for police services as they are for criminals (Tupman and Tupman 1999). This European database was completely innovative, comprises data such as stolen vehicles, undesirable immigrants, wanted criminals, arrest warrants, etc., and is seen as a very efficient and fast system, as it corresponds to the needs of practitioners in the field. The central SIS (C-SIS) is located in Strasbourg (France) and each Schengen signatory country has a SIRENE[13] office with its national database terminal (N-SIS). All queries made to a country have a double interrogation and double reply system: the national database of the police force in question as well as the SIS. It gives real time information and indicates instantly to practitioners whether or not the requested information is within the database by a hit or non-hit. This tool is a European-level creation and offers a multilateral-level 'input', but it remains at a bilateral level in relation to the action to be taken if the hit is positive as its 'outcome' generally occurs at a bilateral level. On such a large scale, it seems to be the tool that works best and which is most used according to the different interviewees.

Other tools that have been identified as useful by the interviewees and also by Maguer (2004) are the Centres for Police and Customs Cooperation (CPCCs). These have been integrated into the daily practices of practitioners and clearly facilitate cooperation in border areas, as the different police forces within the area concerned are effectively under one roof. Officers working in the CPCCs are usually bilingual and aware of criminal justice systems' differences, which are important factors. The empirical data gathered showed that these are quick, used very often to deal specifically with simple real time information and therefore, like the Schengen System mentioned above, correspond to the needs of police officers. They are of great value compared with European and central channels because of the heavy delays these entail. Furthermore, they foster the making of contacts as well as trust, showing once more the relevance of personal and direct contacts. Nevertheless, in spite of their common use, a concern to be stressed is that the practitioners themselves have many doubts about whether the data obtained can legally be used in judicial investigations, as is raised below. One reason for this situation is that traditionally justice has been lagging behind in terms of transnational cooperation and still relies heavily on the old international commission rogatoire to obtain legal data and evidence. In a similar vein, the ELU's efficiency is comparable with the CPCCs', providing the same added value, such as addressing practical needs, and facing similar issues.

Liaison officers and liaison magistrates posted abroad have a unique multi-function task. Among others, they are expected to provide bilingual assistance, have a good knowledge of criminal justice systems with an understanding of any differences, support practitioners in commission rogatoire-related matters, etc., and most importantly they are usually personally known to their foreign counterparts, therefore providing privileged contacts. Even though these can only be used on a bilateral basis, they are clearly seen as invaluable by practitioners. Furthermore, it was pointed out that despite seeing the (EJN) as efficient as well, practitioners would probably tend to contact the liaison magistrate first as he or she will be an 'older figure' – in the sense of a more established institution – and therefore better known. Liaison magistrates act as intermediary persons for contacts in the same way as officers working in the CPCCs and are unfortunately, like the CPCCs, also not available in every country, as they both rely on bilateral agreements signed at a governmental level. The EJN is increasing in importance but still has major disadvantages, such as linguistic issues and the contact points having duties as national magistrates/prosecutors in addition to those of the EJN, and therefore not always being reliable in terms of availability due to their workloads.

Multilateral instruments of cooperation

Increased transnational crime and the demand for security have encouraged governments to implement new structures and new methods and techniques of working for their national policing systems. European policing is therefore increasingly 'intelligence-led' and takes the shape of *informationalized* central 'hubs' of communication (Hebenton and Thomas 1995; Sheptycki 1998a, 1998b, 2002) which are in direct 'competition' with the other well rooted kinds of cooperation, the less formal bilateral channels, that have been discussed above. As we will see, even though these types of multilateral and centralized channels of cooperation are promising and could prove effective, they still suffer from big disadvantages. While Ekengren *et al.* (2006) and Anderson *et al.* (1995) suggest that formal mechanisms can provide for more consolidated and legal responses, therefore avoiding the kind of chaos engendered by informal means of cooperation, other authors such as Bigo (1994, 1996) and Robertson (1994) argue that formal bodies only work thanks to the trust and contacts developed through bilateral cooperation, and that communication is slowed down and less effective when it goes through a central institution. These last points are also confirmed in this research. In that context, a closer look needs to be given to Interpol, Europol and Eurojust as multilateral and central mechanisms of cooperation.

Interpol is interesting as it is the oldest well-known organization for police cooperation. As a consequence, the research discovered that most of the senior police officers exchanging information with other countries used Interpol. Curiously, most of the time, they did not know why they used this means of cooperation as opposed to any other. They admitted to using Interpol on an automatic basis: 'That is the way I have always done it', one interviewee explained. It is not more efficient than other tools, but old habits are the key element. Interpol is the main channel for the flow of international commission rogatoires, which works more or less well, though some police officers who were interviewed said they never used Interpol in urgent cases as real time information and rapid communication could not be provided through this channel. Indeed it has the reputation of being very slow in responding to requests and often no such replies are forthcoming as it is not compulsory for countries to respond, whilst the contrary is true for the SIS.

Europol and Eurojust are probably essential tools for cooperation at a European level but still do not yet work as they should. It has been recognized that they enable the provision of a global vision of criminal trends in Europe but that their conventions are too broad, the volume of bureaucracy involved is too great and awareness of their operation is not sufficient. They both suffer from a lack of incoming 'hot information' from the member states, mostly due to the fear member states have of losing their data into a 'black hole' because they do not trust the institutions, which demonstrates perfectly the reason why bilateral cooperation prevails. This lack of trust impedes the flow of information which in turn leads to Europol and Eurojust not being able to demonstrate their efficiency as the member states feed them with too little information. Gerspacher and Lemieux (2005) argue that by being flexible and having gone beyond its mandate Europol has managed to offer a wider information market, providing better quality data and more relevant and 'hot' information for practitioners, resembling an intelligence entity and referring to the notion of a 'knowledge broker'. However, the results of this present study contrast with Gerspacher and Lemieux's (2005) claim as the majority of the practitioners interviewed and with whom the author has worked/collaborated as well as many civil servants agreed on the particular fact that the relevance and quality of the information hold by Europol was still far too 'low-level' based and therefore remained a major issue to its appropriate functioning not reaching the level of trust required for the member states. The mechanisms of cooperation have created a vicious circle, which can only be tackled by a change of mentality within the member states, focusing on the European organized crime issue instead of sticking to a strong nationalistic vision.

The main areas for improvement are the strong will of practitioners to invest in the cooperation process and to have Europol work much closer to the requirements in the field and with much less political input.[14] Practitioners have mostly agreed that Europol does not work well yet; moreover they also pinpointed that in urgent cases Europol had to be bypassed and Schengen used instead. It has been raised that Europol is seen as a competitor by the police services, which therefore affects their level of commitment to it. In the present situation, the study has shown that an important volume of information exchange undertaken within Europol is on a bilateral basis which is not what was expected from Europol's activities when it was created. Indeed, it was commented on at various times by practitioners, for example, that one of the major frustration for some countries is when the UK makes requests – which it seems happens quite often – which are not related to organized crime, such as when they ask to check a vehicle registration number. According to my interviewees, this kind of request should be done through Schengen, but as the British still do not have an operational Schengen database (at the time of writing) they use the Europol channel when it is not within Europol's remit. However, as these are real needs the work usually ends up being done even though it does not comply 100 per cent with the legislation. As has been picked up in many examples during the research, rules have to be adapted to needs otherwise no action at all would be allowed. Furthermore, when contacts do start via Europol between two countries which usually have little to do with one another, investigations also often end up working on a bilateral basis, especially for reasons of the sharing of information, as the countries involved can avoid the heavy system of data protection within Europol, and of urgency, which are better handled at bilateral level. Thus, Europol is left 'out of the loop'.

As Santiago (2000), Gerspacher (2005) and Gerspacher and Lemieux (2005) have illustrated, Europol has been flexible, going beyond its mandates and allowing direct and bilateral contact in order to gain confidence from the member states and make the institution work. However, the research has clearly shown that Europol's activities are still at present very much rooted on bilateral contacts. The question to be asked is whether the law enforcement agencies want another kind of 'postbox' instrument – or a 'passive facilitator of information' as Gerspacher and Lemieux (2005) term it – such as Interpol, or whether they want Europol to grow into something else. Considerable attention will need be paid to and invested in the future of Europol if it is to become effective on a multilateral basis. This is a key point of discussion, as Europol was set up to be different from Interpol and to give the member states a major tool of cooperation in order to fight organized crime. A variety of questions therefore readily come to mind. Could Europol be evolving as a postbox because this is actually what practitioners need? Or is it because there is not enough emphasis put on cooperation? Is it needed at all? Are its mandates adapted to the needs of law enforcement officers? Mandates do not determine but only limit the way an instrument works, so what does determine the way of working for Europol? Is there a gap between its political creation and idealism, and are the needs in the field far apart from those of politicians? Is there enough will to improve its operation? Do the member states want and/or require Europol, and most importantly, are they prepared to shift from a national vision to a European one?

With Eurojust, we can see a potentially invaluable successful creation as no similar institution/instrument exists in judicial cooperation in Europe in criminal matters, leaving police cooperation initiatives without an equivalent at the judicial level. Eurojust also needs to develop in the right direction, responding to what is required in the field and being proactive in order to prove it is a unique institution of interest. However, the majority of the practitioners interviewed are still uncertain as to what Eurojust actually does, which means that it needs to be better known and to have clearer and better defined remits so that countries across Europe use it in similar ways.

Eurojust still lacks a judicial database but has managed to build up some personal contacts through the national magistrates based in The Hague. However, opinions on Eurojust varied widely between the practitioners using it, depending on the outcomes they personally experienced. This one-to-one personal rate of satisfaction, from one extreme to another, received by the interviewees in relation to Eurojust is not enough to prove any substantive added-value for Eurojust at the moment. Eurojust will have to make the right moves to stand out, emphasizing its multilateral level of activities, as it has managed to achieve, as has Europol, a high volume of bilateral work. However, the point that was mentioned by several senior police officers about the non-existence of a judicial mechanism at a European level brings us to the debate about whether such a tool is important in an eventual future European judicial space, and if so, how this might develop.

If it is to fulfil its potential and mandate, Eurojust will need to become something more than just another instrument of cooperation to be added onto an already existing list. It cannot be allowed to grow as a postbox alone and it needs to be given resources in order to be efficient. It will also need to show a strong and unique purpose, different from that of the liaison magistrates and the EJN, which have been in place for longer. In order to achieve this objective, all the agents involved have to play the game and be willing for it to work: prosecutors, justice, police, experts, civil servants, other European bodies and governments. Mutual assistance and direct contacts between the judicial world and the police world are fundamental for a European judicial space, but a minority of practitioners still argue that there is a real need for a coordination structure. Informal cooperation has to be kept but it needs to be fitted into a formal framework. For the moment most of the decisions taken are 'a lot of "*poudre aux yeux*" which is an easy way for the heads of states to hide their voluntary passivity'.[15] One can suspect there will only be important changes if some major event or perceived need propels these.

Conclusion

As a result, the question here is whether cooperation can work on an informal basis or whether every action has to be made formally. Do we want to achieve full 'Europeanization' of cooperation or is it worth fostering decentralized actions if they are more efficient? Or can we shape a centralized type of cooperation or formal policies to be as efficient as informal means? For the moment, the gap between the 'governmental bureaucracy' (Gallagher 1998: 119) and practical and operational needs is increasingly seen as getting wider, an issue already mentioned more than a decade ago by Anderson *et al.* (1995). As a consequence, practitioners prefer to choose the difficulties involved in overcoming cultural, linguistic and procedural differences and to make direct contacts with colleagues, having to adapt the law to actual practice. Dupuy (1983)[16] correctly stated that 'cooperation is likely to be more effective if participation is performed by actors who are well informed and highly motivated or in other words "those directly concerned"'. Politicians do not yet seem 'directly concerned' about the need for practical action.

It has to be pointed out, however, that even if informal means of cooperation seem to practitioners to be the most suitable way of acting, the macro level must be used at some point if files need further action and then go to court, including formal requests for evidence via international commission rogatoires, etc. Indeed, issues such as extradition and asylum cannot be handled on an interpersonal basis (Benyon 1992). It is evident that treaties and formal structures are necessary even for common routine controls (train, border checks, etc.) but practical problems (uniforms to be worn abroad, talking to a prisoner abroad, etc.) also carry weight and are most of the time left out of formal negotiations, usually dealt with instead by the practitioners on the spot. Formal structures are almost always about the exchange of information, but practical needs and informal cooperation are just as important, especially in a border area setting such as Folkestone where cooperation is a daily matter. As a consequence, the police have to consider the methods they will use to pass on information, whether formally or informally. Interestingly, some parts of the patchwork of informal communication that have developed can be recognized as being so efficient in the context of cooperation that they result in more formalized agreements from the centralized agencies.

None of the cooperation processes, whether bilateral or multilateral, is perfect. Even though bilateral cooperation could be considered obsolete in Europe nowadays, it still prevails. At the moment, bilateral agreements and the exchange of information still remain the most effective means of police and judicial cooperation. However, the author believes that they should only be seen as an interim stage and are no substitute for European integration.

Centralized and formal instruments of cooperation hence need to have their activities improved and promoted. As Elsen (2007: 22) states, multilateral mechanisms of cooperation must not remain a 'paper exercise' and need to be more effectively used. Various factors that come into play as the reason why central instruments are not fully exploited mainly concern a lack of awareness and trust, chaotic and political management and functioning, and issues surrounding firm sovereignty and the sharing of hot information. There is also a need to go further and deeper to guarantee rapid and efficient procedures, to allow for the current system of cooperation in Europe to keep up with the pace of globalized organized crime trends. The right balance needs to be found between the mechanisms of cooperation and the development of trust for a successful outcome. Bilateral cooperation is vital and therefore should never be excluded from any type of cooperation. Even within centralized institutions, a minimum of bilateral contacts – used appropriately – will give the impetus for success.

Notes

1 See Guille (2009) for the complete study and findings.
2 The first planned interviews started in December 2002 and interviewing finished in June 2006. Further update information was given by telephone, conference and e-mail until October 2008. The total number of formal interviews undertaken amounts to 87 to which must be added the numerous informal discussions, phone conversations, informal discussions at conferences and, most importantly, invaluable informal discussions during fieldwork and during the observations.
3 The various observations and internships undertaken commenced in August 2003 and ended in August 2005.
4 The Kent Police ELU was created in 1991, is unique in the UK, and is part of the Kent regional Special Branch which is the second largest in the UK, mainly as a consequence of the Eurostar, the Channel Tunnel terminal and ports activities.
5 The UK CA, based in the Home Office, is seen as a non-useful onerous process which is referred to as a post-box with far too many layers of bureaucracy.
6 See Council of the European Union (2005).
7 It refers to a request addressed by a judicial authority of a country A to a foreign judicial authority or equivalent (country B) to request that authorities of country B proceed with certain actions (a house search, interrogations, etc.) in relation to a criminal investigation country A is undertaking.
8 This theme is further developed in Guille (2009).
9 Autonomous police force from the region of Catalonia.
10 See Guille (2009) for further details.
11 The NCIS no longer exists. Since 1 April 2006, it ceased activities and was integrated within the Serious Organised Crime Agency (SOCA). The information given here on the NCIS is, however, also likely to happen with SOCA, though obviously this cannot be a certainty.

12 Since 18 April 2007 major amendments have been made to the Europol Convention amongst which is the Danish Protocol of 27 November 2003 which allows direct contact between competent authorities and Europol as stipulated in Article 4.2. See OJ C 2 of 6 Jan 2004, 1–12.
13 SIRENE stands for 'Supplementary Information Request at the National Entry'.
14 A full section on the gap between politics, policies and work in the field is provided in Guille (2009).
15 Statement given by a practitioner at a conference in 2003.
16 Cited in Gallagher (1998: 64).

Chapter 3

Towards a governance model of police cooperation in Europe: the twist between networks and bureaucracies

Monica den Boer

General observations about police cooperation in Europe

One can make a number of observations about the theatre of European police cooperation. After nearly two decades of construction, the most visible aspect of police cooperation within the context of the European Union is the vast number of initiatives and the proliferation of instruments that has resulted from it. This steep growth – at least when one considers the quantity and scope of legal instruments – presents a particular challenge to academic experts, lawyers and practitioners. The increase of instruments is partly due to the discovery of security as a new policy arena which has been appropriated by the European Union polity, and which has been shaped as the Area of Freedom, Security and Justice. On the other hand, the increase may be due to the fact that police officers tend to be pioneering actors who are continuously looking for chances and opportunities to cooperate and to transform their initiatives in durable cross-border enterprises. The incremental nature (Walker 2004) of the policy-making process, the gradual layering of new laws and instruments without declaring old instruments obsolete, has been labelled as a form of modern conservatism. These developments cannot exist without consequences for the police profession. In terms of education and knowledge acquisition, police officers who are in training are increasingly being requested to understand and interpret international legal instruments that apply to international cooperation, which include a wide and rapidly developing range varying from anything like a Mutual Legal Assistance Convention to the European Code for Law Enforcement

Ethics. A sound knowledge of the content and strategic orientation of these instruments is, however, indispensable in the establishment of an international law enforcement culture.

A further observation is that from interviews and talks with police officers across several ranks and countries, European police cooperation as it is currently shaped within the European Union is regarded as bureaucratic, difficult to understand and barely workable. Practitioners feel ill-represented in Brussels circles and are frequently of the opinion that their concerns are insufficiently voiced within the EU Council's working groups. The influence on the policy-making process by the civil executive, i.e. non-police officers from the national ministries, is regarded as having grown since the formalization of police cooperation under the Maastricht Treaty in the early nineties. Practitioners also view the 'Brussels instruments' as tedious, too difficult, and even utopian. This can be illustrated by means of the new rules concerning EU Joint Investigation Teams, which have even been characterized as 'judicial spaghetti'. If a criminal investigator feels the route to Europol or Eurojust is simply too long, it may be the case that this formal route remains under-utilized and is neglected to the benefit of informal networks and bilateral contacts. This may hamper potentially successful instruments like the Joint Investigation Teams (JITs) and Europol's Analysis Work Files (AWFs).

Furthermore, European police cooperation has experienced ample progress in the area of strategic policy making; however, the operational or executive cross-border cooperation within the EU framework seems to lag behind. One may hypothesize from this that the subsidiarity principle prevails and that the operational aspects remain situated in the individual member states. Operational cooperation, which may include the use of investigatory or even coercive powers on the territory of another member state, requires a high level of trust and professional tuning. Hence, most executive police cooperation can be found in the pockets of regional cross-border cooperation, which has been strongly facilitated by the Schengen Agreement and the Prüm Treaty, complemented by a series of bilateral or multi-lateral treaties such as the Treaty of Senningen. Well-known examples are the Hazeldonk initiative between the Netherlands, Belgium and France (Corten and Martens 2006). Other examples include longstanding multilateral practices such as the Police Working Group on Terrorism (PWGOT), which also draws members from outside the EU and is focused on the exchange of operational intelligence.

Finally, the proliferation of legal instruments in the field of European police cooperation withstands the design of a comprehensive accountability regime. Transparency, legitimacy and the evaluation of effectiveness and efficiency are standards which are more difficult to measure in an increasingly complex and dynamic international environment. National parliaments have difficulty in scrutinizing the agenda of the Council of Justice and home affairs ministers, but they are gradually becoming more experienced with handling the policy rhythm of EU presidencies and various recurrent items in the action plans. The main challenge is, however, monitoring the follow-up to the JHA Council's decision making: it is often unclear as to which actor carries responsibility and ownership for the implementation of an instrument in the field of European police cooperation.

Policing: a typical sovereign concern?

Sovereignty, a concept explicitly linked to the concept of the nation-state, is supposed to be under pressure as a consequence of shifting governance principles. As a consequence of globalization, multi-level governance, networking and privatization, the nation-state – certainly when placed in the context of Europe – is undergoing fundamental changes. Centralized forms of public administration may be subject to a gradual process of erosion, to the benefit of other levels of governance (Eising and Kohler-Koch 1999: 4). The discourse on the globalization of crime and terrorism has nourished the consolidation of the supranational level of governance (e.g. a reinforcement of multi-lateral polities, such as the United Nations, the G8, and the European Union). The police organization and its representatives from the executive (ministries) could have particular interests in Europeanizing law enforcement matters, e.g. by emphasizing benefits of scale, shared information and intelligence, regarding internal security as a spill-over sector of the economic-financial market, and exploiting the European forum to acquire some attention for domestic security products.

On the other hand, globalization seems to be paralleled by the assertion of local security concerns (Keating 1998: 73, 161 and 164). This double logic in the crime and security discourse is visible in 'glocalization' strategies, where international security problems (e.g. fragile states, ethnic or religious conflicts) are interlinked with local security issues. The gradual erosion of sovereignty cannot be measured properly, as it is essentially a contested and ambiguous concept (Hoffman 1998). Being active and committed within a (legal) international community does not necessarily lead to the erosion of national sovereignty, but may alternatively lead to an articulation of the position of that individual nation-state within the relevant international community; such is the position of liberal intergovernmentalists. In the domain of the police, the military and security, this national assertion is reinforced by the nation-state monopoly of legitimate force: the use of violence is principally delegated by the state to the police and the military because it may be contested by others (Hoffman 1998: 30).

As Johnston and Shearing (2003: 14) maintain, the provision of security is perceived to be the responsibility of state governments, based on the premise that it is the state's right to define – through lawmaking – those things which are deemed to threaten order. Moreover, governments exercise their security responsibilities through the employment of specialised professionals. Such authority grants agents, like police officers, 'the legitimate capacity to apply the necessary coercion' (Johnston and Shearing 2003: 14). However, in a newly emerging security paradigm, security is no longer regarded as the sole or even primary preserve of the state, thus implying that 'its governance is exercised under plural auspices' (Johnston and Shearing 2003: 15). Hence, the pluralization of security governance challenges the state monopoly on governing the activities of public security providers. Hence, shifts in governance are deemed to have an undeniable impact on practices of policing. Except for the process of 'glocalization', there are trends of privatized policing, policing suspect populations rather than sovereign territories, and increased technological capacity for pro active monitoring on the basis of risk factors (Sheptycki 2002).The emergence of plural security governance is taking shape despite the stronghold of nation-states in the intergovernmental arena of police and justice and home affairs.

Supra-national institution-building, paralleled by the maturation of intergovernmental law enforcement bureaucracies such as Europol, Eurojust and Frontex, may be seen as the result of rational decision making within a historical context that was conducive to strong and clearly defined interests of the nation-state governments involved. One of the central assumptions is that enhanced sovereignty can be obtained through assertion and articulation in the European integration process. From the perspective of liberal intergovernmentalism, states are involved in a bargaining process (Schimmelfennig 2004: 77). As regards sovereignty, Schimmelfennig (2004: 80) refers to liberal intergovernmentalism when he notes that 'The degree to which governments favour the pooling of sovereignty (voting by other procedures than unanimity) and the delegation of sovereignty to supranational institutions, depends on the value they place on the issues for a government, and the higher the risk of non-compliance by other governments, the higher its readiness to cede competences to the EU to prevent potential losers from revising the policy'. These observations are particularly relevant in view of the EU's Lisbon Treaty, which entails the abolition of the unanimity voting procedure for non-operational police cooperation issues within the EU. Until now, however, police cooperation has been situated in the wider intergovernmental policy field of Justice and Home Affairs cooperation, which means that the 27 member states can still exercise their veto in this area of decision making.

The multi-level governance theory offers us another perspective on the way police cooperation is governed within the EU, namely as a series of interlinked arrangements 'for making binding decisions that engages a multiplicity of politically independent but otherwise interdependent actors – private and public – at different levels of territorial aggregation in more or less continuous negotiation/deliberation/implementation, and that does not assign exclusive policy competence or assert a stable hierarchy of political authority to any of these levels' (Schmitter 2004: 49). Multi-level governance has become the most omnipresent and acceptable level of governance within the contemporary EU. Multi-level governance develops because the actors/principals (i.e. the member states) that form the EU do not trust each other to respect mutual agreements faithfully and accurately (Schmitter 2004: 50). This is a sub-premise of the theory which is applicable to internal security actors.

Internal security cooperation was only added to the realm of EU competences at a relatively late stage. The national sovereignty spirit precluded the possibility of inserting police and judicial cooperation in criminal matters under the competences of the institutions of the European Community. The European Parliament, the European Court of Justice and the European Commission have merely enjoyed limited competences. In this context, Schmitter (2004: 51) has observed that 'the non-decision to include security issues from the initial (and so far, subsequent) stages of the integration process, deprived the emerging EU-polity of the coercive mechanisms that elsewhere promoted greater administrative uniformity and concentration of governmental authority at the national level – namely military mobilization and centralized taxation'. Within the sub-arena of police and judicial cooperation in criminal matters, actor interests have experienced a shift from the national to the supranational level, and the formation of stable, transnational alliances and coalitions, possibly with their own resources. Hooghe and Marks (2001: 3–4) emphasize that multi-level governance predicts the dispersion of authoritative competence across territorial levels and draws attention to the interconnection of multiple political arenas in the process of governing. In the field of police cooperation, there are several professional platforms and international senior police associations which enable a web of authoritative contacts across the world (Savage *et al.* 2000).

Hence, the multi-level governance perspective encourages us to analyse the responsibility for law enforcement administration as being increasingly shared with other levels than the central levels of government, namely with supranational, regional and local players, as well as with private actors and non-profit organizations (Kettl 2000: 488). In a multi-level governance system, layers of governance are deemed interdependent for the achievement of their objectives (Nomden 2001–2002: 17). Throughout this structure of interdependencies, loci of government may enter into competition and bargaining: the relationship between the centre and the sub-centre (locality/regional entity) may be subject to continuous movement, in which neither side is able to dominate completely (Rhodes 1981; quoted in De Vries 2000: 193–194). Van Kersbergen and Waarden (2001: 8) have characterized this development as a shift in governance location: within the public sphere, we see a gradual, horizontal shift from the public to the semi-public or to private forms of governance, as well as a shift to business. From this perspective, EU-governance has acquired the structure of an 'intricate web of transnational relations between interested parties', also called 'advocacy coalitions', which are organized around policy networks that loosely couple actors in the transnational, the horizontal and the vertical dimension (Kohler-Koch 2000: 88). 'Network governance' refers to the setting of policy making within highly organized social sub-systems, which have specific rationalities (Eising and Kohler-Koch 1999: 5).

International law enforcement networks may gradually evolve into light institutional arrangements. Local and regional configurations in cross-border cooperation areas are increasingly often the subject of institutionalization, e.g. in the form of bilateral or multilateral regional cooperation arrangements (Nogala 2001). An example of the further regulation of concrete cooperation procedures and the establishment of a joint Police and Customs Cooperation Centre (PCCC) in the border region is the Mohndorf agreement of 9 October 1997 between the French and German governments. An important dimension of the network governance is privatized security (Van Kersbergen and Van Waarden 2004: 151; Van Steden 2007): market liberalization and reduced state control have encouraged the transfer of public sector functions to the private sector. European police cooperation also has a private security dimension, for instance in the role of ICT companies in the development of international information systems that have been developed for law enforcement purposes, such as the Schengen Information System (SIS).

Theoretical governance perspectives on European police cooperation

Within the European Union, the challenge to prevent and combat trans-national organized crime has predominantly been responded to according to a state-centrist formula: legal instruments and action plans concluded at EU level have mainly inspired forms of central coordination within the EU member states. Examples – discussed in more detail below – are the creation of Europol, Eurojust and the European Police College (CEPOL). Except for the hectic lawmaking activity at the intergovernmental and supranational level, where bargaining is the preponderant strategy to arrive at optimal solutions which are acceptable for all 27 EU member states, there is a range of police cooperation initiatives which are undertaken by sub-state or private security actors. Security providers operate in a market which holds plenty of opportunities and other actors who are looking for new partnerships. Hence, a trend which can be observed is that alternative governance arrangements emerge which may put the preservation of national sovereignty under pressure. It has even been suggested that the emergence of informal, cross-border, horizontal police cooperation working practices should be seen as an anti-response to the vastly bureaucratic character of the European Union. Hence, police cooperation is also subject to a networked governance perspective, which emerges as a policy field without a single centre of authority. Table 3.1 below shows the different theoretical perspectives which can be laid down concerning the governance of European police cooperation.

The table shows a great variety of impacts for the autonomy of public security agencies when we shift the theoretical governance perspective. The neo-functionalist perspective predicts a situation where police organizations are reluctant players in the international arena: they are loyal followers of the national political authorities and they only enter the international arena when they are requested to do so. In this neo-functionalist scenario, there is little room for pioneering work across the borders, although liaison officers – who are formal attachés seconded to foreign countries – are the 'networked' limbs of nation-states. Within the neo-liberalist model, we can see international law enforcement cooperation as a visible form of action where nation-states can (re-)assert and articulate themselves as the prime interlocutors for security politics: police professionals are given room for manoeuvre, but merely act in a loyal fashion on the basis of political instructions. The multi-level governance perspective and the policy networks perspective clearly show different outcomes compared with the functionalist and the liberal-intergovernmentalist scenarios, certainly when it concerns the policy space which can be enjoyed by sub-central security/law enforcement actors. In a multi-level governance perspective, security actors seek to liaise with other actors in other to exploit newly arising opportunities, and they do so across the vertical layers (the interface between national, regional and local security actors) as well as sideways (the interface between public and private security actors). Crucial variables in the multi-level governance scenario are co-ordination and communication: a sub-central security actor would feel the need (if not the necessity) to inform her superiors, as well as facilitating the implementation of new security strategies within her own organization. In the network model, which is to a large extent compatible with a multi-level governance perspective, sub-central security actors are granted a relatively high degree of discretionary autonomy, to the extent that there is a tolerance or encouragement of local and regional cross-border security initiatives (often against the background of an existing legal framework). Although these scenarios are ideal-typical in their presentation, they can function as a heuristic device for understanding the deeper dynamics of the governance logic and the ways in which security actors can define the limits of their cross-border interventions.

Patterns of governance in European police cooperation

Governance of the European – and the international – police cooperation business is hard to grasp as one single theoretical-analytical framework. The social science perspective is dominant, particularly those of political science and public administration, international relations, social anthropology (Sheptycki 1995) and cultural studies. It is striking that police cooperation governance is hardly ever analyzed from an economic or psychological perspective,

Table 3.1 Theoretical perspectives on the governance of European police cooperation

Theoretical perspective	Key concepts	Key actors	Sovereignty transfer	Applied to police co-operation
Neo-functionalism	Supra-national state-building Spill-over	Elites within the law enforcement sector (police organization and executive), authorized by their states	None, as nation-states remain the prime interlocutors	Police act as state exponent and assist in building supra-national police agencies and in building state-authorized forms of cross-border cooperation agencies
Liberal inter-governmentalism	Rational decision making Bargaining Asymmetrical distribution of power, information	States, represented by politicians and an executive	None, enhanced sovereignty for states as prime interlocutors	Police represented by an executive (within the EU: Commission and Council working groups); is an actor which seeks to influence politicians and executive through professional lobbying process; thereafter it has to implement the (binding) decisions that have been adopted

Multi-level governance	Inter-dependency Continuous negotiation/ deliberation/ implementation Power and influence not explicitly delegated to single actor but shared	Various actors, including the state, but also state and semi-state agencies at a supra-national, sub-national and private level	Some, as the state is no longer able to own, coordinate and monitor all governance levels; nevertheless, the state remains a crucial co-producer, security provider and financer	In a decentralized or deconcentrated police system, police organizations may take independent initiatives across borders and cultivate relationships with the private sector through contracts and covenants
Policy networks	Interdependency Relatively stable, focused on selected (e.g. project-related) interests	State and non-state actors alike, including private actors Centre of power and authority may be absent, several authority and accountability relationships	Some transfer of sovereignty Accountability under pressure	Short- to medium-term forms of cooperation across representatives of the law enforcement sector, focused on selected thematic objectives (e.g. human trafficking, terrorism, crisis-management)

while these disciplines could have an important explanatory value in analysing the choices made by police officers and their organisations, and the considerations they have in participations in international police cooperation initiatives. There are, however, some sound historical works, for instance studies of Interpol as an evolving global policing organization (Anderson 1989) and the historical roots of international police cooperation (Deflem 2002). Within political science and public administration, the distribution of power and authority is an essential subject of analysis, which allows tested and new concepts of policing to be compared with other public agency sectors.

Several academics have sought to identify, systematize and explain the trends in international police cooperation. Due to the proliferation and lack of public transparency of these initiatives, this does not appear to be a simple exercise. The former Centre for the Study of Public Order of the University of Leicester made a distinction between the micro, meso and macro levels of police cooperation (Benyon *et al.* 1993). Building on this work, a research team at Edinburgh University sought to draw a distinction between formal and informal levels of police cooperation, and 'old' and 'new' systems of police cooperation (Anderson *et al.* 1995). Following Van Reenen (1989) and inspired by the multi-level governance theory, Den Boer (2001) sketched the structures of international police cooperation on a vertical axis (top-down) and horizontal lines:

Table 3.2 presents a crude overview of the several practices in the arena of European police cooperation. In reality there are several mixed examples and the diachronic perspective is instructive to the extent that practices may gradually adopt a more institutionalized or formal character (Den Boer 2005: 192). This illustrates the incremental path of the governance of European police cooperation (Walker 2004): old systems remain whilst new structures are continuously added and changed. The other aspect that makes cooperation practices more hybrid in reality is that agencies that have been furnished with an institutional structure and mandate – like Europol and Eurojust – are themselves taking on new challenges by developing networks and taking part (in a supportive capacity) in sub-central practices such as JIT. From a governance perspective, a series of international law enforcement hybrids is emerging on the scene: traditional institutional agencies distinctly marked by a hierarchy which are gradually seeking to unleash themselves, as well as small-scale informal initiatives across the border that are gradually folded into a standing law enforcement structure.

Table 3.2 Vertical versus horizontal governance in European police cooperation

	'Vertical' police cooperation	'Horizontal' police cooperation
Institutional appearance	Europol, OLAF,[1] Eurojust, Task Force Chief Police Officers	Schengen and Prüm Treaties, bilateral and multilateral treaties such as Senningen and Enschede, covenants and Memorandums of Understanding
Levels of cooperation	Formal, strategic, preparation and facilitation of policy, supportive, emphasis on inter-state diplomacy	Informal, policy preparation, facilitation and execution, emphasis on information-exchange and regional or cross-border (operational) cooperation
Key actors/ interlocutors	National politicians, senior civil servants (e.g. Directors General Safety, Senior Advisors relevant Ministries); national civil servants in the Committee of Permanent Representation; officials of the European Council Secretariat and the European Commission; top representatives of the national police and judicial bodies of the EU member states	National, regional and local politicians, civil servants and practitioners from police services and regional departments of the public prosecution service; multi-disciplinary cooperation with local customs, border control and immigration and naturalization services
Key policy objective	Convergence through the inter-ministerial negotiation and adoption of legal instruments; centrally coordinated exchange of best practices, information and intelligence, focus on supranational security issues such as transnational terrorism and organized crime central; subsidiarity is the leading principle; financial facilitation and support of regional cross-border cooperation practices	Sub-central or local approach to security issues, room for differentiation and pluriformity, tailor-made solutions and flexibility; focus is on cross-border, bilateral, Euroregional cooperation; common culture and trust enhances the likelihood of operational cooperation, e.g. in the form of Joint Hit Teams

Selected practices of European police cooperation: Europol, Schengen and Liaison Officers

In order to analyse the practices of European police cooperation in more detail, we have selected three arenas where police cooperation takes place: Europol, Schengen and the police liaison officers' network.

Europol

The European Police Agency, or Europol,[2] was created with the adoption of the Maastricht Treaty on 7 February 1992. The member states of the European Union decided that an organization should be created for the analysis of criminal intelligence, and this was done by virtue of article K.1.9 of the Maastricht Treaty. Europol was originally launched with a limited mandate, namely the fight against international drugs trafficking and related money laundering offences, and it was named the European Drugs Unit (EDU). The Europol Treaty, which was signed in 1995 by the member states and fully ratified in 1998, extended this mandate to other fields of crime. The leading principle was the subsidiarity principle: Europol is only allowed to offer its services when the interests of two or more member states are undermined by the relevant crime.

On the one hand, Europol is not a full-blown police agency. Similar to Interpol, it does not enjoy operational powers, but merely investigatory powers. These investigatory powers are primarily vested in the member states themselves: Europol analyses the information and intelligence which is submitted by the member states. In that sense, the agency and its success depend on the cooperation of the national law enforcement authorities, who send their information via their Europol National Units (ENUs), who are supposed to process the information from the regional and local police agencies. The kind of information processing is mostly of a strategic rather than a tactical nature. For instance, in its Trends and Situation Report on Terrorism (TE-SAT), Europol presents a broad overview of the developments in the field of terrorism. Moreover, the officials who work within Europol come from a variety of law enforcement backgrounds (police, customs, immigration and naturalization services) and security services, which implies that this agency has adopted a multi-disciplinary and multi-national profile.

The work of Europol is embedded in a political-strategic context. The Justice and Home Affairs Council lays down the strategic programme for Europol and appoints its director. Europol reports to its Management Board, in which all 27 member states are represented. Its data exchange is controlled by the Joint Supervisory Board, which comprises the heads of the national data protection authorities of the member states. The European Parliament can be informed or consulted, but it has hitherto not had inspection powers. In the future, with the entry into force of the Europol Council Decision, Europol will adopt the status of an EU agency and this will allow the European Parliament to approve of or scrutinize Europol's annual budget (Den Boer and Bruggeman 2007). In the meantime, Europol has grown into an agency with around 500 employees and an annual budget of about 60 million Euros. At the moment, Europol accommodates around 100 Europol Liaison Officers (ELOs) from the member states. They are responsible for the information flow between their national agencies and Europol, as well as for information exchanges with the liaisons of other countries.

Europol is in the process of developing and applying new products, in particular the Organized Crime Threat Assessment (OCTA) and the European Crime Intelligence Model (ECIM). OCTA is regarded as a move away from the retrospective and descriptive annual reports on the activities of organized crime groups in the member states to a more proactive approach which is based on the assessment of intelligence and the prediction of security risks. Hence, while OCTA is meant to take a more forward-looking perspective, the objective behind ECIM is to introduce a standardized management of intelligence and knowledge within the national police organizations. Other products of Europol are, excepting its Europol Information System, the delivery of strategic support and the co-ordination of international (parallel) investigations. Since the entry into force of the Amsterdam Treaty, as well as the implementation of the EU Framework Decision on Joint Investigation Teams, Europol can offer supportive services to JIT, or – as seems to have happened – in the performance of a cross-border controlled delivery[3] (Storbeck 1996: 86). Although there is no 'criminal justice chain' as such within the European Union, Europol is supposed to closely cooperate with its judicial counterpart Eurojust. In our governance schedule, Europol is exemplary of a vertically styled form of police cooperation, characterized by formal rules of decision making and institutional anchorage, as well as by centrally co-ordinated information exchange.

Schengen

In contrast to Interpol or Europol, 'Schengen' is not an agency or institution but an ambitious and wide-ranging framework for internal security cooperation in Europe. The Schengen cooperation formula is seen as a successful arrangement, as the participation of both EU member states and non-member states (Iceland, Norway, Switzerland, and at the end of 2009, probably also Liechtenstein) has been secured. The principal objective of the Schengen cooperation framework is to compensate for the so-called security deficit which has been caused by the abolition of internal border controls within the EU, due to the realization of an area of the free movement of persons. Not all EU member states are full cooperation partners: the United Kingdom and Ireland prefer to keep their Common Free Travel Area and do not want to lift their external border controls; of the member states that joined on 1 May 2004, only Cyprus has not yet fully implemented the Schengen rules and requirements because of the external border with Turkey; and Bulgaria and Romania, which joined on 1 May 2007, are not fully in Schengen yet as they first have to guarantee the quality of their external border controls.

The first Schengen agreement was signed in 1985 by France, Germany, Belgium, the Netherlands and Luxembourg, or between the countries that shared the Saarbrücken Agreement and the Benelux. The Schengen Implementing Agreement dates from 1990 and shaped the compensatory measures in 142 articles, ranging from cooperation in the field of illegal immigration and asylum, to police, customs and judicial cooperation, as well as information exchange by means of a Schengen Information System. By virtue of the Amsterdam Treaty, the whole intergovernmental Schengen acquis was lifted into the legal and institutional framework of the European Union.

Police cooperation establishes an essential part of the Schengen acquis, making it possible for Schengen partners to allow operational cross-border police activities on each other's territory, including information exchange, hot pursuit, controlled delivery and cross-border surveillance, in combination with standardized measures for the execution of external border controls. The basic idea behind the cooperation was still that national authorities could exercise their sovereignty by means of granting explicit authorization for the use of cross-border police powers. Subsequently, the rules have been bent to some extent, e.g. in treaties such as Enschede and Senningen. In May 2005, a selection of Schengen countries signed the Prüm Treaty, which extended the powers of Schengen in the area of internal security considerably, such as demanding from member states that they create a national DNA database, allowing for the collection of fingerprints, biometric data and vehicle registration, and extending the Schengen competences beyond ordinary transnational crime to include terrorism. At the same time, work has been underway to expand the capacity and to adapt the technological aspects of the Schengen Information System, which currently comprises around 30 million data. In terms of governance, the Schengen framework offers a minimum menu of rules and instruments to the various participant countries, and in practice it turns out that – through enhanced cooperation – they can build deeper forms of cooperation by adding new bilateral or multilateral treaties. Although the negotiators of Schengen are usually representatives of the ministries, the output of the law enforcement sector is usually higher than in the EU Council working groups. Hence, there are several indications that the taking into account of professional rationality enhances the practical relevance of this form of cooperation, especially in border zones (Block 2008b). This has culminated in the creation of joint police commissariats and police information exchange centres (Nogala 2001). Police cooperation within the Schengen framework can thus be regarded as a hybrid and horizontal form of cross-border co-operation, originally negotiated and governed, however, through the various signatory states as the primary interlocutors.

Liaison officers

The role of international liaison officers is deemed important in the field of international police cooperation (Den Boer 2005: 196). As personifications of the foreign policy of nation-states, they are usually posted at embassies, consulates or international organizations. Bigo (2000: 67) argues that the principles of free trade and free movement have made the liaison officer role crucial for policing in Europe, because it is they who manage the flow of information between their respective agencies. Hence, Bigo (2000: 74) regards them as 'the human interface between various police forces'. Their tasks include giving recommendations to their own national law enforcement organization, taking care of (operational) information exchange, the distribution of management information through reports about crime policy, the political situation, and the organization of police and justice (Parlementaire Enquêtecommissie 1996: 448). Zagaris (2002: 156) noted a trend to expand the use of specialized liaison officers by the US and other countries in areas like drug-trafficking, customs, immigration, tax and counterfeiting. The management of data flows is seen as the most important task of liaison officers, and acting as cultural-linguistic brokers. Hence, liaison officers fulfill a number of different roles (Vanderborght 1997: 182–188), such as facilitator, broker, negotiator and trustor. Moreover, as Zagaris (2002: 156) maintains, liaison officers are crucial 'to the success of selecting and conducting transborder criminal investigations and helping to prosecute transnational criminals'.

More concretely, in the wake of the attacks on 11 September 2001, there was a push for a more multi-disciplinary representation of liaison officers at Europol, including from the national intelligence services (Den Boer 2003: 199). Counter-terrorism liaison officers were also exchanged between the US and Europol and Eurojust respectively (Den Boer 2003: 201). Nadelmann (1993) has documented the American web of liaison officers in Europe and beyond. The US Drug Enforcement Administration (DEA) has numerous liaisons in at least a quarter of all the countries in the world, whose mission includes the conduct of bilateral investigative activities, the coordination of intelligence gathering, engagement in foreign liaison, the coordination of training programmes for host country policy agencies, and assistance in the development of host countries' counter-narcotics law enforcement institutions (Zagaris 2002: 157). As liaison officers often enjoy diplomatic or consular immunity (Zagaris 2002: 168), issues of legal accountability concerning the use of investigation methods may arise. However, liaison officers must act under the authority of the foreign jurisdiction where they are based and have to abide by the rules and procedures of that particular jurisdiction. It could be argued that according to the governance schedule above, the liaison officers cannot be regarded as a pure form of network governance, as they act strictly on behalf of their national authorities, i.e. they do not act autonomously at a sub-central or private level of governance. On the other hand, however, as they are not institutionally embedded in law enforcement bureaucracies, they enjoy a relatively large margin for autonomy, which means we can categorize them as a form of horizontal cross-border form of law enforcement governance.

Good governance perspectives on international police cooperation

Shifting patterns of governance culminate in more fragmented and even deficient accountability (Sheptycki 2002; Van Kersbergen and Van Waarden 2001: 27), and this also applies to policing. For law enforcement organizations that are competent enough to investigate and prosecute transnational organized crime, the potential accountability deficit may present a challenge. For instance, how can the judicial and law enforcement authorities trust their partners on the other side of the border (Anderson 2002)? The latest instruments which have been called into being within the realm of the EU Area of Freedom, Security and Justice have promoted the principle of mutual recognition, which harbours the idea of symmetry and mutual trust in the quality of each other's judicial system. The principle of mutual recognition was introduced in the 1999 Tampere Action Programme and has since become the cornerstone for the EU Framework Decision on the Arrest Warrant and the Evidence Warrant. However, as we have seen with the fate of the principle of availability, which advances the automatic exchange of information between law enforcement officials, it is more difficult to enshrine the principle of trust at a sub-national or interregional level.

As this chapter has illustrated, there are several forms of informal, horizontal, regional and network-like practices of police cooperation. One of the potential detrimental effects of networked governance is the accountability or legitimacy deficit, which arises from an absence of written rules of process, authorization, transparency, or judicial review (Den Boer *et al.* 2008; Peterson 2004: 125). On the other hand, informal bargaining within networks can help build consensus. Policy networks can thus 'diffuse norms of good governance' (Peterson 2004: 125), but private actors may gain a sense of ownership in EU policy making ('co-production'). Hence, within the security arena, networked governance continues to be regarded as a successful form of transnational governance, despite the risk that it may lead to pioneering efforts in a legal grey zone. Yet, various cross-border and interregional initiatives have been able to function and expand in spite of maximum accountability assurances: we may think of the Cross-Channel cooperation initiative in which law enforcement partners from the UK, France, Belgium and the Netherlands are involved, and of the Euroregional cooperation initiative NEBEDEACPOL (Brammertz *et al.* 1993) and the creation of a European Police Information Centre (EPIC) between (regional) actors in Germany, Belgium and the Netherlands.

As the embryonic phase of European police cooperation is now well behind us, there remains the question of which direction the juvenile will follow. Some envisage a full-blown European police organization which can act effectively when it is given more supranational powers; others argue for the likelihood of a continued incremental growth such as we have seen over the past two decades. More specifically, a European police organization may have to be embedded in a fully furnished EU criminal justice chain, where a EU criminal law and criminal procedure code would lay down the rules for penalization, procedures and sanctioning. Moreover, the different trends that have been identified in the arena of policing (Jones and Newburn 2002) will also have an effect on European police cooperation. The pluralization of policing, which entails processes such as multi-lateralization and privatization, has already gained firm ground in the several action programmes that have been adopted in the EU Area of Freedom, Security and Justice, including the prevention of crime through multi-agency cooperation. Hence, it is not a question of whether plural and networked policing will gain ground in Europe, but of how this unruly business will be governed with instruments that may well be past their sell-by date.

Issues of accountability and legitimacy present themselves most acutely in the realm of international information and intelligence exchange. Data protection instruments may be solid, but are they in step with the vast volumes of information that are collected about European citizens each day for law enforcement purposes? Do the classical principles of subsidiarity, proportionality and finality sufficiently protect citizens against the surveillance potential of the European polity? The European governance of police cooperation can only become mature if the growth of cross-border police competences is matched by a professional culture of checks and balances. Gradually, the EU Area of Freedom, Security and Justice may absorb the necessary ingredients that have become part and parcel of national police systems, namely democratic, legal and social accountability. Only a balanced governance system will overcome the link between informal law enforcement networks and formal police cooperation bureaucracies.

Conclusion

European police co-operation can be characterized by several different – and sometimes contradictory – trends. The first observation is that the field of relevant activities has proliferated, which draws several actors into venues for transnational cooperation when it concerns crime strategies and law enforcement training. Second, the field looks divided when it takes into account the different appreciations of Europeanization processes in law enforcement: professionals are of the opinion that politicians and executives have a different rationality when it comes to coining different instruments of cooperation, which may eventually hinder the practical implementation. Third, and this is where the contradictory logic comes to the fore, fear of the erosion of national sovereignty within the EU means that the veto keeps its stronghold for the time being. However, realists anticipate the sharing of sovereignty within the internal security arena: significant in this context is the re-assertion of local security issues as well as the creation of (mostly informal) transnational security alliances.

Public security actors find themselves positioned on a complex and dynamic board of chess, where several opportunities and obstacles present themselves. Security actors who wish to engage in cross-border law enforcement co-operation must first appreciate the contours and the complexity of their governance arena before they can make a move. Hence, the landscape of European internal security is full of learning law enforcement organizations that manage to adapt their governance and administration to the contradictory logic of sovereignty, subsidiarity as well as globalization and networking. Europol and Interpol are increasing their accessibility and have begun to incorporate network-type features, whilst smaller pockets of law enforcement cooperation seek to stabilize and anchor themselves by adopting vertical governance characteristics. Ultimately, the question will be whether widely proliferating European law enforcement initiatives can be properly governed under the currently existing fragmented regulatory regime.

Notes

1 Office de la Lutte Anti-Fraude, European Commission.
2 www.europol.eu.int
3 Framework Decision, 13 June 2002, OJ L 162, Vol. 45.

Chapter 4

A market-oriented explanation of the expansion of the role of Europol: filling the demand for criminal intelligence through entrepreneurial initiatives

Nadia Gerspacher[1] *and Frédéric Lemieux*

Introduction

The regionalization of markets and the creation of common economic spaces have generated new social spaces plagued by security problems that states do not necessarily have the capacity to address unilaterally (Hall and Bhatt 1999; Manning 2000; Sheptycki 2000). The unintended consequences of the development of common economic markets include several threats to security and prosperity in the face of transnational crime. Thus these new spaces require heightened control of movement of goods and people and the securing of border areas. This demand for security has provoked a need for greater collaboration between national police services and has led to a myriad cooperation treaties in police and justice matters (Hass 1972; Occhipinti 2003). Consequently, there has been a rise in 'common security spaces' in which police agencies are asked to share information and expertise (Manning 2000). Particularly, international police cooperation organizations have emerged and national police authorities have enjoyed opportunities for participation outside their jurisdictions through mutual legal assistance treaties (Benyon *et al.* 1993; Fijnaut 1993b; Nadelmann 1993).

In concrete terms, we can observe a strong progression of police and judicial cooperation inside free exchange zones, such as the Plan of Action against Transnational Criminality initiated by ASEAN countries in 1999 which was meant to create the Centre for Combating Transnational Crime (Pushpanathan 1999).[2] In addition, ASEAN countries have recently adopted a mutual assistance treaty in matters of justice (2004) and some have also signed an agreement to share police information and develop a communication network (2002).[3] These arrangements have a support function for investigators of member countries as they promote intelligence exchange and undertake the coordination of operations that involve police forces from more than one country. In the North American free exchange zone, we can observe a proliferation of police initiatives that rest on bilateral agreements between the United States and Canada and between the United States and Mexico since the late 1990s (Deflem 2001). Cooperation between the police authorities of these three countries implies numerous joint ventures in the surveillance of borders in the fight against drug trafficking, in national security activities, and in the training of police officers.

In Europe, police cooperation has been in practice since the end of the nineteenth century (Occhipinti 2003: 239). The implementation of a common European space has largely contributed to the development of numerous legislative measures to allow for the formalization and structurization of collaboration between police services. From the Treaty of Maastricht (1992) to that of Amsterdam (1997), including Schengen (1985) and the The Hague Programme (2004), the parameters of European police cooperation have continued to expand. We can witness a growing willingness to structure police activities aimed at combating transnational crime, specifically under the auspices of the European Office of Police (Europol). We should also note that member states of the European Union have also adopted a centralizing approach in the area of police training (CEPOL) and judicial cooperation (Eurojust). And cooperation mechanisms in the area of security take shape internally in international organizations whose missions and competencies are traditionally reserved for national police services.

Besides economic and socio-political explanations for why states have opted to institutionalize police cooperation in Europe, little attention has been given to the reasons for the transfer of competencies and the gradual erosion of sovereignty and the principle of subsidiarity (Occhipinti 2003). Most studies on this topic focus on the target of police cooperation (e.g. the fight against drug trafficking and other forms of organized crime), on the interactions between national police services, or on the challenges surrounding the democratization of the process and respect for human rights (Bigo 1996, 2003; Bruggeman 2002; Den Boer 1997, 2002d; Sheptycki 1995, 1996, 2000, 2005). In this chapter, we show that Europol has made significant operational gains by tracking the evolution of the mandate to facilitate cooperation in the fight against organized crime. We argue that the role of Europol has considerably evolved since its inception as the European Drug Unit (EDU) in 1993 and is gradually becoming a knowledge broker. We pay special attention to the factors that have contributed to the expansion of the mandate of Europol even with its normative framework that strictly constrains its activities (mainly via its convention) due in part to a complex legal and political environment. More specifically, we examine the initiatives undertaken inside the organization (the practices and processes introduced) and those that result from outside stimuli (interstate relations).

Our argument rests on a series of interviews conducted between 2001 and 2005. Firstly, we visited a dozen officials at the secretariats of Interpol and Europol in order to identify the constraints that have been imposed on the respective structures and responses of these international bodies in their quest to fulfill their missions (Gerspacher 2002, 2005). Secondly, we interviewed a separate group of individuals as part of a comparative analysis of the norms and current practices within the area of criminal intelligence (Lemieux 2006). Based on a collection of semi-structured interviews of staff members of Europol, Interpol, the National Criminal Intelligence Service (NCIS) of the UK, the federal police in Belgium and the Franco-Swiss Police and Customs Cooperation Centre, we were better able to understand the normative frameworks that shape information exchange in the European police cooperation context. These interviews also enabled us to put in perspective the various modes of application of the collaboration that takes place and to identify the organizational, cultural and individual constraints that hinder the implementation of cooperation mechanisms. In addition, in June 2005, we visited Europol and interviewed eight additional Europol staff to deepen our understanding of the increase in operational activities that we observed. More precisely, we conducted semi-structured interviews with directors of administration, development and planning, members of analysis teams, legal affairs, the processing of nominal and ordinal data and liaison office managers.

Europol: a mandate in evolution

The idea to create a European police organization came to light in the 1980s following a realization by national police services that it was desirable to establish common information exchange mechanisms (Busch 2002). In 1992, Europol was officially born via the European

Union Treaty and translated into the first commonly defined cooperation policy in matters of police and justice (Guyomarch 1995: 249).

While it was largely left out of European politics before 1992, this initiative was a formal response of sorts to the need to improve cooperation between national police services. Since the Maastricht Treaty, the mission of Europol included two aspects: the instrumental and the functional (Grewe 2001: 80–81). It is instrumental because its aim is to combat transnational organized crime, albeit restricted to drug trafficking cases between 1995 and 1998. And it is functional as Europol was designated to facilitate information exchange between member states, to collect and analyse voluntarily shared police data, and to produce strategic finished intelligence that would be useful in the operations conducted by national police services.

Even if Europol can be seen as the centrepiece of the EU's fight against transnational crime (Hebenton and Thomas 1995: 51), there is no certainty that Europol will establish a hegemonic presence in the repression of organized crime in Europe (Walker 2003). However, we can observe a notable progression in the nature of Europol's activities since its inception in 1992 (Anderson 2002; Bigo and Guild 2003; Busch 2002). Not surprisingly, the language of the convention leaves significant room for interpretation of the role of Europol which also leaves the door open for the expansion of its activities, specifically as this relates to an involvement in national police operations. In fact, between the drafting of the convention of Europol in 1992 until the Tampere Programme (2001), we can see an evolution in Europol's involvement in national investigations and initiatives of support for the investigations and operations of member states (Anderson 2002). Europol's 1998 annual report had already invoked its participation in several operational missions.[4] The role of Europol in these investigations was limited to facilitating information exchange, to performing tactical crime analysis in collaboration with investigating officers from member states' police services, to coordinating controlled deliveries and to providing a forum for operational joint strategy sessions. Several of these operations have taken place in collaboration with national police services and magistrates from outside the Union, without any legal frameworks, agreements or official arrangements authorizing or promoting these initiatives. The initial mission did not stand the test of time ever since the very beginning: the Treaty of Amsterdam (1997, art. 30 § 2) officialized Europol participation in police investigations. Moreover, in 1999 the Council of Tampere granted Europol the authority to process police information of an operational nature.

⟩ (2002) states, since its inception in 1999, the Europol ⟩as rarely been pivotal for the development of Europol ⟩ecame outdated soon after its inception. Because the ⟩.endment process of an international treaty is lengthy, its objective is more to render official practices already in place rather than to introduce new directives for the international organization. Thus, the mandate of Europol has evolved in several dimensions. Europol started out as an international organization to facilitate voluntarily shared criminal intelligence (passive participation) and now assists, coordinates, guides and even shapes police services at the operational level (active participation). This progression can notably be explained by the fact that the implementation of new initiatives can be accomplished without requiring state ratification or the authorization of the European parliament. Interestingly, the legal dispositions represent a *post factum* officialization of practices that are already part of the normative behaviour of police services that engage in international cooperation. For example, the common investigations on drug trafficking have generated a demand from the European Unit for intelligence on drug trafficking. Once in place, this project was integrated into the TREVI action programme. Furthermore, the essential elements of the EDU were inserted into the Europol convention in 1995.

The areas of intervention of Europol have also become considerably diversified. In fact, since the Treaty of Amsterdam Europol has made considerable gains in its ability to participate in police operations across the membership of the EU. These gains have been highlighted and particularly promoted in The Hague Programme (2004). Today, Europol is competent in the coordination and active participation in several joint investigations conducted by national police services (Berthelet 2005; Programme de La Haye 2004). While in 1995 its only competence was in the area of drug trafficking (Convention Europol, article 2 (1), 2 (2) and appendix) since 2002 Europol's mission to support the repressive activities of member states included 18 forms of crime. Then, in 2003, under the auspices of a Mutual Legal Assistance Treaty which incited member states to become further implicated in the multilateral fight against transnational crime, new initiatives have lent additional operational dimensions to the services offered by Europol. First and foremost, joint investigation teams were formed under the umbrella of Europol in order to ensure the constant presence of a legal authority during transborder investigations. Secondly, member states are engaged in the transferring of evidence in order to allow their foreign colleagues to lead investigations and proceed with prosecutions. Thirdly, a mechanism of evaluation was put in place in order to perform audits of the national information exchange systems to identify problems and to issue recommendations for the proper functioning of cooperation mechanisms to national governments. Finally, Europol has obtained the right to request the initiation of an investigation when the crime analysis they perform suggests the need for one.

The Hague Programme (2004) also encourages member states to grant Europol the right to play a central role in police cooperation in general and, more specifically, in the fight against transnational crime and terrorism. To that end, the programme has introduced new initiatives aimed at reinforcing the role of Europol in these areas. Europol was mandated the production of threat assessment reports of organized crime destined not only for national police services but also for the Council of Europe so as to set future actions in motion. Thus, we can observe that the area of activity mandated to Europol has been significantly widened. For example, Europol is the official central coordinator for the repression of Euro counterfeiting and the point of contact for third states in this area. In addition, The Hague Programme encourages national police services to constitute joint teams and recommends that Europol become the authority in the coordination of these activities, notably by supplying logistical support, technical assistance and expertise. Consequently, we can see that the voluntary nature of information exchange erodes *vis-à-vis* the principle of disponibility which stipulates that any police officer from one member state which needs intelligence can obtain this from a police officer from another state upon request (Berthelet 2005). Because of the adoption of this principle and in the framework of joint investigative teams, Europol is able to formulate a request for information from national police services.

While the initial mandate for Europol did not grant it any executive powers allowing it to arrest, pursue, or even to question foreign suspects, interviews overwhelmingly reveal that Europol participates actively in common investigations by collecting and analysing criminal intelligence that can serve to target perpetrators both inside and outside the European Union.[5] Moreover, Europol also promotes sophisticated techniques of criminal analysis and the harmonization of investigation techniques to member states. In order to ensure the diffusion of best practices and the development of networks, Europol regularly organizes training seminars for police and customs officials. And Europol also supervises the installation and management of a complex information system aimed at facilitating diffusion, access, and the analysis of data which come from national police services inside and outside the EU (the TECH system). Although police, judicial and political actors have systematically attempted to slow down this type of growth, it is important to better understand how Europol, acting as a vector for information exchange, is today capable of actively participating in multilateral police investigations and to foster the development of norms and best practices in police cooperation.[6]

Europol and a market for information

Because they wanted to ensure the protection and stability of social, economic and political institutions, several member states invested considerable resources in the development of information technology and the restructuring and reform of their police and customs services in order to improve cooperation in the fight against transnational crime. The whole of the transformations which have stemmed from either individual or collective initiatives has resulted in the birth of a police information market: a market in which the need and the demand for intelligence are formulated and come to shape the quality and quantity of the information exchange process.

During the decade covering 1980–90, the transfer of military technologies toward the police sector combined with the cuts effected in the area of national security have hindered reform activity for many national police services (Bayley and Shearing 1996; O'Malley 1997). One which is of special significance is the development of a new managerial approach which emphasizes the strategic utilization of police resources in proactive operations guided by criminal intelligence: *intelligence-led policing* (Maguire 2000). The acquisition of a technological arsenal has given police services a significant capacity to collect and analyse information coming from social and criminal environments. Police services quickly sought databases that allowed them to develop practical and useful knowledge to guide criminal investigations, to profile delinquents, and to plan repressive operations. Moreover, sophisticated information technologies stimulated the development of new communication channels by offering information exchange mechanisms that were evermore rapid and effective. And technological advances have led to the identification of solutions to the emerging problems of standardization of data and of harmonization of computer systems.

The increased utilization of new technologies and the non-stop quest for performance in the fight against transnational crime have provoked a concentration of information and the centralization of intelligence collection and analysis in member states (Den Boer and Doelle 2000).[7] Although the centralization of information simplifies the exchange of national intelligence, there are centralized structures which in certain conditions can authorize local police services to exchange information directly with other police agencies (domestic and foreign). In addition, it seems that a significant amount of European countries still maintain decentralized police infrastructures whereby it remains at the discretion of particular law enforcement agencies to decide whether or not to share the intelligence they gather. In other words, the national markets for police information can be characterized by a constellation of actors who exchange intelligence inside diversified, fragmented, and sometimes informal, channels of communication.

These national and European initiatives structure the market for information by housing a massive data management mechanism which is necessary for the multilateral fight against transnational crime. They also result in the creation of organisms which can respond to the specific needs of national police services (the CCPD, BCCP). Nevertheless, the organization of the market for information in Europe is problematic as it relates to the transfer of police data. On the one hand, this information is often perceived as the property both of states and of the police services who obtained it. On the other hand, the issue of universal access to data is a sensitive debate that continues to take place throughout the political and operational law enforcement communities. Moreover, there is lack of trust and reciprocity in the process of information exchange which fosters the development of inter-organizational relationships which often stem from interpersonal relations.

Europol already faced considerable obstacles including 1) a fragmented and heavily regulated information market; 2) competing mechanisms and structures that were well established; and 3) a demand for criminal intelligence at its inception. Not only did the services of Europol not correspond adequately to the expectations of several national police services (the production of strategic analysis), they also faced stiff competition by well established organizations that provided several services which were perceived as similar. While the success of Europol rests on the voluntary participation of national police services, without the intelligence they hold they are limited in their ability to perform strategic threat assessments and other analyses. And even though Europol comprises police personnel, the lack of executive powers results in Europol not being considered as a 'sister agency' by national police services. Instead, it is perceived in interviews as a lumpen bureaucracy in which politics has priority over policing.

In order to be functional, Europol has had to reach two main objectives: 1) to gain the trust of national police services; and 2) to enhance informational capacity. To that end, Europol implemented strategies which represented an added value beyond those offered by existing mechanisms. First and foremost, the national central bureaux lend direct access, albeit limited to the police services of member states. In fact, although the national bureaux can provide bridges for information exchange, the rates of participation have varied from state to state, leaving Europol to respond to requests for information from national police services. Moreover, besides having informal channels of communication, Europol had few contacts with national police agencies in those member states with a decentralized police apparatus.

With the aim of reducing the distance that separated national police services and to obtain privileged access to first-hand intelligence, in 2000 Europol created an analysis service to assist international investigations. Analysts were invited to participate in joint operations and their role was to present the information collected from national police services to guide investigators. In cooperation with the national police services they created, specific databases categorized criminal activities of interest. At its onset, this service was only offered in a bilateral manner to guarantee the exclusivity of such information and to develop trust between foreign police services. Nevertheless, these databases escaped from the control of many member states and were thus outside the confines of the convention, especially because they contained nominal data. Facing pressures by the European Community and the Council of Europe, Europol was constrained to modify this strategy in 2002–2003.

According to Europol's crime analysis unit, this shift in the approach to working with national police services has considerably destabilized the information exchange mechanisms. In fact, the Analysis Work Files (AWF) system does not guarantee a reciprocity of information exchange because the case files are available to all national police services within the membership. In order to ensure a continuous participation by police services, Europol has reorganized the way they put together the AWF by regionalizing the analysis files. Although there are negative consequences to producing strategic analysis strictly for European states, as they risk being estranged from the operational preoccupations of police officers, Europol is able to produce operational analyses to support joint investigations. As a result, each of the AWFs focuses specifically on one type of criminal activity (drug trafficking or people smuggling, etc.) and regroups a varying number of national police services that are directly concerned with the phenomenon in question.

This initiative has several advantages for the central bureaux and generates considerable benefits for Europol. On one hand, the reorganization of AWFs brings an added value to the existing structures such as trans-border cooperation agreements. By adopting a regional perspective, AWFs reach beyond information exchange between border authorities by integrating national police services whose investigations can benefit from comprehensive intelligence. Further, this approach allows the national police apparatus to gain a bigger picture of a transnational criminal phenomenon as the analyses are better and more narrowly targeted. On the other hand, this procedural change allows Europol to fulfill its mandate more adequately. Taking part in joint investigations, controlled drug deliveries or other operational activities has allowed Europol to obtain first-hand access to information which is crucial to the accuracy and integrity of the finished intelligence. Consequently, the more specific the strategic analysis is, the more useful to police services the threat assessments are, as their degree of accuracy increases. Moreover, by participating in joint investigations, Europol is closing the gap that separates national police services all the way to local police departments by constantly improving the national information flow system. Finally, the accumulation of operational experiences lends Europol a level of expertise which is significant enough to coordinate joint investigations and even to prescribe standards for transnational investigations and criminal analysis. The gradual gain in recognition of Europol's expertise by police services contributes to establishing its legitimacy, develops relationships of trust and increases the volume of information exchange even with the most reluctant member states.

Beyond the mandate, before the mandate

In order to understand better how Europol was able to extend the reach of its activities so quickly after its inception, we must examine the principal factors that explain how an international organization, bound by the principles of sovereignty and a respect for state supremacy, can expand its field of activities so quickly and significantly. These operational gains were realized despite a constraining mandate whereby states requested information or fed information into the system on a voluntary basis when it was in their interests to do so. And these gains are considerable when compared with other international agreements concerning cooperation initiatives such as with Interpol and UN agencies (the UNDCP for example) and even transborder agencies such as the CCPD or BCCPs. In order to understand the origin of these gains, we must scrutinize the source of those initiatives that allow Europol to exert influence over national policies and procedures and assume an active role in the fight against transnational crime. Does the influence come from the formulation of national security policies? Are there other forces that shape the expansion of the mandate of Europol? How is this proactive, even interventionist, approach being received and implemented by states?

Interviews with Europol staff suggest that a significant number of the initiatives discussed above have arisen out of interactions between the 'entrepreneurs' who staff the Secretariat, the liaison offices, and various individual police officers in member states. Even though the demand for international intelligence was imprecise before the creation of Europol, the fact still remains that this demand was shaped by the needs expressed by national police services. Because of the disparities between the expectations of the political realm (public opinion) and operational considerations, the enlargement of the mandate of Europol addresses the obstacles that police services must tackle in their efforts to cooperate. According to Hebenton and Thomas (1995: 200), cooperation between police agencies is hindered by a lack of competence, expertise and commitment and also by the lack of essential structural conditions for the proper flow of information.

Because of the reality that European police cooperation is restricted by a normative framework that discourages any ambition by Europol to gain executive powers, it could be possible that the complexity of legal and political environments has contributed to the emergence of an 'informal entrepreneur' who is attempting to fill a demand for criminal intelligence that impacts police operations. Europol has readily realized the weak capacity of member states to participate systematically in an international system of cooperation based on the voluntary exchange of information (Gerspacher 2005).

This less than stellar commitment to police cooperation affects the quality and pertinence of the output. The irregularity of information flows at the national level, the lack of adequate technology and judicial and political constraints, the heterogeneity of judicial systems and investigation techniques, and the respect for human rights all contribute to a rather erratic implementation of international collaboration policies. In such a context, Europol takes the reins and strives to counterbalance the negative effects of these constraints by allowing it to stimulate the demand for international strategic intelligence with the aim of subscribing to its own organizational objectives.

In order to overcome the numerous obstacles which limit the exchange of information, the experts, analysts and liaison officers have developed numerous procedures to help create, and even shape, a favourable environment for police cooperation. The tools have been developed largely outside the mandate of Europol but are necessary prerequisites to the mission that was initially given to Europol (e.g. the collection and analysis of information). Through the elaboration of training programmes[8] and conferences hosted by Europol and offered to the national police services, these initiatives foster the development of networks of police services throughout the membership and promote the exchange of inter-organizational knowledge and competences (experiences, expertise, etc.). The benefits of such exchanges are widely recognized today. It should be noted that the work of liaison officers has been adjusted at several occasions to respond better to the needs of national police services during seminars organized by Europol. These initiatives are implemented inside Europol. As one Europol official pointed out, 'If member states don't act, Europol will step in'.[9]

Interviews also reveal that officers who have been seconded to Europol, and thus are taking leave from their national police service functions and whose duties are re-orientated towards an internationally-minded mission, enjoy a privileged position. This new perspective allows them to experience at first hand the nature of the needs and failings in member states' international cooperation systems. They are also better placed to identify the most appropriate and viable solutions and approaches in the fight against transnational crime. This observation goes against conventional wisdom which stipulates that states are the principal agents of change in the mandate of Europol (Lake and Powell 1999). Thus, the delegation of operational tasks is not always a state's doing but seemingly results from an informal implementation of products/services that are either requested by national police services during conferences at Europol or via the intermediary of networks established between former colleagues and new contacts in a new international cooperation environment. Just as interpersonal relations between liaison officers have been considered to act as motors of transformation in information exchange systems between border police (Sheptycki 2005), we should not underestimate the role of networks between subnational and international actors (Gerspacher and Dupont 2007). Therefore the simple presence of police networks is crucial to cooperation. All in all, the implementation of initiatives that generate operational benefits takes place via 'police entrepreneurs' who come from central national police services and are acting as international actors (as officials of Europol).

Even if the introduction of new operational services takes place outside official channels, cooptation takes place inside a forum which possesses neither decision-making powers nor autonomy in the determination of its mandate and activities. Nevertheless, these initiatives must be accepted, or albeit adopted, by member states and then integrated into the official mandate. This practice ensures the necessary degree of legitimacy for these initiatives, an especially important component when dealing with non-cooperating or non-initiating states. In the opposite case, the legitimacy of Europol's actions would be compromised and this would risk meeting significant legal challenges at the national level. Nevertheless, the ratification of international agreements takes time. Their content is often rendered vague in order to satisfy the interests of a relatively heterogeneous mix of member states, especially those states who exhibit a natural reluctance to participating in the Europol system. In such a context, Europol seems to prefer an approach that allows it to demonstrate *de facto*, at the heart of the market, the utility of these new services by promoting the benefits via networks of Europol officers which include both police and political actors. Our visits to the Europol Secretariat in The Hague gave us the opportunity to witness a regular flow of exchange with the directorate which vehemently defends the interests of Europol and European ministers. Europol's informal activities weaken the supremacy of member states (impunity, democratic deficit, delegation to international organizations and intervention in judicial systems), as these constrain member states in acknowledging the contributions and benefits of these initiatives which in turn stimulate a rethinking and renegotiation of its mandate.

Conclusion

Throughout this chapter we have argued that there have been significant changes in Europol's activities, lending it a more active role in the facilitation of international police cooperation. We made the case for an expansion of its role by putting forth the lack of capacity of member states to implement a national system which is conducive to the participation of its police services at an international level and an evident request for information exchange with operational implications. We first presented the progression of the mandate of Europol with a focus on the speed of the changes that have ensued in its field of expertise and activity. We must not forget that in 1992 Europol was created to facilitate cooperation between police services in the fight against drug trafficking only. Since 2000, Europol has fostered the exchange of information, performed analyses, and coordinated joint investigations in 18 different international crime areas. This wider field of activities suggests that due to its operational involvement Europol has begun to resemble more an international intelligence police entity than a facilitator of information sharing, particularly when compared with Interpol and Schengen.

To support this claim, we showed that the role of Europol has changed significantly. We argued that Europol is becoming a knowledge broker and has contributed to the identification and shaping of the demand for coordination of joint investigations to compensate for a lack of adequate organization and national institutions and for the limited expertise of the national police services in the area of international cooperation. In fact, Europol has not only utilized its status as a forum for information exchange, it has also capitalized on the analysis of operational information exchange in order to respond better to the demands of member states and to adjust its services and procedures to better meet the expectations of police services who were largely unsatisfied by the strategic activities of Europol which they had judged as marginal contributions. Thus, Europol fills a void by acting as a broker between the demand for assistance and the provision of those essential services necessary for the facilitation of international police cooperation – its initial and ultimate *raison d'être*. These services have, for the most part, operational value and they are provided at the margins of the mandate. Consequently Europol acts informally without the official authorization of the European parliament or any ratification by member states.

Finally, our interviews allowed us to highlight the capacity of an international organization to exert sufficient influence on member states to ensure the enlargement of its mandate when its ability to reach its goals seemed threatened. This observation is particularly interesting because it goes against conventional wisdom which stipulates that states have supreme authority, being the only actors allowed to enlarge, or modify, the mandate of the international organizations that they create and support. While states have delegated their authority to Europol in order to respond more adequately to the needs of national police services and to facilitate cooperation between them, we must also recognize that officers who work at the international level and whose interests reflect more that of the European Union than of any one member state have significantly contributed to the enlargement of Europol's mandate.

The influence that the 'police entrepreneurs' of Europol have on national political agendas is particularly interesting since the innovations and implementation of new services are effected outside the margins of international agreements, in short, defying or simply bypassing the limitations of the mandate. However, the added value attached to these initiatives must eventually be recognized officially in order for the products and services to become legitimate practices that are susceptible to benefit those states who are most reluctant to cooperate and who hesitate to become implicated in the informal initiatives deployed by Europol. This phenomenon challenges earlier studies that stipulated international police cooperation is constructed around a demand which comes from member states and is gradually structured via the intermediary of official channels such as agreements, treaties and conventions (Kube and Kuckuk 1992). Rather, after careful scrutiny of the Europol case, we can observe that police cooperation is developed in a market for information in the hands of individuals who have the requisite competences, expertise, resources and contacts to identify and adequately respond to the needs of national police services (first operational and then strategic, rather than the other way around). The collateral impacts of these initiatives lead to the ability of an international organization to 1) establish norms and standards in judicial matters (joint investigations); 2) intervene in member states by targeting individual suspected perpetrators through operational analyses (circumventing the principles of sovereignty and subsidiarity); and 3) establish new channels of communication and expand the information flows between member states.

Meanwhile, the interpretation that we offer essentially rests on first-hand information and observations collected at the Europol Secretariat. Nevertheless, suggestions about the intervention and self-determination that we describe may also be found in recent debates that denounce the lack of democratic control over Europol and the influence that the organization exerts on national police services. Moreover, the interviews we conducted with national criminal intelligence services have allowed us to observe that those who do not hold executive powers demonstrate a strong capacity to innovate which often surpasses the scope of their mandate, in order to offer services and products that allow 1) the establishment of their own credibility *vis-à-vis* national law enforcement agencies; 2) the securement of a privileged place in the national market for police information, and 3) the shaping of the police cooperation environment by introducing standards and best practices in the exchange of information as well as in joint investigations. This observation seems particularly true when the criminal intelligence personnel of national services comprise police officers who come from agencies that hold law enforcement authority. In order to expand on the thesis that we have put forth here, future research projects should focus on the 'sociability' of police cooperation agencies (national and international) in order to understand better how they can develop and utilize the ties they make with other organizational and institutional actors. In addition, we would also find it pertinent to evaluate the impact of initiatives deployed by international police cooperation organizations on the volume of exchanges between national police services.

Notes

1 Nadia Gerspacher contributed to this article as a post-doctoral fellow at the Center for International Compared Criminology at the University of Montreal, Montreal, Canada.
2 This is an intergovernmental initiative which aims to promote the exchange of police information, a harmonization of the policies, justice systems and regulatory measures of member countries, as well as the drafting of a strategic analysis of transnational crime.
3 The signatories are: Indonesia, Malaysia and the Philippines.
4 Among the operations in which Europol has participated are Opération Carl (1997–98), Opération Primo (1997–98), Opération Bellomo (1998), Opération Calabaza (1998), Opération Pristina (1998) and 32 controlled deliveries of narcotics (Europol, Annual Report – 1998).
5 In 2005, Europol contributed to the identification of individuals involved in Euro counterfeiting in Colombia. The results of this operation led to the arrest of a suspect, the issuance of arrest warrants for several suspects, and the seizure of 2.5 million counterfeited Euros and sophisticated material.
6 We particularly refer to the development of better practices in the control of police informants, drug lab dismantling operations, and the publication of operational manuals to guide the services offered by the liaison bureaux.
7 The German government has designated the BKA as the coordinator of information exchange between Lander police services as well as having a duty to communicate at the international level. In the UK, the NCIS was created to produce intelligence to support local and national police services. Now merged into SOCA it was responsible for the exchange

of information between foreign police services. We also should mention that the implementation of federal police in Belgium (Fedpol) has led to the centralization of police data in one national databank, *carrefours d'informations d'arrondissements* (CIA), which is linked to Fedpol and responsible for border zones information exchange. Finally, we can note that the Netherlands has centralized its management of police information at the National Corps of police services (KLPD) whose mission includes the coordination of information exchange between the 25 regional police services and foreign police agencies.

8 This refers to the identification and dismantling of synthetic drug labs, the counterfeiting of Euros, and the drafting of analysis reports.
9 Interview of Liaison Officer at the Europol Secretariat, January 2005.

Part 2

Applied police cooperation:
initiatives and limitations

Chapter 5

Iterative development of cooperation within an increasingly complex environment: example of a Swiss regional analysis centre[1]

Olivier Ribaux and Stéphane Birrer

Introduction

Law enforcement agencies are externally linked with a broad set of institutions (public and private), communities and people. These links between entities are of different natures and continuously evolve, for instance in the function of changes of policies, laws, organizations, models of policing, technologies, the perception of problems, and the dynamic of informal confidence relationships. This complex multi-agency system seems increasingly difficult to understand within a contemporaneous context that incites to shift towards an intelligence-sharing attitude. The interlinked dimensions to take into account are various and numerous. More often than not, they are not considered holistically. This is particularly evident when salient weaknesses of intelligence systems, such as an incapacity to 'connect the dots', are detected. Any solutions found might cause uncontrolled consequences in a chain reaction, potentially creating more problems than they solve.

Different methods and models have been suggested for supporting the global understanding of this increasingly complex structure. For instance, symbolic representations of entities connected by links of various types can be used to model the network dimension of co-operative police systems (Gerspacher and Dupont 2007). Theories related to crime intelligence (Ratcliffe 2008) and formalizations of intelligence-led systems (GNIM 2005) have the potential to structure the use of new communication channels opened up within the new national and international cooperation landscape. Indeed, combining studies on networks and the nature of knowledge used in police intelligence systems seems a very promising modelling approach (Brodeur and Dupont 2006).

However, despite those valuable efforts we can assume that fundamental difficulties underlying new intelligence cooperation frameworks are still not always understood and recognized. Indeed, it is obvious that formalized intelligence-sharing systems do not contain a comprehensive modelling of relevant factors and their relationships (Sheptycki 2004).

These considerations provide the motivations for studying existing police intelligence systems in more detail. Of importance here is not only how they work now, but rather how they have evolved and adapted over time within their singular demanding environment. We would argue that, beyond the implementation of formal systems within organizations, structures have mainly evolved iteratively, via small and tractable adaptations. These changes have been stimulated in the main on the initiative of the practitioners themselves. These developments are also often ignored, and even occasionally seen as undesirable by management. They are generally poorly formalized by their inventors who have little interest and time for theorizing. Successful paths of adaptations should be studied more in order to evaluate the possibility of recognising that an adaptive and iterative approach can form the basis of a possible complementary method for coping with the complexity of the environment.

This chapter relates the specific development and evolution of a regional analysis centre in Switzerland considering this perspective. It first justifies the approach by describing how difficult it is to recognize the intractable difficulties within systems that are in need of rational frameworks. However, in related domains that have to cope with a complex and continuously changing environment, there is a movement toward more iterative and adaptive methods. By analogy, we will interpret the evolution of a specific regional analysis centre over several years as a process of successively adapting the system in regard to encountered obstacles.

In particular, we claim that original developments have resulted from this approach. Once formalised, they have been published in the scientific literature. These considerations will open a final discussion about the lessons learned, in particular how the academic world has joined in with the process.

Recognizing the difficulty

Within police intelligence systems, the timely understanding of continuously changing crime problems is ideally obtained from the collaborative contribution of distributed, efficient and analytical capacities that spread over several organizations and cover the whole range of territories and competencies, from a local to an international level, from the treatment of petty to serious crimes, and from tactical to strategic assessments. This should result from a subtle, formalized equilibrium that integrates a broad set of relevant interacting dimensions, ranging from technical considerations to all aspects influencing the context of intelligence activities. The aim of most formalizations of intelligence systems, from legal frameworks to standard operating procedures, is to prescribe how information should be processed within such a context.

However, one must also recognize that we are far from having reached an optimal arrangement of these different pieces. Indeed, it may be asked whether this complexity involving so many nations, regulations, organizations and individuals is really tractable or not. Despite regular efforts to formalize management strategies, and to devise the flow of information, real-life situations show that intelligence-sharing still suffers from various types of pervasive pathologies that come from the environment in which these are deployed (Sheptycki 2004). Evident and salient weaknesses such as the inability/incapacity to 'connect up the dots' or linkage blindness[2] are recurrent particularly when manifold agencies are expected to cooperate. These universal factors underlie failures in investigations, intelligence or puzzle solving.

Indeed, intelligence represents a trade-off between various factors operating in tension with one another. There are many obvious examples of the necessity to balance arguments. Series of individual (rivalries), organizational (hierarchies) or national interests compete with the project of elaborating harmonious networked system. Intelligence sharing endangers privacy and civil liberties, and increases the risk of informing the adversaries of intentions and means. The application of detailed procedures, bureaucracy, quality control, and other management tools has an effect on motivation, imagination and creativity. Adequate analysis can be hampered by costly and time-consuming plans for collecting detailed but unnecessary information.

In such an interlinked environment, unexpected forms of linkage blindness then arise as a side effect of the corrective measures taken. For instance, because of the detection of obvious weaknesses, there is a recent aspiration to shift toward a 'need to share' attitude. This trend influences, directly or indirectly, a broad variety of other dimensions to the problem. Rules for safeguarding privacy and secret information are debated on this new basis, potentially changing the regulations substantially. This is compounded by the consequences of opening new communication channels that are susceptible to being inappropriately used and cause information overflow. Finally, informal confidence networks and motivation may even be damaged by the burdens of bureaucracy that implement these new formal procedures. Further consequences are probably manifold, producing a chain reaction that is impossible to anticipate. These difficulties already pervade at the level of a single organization, but are amplified when different agencies are expected to cooperate when dealing with common crime problems.

All these considerations should not deflect our attention from the more fundamental aspects pertaining to the treatment of vast quantities of imperfect information. The limits to human cognition, our use of computers and algorithms, and the quality of available data are also occasionally difficult to admit. Numerous factors are thus increasingly interlinked: when changing one of them the consequences become more and more difficult to anticipate. From one reform to the next, there is an evident risk that the salient weaknesses of the whole system are the focus of efforts that can lead to simplistic and apparent obvious measures that can cause more problems than they solve. We must recognize that the ideal trade-off or subtle equilibrium to be found can hardly be devised within such a continuously changing, increasingly complex, and largely unpredictable and unknowable environment.

Iterative and adaptive approach

This underlying complexity must be captured in a certain way or at least dealt with. Many new policies and agreements, reorganizations, platforms for communications or ambitious developments of computerized systems have failed while others have succeeded. The reasons for such failures and successes are sometimes related to the competence of the project management or the motivation of the participants. But they are rarely related to the realization that certain key parameters were simply uncontrollable, depended on individual perceptions, and went beyond what was laid down in official procedures. In other cases, entirely outside of formalized organisational projects, best practices, individual initiatives or prototyped computerized systems have occasionally obtained an official existence through their recognized effectiveness.

Rather than rejecting those kinds of successful developments as being undesirable exceptions, we propose to make these explicit as a possible complementary methodology for overcoming the above mentioned limits for developing cooperative intelligence systems.

This proposition can be related to movements in several disciplines facing the devising and integration of methods and tools within complex and changing environments. For example, some schools of thought in computer science maintain their distance from the traditional software developments made of well structured cycles based on the formalized flow of information. Better situating the designer and the user within his/her continuously changing and largely intractable environment was the keytone of the argument here (Hofmann *et al.* 1993). The authors asked for a recognition that the official and formal tasks of potential system users were not the sole basis for devising a system. It was more important to consider perceptions and confront the viewpoints of participants interacting within a changing environment.

The movement created around so-called *agile developments* methodologies rests on the rapid development of a software system that is articulated around a core architecture. This is a basic system explicitly considered as a starting point. New functionalities are then integrated iteratively, in the function of new demands and how the system and users behave in their real environment. These methodologies are aimed at overcoming the incapacity of future users to formalize their needs exhaustively at the beginning of a project and then adapt to changes in a flexible way, rather than trying to follow formal procedures to the letter. 'Agile development excels in exploratory problem domains – extreme, complex, high-change projects – and operates best in a people centered, collaborative, organisational culture. This approach has proved to be effective at solving many problems and at forging attractive work environments in many organisations' (Cockburn and Highsmith 2001: 133). Successful specific computerized systems and databases have been created in police intelligence environments. These were mostly developed on the basis of individual initiatives, with only an amateur knowledge of programming. Agile development is certainly a possible model of how these were effectively elaborated.

From a more general perspective, we can claim that the evolution and adaptation of some intelligence units, methods and tools have followed similar patterns within their respective contexts. These started with a core set of initial missions and activities and have evolved and adapted iteratively along all dimensions (legal, organizational, methodological and technological) of a continuously changing and complex environment. We propose scrutinizing these kinds of developments using our viewpoint. We assume that this perspective will provide indications of a possible methodology for supporting the development of suitable intelligence-sharing frameworks in an iterative and adaptive way.

The evolution of a Swiss regional analysis centre will illustrate this proposition. The whole Swiss security system is particularly scattered by keeping the main security competencies at a rather local level. Switzerland is definitely a fertile area for cumulating all types of problems between all types of organizations, from a local to an international level.

However, despite this seemingly fuzzy and continuously changing environment, regional analysis centres have grown up during the past years. They materialized some kind of agreement for turning toward a more intelligence-led style of policing at a regional level, in order to improve the coordination and cooperation between the different forces.

The initial project stated this global aim. But all the dimensions of the problem, in particular the methodological and technological content, were to be developed almost from scratch since 1994. From this point, contributors to the system have permanently searched for some equilibrium and thus gone in some contingent directions outside of what have become 'traditional frameworks' since this time. The environment was not always favourable for this police network, not to say occasionally showing some hostility. Indeed, the development of the structure has been mostly iterative. It was elaborated by individuals situated within a demanding, changing, and largely unpredictable and unknowable environment. The result obtained is far from perfect and still shows evident weaknesses. However, several experiences have led to original published methods that may enrich these already formalized frameworks. The experience will be described with this iterative and situated viewpoint.

The context

Some aspects of security and police in Switzerland

The location of Switzerland at the centre of Western Europe contrasts with its political position on the border of the European Community. The country is also frequently the target of groups of itinerant criminals. It cannot be contested that the structure of criminality at a European level crosses jurisdictions and largely concerns Switzerland. This has been an argument for participating in the new European security landscape. Cooperation agreements have been signed with Europol and all neighbouring countries and the integration into the Schengen space is now also effective.

A federal police conducts investigations mostly in fields related to organized crime. Otherwise, its tasks are largely related to the security of the state, the protection of personality tasks, providing a platform for exchanging data with foreign countries, and internally supporting and coordinating efforts with other police forces. Because of international developments and new agreements, the importance of this structure as a hub in international exchanges of information has considerably increased over the past years. Finally, centralized databases have been developed in the field of organized crime, wanted persons, and object and vehicle searches, as well as in the treatment of forensic case data (fingerprint and DNA databases).

Despite a growing role for the federal police within the country, the organization of the judicial system and the police is essentially part of the internal affairs of each of 26 autonomous regions called cantons. These organizations vary greatly in size, and the territories covered by the different forces are extremely disparate, ranging from urban areas to rural or mountainous regions. This diversity is completed by a layer of municipal police forces in most of the cantons. Two cities also have full investigative competences in their territories (Lausanne and Zurich). Police regulation is itself dispersed over the national, cantonal and municipal levels.

Beyond these police structures, important contact points have been implemented as a result of bilateral agreements with neighbouring countries. In particular, the cooperation centre between Switzerland and France has been operating since 2004, allowing Swiss and French law enforcement agencies to exchange certain types of information by using a one-window system (a centralization of all demands). The role of this centre will be discussed further.

Switzerland is resolutely a federalist country, and this is directly reflected in its police structure. The contemporary police system has its roots mainly in the *'Acte de médiation'* signed by Napoleon in 1803. The emperor tried to establish a central republic, but resistance was too strong. He finished by accepting a system based on an assemblage of its cantons in order to respect the diversity of the cultures that distinguished the different regions. Switzerland is also a multilingual country, with four official languages for fewer than 8 million inhabitants. The languages effectively spoken consist of a broad diversity of very specific dialects. Thus, the country is also divided into linguistic regions that can also have an impact on police practices and cooperation.

Top-down and bottom-up approaches to adaptation

Of importance is that this system is regularly challenged by a series of ambitious projects of reforms initialized at the level of the confederation (central level). This is typically a top-down approach that may also be externally stimulated, for instance by developments in neighbouring countries or as a result of other influential tendencies. However, most of these attempts have globally failed for different reasons. For instance, a very ambitious project named USIS[3] in the early 2000s was supposed to dramatically impact the whole security system. The motivation of this reform was based on recurring identified weaknesses, and the necessity of better situating Switzerland within the changing European security system. However, after several years and many working groups and evaluation reports, the project was rejected politically. It may be that it was too complex, involving too many competing institutions and persons. Fears of endangering data protection by more centralization and some pervasive conflicts on preserving autonomy and interests, as well as difficulties in elaborating fair budgets between the different political levels, finished off these processes.

However, after each similar attempt, some components of the original plan were finally implemented. For instance, the new centralized index for searching a canton's police records is about to be implemented at a national level, although it was originally part of the bigger, abandoned project. And Switzerland is finally also connected to the European system. Small steps towards more centralization have resulted from the remnants of the big projects. Another movement led to reforming and adapting processes towards a more structured cooperation between cantons. A series of conventions and agreements were signed at a regional level for sharing resources and expertise in fields such as order maintenance, logistics, training and crime intelligence. This is another way of implementing small steps, but in a bottom-up rather than a top-down approach. Broadly speaking, the results of both approaches are the same globally, even if the method is entirely different for each. From ambitious projects, tractable components are extracted and implemented in the top-down approach, while the bottom-up strategy rests on delineated problems treated from the viewpoint of the cooperation of several cantons. The whole system seems to evolve iteratively on this dual, occasionally conflicting, way. The regional analysis centre called CICOP[4] was created in this context through an alliance created between some of the cantons.

The regional analysis centre (CICOP)

Since 1990, a group of investigators has been charged to develop a system for the analysis of repetitive crimes within a police force at the level of a single canton. Due to the mobility of some groups of offenders that were operating all over Europe, and in particular crossing over the different regions, the necessity to extend this approach was accepted by the French and Italian speaking cantons in 1994. CICOP was born, followed soon after by the creation of other structures that grouped cantons in the German part (see Figure 5.1).

Figure 5.1 Map of Switzerland showing the delineation of the cantons and their groupings in regional analysis centres

The regional analysis centre has an explicit existence through a convention signed by several cantons. At this point, the structure is answerable to the association of chiefs of police. Two positions are shared by all the contributors and they are administratively linked to one leading canton. Each canton organizes its own structure, and autonomously devises the size and position of this structure in its own organization. Similar structures have been developed across the country. They constitute vital bridges between linguistic regions.

Their missions were originally relatively broad. These related mostly to an understanding of the criminal environment in order to stimulate cantons to coordinate their efforts and share their resources so they could disrupt the activities of itinerant criminals, mostly thieves and burglars.

Models, methods and technology had to be developed from scratch. Even though models for intelligence-led policing and methods for crime analysis were already available in the Anglo-Saxon literature, these were relatively new and of limited visibility in this operational environment and for non-English speaking policemen. Moreover, at the beginning of the process, police forces and academics chose to keep their distance.

Various formal processes have been developed to carry out common analyses of problems that concern the whole region. Broadly, each canton is responsible for the coverage of its region. The mechanisms for the analyses are thus mainly locally based and then aggregated at a regional level. Each police force uses its own internal cooperation framework and adopts intensively informal local communication networks with the forensic unit, CIDs, other policemen, informants or the public in general. Moreover, interpretation of information at a local level allows knowledge about the specific environment to be used, which is less possible at a more centralized level. Connections with local institutions are obviously also of importance for collating manifold data, for instance with the municipal police or other private security services. Of course, specific hypotheses developed during an analysis in one canton may ask for specific comparisons with data in another canton. This kind of hypothetico-deductive reasoning process across police boundaries can be carried out without encountering a lot of obstacles via the regional centre, and performed locally with the support of a set of local databases, for instance distributed footmark collections dedicated to the detection of crime series.

The analysis is enlarged by extensive use of the forensic case data, such as DNA links extracted from the centralized database for detecting crime series. This is combined with the use of footmarks, tool marks, earmarks or even glove marks. Integration of information coming from specific investigations is also a very common trait favoured by the physical proximity of the analysis centre to the CID offices.

Complementary to an aggregation strategy, a central analysis is carried out on the basis of a shared database that is fed into by all the contributing analysts, as well as during a monthly analysis meeting. It integrates the most relevant forensic links detected and thus provides a general overview of the crime series detected at a certain time.

Methodologically, these activities are guided at every level and over most of the country by a harmonized and very simple classification system that has been specifically devised for recognizing and isolating within crime data a series of relevant and recurrent crime problems. It allows a follow-up on the main detected phenomena under its competency in Switzerland, and also feeds into European knowledge by creating profiles, such as the activities of itinerant burglars, or other offenders playing confidence tricks, or crime problems such as metal thefts (or even the theft of engines from private boats that is currently a proliferating occurrence). This system has been based on using the Italian language (a minority in Switzerland), which is a common way to solve multilingualism issues in Switzerland.

The main product of the centre consists of a weekly synthesis dedicated to investigators, chiefs of operations and border guards. The document is then finalized by the leading canton. In certain cantons, specific documents extracted from the global synthesis are produced. These provide a basis for making decisions at the level of each force.

Manifold activities complete the work, such as supports for joint investigations, an ad-hoc structure for punctual analysis, a network of people across different organizations, or the provision of other advice when connections beyond the border of an individual canton are needed. In particular, CICOP serves as a hub in the connection with a contact point shared with France, the federal police, and border guards.

Despite a lot of obstacles encountered within this complex multi-agency assemblage, this structure has developed, structured its methodology, influenced other developments in Switzerland, and grown over time. The developed forms of analysis can mostly be classified under the operational and tactical categories, relatively proximate to the investigation (modus operandi, follow-up of crime problems, target profiles analysis, detection of crime series etc.).

However, strategic assessments may also occasionally be based on an analysis at this regional level.

Relationships with the academic world have also developed over the last several years, in particular with the School of Criminal Justice of a nearby university and its forensic science department. This has definitely had an effect on the formalization of the process by grounding its theoretical basis and supporting an iterative strategy through a series of experiments on the treatment of data. These studies covered the integration of data mining technologies into such processes, more global considerations on combining forensic case data, or the situational dimensions of the developed classification system. A series of published work is a direct consequence of these kinds of relationships with the academic world (for a review of these works, see for instance (Birrer and Ribaux 2008; Ratle *et al.* 2006; Ratle, Gagne *et al.* 2007; Ratle, Terrettaz-Zufferey *et al.* 2006; Ribaux and Margot 1999, 2003; Ribaux, Girod *et al.* 2003; Ribaux, Walsh *et al.* 2006; Terrettaz-Zufferey, Ratle *et al.* 2006; Walsh, Ribaux *et al.* 2004).

However, it has to be recognized that CICOP is still under pressure, caught between a rock and a hard place: top-down initiatives from the central level may endanger its existence. Weaknesses in the alliance of the cantons may also cause its collapse. There is still no central intelligence-led philosophy where CICOP could be situated. At least recently, thanks to these developments, the federal level was able to present the European commission with a three-level analysis structure (local, regional and central) that satisfied the evaluation preceding the effective initiation of the integration of Switzerland into the Schengen security space. It may be that this role will consolidate its position and improve its national recognition.

Example: the development of intelligence databases

When the intelligence structure was set up, the available computerized systems consisted mostly of unrelated databases, uniquely devised by each canton. These stored reported criminal events and criminal records. However, for several reasons these were not suitable for carrying out intelligence tasks.

- When a case was reported to the police, several weeks were necessary for entering data into some of the systems, which obviously did not allow for an up-to-date analysis.

- Data were mostly organized around criminal codes and modus operandi, which had been demonstrated to be unsuitable for analytical purposes.

- Methods for entering data and the technologies used were incompatible between the different cantonal systems.

There was clearly a need to develop new and specific tools that were better adapted to intelligence tasks. This process started at the level of a single canton. Local use of another database, called the 'journal', was chosen for storing criminal events. This database recorded very synthetic information on manifold events faced by the police. At the beginning it was distributed on a daily basis, in a printed format that was widely distributed across the organization. This information had the advantage of being available immediately after the first intervention by the police at the scene. However, it was not directly accessible to the intelligence unit and the data were not technically extractable. Thus, relevant information had to be selected from the printed document and re-entered manually into a simple database developed by the analysts themselves. This was somewhat absurd but there was no other solution. Yet from the beginning, this intelligence database was merely tolerated by the police force because a new ambitious computerized system then under development was supposed to integrate all the functionalities required. But for different reasons, mostly pertaining to the intractable complexity of the project, this system never fulfilled its promise. Iteratively, the small but flexible database developed in several adaptation phases. Automatic extraction from the journal system was finally made possible, and the structure of the database was adapted according to the evolution of the crime patterns and the lessons learned. On top of this function, analysis and visualization tools were interfaced and an automatic reporting system was also implemented.

Finally, after about ten years of iterations and adaptations, the system was transformed into an official intercantonal platform, automatically collating information from the manifold databases located in several cantons, accessible to all the analysts across the different police forces, and perfectly integrated into the methodology that itself had developed over time. During the period it has been available, this intercantonal version of the database has already been the object of about 300 adaptations. A consolidated project that may have a national ambition will probably follow. In this example, the tensions between ambitious projects and iterative and adaptive developments are very clear. However, this example does not intend to discredit structured projects emanating from the organization. Rather, we would claim that this kind of development should be understood more as an intelligence project than as a computer science project, and thus it needs a mature formalization that can only be reached through aspects of more limited experiences.

Discussion: the rational gap

This description has highlighted further tensions within intelligence systems. On the one hand, the regional centre has existed for a long time, has developed structured methods, and, even modestly, has improved police cooperation. On the other hand, the global situation, the goals and the integration are fuzzy within a highly complex system made up of numerous autonomous entities. Despite its apparent weaknesses, the structure has reached some kind of equilibrium within this difficult environment. This is challenging from our traditional, rational point of view. Indeed, an ideal framework as described in Table 5.1 can summarize some aspects of this apparent gap. The effective situation seems far from favourable.

The value of the main descriptions of intelligence models or the standard operating procedures that are proliferating is not contested. Nor is the value of available technologies for exchanging and processing information. But we would argue that these formalizations should more explicitly rely on the real substance of analysis which is developed iteratively.

Resisting irrelevant solutions

However, the activity is regularly challenged by external influences. Commercial companies, or other individuals and institutions, will try to impose solutions that directly derive from what is assumed to be an irrefutable statement. More often than not, any proposals are based on technologies. Upon first examination, these can seem reasonable and rational to management. However, when considered more holistically, the relevance of an approach can become less evident.

For instance, mapping incidents has an evident interest (the irrefutable statement). Recurrent brilliant presentations seem rational (one particular case solved for instance), and directed toward the future (technology). These are often welcomed by management.

Table 5.1 Some basic requirements for building an 'ideal' integrated intelligence-led system at the level of a country (for instance based on the National Intelligence Model (GNIM 2005))

	Requirements for crime intelligence	Actual model
Structure	Integrated. Mostly based on a three-level model: local, regional and central.	Mainly local (cantons) and central (confederation).
Legal framework	Homogeneity. Clear formalization.	Scattered, different levels for different competences. Not always very clear about the exchanges of information.
Political and management outcomes	Coherent strategies and objectives on all three levels.	Strategies and priorities are manifold and may occasionally compete.
	An intelligence-led strategy that is established and formalized.	Intelligence-led strategies not yet identified globally as a management philosophy.
Processes	Communication models and infrastructures for collating and analysing data.	Obstacles are manifold.
	Methods and capacity for analysing data. Dedicated training, formalized job descriptions and specific selection processes.	Mainly bilateral exchanges (investigations). Scattered data.
		Various capacities and understanding. Scant training, manifold job descriptions and selection processes.
	Well formalized decision-making processes on the basis of well-structured basic intelligence products.	Mutual assistance.
		On a 'voluntary' basis (confrontation of priorities). Difficult to coordinate.

However, crime mapping goes far beyond sticking pins on maps. Beyond the technology itself, more importance rests on how this technology is integrated into a crime analyst's reasoning process by using various sources of information and the way it is used for communicating information and intelligence. Crime mapping can bring a lot to the practical world, but only if it is well integrated into a more global methodology. Otherwise, it will cost money, time and energy before being eventually discarded.

There are also systematic demands for information sharing through the use of centralized databases (the irrefutable statement). Today, existing technologies provide the support for retrieving relevant information from huge amounts of stored data (the technology). However, depending on what the strategy is to feed these, the systematic use of centralized databanks may cause many false positive results. In turn these create a burden via the data treatment or increased risks of misdirecting justice. Indeed, the cumulating use of certain databases can cause an implicit adoption of a 'database-led policing strategy'. Each hit from the manifold available databases absorbs, in a reactive way, a substantial amount of the available resources to be treated. This fallacy is particularly evident when concentrating at the central level information that needs a local or regional contextualization for its proper interpretation. Aggregations at a higher level should generally occur only as a second step. Analysis and information must be distributed in a subtle equilibrium that takes into account the nature of the data and the reasoning processes in which they are used.

When considering the storage of criminal events, the construction of databases is generally based on the premise that the more the information is detailed the better it will meet the needs of the police (the irrefutable statement). However, more often than not, working groups will spend untold hours collating information from 'specialists' to formalize, for instance, modus operandi files or classification systems. This approach generally results in systems that can separate data by criminal codes and describe modus operandi using hundreds of detailed attributes. This is the result of stacking up individual experiences. Beyond the burden of encoding data and an unavoidable lack of liability, these systems generally support analytical tasks very poorly (Goldstein 1990; Ratcliffe 2008). Moreover, analysis is only one possible use for the police's information within a set of entangled processes fulfilling different purposes. This complexity is often the reason for the recurrent failures of ambitious police databases.

When trying to develop a cooperation framework, opening up communication channels with network technologies is seen as a necessary solution (irrefutable statement and technology). However, the opening of new communication channels has already caused an information overflow and submerged units dedicated to the management of information exchanges.

The multi-dimensionality and simplicity of the system developed by the regional analysis centre differentiate it from these traditional developments. The use of databases, other technologies and communication channels should definitely be well integrated into a global strategy that searches for an ideal trade-off between the factors under tension. Such a system is permanently seeking this equilibrium. It is confronted with failures, conflicts, successes, pressure and hostility from a demanding environment that forces actors to continuously imagine new solutions.

This trade-off can only be obtained by the fine and permanent tuning of a series of parameters. This can be obtained by explicitly adopting a more iterative and adaptive strategy for developing intelligence-sharing.

Relations with the academic world

The explicit iterative and adaptive process consists of the activity of grouping similar experiences into recurrent problems and searching for specific solutions. The evaluation of technologies at an office level and the formalization of analysis and reasoning processes are other important concerns. This typically goes onto a research agenda. However, more often than not, official research and development units are very rare within police organizations. Collaborations with universities are often reduced to punctual projects of limited duration and related to specialized fields. These can hardly be interpreted within the viewpoint of the suggested iterative strategy.

A long-term collaboration with shared objectives is usually very difficult to establish. Beyond some criminological schools, universities are generally very ignorant about the needs of the police, and the police are reluctant to allow external intrusions into their daily activities. Moreover, universities will often search for the broadest applicability of existing theories and models. For instance, general models and methods developed in data mining or geographical information system disciplines can find some interesting applications for crime data. Indeed, academic researchers specialized in these fields are generally enthusiastic about participating in police research projects. But modelling the holistic treatment of imperfect crime data coming from manifold sources is not really the main focus of these studies. This is exactly the kind of misunderstanding and implicit conflicting interests of different communities that often lead to disappointing results. In our view, any added value will not come from testing prefabricated models to detect their potential for use with crime data. Rather, relevant methods, models and technologies are systematically sought in functioning with the variety of problems with which crime intelligence activities are faced.

This is probably the tradition at the University of Lausanne: to group forensic science, criminology and penal law into the same unit so as to favour the implementation of this kind of research strategy. This is compounded by one hundred years of systematic collaboration with the police. The part-time jobs of several researchers within the police structure have favoured the design of relevant studies and helped in the search for research grants. Accessibility to crime data is also an advantage when formalized frameworks are defined and simplified for a whole collaboration and not for punctual projects. The systematic participation of the university in important police working groups and consultancy, as well as in police academy structures, allows for the proper application of an iterative research process.

From the university's viewpoint, this is a very proximate way of collaborating and developing research for the development of police intelligence methods that are preferable to theoretic studies on the police. However, this occurs together with a mutual respect for the autonomy of each structure that shares the goal of increasing capacities and developing knowledge in police intelligence activities.

Federalism and locally based analysis

Along with relationships with academia, the specific Swiss context has certainly favoured the use of generally very poorly used crime data. This covers for instance forensic case data or digital traces that are abundant in the information society. Distributed models in a federalist country also favour other forms of local relationships with CIDs and other actors within the criminal justice system, as well as with private security companies. In such a system, communities of forensic scientists, CIDs and analysts will meet each other daily, collaborate at the crime scene, and then contribute to the global resolution of problems by sharing knowledge through implicit confidence networks. It may be that the irrational situation of a federalist system also has some virtue in allowing the rise of original solutions to be iteratively formalized and integrated into the general body of available knowledge.

Conclusion

An environment of numerous interlinked entities is supposed to deploy efficient intelligence-sharing, in particular through the use of new communication channels. Holistically modelling this activity is far from obvious, despite the proliferation of regulations, organizational charts, and standards for selection, training and procedures. However, beyond formalized processes, information exchanges proceed through implicit confidence networks that largely circumvent these models. It may be that the modelling task is even intractable.

We would argue that for building a global framework for cooperative police intelligence, the practical adaptation of specific units within their continuously changing and largely unpredictable environment should be studied more seriously. Indeed, both the devising of general prescriptions and the local scrutiny of singular complex environments should form the basis of a global methodology. Undoubtedly, a specific approach should be developed around the idea that local realistic solutions are to be found within this demanding environment. The trade-off found between factors under tension can then be discussed and possibly proposed as a more global solution.

The approach has been illustrated by considering the development of a regional analysis centre that tries at best to exploit the available information and knowledge that are spread over a large quantity of individuals and stored under many forms within scattered databases. Individuals are regrouped into many units (forensic department, investigators, beat policemen, etc.) and organizations. They work using different languages and at different levels (local, regional or central) under manifold legal frameworks.

It can be said that, even with its apparent irrational model, from a cooperation perspective Switzerland has acquired the faculty of carrying out valuable local, regional and central analyses using a strategic, operational and tactical perspective.

The implementation of an iterative approach has been made possible because of flexibility, support from the management, and a structured collaboration with the academic world. But it is not in line with the long-term plans and budgets asked for by the administration. Thus, those kinds of developments are still fragile and contested.

The structure can collapse for numerous and apparently 'rational' reasons. Therefore it is vital that one recognizes iterative and adaptive methodology as a possible approach for coping with such complex and interlinked police and crime environments.

Authors' note: Any opinions expressed in this paper are those of the authors and do not constitute policy of the mentioned organizations.

Notes

1 The authors would like to thank Simone Gittelson for her great help in proofreading and correcting the English of this work.
2 Here we interpret 'linkage blindness' in a broad sense. It occurs whenever organizations are not aware of existing connections between entities (crimes, objects, persons, etc.). The causes here are manifold.
3 In German: *Überprüfung des Systems der Inneren Sicherheit der Schweiz.*
4 In French: *Concept Intercantonal de Coopération Opérationnelle et Préventive.*

Chapter 6

The Meuse-Rhine Euroregion: a laboratory for police and judicial cooperation in the European Union

Cyrille Fijnaut and Toine Spapens

Introduction

Over the past few decades, economic and social integration within the European Union (EU) has rapidly gained momentum. This integration has been largely facilitated by the Schengen Implementation Convention of 1990, which abolished border controls between the member states.[1] However, this easing of border controls has also improved and expanded the opportunities for criminals to engage in cross-border illegal activities. Therefore, police and judicial cooperation has now become a high priority on the European Union's agenda.

The authorities in urbanized border areas are usually the first to be confronted by new developments in cross-border crime. As a result, opportunities for law-enforcement cooperation are quickly grasped, and practical innovations are devised as far as the conventions permit. Hence, border areas often serve as 'laboratories' for police and judicial cooperation. A clear example of this is the Meuse-Rhine Euroregion, located in the border areas of the Netherlands, Belgium and Germany.

From a scholarly point of view, jurists have largely dominated the discussion about police and judicial cooperation (Corstens and Pradel 2002; Peers 2000; Sabatier 2001). This is easily explained by the fact that up until now criminologists have conducted relatively little empirical research on this topic. However, the Meuse-Rhine Euroregion is an exception to the rule, as several studies about police and judicial cooperation with regard to the area have been published over the years (Hofstede and Faure 1993; Spapens 2002, 2008a; Spapens and Fijnaut 2005).

Here, we will first address developments in cross-border crime and safety in the Meuse-Rhine Euroregion, as well as examine questions with regard to police and judicial cooperation, and discuss the practical solutions devised to enhance law-enforcement cooperation. Second, we will outline developments considering the legal framework for police and judicial cooperation in the broad context of the European Union on the one hand, and specifically in regards to the Netherlands, Belgium and Germany on the other.

A portrait of the Meuse-Rhine Euroregion

History, people and economy

The Meuse-Rhine Euroregion comprises the Belgian provinces of Liège and Limburg, as well as the German-speaking part of Belgium (the *Ostkantons*), the German *Landkreise* of Aachen, Heinsberg, Düren, and Euskirchen, and the southern part of the Dutch province of Limburg. The Meuse-Rhine Euroregion contains several major cities, such as Aachen, Liège and Maastricht, but there are also very rural areas such as the Hautes-Fagnes Nature Park. On average, the Euroregion is one of the most densely populated border areas within the European Union, with approximately 3.7 million inhabitants. Three official languages (German, Dutch and French) are spoken, as well as a common dialect.[2]

In the Meuse-Rhine Euroregion, cross-border economic and social mobility has always been substantial. This is due to the mining industry having been a major economic activity in all parts of the border area and a redrawing of the map on several occasions due to conflict. Accordingly, the German-speaking part of Belgium represents a good example of border shifting. It was annexed to Belgium after the First World War but, following its occupation by the Nazi regime, it was returned to Germany in 1940. After the end of the Second World War, the *Ostkantons* once again became part of Belgium.

The pace of economic and social integration in the Meuse-Rhine Euroregion increased substantially after 1995, when the Schengen Implementation Convention came into effect. This allowed people to move freely across the borders, and it also became much easier to live, work or start businesses in a neighbouring country. At present, it is fairly common for a Dutchman to live in the Belgian part of the Euroregion and work in the Dutch part of the border area or vice versa. A large number of people cross the border every day for purposes of shopping, recreation, socializing, and so on (Hermans *et al.* 2007).

However, rapid economic and social integration also came with a downside, as problems regarding crime and safety have increasingly come to involve the entire border area.

Questions of public safety, public-order policing, and cross-border crime in the Meuse-Rhine Euroregion

In the past few decades, both public-order policing and serious and organized crime involving indigenous groups have rapidly become internationalized in the Meuse-Rhine Euroregion. In particular, the dealing and trafficking in and the production of illicit drugs have developed into a major problem. These questions are scrutinized in more detail in the following sub-sections.

Public safety and public-order policing
The Meuse-Rhine Euroregion is tightly interwoven both economically and socially. In some municipalities, such as Kerkrade (NL) and Herzogenrath (G) and also Maastricht (NL) and Lanaken (B), built-up areas have virtually merged. This evokes several questions with regard to everyday policing, such as traffic offences, accidents, petty crime, and the relational conflicts that regularly involve persons from different parts of the border area (Spapens and Fijnaut 2005). For instance, a drug addict from the Netherlands may be apprehended in Belgium while trying to steal a radio from a car. A Belgian may be arrested for drinking and driving in the Dutch part of the Euroregion after visiting a discotheque in the German part. A German may be questioned in the Netherlands in response to accusations of domestic violence with regard to his Dutch girlfriend. Numerous cases can be added to these examples. Statistics compiled by police in the South-Limburg district, which constitutes most of the Dutch part of the Meuse-Rhine Euroregion, reveal that 12 per cent of the suspects apprehended in 2002 originated from Germany or Belgium (Spapens and Fijnaut 2005: 65). This figure serves as a minimum, as it only concerns those persons who were apprehended on the scene and does not include suspects who were arrested only after they had returned to their country of origin.

In light of these scenarios, it is no surprise that a large number of requests for mutual legal assistance are exchanged annually. Between June 2002 and June 2003, the German and the Belgian police sent about 25,000 requests for information to the Dutch part of the border area (Spapens and Fijnaut 2005: 63).[3] Almost half of these requests concerned vehicle registration data. Moreover, the Dutch judicial authorities in the Meuse-Rhine Euroregion exchanged about 4,000 letters rogatory with Belgium and Germany. About 80–90 per cent of these letters concerned traffic offences, accidents, petty crime or administrative questions, such as checking with the Registry Office to obtain a person's address.

Apart from public-order policing, maintaining public safety also regularly requires a coordinated effort. Large-scale public events, such as soccer games, Christmas markets, and the annual Formula One race at Spa-Francorchamps, attract large numbers of visitors from the entire border area and beyond. This is also true for incidental events. For instance, when President Bush visited the Netherlands in 2005 he also went to the United States war cemetery of Margraten which is located in the Meuse-Rhine Euroregion. The Margraten war cemetery is about ten kilometres from the German border and only five kilometres from the Belgian border, so safeguarding the dignitaries involved not only the Dutch police but the Belgian and German forces as well (Politieregio Limburg-Zuid 2005: 5).

Serious and organized crime

Though a relatively small portion of the total number of requests for mutual legal assistance concern serious and organized crime, handling these requests often requires a major effort on the part of the police and judicial authorities. From October 2006 to October 2007, some 300 rogatory letters requiring substantial investigative action were exchanged between the South-Limburg police district and the German and Belgian parts of the Meuse-Rhine Euroregion (Spapens 2008b: 110).[4] These requests concerned the interrogation of suspects and witnesses; the transfer of evidence; specific information about persons, vehicles, or financial transactions; cross-border observation; the interception of telecommunications; and house searches (Spapens 2008b: 113). Serious and organized crime in the Euroregion can be divided into three major types.

First, criminal groups in the Meuse-Rhine Euroregion commit predatory crimes in two or more different parts of the border area.

There are both indigenous as well as itinerant groups of criminals, originating from Eastern and Southern Eastern Europe, committing these crimes.

Of the indigenous groups, the Dutch seem to 'specialize' in committing thefts of commercial vehicles and transported goods, the thefts of private cars or motorcycles, and burglaries at commercial premises, sometimes by means of ram raids. The Belgian groups seem to specialize in bank robberies and the holding up of money transports across the border. German criminals, however, are very rarely suspected of predatory crimes committed in other parts of the Meuse-Rhine Euroregion.

The itinerant, roaming, or travelling crime groups originating from Eastern Europe are mainly from Lithuania and Poland. Lithuanian groups specialize in the theft of vehicles and valuable vehicle parts, such as airbags, which are stolen from parked vehicles. The Polish crime groups are associated mainly with hold-ups and organized shoplifting (Korps Landelijke Politiediensten 2005). Southern Eastern European groups, mostly originating from Romania, Albania and the former Yugoslavia, usually perpetrate a variety of predatory crimes (Federale Politie 2007). One specific illegal activity of some of these groups is skimming debit or credit cards. The information is then copied onto cards that are illegally manufactured and used to plunder the accounts of the original cardholders. These particular groups are highly mobile and do not limit their criminal activities to the Euroregion.

Second, integrated crime groups have evolved in the Meuse-Rhine Euroregion. These types of groups are no longer based in one country, but operate throughout the border area, predominantly in the Dutch and Belgian parts. One reason for the emergence of integrated crime groups is that a substantial number of Dutch criminals, some of them notorious, have moved to Belgium in the past few years. They continued their illegal activities in the Netherlands and also established new contacts with their Belgian counterparts. Moreover, parts of the logistical processes of criminal activities were moved to the neighbouring country. A group of XTC producers, for example, tried to reduce the risk of being detected by the police by regularly moving their laboratory from the Dutch to the Belgian part of the Meuse-Rhine Euroregion and vice versa (Van Daele *et al.* 2008).

Integrated crime groups are involved mostly in the production of synthetic drugs and cannabis, VAT frauds, swindling schemes, money laundering, and the fencing of stolen goods. For example, expensive cars or luxury goods are shipped to the Middle East, whereas excavators and vehicles that can be used for road construction are smuggled to Africa.

Finally, there are criminal groups whose activities are only in small part related to the Meuse-Rhine Euroregion. The perpetrators are usually involved in smuggling operations that may span a large part of Europe or even the globe. Examples of these activities include the import of illicit drugs, cigarette smuggling, illegal immigration, and the trafficking of women for sexual purposes. Illegal immigrants travelling from China to the United Kingdom or Canada may be temporarily lodged in safe houses somewhere in the border area. Investigating these types of groups sometimes requires intensive law enforcement cooperation, though in most cases, this does not directly involve the police or judicial authorities within the Euroregion itself.

The drug problem
Undoubtedly, the drug problem is one of the most pressing types of organized crime in the Meuse-Rhine Euroregion. The Netherlands in particular has developed into a major marketplace for illicit drugs, as well as an important production base for synthetic drugs and marijuana. At the root of this problem is, to a large extent, the decision of the Dutch government to revise its drug policy in the mid-1970s. A distinction was made between 'soft drugs' (marijuana, hashish) and 'hard drugs' (heroin, cocaine, synthetic drugs, etc.). Subsequently, the selling and use of soft drugs became more and more accepted. The so-called coffee shops emerged, where marijuana and hashish were sold, and these shops were gradually allowed by the local authorities. Nowadays, coffee shops need a licence, which is only issued under strict conditions. Additionally, customers are only allowed to buy soft drugs up to a maximum of five grams per person and must be over 18 years of age (Boekhout van Solinge 2005).

The main policy goal of the government was to separate the markets for soft and hard drugs and thus to prevent users of marijuana or hashish from progressing to heroin or cocaine. As the number of hard drug addicts in the Netherlands is fairly low, and the prevalence of soft drugs use is not exceptional when compared with other European countries, this drug policy has long been considered successful. However, it has also had a number of unforeseen side effects, which manifest themselves particularly in border areas (De Ruyver and Surmont 2007).

First, coffee shops in towns close to the border attract customers not only from the Netherlands itself but also from other countries. Mobility has substantially increased over the past few decades, and many youngsters now possess a car of their own. Moreover, crossing the border became much easier after fixed border controls were lifted in 1995. All of this has resulted in a steep increase in the number of foreigners buying drugs in the Netherlands. Some of them will not hesitate to travel 1,000 kilometres or more, although the bulk of customers will come from within a radius of 100–200 kilometres. Most of the buyers are from Belgium, Germany and France. Every day, an estimated 7,000 'drug tourists' visit the Dutch part of the Meuse-Rhine Euroregion. Although buying soft drugs at a coffee shop is allowed, drug tourists are a constant nuisance because of littering, parking problems, etc. (Spapens 2008b).

Second, some of the users who travel to the Netherlands actually want to buy hard drugs instead of soft drugs, or want to acquire amounts that are larger than five grams. As a result, parallel to the coffee shops, an infrastructure for drug dealing has also developed. The drugs are mainly sold at drug-dealing houses, the number of which is currently estimated at 150 in the South-Limburg District. The dealers operating from such drug-dealing houses also employ 'drug runners,' mostly youngsters of Moroccan descent, who sometimes aggressively approach anybody who is considered a potential customer on the motorways leading to Maastricht (Fijnaut and De Ruyver 2008: 149).

Third, suppliers operating in border areas periodically ship larger quantities of drugs directly to dealers in Germany and France. A foreign dealer may have a weekly order of two kilos of marijuana, 1,000 Ecstasy pills, 500 grams of cocaine, and 50 grams of heroin, depending on his customer base. The Dutch dealer will then contact his suppliers of different types of illicit drugs using the 'shopping list' submitted. Next, a courier will drive to the Netherlands to pick up the order. Because the risk of apprehension is virtually nil, drug deliveries have developed into an almost on-demand service (Spapens 2008b).

Fourth, coffee shops and drug dealers also need to be supplied themselves. Heroin, cocaine and hashish are imported from abroad, but marijuana and synthetic drugs are produced domestically. Criminal groups, who import the illicit drugs from source countries such as Colombia (cocaine), Turkey (heroin), or Morocco (hashish), are also active in the Meuse-Rhine Euroregion (Europol 2006).

The history of law enforcement cooperation in the Euroregion

As outlined above, the economic and social ties in the Meuse-Rhine have always been strong and cross-border crime is not a phenomenon that is new to the region. The need for good police and judicial cooperation has long been present.

Shortly after the Second World War ended, Dutch, German and Belgian police chiefs began to consult on the approach to cross-border crime problems. The main question at that time was how to better control the smuggling of scarce goods such as food and clothing. Later the emphasis shifted to combating all sorts of theft (burglaries, car thefts), traffic violations, acts of violence and the drug trade.

In the beginning, cooperation was based on police partnerships that had been formed before the war (on a diplomatic level) between Germany, the Netherlands and Belgium. At the end of the 1950s, the first multilateral conventions on law enforcement cooperation were signed. Of great importance was the European Convention on Mutual Assistance in Criminal Matters (1959), drawn up by the Council of Europe.[5] Then, on 27 June 1962, Belgium, the Netherlands and Luxembourg (the Benelux) signed a treaty on extradition and mutual legal assistance.[6]

The 1959 Convention primarily aims at enhancing judicial cooperation by introducing a framework for the exchange of rogatory letters. However, the convention also includes specific provisions for the interrogation of suspects and the taking of witness statements, house searches, and the exchange of information from criminal and judicial records. Meantime the authors of the convention still regard Interpol as the main channel for police cooperation.

The 1962 Benelux Treaty more specifically addresses several forms of police cooperation. Articles 26, 27, and 28 explicitly provides for cross-border pursuits by police officers and implicitly enables cross-border observation. In addition, the treaty allows police officers in one country to assist their counterparts abroad with tracking criminals.

The need for police cooperation further increased in the 1960s. In 1969, the *Polizeipräsident* (Chief of Police) of Aachen initiated the establishment of the NeBeDeAgPol (*Niederländisch-Belgisch-Deutsche Arbeitsgemeinschaft der Polizei*), a Dutch-Belgian-German association on police cooperation. Within the Meuse-Rhine Euroregion, NeBeDeAgPol contributed to increasing the reciprocal knowledge of the various police services; organizing direct radio and telex links between the police services in the region; exchanging information about crime and criminals; setting up language courses for police officers; and appointing contact officials within the police forces involved (Brammertz 1999).

Over the course of the 1970s, a trilingual form for the reporting of criminal offences was developed, the heads of the investigation departments in the region met on a regular basis, and direct communication links between the incident rooms of the various police services concerned were created (Fijnaut and Van Gestel 1992).

These successes encouraged the development of proposals for further expansion of police and judicial cooperation within the Euroregion, such as giving police officers broader powers on foreign territory under the supervision of the local public prosecutor and under the direction of the police. Another idea was mooted to enable police officers to interview suspects in a neighbouring country. Furthermore, they would be able to participate in house searches abroad and to perform seizures. However, these ideas met with little support because they seemed to conflict too much with the sovereignty of the states involved.

Things gradually started to change when the European Economic Community established a common market. This implied, among other things, the abolition of fixed controls on the interior borders. For most of the countries involved, including Germany, Belgium and the Netherlands, this radical decision was only acceptable if police and judicial cooperation was intensified. This was clearly articulated in the Schengen Agreement signed by Germany, France, the Netherlands, Belgium and Luxembourg on 14 June 1985. Here, the parties agreed on strengthening their cooperation in combating crime, focusing in particular on the illegal trade in narcotics and firearms. Practical provisions were worked out in the Schengen Implementation Convention of 1990, which went into force in 1995.[7] The Convention echoes the 1962 Benelux Treaty and includes, for instance, provisions for speeding up information exchange in border areas (Arts. 39 and 46), cross-border observation (Art. 40) and cross-border pursuits (Art. 41), and controlled delivery of narcotic substances (Art 73).

The Schengen Implementation Convention also includes organizational measures to be taken by the Parties (Fijnaut 1992). The most important is the introduction of the Schengen Information System, which is used for signalling wanted persons and stolen vehicles. The Convention also provides for a legal framework for the exchange of police liaison officers (Art. 47). Furthermore, particularly in border areas, mutual cooperation is to be facilitated by the installation of standardized and compatible communication systems.

Apart from Schengen, the 1992 Treaty of Maastricht was instrumental in further developing police and judicial cooperation which in turn influenced other types of practical cooperation in the Meuse-Rhine Euroregion.[8] These other cooperative efforts will be discussed in the next section.

The framework of the Treaty on the European Union

The Treaty of Maastricht, being the first treaty on the European Union, addressed the topic of police and judicial cooperation, albeit briefly. At that time, most member states were resistant to the idea of integrating law enforcement cooperation into the institutional framework of the European Union (Fijnaut 1993a). Only Germany opted for the solid and immediate organization of police and judicial cooperation at the Union level.

Title VI of the Treaty of Maastricht included a number of general provisions on cooperation in the areas of justice and home affairs. Article K.1 defined specific areas as matters of common interest, including judicial cooperation (Art. K.1.7) and police cooperation for the purposes of preventing and combating terrorism, unlawful drug trafficking and other serious forms of international crime [...] in connection with the organization of a Union-wide system for exchanging information within a European Police Office (Art. K.1.9). The latter stipulation led to the formation of the Europol Drugs Unit, the forerunner of Europol. However, all decisions on cooperation within the realms of justice and home affairs, the so-called Third Pillar, were intergovernmental and subjected to the rule of unanimity between the member states.

In 1998, the Treaty of Amsterdam amended the Treaty on the European Union.[9] Here, law enforcement cooperation received its due emphasis, as evidenced by the fact that Title VI was renamed as 'Provisions on police and judicial cooperation in criminal matters'. Article 29, which replaced Article K.1, now states that one of the Union's primary aims is 'to provide citizens with a high level of safety within an area of freedom, security and justice by developing common action among the Member States in the fields of police and judicial cooperation in criminal matters'. To this end, closer cooperation between police forces, the customs authorities and other competent authorities in the member states is to be developed, both directly and through Europol (Art. 29). Article 30 mentions a number of common actions, such as operational cooperation between the competent services; the collection, analysis and dissemination of information; initiatives regarding joint training and equipment; and a common evaluation of particular investigative techniques in relation to the combating of organized crime. Article 31 mentions common actions with regard to judicial cooperation, such as facilitating extradition between member states and ensuring compatibility with regulations applicable in the member states (Fijnaut 2004).

The Treaty of Amsterdam also amended the decision-making process in the Third Pillar. The European Commission, which had had little influence in matters concerning justice and home affairs until this point, now became fully involved in the activities contained within the Third Pillar (Art. 36). Moreover, the European Council is obliged to consult the European Parliament in a number of cases (Art. 39). The unanimity rule, however, remained in place. Therefore, any enhancement of the framework for police cooperation remains a slow and difficult process. The EU formulated two action programmes in order to promote the implementation of the Treaty of Amsterdam, which also addressed law enforcement cooperation.

First, the 'Action plan of the Council and the Commission on how best to implement the provisions of the Treaty of Amsterdam on an area of freedom, security and justice' (Vienna Action Plan) was adopted on 3 December 1998.[10] This plan paid a lot of attention to the development of Europol into an office that could take on an operational role in combating cross-border crime in the European Union. The plan also promoted direct cooperation between the police services.

Second, the European Council adopted an action programme at the Tampere Summit on 15 and 16 October 1999.[11] This action programme covered the 2000–2005 period and was more robust than the Vienna Action Plan on a number of points. However, the Tampere programme had little to offer with regard to either operational police cooperation or practical measures to be implemented on short notice. Important for the longer term were proposals for forming a task force of chiefs of police and a European police college, which were indeed realized.

For practical police cooperation, the Treaty of Amsterdam stimulated the signing of the Convention on Mutual Assistance in Criminal Matters between the member states of the European Union on 29 May 2000.[12] This convention provides for the intercepting of telephone conversations and cross-border covert operations. It also formally introduces Joint Investigation Teams (JITs) as a means of operational police cooperation. A JIT can be established for specific periods of time and for specific objectives. JITs are to act in accordance with the law of the country in which they were established, but team members from other countries can participate directly and actively in investigative action undertaken on foreign territory. At the same time, they may also gather information in their own country and exchange this with other team members directly, thereby not requiring formal (written) requests for mutual legal assistance. Finally, the convention extends the existing provisions for witness and expert testimony and for controlled deliveries.

In 2005, the 'Hague Programme' was developed to follow the Tampere Programme to cover the period of 2006–2010.[13] This new programme was already anticipating the draft Constitutional Treaty for the European Union (Fijnaut 2006). The Hague Programme contains four major topics with regard to police cooperation.

First, it aims at improving the coordination of operational co-operation between member states, particularly by proposing the formation of a Committee on Internal Security as provided for in the draft Constitutional Treaty. Second, it introduces the 'principle of availability' as a means of speeding up the exchange of information. This principle implies that the police, under specific conditions and according to specific procedures, can obtain all the information available in another member state that is relevant to an ongoing investigation case. Third, the programme calls for intensifying the external police policy, particularly by means of closer cooperation with non-EU countries in combating terrorism. Finally, it proposes to extend practical cooperation among the police services in the European Union. This would result in a wider involvement by Europol in cross-border investigations and a strengthening of law enforcement cooperation in border regions.

Step by step, the policies articulated in the Treaty of Amsterdam and the Hague Programme in particular have been implemented almost in their entirety. Specifically with regard to police cooperation in EU border regions, Belgium, Germany and the Netherlands have acted as forerunners, prompted by increasing cross-border crime problems in their common border areas. The next section will address the recent bilateral, trilateral and multilateral conventions that are particularly relevant for law enforcement cooperation in the Meuse-Rhine Euroregion.

Recent bilateral, trilateral and multilateral conventions on police cooperation

The first convention of relevance for police cooperation in the Meuse-Rhine Euroregion was the Benelux Police Cooperation Treaty.[14] This was signed on 8 June 2004 by the Netherlands, Belgium and Luxembourg. The convention includes provisions for police cooperation in the areas of criminal investigation and public-order policing. In addition to the legal framework of the Schengen Implementation Convention and the Convention on Mutual Assistance in Criminal Matters between the member states of the European Union in 2000, the Benelux Police Cooperation Treaty aims at further simplifying and speeding up information exchange. For instance, it allows for online access to vehicle registration data and anticipates an extension of this to other databases in the future. This convention expands the existing regulations for cross-border pursuit and cross-border observation and also for the use of technical equipment during observation operations. Specifically, it allows for the establishment of joint police stations. With regard to public-order policing, the treaty enables the police to provide assistance abroad both on request and in situations that required immediate action. Furthermore, arrangements are made for the composition of mixed police patrols and the execution of joint controls by the various police services involved. Finally, the treaty emphasizes the importance of joint training and exercises for police personnel and the exchange of communication resources and equipment. Clearly, the provisions incorporated in the Benelux Police Cooperation Treaty are of great importance to police cooperation in border areas.

Germany and the Netherlands signed a treaty regarding 'cross-border police cooperation and cooperation in criminal matters' on 3 March 2005.[15] This treaty is largely comparable to the Benelux treaty on police cooperation, although it also contains some specific provisions. It enables, for instance, 'diagonal' communication between the police and the prosecution services of Germany and the Netherlands. This is of importance because a public prosecutor leads criminal investigations on a daily basis in the Netherlands, whereas in Germany the police handle tactical questions independently. Thus, the German police and the Dutch public prosecutor can communicate directly about practical issues, which saves much time. The treaty is also more extensive with regards to criminal investigation and contains provisions for the securing of evidence, the comparison of

DNA profiles, controlled delivery, and infiltration. However, it does not specifically provide for the formation of joint police stations.

Third, Germany, France, the Benelux countries, Spain and Austria signed a treaty 'on the stepping up of cross border cooperation, particularly in combating terrorism, cross border crime and illegal immigration' (the Treaty of Prüm) in 2005.[16] This is intended to facilitate the exchange of information by allowing all parties online access to databases of DNA profiles and fingerprint evidence on a hit/no-hit basis. In other words, the police can check online if a matching DNA profile or fingerprint is available abroad. If this proves the case, further details can be obtained by means of a request for mutual legal assistance. The treaty also enables online access to vehicle registration data. In addition it lists a number of sources from which the police can directly request information, without having to use the Interpol channel. This arrangement represents the most far-reaching and extensive application of the principle of availability. Finally, the Treaty of Prüm contains articles specifically concerning public-order policing. Recently, the Council Framework Decision 2008/615/JHA integrated the larger part of the Treaty of Prüm into the legal framework of the European Union (Bellanova 2008).[17]

Enhancing police and judicial cooperation in the Meuse-Rhine Euroregion

We described previously how public-order policing, and the investigation of serious and organized crime (specifically the drug problem), are issues that cut across national boundaries within the Meuse-Rhine Euroregion and frequently require intensive cooperation between the police and judicial authorities. In this section, we will explore the main problems that can arise from this type of practical cooperation, as well as some solutions for overcoming them that have been implemented in the region. Though these solutions fully exploit the opportunities provided by the legal framework discussed in Section 5, there remains a need for further innovations.

Cooperation with regard to public safety and public-order policing

The treaties described previously create an extensive additional legal framework with regard to public safety and public-order policing. The bases of the Benelux Police Cooperation Treaty and the Dutch-German Treaty on police cooperation resulted from a careful study of the practical difficulties confronted by the police, so both conventions do provide effective solutions with regard to most of these problems.[18] However, the disproportionate burden put on the system of law-enforcement cooperation by the large number of relatively simple requests for legal assistance is an issue that needs to be addressed further.

These treaties provide an initial step towards reducing the number of administrative requests for legal assistance by granting the parties involved direct access to each other's vehicle registration databases. The bulk of requests for information concern vehicle registration data, as was noted earlier in this chapter. Therefore direct access, which is currently in the phase of technical implementation, would substantially decrease the number of requests for information. However, experts doubt that this will decrease the number of requests altogether, as the number of follow-up questions – for instance, about the owner of a vehicle – is likely to increase.

To a large extent, other requests for mutual legal assistance concern relatively minor cases. The Belgians, for instance, still send many rogatory letters to the Netherlands (and Germany) concerning minor traffic offences, such as speeding or parking violations, requesting an interrogation of the drivers involved. In the Netherlands, minor traffic offences are dealt with administratively and no longer require police involvement. As a result, the Dutch police consider these requests from outside countries an unnecessary burden and give little priority to handling them. This, of course, frustrates Belgian public prosecutors.

The discussion now rests on whether the system for handling requests for mutual legal assistance should be relieved of those cases that are relatively simple or purely administrative. With regard to traffic offences, for instance, it would be much simpler to hand over the case to the authorities in the offenders' country of origin and have it settled according to their domestic regulations. However, there is as yet little progress towards this potential solution.

Identification of cross-border criminal activities in the Euroregion

Tackling serious, organized cross-border crime first requires the identification of active crime groups at the earliest possible stage. Second, personnel and resources have to be assigned to the investigation of specific perpetrator groups. Here, we will explore initiatives directed towards an 'early warning' for criminal activities in the Meuse-Rhine Euroregion. Later we will also address organizational aspects of cooperation in the investigation of serious and organized crime.

Whenever information about criminal groups' activities in the border area is not properly shared between the law enforcement agencies of different countries (or even jurisdictions within a country), it will take greater time before such criminal groups are identified and the gravity of their illegal activities is assessed. Hence, it will also take longer before the police can implement adequate countermeasures. In the case of itinerant groups, the perpetrators may have already moved elsewhere before an investigation is started.

The Schengen Implementation Convention of 1990 in particular can be considered an important step forward in the sharing of vital information, as it enables the authorities in border areas to exchange information directly, bypassing the Interpol channel. Based on this, an online system for the exchange of information, called EMMI-PALMA, was implemented in the Meuse-Rhine Euroregion in 1995 (Verbeek 2004).[19] EMMI-PALMA enabled the German, Belgian and Dutch police in the border area to exchange requests for information electronically on the basis of Article 39 of the Schengen Implementation Convention. From then on, requests for information were usually answered within 24 hours. Previously, a request sent via the Interpol channel would have received a response several weeks later. In 2005, a joint face-to-face information centre, called EPICC (Euroregional Police Information and Communications Centre), succeeded EMMI-PALMA. Here, police officers from Germany, Belgium and the Netherlands work side by side. Requests for information that used to be sent electronically can now be exchanged between police officers working in the same building or even in the same room who can immediately access their information systems to retrieve information about a person, an address, a vehicle, and so on.

Although EPICC has increased the pace at which information is exchanged, there is still room for improvement in the early warning aspect of dealing with crime. First, in order to identify groups committing predatory crimes, various pieces of information (i.e. similar crimes committed elsewhere in the border area) have to be constantly analysed. For this reason, the authorities in the Meuse-Rhine Euroregion are planning to attach Belgian, Dutch and German crime analysts to EPICC.

Second, perpetrators committing 'victimless crimes', for instance, drug trafficking or drug production, cannot usually be identified solely from reports to the police. Instead, criminal intelligence, provided by informers who are themselves involved in illegal activities, is normally essential. Therefore, in order to quickly identify these types of criminal groups operating across the borders, the exchange of criminal intelligence is also critical. However, the police are often reluctant to share intelligence with their counterparts in other countries for fear of possible disclosure, thereby putting their informers at risk. Until recently, sharing intelligence was also difficult because of the lack of a legal framework, but this has changed with the implementation of the 2006 EU Framework Decision on simplifying the exchange of information and intelligence between the law enforcement authorities of the member states of the European Union.[20] Although intelligence has been exchanged informally between the police in the border area for many years, it was not pooled structurally or used in threat analyses with regard to cross-border crime groups.

Third, efforts to ease the exchange of information have focused primarily on written information. However, other sources of information, such as DNA and tracing evidence, CCTV footage and cell-phone traffic data, have become increasingly important for the identification of perpetrator groups. In the near future, technical improvements based on the Prüm Framework Decision of 2008 will enable an online comparison of DNA profiles and dactyloscopic data. However if, for example, CCTV footage or traffic data from a cell phone need to be collected and exchanged, this will still require the sending of rogatory letters. It is evident that simplifying the exchange of this type of information will need to take a prominent place on the agenda in the near future (Spapens 2008b).

Aligning priorities and assigning personnel and equipment to the investigation of cross-border crime groups

After identifying criminal groups, the next step is to actually stop their illegal activities by means of investigation and prosecution. In practice, it appears that in the Meuse-Rhine Euroregion policy and organizational problems regularly interfere with criminal investigations.

To begin with, each country determines their investigation priorities independently. To some extent, that same practice applies to individual districts since they can designate specific regional priorities. Indeed, there are substantial differences between Germany on the one hand, and Belgium and the Netherlands on the other. In Germany the principle of legality applies, which means that a criminal investigation always has to be conducted when the police or the public prosecutor become aware of crime. The investigating authorities are obligated to do so. In Belgium and the Netherlands, however, the opportunity principle applies, which gives the public prosecutor more freedom of choice about whether to investigate or not.

The possibilities of conducting a criminal policy are relatively restricted in Germany because of the legality principle. In addition there are differences in the investigation priorities between the Netherlands and Belgium. For example, in the Netherlands the investigation of property crimes, except for burglaries, is not a high priority, though it is in Belgium.

Second, investigative priorities have consequences in the assignment of personnel and resources to specific criminal investigations. Both in the Netherlands and in Belgium the number of detectives is relatively limited. Particularly in the Netherlands, only cases that have been given priority status can actually be investigated. In Germany the situation is more rosy since, because of the principle of legality, more detectives have to be available.

Not surprisingly, differences in priorities and in available manpower and resources regularly give rise to conflict. When the Belgian authorities start a large-scale investigation that, over the course of it, requires a substantial contribution from the Netherlands, progress will be seriously hindered if the Dutch police cannot, or will not, provide the necessary effort.

In the Meuse-Rhine Euroregion in recent years, several initiatives have been established to deal with these problems. At the public prosecutor level in all three countries, the *Bureau Euregionale Samenwerking* (BES: Office for Euroregional Cooperation) was created, based on an informal agreement. Here, magistrates from the three countries regularly consult on planned and ongoing criminal investigations. This offers the opportunity to synthesize the cooperation efforts in advance. It also informs the parties involved in a timely way that a substantial contribution will be requested and thus appropriate preparations can be made. The BES itself, however, has no hierarchical powers to assign detectives to specific cases.

The second initiative is the organizing of semi-annual conferences of judicial, police and administrative authorities. One of the goals of these meetings is to better coordinate various investigative priorities. Toward this end, working groups are established to improve cooperation and reflect these joint priorities. In 2008, for example, working groups were created for home burglaries and for the trafficking in women for the purpose of prostitution.

To arrive at a structural solution, several parties have suggested the establishment of a more permanent team tasked with the investigation of serious and organized crime in border areas (Spapens 2008b). District-based public prosecutors in the three countries of the Meuse-Rhine Euroregion would be responsible for directing this team. Team members would operate as a JIT in the execution of specific criminal investigations. Attempts to create such a team have so far been unsuccessful because the police and prosecution services fear losing control over the use of 'their' people and resources.

An integrated approach to the drug problem?

We noted previously that one side effect of Dutch drug policy is that the border areas have become important marketplaces for drug tourists and drug dealers from neighbouring countries. This has annoyed the German and Belgian authorities for quite some time.[21] The Germans, for instance, contend that a large part of the drugs seized originate from the Netherlands. Dutch police and judicial authorities generally give little priority to the investigation of couriers who smuggle relatively small amounts of drugs. German requests for assistance that would involve a substantial effort (for instance, the monitoring of controlled deliveries) are likely to fall on deaf ears in the Netherlands because observation units are needed for more serious and pressing investigations, such as drug production.

On the Belgian side, the problem is different. The Belgian authorities themselves report fewer incidents involving drug dealers who are supplied from the Netherlands. Instead, the Belgian authorities must cope with the consequences of actions undertaken by the Dutch authorities.

First, the intensified investigation of drug production in the Netherlands has caused some Dutch crime groups to shift their activities to Belgium. Reining in synthetic drug production had become a major priority from the second half of the 1990s onward. Hence, a number of ecstasy producers decided to move to Belgium, where synthetic drug-making laboratories were increasingly established as well. More recently, a rising number of cannabis plantations have been found in Belgium, especially in border areas. In many cases, Dutch nationals are involved. This development is also attributed to the fact of the Dutch authorities having taken action to reduce cannabis cultivation.

Second, police teams called Joint Hit Teams (JHT) have been created, which focus on drug-dealing houses and drug runners.[22] The first team was formed in 1998, based on an agreement between France and the Netherlands (De Bie *et al.* 2004). JHTs are now active on the main motorways leading to the Dutch part of the Meuse-Rhine Euroregion. A team of police officers from the Netherlands, Belgium, Luxembourg and France monitors the roads into Belgium and France. Recently, a German-Dutch JHT was also formed that concentrates on smuggling routes into Germany. The foreign buyers of illicit drugs are followed to dealing houses and then apprehended upon their return home if they possess such drugs. Subsequently, the dealing house involved will be raided by the police. However, in reaction to actions undertaken by JHT, drug dealers have also started to set up dealing houses in Belgium. Once again, the problem has shifted across the border.

In 2008, discussion about the drug problem intensified when the mayor of Maastricht proposed relocating some of the coffee shops from the centre of the city to the outskirts, which happened to be near the Belgian border. The idea generated considerable protests from the Belgian authorities, as they saw this as a unilateral step by the Dutch that was primarily intended to send the drug tourists and associated problems their way.

These examples illustrate the interconnectedness of the problems surrounding the drug trade, smuggling, and production in an area like the Meuse-Rhine Euroregion. It is no longer possible for one country to achieve success in reining in their own problem without repercussions that may negatively affect a neighbouring country. The solution is not merely an improvement of practical police and judicial cooperation in the ways outlined above. It requires a substantial joint policy not only on the level of the police, but also on the administrative level. Leading Belgian and Dutch criminologists recommended establishing a permanent entity for cooperation, run by the authorities responsible for the administration, judiciary, and police in the Belgian, German and Dutch parts of the Meuse-Rhine Euroregion (Fijnaut and De Ruyver 2008). This entity has been given the working name of JustPol.

JustPol would integrate the present facilities such as the *Bureau Euregionale Samenwerking* (Office for Euroregional Cooperation), the JHT, and EPICC. The same would apply for a future permanent JIT. These proposals are at present at the discussion stage.

The potential impact of the Lisbon Treaty and future group reports

The proposals for JustPol may seem radical to some of the parties concerned and even too far-reaching. However, they fit well with the principles articulated in the Reform Treaty, or the Treaty of Lisbon: 'amending the Treaty on European Union and the Treaty establishing the European Community'. This convention replaced the Constitutional Treaty, which had to be withdrawn after a majority of the voters rejected it in referenda in France and the Netherlands. The Lisbon Treaty was signed on 13 December 2007, but at present not all the member states have ratified it yet.

This treaty is actually more revolutionary than is ordinarily thought, especially with regard to the Third Pillar, precisely because it indicates the 'area of liberty, security and justice' as one of the shared competences of the member states and the European Union. Up until now, all decisions with regard to justice and home affairs were subject to the unanimity rule. In the Lisbon Treaty, however, this principle is dropped.

The European Council now has the authority to draw up 'strategic guidelines for legislative and operational planning'. Moreover, a standing committee will support the Council 'in order to ensure that operational cooperation on internal security is promoted and strengthened within the Union'. Finally, the Commission is given the authority to 'conduct objective and impartial evaluation of the implementation of the union policies' in cooperation with the member states.

These provisions manifestly demonstrate the determination of the European Union to strengthen operational police and judicial cooperation between member states. This is especially true when it comes to the Union's traditional priorities in its criminal policy: terrorism, human trafficking, the drugs trade, the arms trade, and fraud. In the Meuse-Rhine Euroregion, the formation of JustPol mirrors these ideas.

At present, the Council of Justice and Home Affairs of the European Union are in the process of preparing a new action programme, the Stockholm Programme, based on the ideas underlying the Lisbon Treaty. This is to be accepted under the Swedish presidency in the second half of 2009. An informal high-level advisory group on the future of European home affairs policy, the 'Future Group', was installed at the beginning of 2007 to prepare the new programme in the named field.

This group reported in June 2008 (High Level Advisory Group 2008a).

In this report, the *convergence principle* was introduced. The aim of this idea is 'to bring Member States closer not only by means of standardization when necessary, but also by operational means. Common training programs, exchange networks, solidarity mechanisms, the pooling of some equipment, simpler cooperation procedures, and, of course, information exchanges are essential ways of reaching true and genuine operational cooperation between the Union's Member States' (High Level Advisory Group 2008a).

One of the proposals is to train the member states' police forces at the European level, in order to ensure mutual understanding and an exchange of best practices. Joint training of police officers and members of the public prosecution services has already started in the Meuse-Rhine Euroregion in the wake of the Benelux Police Cooperation Treaty.

Second, the convergence principle is expressed by proposals to promote joint investigation teams and to set up joint Police and Customs Cooperation Centres (PCCCs). In individual cases, JITs have already proved their worth in the Dutch border regions, and discussions are now in progress about the benefit of mounting a permanent JIT to combat cross-border crime in border areas. Indeed, a joint police station (EPICC) has been set up in the Meuse-Rhine Euroregion.

Third, the proposals of the Future Group are intended to broaden and expedite the exchange of information. The full implementation of the Framework Decision 2008/615/JHA on the stepping up of cross border cooperation, particularly in combating terrorism, cross-border crime and illegal immigration, is one of the policy goals. In border areas the swift exchange of information is of utmost importance, certainly for boosting the capacity to be proactive against cross-border crime groups.

Finally, the Future Group proposes the strengthening of Europol but without its development into an executive police force as yet. Europol could aid primarily in combating the itinerant groups and crime groups operating within border areas whose activities are only partly related to the border areas, for example, by charting any illegal activity that may involve the same groups elsewhere in the EU. Based on this, concerted efforts towards combating these crime groups in different member states could be organized more effectively.

By introducing the convergence principle, the Future Group on Home Affairs took a worthwhile approach to police cooperation partly reflecting initiatives that are already in existence in the Meuse-Rhine Euroregion, such as EPICC. However, the ongoing integration of illegal activity in the border areas calls not only for tools to enhance cooperation during actual cross-border criminal investigations, but also for the means to respond to the growing need for a coherent and coordinated criminal policy towards crime problems shared by the border areas. Therefore, JustPol, if agreed upon, would be exemplary in the practical implementation of the convergence principle. Finally, it is worth mentioning that a second high level advisory group reported on the future of European justice policy (High Level Advisory Group 2008b). In this report, however, police cooperation received little attention.

Conclusion

This chapter clearly shows the interaction in the discussion regarding police and judicial cooperation between the European Union, the national authorities, and the authorities in a border area where criminal investigation and public-order policing increasingly require cross-border cooperation.

It is also clear that the need for more intensive law enforcement cooperation differs from region to region within the EU. The problems occurring in the Meuse-Rhine Euroregion may be comparable to those in other densely populated European border regions, but the need for cross-border cooperation is obviously not as pressing in rural areas and districts that are further away from the borders. Therefore, it is not surprising that developments take place at various speeds. However, innovations with regard to police and judicial cooperation developed in regions such as the Meuse-Rhine Euroregion can only be implemented in conjunction with frameworks constructed on the national and European levels.

Any further development of legal and organizational frameworks for police and judicial cooperation is a complex and dynamic process. In this, border areas like the Meuse-Rhine Euroregion play an important role. Here, new developments in cross-border crime constantly confront the police and judicial authorities. Not surprisingly, it is also here that the need for comprehensive cooperation is obvious.

The border areas thus serve as a laboratory, informing the procedures and innovations implemented elsewhere only much later. Innovations in police and judicial cooperation do not proceed without discussion and sometimes require substantial consultation across national frontiers. The experiences in the Meuse-Rhine Euroregion show that making progress primarily requires pragmatism and flexibility on behalf of the parties involved. Differences of opinion, priority and policies between countries with regard to justice and home affairs make this a permanent and demanding task.

Notes

1 *Official Journal of the European Union* L 239, 22 September 2000.
2 See www.euregio-mr.org (accessed 24 May 2009).
3 These are comparable to requests sent through the Interpol channel. In Article 39 of the Schengen Implementation Convention (1990) the opportunity was created to exchange requests for police use directly, thus bypassing the Interpol channel. However, the direct exchange of information is restricted to border areas.
4 With regard to serious and organized crime, the number of requests 'for police use only' is unknown, as the reason for making such a request does not necessarily have to be revealed.
5 The Convention is available at the website of the Council of Europe. See www.coe.int (accessed on 11 May 2009).
6 The text of this treaty (in Dutch and French) is available at www.benelux. be (accessed 24 May 2009).
7 *Official Journal of the European Union*, L 239, 22 September 2000.
8 *Official Journal of the European Union*, C 191, 20 July 1992.
9 *Official Journal of the European Union*, C 340, 10 November 1997.
10 *Official Journal of the European Communities*, 1999/C, 19/01, 23 January 1999.
11 The text of the Presidency Conclusions is available at http://www. europarl.europa.eu/summits/tam_en.htm#c (accessed 25 May 2009).
12 *Official Journal of the European Union* C 197, 12 July 2000.
13 Council of the European Union, *The Hague Programme: Strengthening Freedom, Security and Justice in the European Union*, Brussels, 13 December 2004.
14 The text of this treaty (in Dutch and French) is available at www.benelux. be
15 *Tractatenblad van het Koninkrijk der Nederlanden*, Jaargang 2005, Nr. 86. The text is available in Dutch and German.
16 See Council of the European Union, Treaty of Prüm, 10900/05, Brussels, 7 July 2005, for an English version of the Treaty of Prüm. Available

at http://www.statewatch.org/news/2005/aug/Prum-Convention.pdf (accessed 23 March 2009).

17 *Official Journal of the European Union*, L 210/12, 23 June 2008.

18 Studying cooperation problems was tasked to informal working groups of Dutch, Belgian, Luxembourgian, Dutch and German police officers respectively. Their findings were not formally reported but used as input during negotiations about the content of the treaties.

19 EMMI stands for *Euregionale Multimediale Informatievoorziening* (Euroregional Multimedia Information Application). PALMA stands for *Politieverbindingen Aachen-Liège-Maastricht* (Police Communication Service Aachen-Liège-Maastricht).

20 *Official Journal of the European Union*, L 386/89, 29 December 2006.

21 The French authorities have also severely criticized the drug policy in the Netherlands.

22 JHTs are not to be confused with JITs.

Chapter 7

Convergent models of police cooperation: the case of anti-organized crime and anti-terrorism activities in Canada

Chantal Perras and Frédéric Lemieux

Introduction

In recent decades, ad hoc police structures, such as multi-jurisdictional investigative teams, have become widespread in the United States (Coldren and Sabath 1992; Jefferis *et al.* 1998). In their intensified fight against organized crime, police authorities have been required to improve both the flexibility of criminal investigations and the coordination of the resources devoted to the dismantling of criminal organizations. In parallel, the war against drugs, the proliferation of firearms in problematic neighbourhoods, and the emergence of particularly violent street gangs have necessitated a reconfiguration of police responses. Police agencies may thus be understood as open organizational systems; that is, systems that interact (positively and negatively) with their socio-political environment and learn expectations of and propose appropriate responses to that environment.[1]

Significant socio-political changes have favoured the emergence of joint police units as a response to public insecurity in the face of complex social problems. To accomplish their mission effectively, police organizations must adapt to the new issues raised in the new socio-political environment. To overcome the unwanted duplication of investigations and reduce the extent of jurisdictional confusion normally attendant on large-scale police operations, the police services have adopted structures that allow the lateral integration of partners from the judicial arena. These structures also allow the police to develop stronger investigative files on drug dealers or criminal organizations that operate in more than one jurisdiction (OCJS 1994).

Although Perrow (1987) demonstrated that police agencies are bureaucratic organizational entities, multi-jurisdictional investigative teams are noteworthy by virtue of their distinct organizational structure. Research by Perras (2006) indicates that these teams are characterized by a flexible decision-making process within a decentralized organizational structure. This configuration allows multi-jurisdictional teams to adapt to perceived variations in the criminal environment (Jefferis *et al*. 1998). It should be noted that a decentralized structure also allows authority to be delegated to investigators and analysts directly involved in investigations. As a result, multi-jurisdictional teams exhibit little vertical, occupational, or functional differentiation, in contrast to the pattern generally observed in other types of police structures.

It should also be mentioned that the organizational configuration of multi-jurisdictional investigation teams primarily reflects two facts. The first is that the relationships between team members are characterized by sustained contacts, continuous communication, and a permanent structure (Jefferis *et al*. 1998). These improve the coordination of resources and the collection of information necessary for effective investigations (Reaves 1992). The second is that the structure of the relationships between team members is a function of interdependence and coexistence based on reciprocity and stability. Furthermore, multi-jurisdictional teams are known for their informality – i.e. fluid supervision, informal operational rules, and flexible internal policies – which facilitates the conduct of investigations.

The lack of study on joint investigative teams is quite surprising when one recalls that enthusiasm for multi-jurisdictional investigative teams rapidly grew beyond regional police forces and became entrenched in both national and international police practice (Coldren and Sabath 1992; Gerspacher and Lemieux 2005). It has been estimated that more than 1000 drug task forces have existed in the United States since 1992 (Jefferis *et al*. 1998). Furthermore, 95 per cent of the 387 police organizations studied by Weisel (1996) stated that they were part of a drug task force. Levine and Martin (1992) consider multi-jurisdictional teams a promising approach to the fight against drug trafficking. The apparent success of this investigative practice seems to lead to the use of joint investigative structures to tackle other threats to security.

In this chapter, we examine how joint investigation structures adopted by the police in the 'war' against organized crime were applied to other types of security problems, especially terrorism. More specifically, we scrutinize whether there has been a transfer and dissemination of innovative practices between police agencies and national security services, particularly from the former to the latter. This research interest emerges from the observation that other security agencies, including border control, immigration, customs and excise, and port security have, in recent years, implemented joint investigative team structures similar to the ones designed to tackle organized crime (Dupont and Perez 2006).

The decision to examine the transfer and application of an organized crime joint investigative team model to the activities of terrorism, rather than to other security sectors, was motivated by the cultural and legal distance that separates high and low policing missions (Brodeur 1983; L'Heuillet 2001). In fact, the organizational culture and legal framework of police agencies are in many ways similar to those of the services responsible for applying laws related to customs and excises, commercial transit zones such as ports, and the trans-border traffic of goods and persons, when compared with those of anti-terrorism agencies. We therefore attempt to determine whether there are limits to the adoption or application of a joint investigative team structure by anti-terrorism agencies. It should further be noted that no Canadian study has examined joint anti-terrorism teams. Finally, the core thesis of this chapter is that the structural adaptations, both within joint investigative teams and between police agencies and joint anti-terrorism teams, can be explained by the interaction between social learning and knowledge transfer. These structural adaptations can be divided into three categories: approaches to crime-fighting, investigative techniques, and organizational structures (Bouchard and Leduc 2007).

The following analysis is based on the examination of the structural adaptations of Regional Integrated Squads (RISs) and Integrated National Security Enforcement Teams (INSETs), two specialized investigative teams formed with the idea of maximizing partnership and cooperation between police organizations (Perras 2006). RISs are involved in anti-organized crime activities in the province of Quebec, and INSETs are involved in anti-terrorism activities throughout Canada. For the purposes of this analysis, we define 'structural adaptation' as any change in the structure of the group intended to facilitate the achievement of objectives defined by group members (Perras 2006). In 2005, semi-structured interviews were conducted with investigators, managers, analysts, and prosecutors working with the Montreal RIS during the investigation leading to Operation Springtime in 2001. In addition, we interviewed members of the INSETs, some of whom had already been interviewed during the round of RIS interviews.

Social learning, structural adaptation, and police cooperation in Joint Task Forces

In this section, we examine how social learning affected the operation of a complex joint investigation team involving many officers from Canadian police forces whose professional practices were sometimes quite dissimilar. Specifically, we focus on the working relationships of police officers during a joint criminal investigation which culminated in national and international arrests and warrants (Operation Springtime 2001). Bandura's (1977) research on social learning provides a relevant conceptual framework within which to explain how individuals in a given work environment are able to learn, internalize, and effectively reproduce techniques and values, and even act as conduits of information transport among and between colleagues.[2]

It should be noted that external reinforcement is not the only mechanism underlying social learning: it appears that other factors, such as feelings of pride, satisfaction and accomplishment, also play a crucial role. Finally, it should be acknowledged that social learning is a multi-stage process comprising 1) attention and concentration; 2) information retention and processing; 3) the reproduction/imitation of procedures and behaviours; and 4) the motivation to learn, which is generally influenced by a symbolic system of external and/or individual rewards and sanctions. In addition, Lave and Wenger (1990) have shown that social learning is shaped by the activity, context, and culture of a given workplace. Social interaction is a key component of learning, as it allows individuals to become part of a 'community of practices' that favours the assimilation of specific behaviours and beliefs.

While there are several ways for social learning to be operationalized in police forces, the most common strategies are mentoring, the buddy system and teamwork. These practices are good examples of the learning process, and reflect human resources management strategies that facilitate knowledge transfer and the consolidation of learning. To date, few Canadian studies have been conducted on the operation of investigative units, and even fewer on multi-jurisdictional structures. In fact, the only studies in this area are Manning's (1980) study of US drug squads, and Ericson's (1981) study of a Canadian homicide investigation squad. To our knowledge, these two authors are the only ones to have studied the effect of a specialized investigative structure on police officers' perception and understanding of specific criminal activities. However, two more recent studies have examined joint investigative teams that specialized in anti-organized crime activities in Quebec. In her study, Perras (2006) looked at the effect of organizational structure, roles and the leadership of joint investigative teams on the capacity of these squads to achieve their goals.

Also, Turcotte (2003) scrutinized the knowledge transmission processes in specialized investigative squads and their impact on police work. The author studied veterans of the Wolverine Squad, a joint force created in 1995 to counter a wave of violence stemming from a conflict between two outlaw motorcycle gangs (Hell's Angels and Rock Machine) over drug trafficking territories. The Wolverine Squad was composed of members of the *Service de Police de la Ville de Montréal* (City of Montreal Police Department), the *Sûreté du Québec* (Quebec provincial police), and the Royal Canadian Mounted Police (RCMP). Between 1994 and 2001, armed violence between the Hell's Angels and the Rock Machine was responsible for 363 victims, 192 of whom were directly linked to outlaw motorcycle gangs (Tanguay 2003). These clashes threatened social order in Quebec, particularly in the regions of Montreal and Quebec City. The situation soon instilled a deep sense of insecurity in the public, who exerted pressure on the government to end the hostilities between the rival gangs.[3]

It was against this backdrop that the government of Quebec urged police forces to work together and stem the tide of conflict between the two outlaw motorcycle gangs. The establishment of the Wolverine Squad was considered an unprecedented initiative in the fight against organized crime in Quebec and, more generally, Canada. The innovative joint structure marked the first time the three levels of police undertook a formal cooperative effort against organized crime (Turcotte 2003: 39). The Wolverine Squad appears to have targeted the most vulnerable criminal group (Rock Machine) in its seizures of weapons and explosives. The targeting of one antagonist group in particular left the field free for the other (Hell's Angels), that then seized the territories vacated or left considerably weakened by the Wolverine Squad's activities.

Turcotte's study demonstrated how veterans of specialized joint investigative teams transmitted their knowledge to rookies, and analysed the mechanisms underlying, and factors affecting, this knowledge transfer. Her results indicated that veterans relied on a variety of institutionalized mechanisms that ensured knowledge transfer, and the substance of this transmission concerned criminal targets and squad practices. Furthermore, information exchange was not a static process, as it appeared to evolve in response to the needs of different groups of police officers. To a large extent, organizational knowledge is based on individuals' representation of the environment that cannot be questioned or disregarded in actual practice at the risk of being marginalized by co-workers. This situation is a pertinent illustration of how a sanction may serve as reinforcement in a learning process associated with the conception of criminal patterns or phenomena. The results of this study, as well as observed flaws in police cooperation protocols, raise serious questions about the capacity of organizations to control knowledge transmission.

Once public safety was restored, however, problems that were typical of police partnerships resurfaced. In fact, disagreements over the leadership and visibility of the constituent police forces resulted in the break-up of the Wolverine Squad. In 1999, the establishment of anti-organized crime units known as Regional Integrated Squad (RISs) ushered in a new investigative framework based on a renewed philosophy of police cooperation. RISs were strategically implemented in the six regions of the province of Quebec in which the criminal activities of the Hell's Angels were concentrated. The six RISs integrated 23 municipal forces and three large-scale organizations: *Service de Police de la Ville de Montréal, Sûreté du Québec*, and the Royal Canadian Mounted Police. Although the RISs' mission was an extension of that of the Wolverine Squad, their primary objective was the suppression of outlaw motorcycle gangs 'in order to eliminate their influence, by adapting to regional needs and priorities, collaborating with existing squads, and collaborating, in operational and informational terms, on the provincial strategy' (RISs procedural guidelines, 31 May 1999). Furthermore, this joint effort lent itself to the establishment of partnerships (in the form of groups of projects) which improved the structural and interactional stability of the constituent police forces over time.

The traditional problems of leadership and visibility encountered within the Wolverine Squad were partially neutralized by a clearer definition of the constituent police forces' mandates and roles. The *Sûreté du Québec* was designated the lead agency of the RISs, with responsibility for coordination and primary responsibility for the mobilization of investigative resources required by the six RISs. The other police forces provided complementary human and material resources (expertise, equipment, supplies, etc.), reducing tensions and competition to tolerable levels that seemed to foster collaboration between the police forces.

The RISs employed the strategy of targeted profiling which means according priority to high profile individuals designated as dangerous or posing a serious threat. Information was collected in several ways, including the use of human sources as well as physical and electronic surveillance. The decentralized work structure of the regional RISs allowed them to share tasks flexibly across multiple investigations. Their strategy was to target the Hell's Angels' upper ranks and affiliated outlaw motorcycle organizations. To this end, specialized investigators were grouped into work units on the basis of the individuals or groups targeted. These units were themselves divided into two sub-units: RUSH for investigations of key players in narcotic trafficking, and OCEAN for the proceeds of crime. These two sub-units were the main participants in Operation Springtime 2001.

This first permanent joint investigative team brought together investigators, prosecutors, and civilian analysts into a decentralized and ad hoc operational and organizational configuration, requiring them to work in close collaboration.[4] In fact, depending on the circumstances and available resources, some investigators active in one sub-unit were authorized to work temporarily on investigations belonging to the other sub-unit. At critical moments, investigations from the two sub-units of Operation Springtime 2001 were merged together, as a result of convergent information on, and evidence related to, criminal targets. In addition, RIS members were routinely invited to working meetings at which investigators from the two sub-units shared information. These meetings also allowed the strategies and investigations to be revised as needed. The flexibility and fluidity of the RISs' organizational configuration were both instrumental in the development of information exchange and knowledge transfer between the professional groups (investigators, prosecutors and analysts) as well as between the investigation's sub-units.

Also, we observed that Operation Springtime 2001 was fertile ground for the implementation of several initiatives, three of which are particularly noteworthy. Firstly, prosecutors played a leading role throughout, in contrast to usual investigative practice. In fact, prosecutors were the principal architects of the investigation strategy and collaborated closely with investigators in the collection of evidence. It was the prosecutors who advised the investigators of the evidence and information they would need to build a judicially solid case in light of recent anti-organized crime amendments to the Criminal Code of Canada (Bill C-24). The prosecutors' legal and procedural knowledge was very helpful to the investigators who found themselves, for the first time, working on a police operation whose legal foundation had never before been tested.

Secondly, working in independent units allowed investigators from different police forces to share their investigative techniques, knowledge of the criminal world, and network of contacts. One of the results of this exchange of information was a 'natural selection' of best practices throughout the operation, which in turn meant that specific tasks were allocated to specific police forces (surveillance, management of sources, etc.). Furthermore, the decentralization of Operation Springtime 2001 into units and sub-units allowed investigators to develop specific knowledge concerning: 1) the criminal activities of targeted individuals and outlaw motorcycle gangs; 2) the strategies and methods adopted by outlaw motorcycle gangs to manage their illegal profits; 3) the infrastructure of the Hell's Angels; and 4) the culture and traditions of the criminal groups under investigation.

Thirdly, Operation Springtime 2001 was largely responsible for the creation and recognition of the criminal analyst function. Analysts routinely organized the information accumulated by investigators and performed on-demand analyses of the chronology of investigative activities. These analysts offered investigators a framework in which they could follow the progress of the investigation, revise the direction of the operation, and identify the activities that were still to be performed. The work of the analysts was also very useful to the prosecutors, who relied on it to follow the investigators' progress and advise them on future work. It should also be noted that the analysts were also active in the management, archiving, and analysis of evidence following Operation Springtime 2001.

In summary, the structure of the Regional Integrated Squad, the multi-jurisdictional and multi-functional composition of the task force (prosecutors/analysts), and the managerial approach (project management incorporating information sharing, processing and communication) favoured social learning and, by extension, structural flexibility. In fact, the horizontal communication of knowledge and expertise that resulted from the establishment of practice communities (e.g. prosecutors, investigators, analysts) advanced the progress of investigations and even allowed investigations to merge or split in light of new leads. In all, RIS investigations led to the seizure of $12.5 million in cash, drugs worth $363,857, 89 firearms, 42 vehicles, and 13 motorcycles; 150 arrests (including the arrest of 138 members of outlaw motorcycle gangs); and the conviction of 131 accused individuals[5]. Of course, membership of this multi-jurisdictional squad specializing in anti-organized crime activities was a source of pride for many police officers, several of whom identified more strongly with this structure than with their originating police force.[6] This new organization rapidly became the symbol of efficiency and effectiveness in anti-organized crime investigations, to such a point that we hypothesize it may have played a significant role in the establishment of a similar structure for anti-terrorism activities.

Knowledge transfer, structural adaptation, and police cooperation in integrated national security enforcement teams

The transfer of police knowledge to organizations that are not responsible for the application of the law is a well-known phenomenon. Ericson and Haggerty (1997) demonstrated that the police regularly transfer information and criminal statistics to banks, insurance companies, automobile registration agencies, and many other non-police organizations. Furthermore, it is also known that the private sector profits from an 'old boys' network' and, above all, from the network of police officers who leave the police force to work in the private security sector (Van Outrive 1998). In this last connection, it should be noted that the 'blue drain' has provided the private sector with access to specialized knowledge and techniques from the public security field and to an array of police resources.

The movement of personnel from police forces to the private sector may also be relevant in the fight against terrorism. *A priori*, the relationship between law enforcement forces and national security forces appears more natural than the relationship between public and private police forces, since the fight against crime and the fight against terrorism remain largely the prerogative of public authorities. However, Canada possesses unique rules with regard to the institutional and operational separation of the judicial and political police. In 1981, the McDonald Commission recommended the creation of a new civilian information service and of an advisory oversight council composed of members of parliament and senators. In 1984, the Canadian government followed up on these recommendations and passed *An Act to Establish the Canadian Security Intelligence Service* (1984), thus creating a civilian security information service, albeit one with no real operational power in the judicial sense of the term. Investigations related to the national security of Canada are the exclusive responsibility of the RCMP. However, testimony has repeatedly and clearly shown that several RCMP officers assigned to national security found themselves 'civilian members' of the Canadian Security Intelligence Service (CSIS), the organization created to ensure a certain degree of cultural and organizational distance between the judicial and political police forces.[7] Thus, the extent of the change imposed by public authorities appears to have been limited by the transfer of police personnel (know-how, factual knowledge, etc.) to a civilian national security agency (Lester 1998).

More recently, the terrorist attacks of 2001 led the Canadian government to review its anti-terrorism strategy and create a multi-jurisdictional structure headed by the RCMP and comprising the Canada Border Services Agency (CBSA), Citizenship and Immigration Canada (CIC), the Canadian Security Intelligence Service (CSIS), and several municipal and provincial police forces. Thus, in 2002, the Integrated National Security Enforcement Teams (INSETs) were created to monitor and eliminate terrorist threats against Canada. As with the case with the RISs discussed above, the INSETs were established in a turbulent socio-political climate in which great pressure was exerted on the Canadian government, by both its citizens and the United States, to secure Canadian territory against terrorist attacks. The similar contexts in which the RISs and the INSETs were created reflect the classic distinction between planned change that is desired by an organization and change during crisis which is imposed upon an organization. In fact, neither the RISs nor the INSETs were created as the result of negotiation, but rather were imposed by public authorities seeking to re-establish or maintain social peace and order. According to Batley and Larbi (2004), imposed change can only be rapidly effective if there is a fluid managerial approach, dynamism in interventions, and an openness to knowledge transfer.

To create four regional INSETs (Eastern Canada, Central Canada, National Capital, Western Canada) the RCMP was obliged to reorganize several units of the National Security Criminal Investigations service. As with the RISs, decentralization of the INSETs should favour the integration of regional police forces and improve the collection and exchange of information, the performance of inter-jurisdictional investigations, and the analysis of information on national security threats. More specifically, the INSETs have a three-fold mandate:[8]

1 Increase the capacity of partners to collect, exchange and analyse information on targets (individuals) who threaten national security.
2 Increase the capacity of police to bring those targets to trial.
3 Improve the collective capacity of the partner organizations to counter national security threats and fulfill their specific mandated responsibilities.

These three primary objectives are similar to those pursued by the RISs in the fight against organized crime. The transfer of resources observed in 1984 following the creation of the Canadian Security Intelligence Service did not occur to the same degree when the INSETs were created. Nevertheless, it is true that members of the RCMP who played a leading role in the establishment of the RISs and the planning of Operation Springtime 2001 were reassigned to the INSETs upon the latter groups' creation. Information on the dissemination of cooperative anti-organized crime investigative models (RISs) and the application of such models to anti-terrorism activities was collected during interviews with investigators who had been transferred to INSETs. The information gathered from interviews indicated three forms of dissemination as follows:

1 Widespread dissemination of the joint investigation model into the area of anti-organized crime activities:

They [the RISs] were a model in Quebec. And I also think that the Bikers' Enforcement Units in Ontario sort of followed the same principle as the RISs in Quebec when it came to bikers. Anyway, I think that that's the future. I'm totally convinced of that.

2 Specific dissemination of techniques from criminal joint investigation to complex investigations involving anti-terrorism activities:

There was a plane that was blown up by terrorists ... the plane took off from Montreal ... Air India. They came to see us. Because of the mountains of documentary and video evidence from the Air India trial. There was also the investigation into the plane crash at Peggy's Cove ... Swissair. Anyway, these were big deals with lots of documents. They attended, they came to see how we managed evidence. It wasn't only police people. People came from all over.

3 Dissemination of specific roles from criminal joint investigation to anti-terrorism activities:

[in RISs] We used analysts a lot. In the INSETs, I try to ensure that those people are used.

The importance that I place on the analysts, the importance that I place on discussion with prosecutors. I can talk about my own experience; I brought them with me [to the INSETs]. We don't have the advantage of having the attorneys in our INSET offices.

This testimony comes from two senior federal police officers assigned to the Montreal INSET at the time of interview. These individuals drew on their experience with the RISs to improve the dissemination, and even the adaptation, of strategies and practices developed in the fight against organized crime to the fight against terrorism. Although organized crime and terrorism have quite different features, we noted that there are several similarities in the police response to each of them. We believe that these similarities may be explained by organizational, legal, operational and cultural factors, despite the different nature of law enforcement and national security operations. Table 7.1 illustrates how these factors converge, independent of the security problem in question (organized crime *vs.* terrorism).

Firstly, the regional character of both the RISs and the INSETs favours a targeted integration of partners on the basis of regional features and priorities (political, jurisdictional, border-related, etc.). The independence that comes from this decentralization enables these multi-jurisdictional teams to create organizational approaches to decision making and its corollaries, administrative procedures and operational planning that differ from those of large bureaucracies. In fact, multi-jurisdictional teams/units exhibit a more or less formal work structure and leadership built around flexible strategies and interchangeable practices (law enforcement *vs.* national security). It is thus hardly surprising – given the absence of precedents in the creation of multi-jurisdictional structures and the general mobilization to counter imminent threats from organized crime and terrorists – that inter-personal and inter-organizational work relations tended to be fluid. Finally, decentralization also allowed the leadership of the agencies involved in the regional units/teams to make adjustments (commensurate with the resources they invested and their jurisdictional authority) designed to avoid the undesirable effects of an unhealthy competition between police forces.

The fight against terrorism not only drove changes in the con-figuration of police structures, but also compelled the Canadian government to promulgate legislation conferring more legal and operational latitude upon police forces (Table 7.1, Point 2). Nevertheless, the 2001 Anti-Terrorism Act has not been truly tested so far. The first charges under this law were laid in March 2004 against Mohammad Momin Khawaja, but that case has unfortunately not yet come to trial. Another more ambitious attempt to apply this law followed the arrests associated with the dismantling of a terrorist cell in Toronto in June 2006. It is worth noting that, prior to this investigation, the Canadian government primarily relied on a legal procedure from

Table 7.1 Convergence between the RISs and the INSETs

Convergence	Anti-Gang (RISs)	Anti-Terrorism (INSETs)
1. **Organizational framework**	Joint investigative structure Decentralized structure Provincial regionalization	Joint investigative structure Decentralized structure National regionalization
2. **Legal framework**	Criminal Code: Anti-Organized Crime Act	Criminal Code: Anti-Terrorism Act
3. **Operational framework** (investigative techniques)	Detection of drug conspiracies Electronic surveillance Physical surveillance Profiling of targets Human sources, special witnesses Controlled drug deliveries	Detection of terrorist plots Online (web) surveillance Human sources Profiling of targets Controlled explosive deliveries
4. **Structural framework**	Police forces Prosecutor	Police forces Canadian Security Intelligence Service (civilian) Immigration service Prosecutor

immigration law known as a *security certificate* to counter terrorism. These certificates can be issued against any individual who does not hold Canadian citizenship and who is reasonably believed to be a member of an organization engaged, or likely to engage, in terrorism. The issuance of a security certificate by the Canadian government authorizes police forces to detain such individuals and not to divulge (out of interest for national security or the anonymity of human sources) information incriminating them. However, in the case of the 2006 Toronto arrests it was impossible to use security certificates as most of the individuals involved were Canadian citizens. Just as Operation Springtime 2001 was the first opportunity for police forces and government departments to apply the anti-organized crime law of 1997, the arrests related to the 2006 terrorist plot were the first opportunity to apply the 2001 Anti-Terrorism Act (Ramraj and Roach 2005).

According to media reports, the Canadian Security Intelligence Service had been monitoring the suspected terrorist cell dismantled in June 2006 since 2004.[9] More specifically, the investigation started when intelligence agents detected suspicious communications while monitoring Internet chat sites. CSIS determined that a group of 17 individuals were plotting several terrorist attacks and apparently intended to detonate explosive-laden vehicles in southern Ontario.[10] The RCMP has stated that there had been no real danger of explosion since the police had replaced the explosives (made up of ammonium nitrate) with a harmless substance in the course of a controlled delivery operation. The investigation ended on 2 June 2006 with the arrest of the suspects, and has since been described as the investigation with the greatest number of terrorism-related arrests in North America.[11] It appears that the Toronto INSET played a major role in the dismantling of the alleged Islamic terrorist cell. In fact, the investigation appears to have benefited considerably from the inter-jurisdictional nature of the INSETs, since the operation involved several police forces from southern Ontario and the Toronto area.

In the fight against both organized crime and terrorism, legislative modifications required police forces to develop a more elaborate investigative strategy which then demonstrated the presence of a conspiracy and of a criminal group or alleged terrorist cell. In both cases, the dismantling of a network of individuals (Hell's Angels and the alleged terrorist cell in Ontario) was the result of the application of the following established methods of judicial investigations: 1) the use of electronic surveillance methods to detect suspicious activities during drug transactions or discussions related to the proposed targets of attacks; 2) the collection of evidence by physical surveillance or surveillance of discussions in Internet forums; 3) a reliance, in both case, on sources (in the criminal group or alleged terrorist cell); 4) controlled deliveries (drugs in the case of organized crime, explosives in the case of the alleged terrorists); and 5) the key role of extensive integration of legal and analytical expertise.

With regard to this last point it should be mentioned that, contrary to tradition, RIS investigators forged close ties with prosecutors who specialized in the fight against organized crime. This facilitated the design of an investigative strategy that favoured the sharing of knowledge and know-how. The INSETs, which had at their disposal a group of prosecutors specialized in anti-terrorism activities, adopted a similar model. It should also be mentioned that it is impossible to draw conclusions about the true scope of this similarity, as these investigations into terrorism have not yet resulted in trials. Of course, all these practices had as their goal the bringing of charges under the Criminal Code, which necessarily influenced the manner in which the two investigations were conducted. In summary, there is no doubt that both the relationship to the judicial system and the rules of criminal procedure affected the choice and operationalization of investigative strategies.

Finally, we saw in the previous section that social learning helped investigators involved in Operation Springtime 2001 to consolidate, refine, and adjust their investigative methods. The implementation and effectiveness of such mechanisms are particularly dependent on the presence of common traits, and especially of a shared cultural framework. This last point raises the question of the organizational culture in which actors involved in the cooperative effort against organized crime or terrorism operate. As Table 7.1 illustrates (Point 4), the two cooperative structures have a considerable number of actors drawn from the legal world, i.e. with responsibility for the application of the law or criminal procedures. RISs and INSETs have several cultural features in common, reflecting their common vocation, the institutions in which they work (justice, public security, civil protection), and a number of shared beliefs, standards and values. All these cultural traits link the actors involved in police cooperation together and allow them to establish communication channels which can facilitate the transmission of knowledge about targets and professional practices. These observations are also true of the INSETs, as those cooperative police structures encompass a large number of actors from the judicial and law enforcement spheres. Nevertheless, as we shall see in the conclusion, these similarities have some limitations that produce nuances regarding the convergence of police cooperation models in the areas of organized crime and terrorism.

Conclusion

Although the models of police cooperation that we examined exhibit many similarities, it is also true that the multi-jurisdictional character of anti-terrorist activities exhibits a unique feature that differentiates it from anti-organized crime activities: the confidentiality of national security questions. This last point is a crucial challenge to inter-agency cooperation and, especially, to the extent of collaboration in law enforcement and national security agencies. In point of fact, the sensitive nature of the information held by security intelligence services, and the often questionable techniques that these services use, render them disinclined to share what they know with organizations which are obligated by law to divulge any evidence they hold concerning individuals. This difference is a recurrent source of tension and conflict between law enforcement and anti-terrorist intelligence agencies. In the United States, this type of conflict has marked the relations between the Federal Bureau of Investigation (FBI) and the Central Intelligence Agency (CIA) over the years, sometimes leading to relations that could fairly be described as counterproductive.[12]

However, there is a difference between the place and role of analysts in RIS investigations and INSET investigations. Firstly, it appears that RIS analysts have always concentrated on specific (tactical) files. While there is little known about the use of analysts in INSETs, members of the RCMP interviewed mentioned that the analysis of nominal (i.e. individual) information was uncommon, and that strategic analysts were primarily provided by the CSIS, an INSET member. In practice, anti-organized crime activities rely more heavily on tactical analysis, while anti-terrorism activities rely more heavily on strategic analysis. In this connection, it should be recalled that the commission on the September 11, 2001 attacks severely criticized the under-utilization of information analysts, and encouraged national security organizations to take greater initiative in this area (Kean and Hamilton 2004). One of the most frequently mentioned reasons for the low participation of tactical and operational analysts is the absence or scarcity of cases involving terrorist activities. Thus, at the time of interview, the interviewees stated that their work consisted primarily of two activities: 1) verification of the credibility of terrorist threats reported to authorities (detection); and 2) surveillance of the development of terrorist phenomena or groups (strategic analyses).

There are similarities in the nature and participation of non-police organizations in RISs and INSETs. It should be emphasized that in both cases non-police agencies remain behind the scenes, in contrast to their police partners. In INSETs, for example, it is the members of the police forces who make decisions, with prosecutors and members of CSIS confined to an advisory role. Non-police organizations attend monthly meetings but are not necessarily invited to other (weekly, daily) meetings, which are operational. On the other hand, differences in the targets of these multi-jurisdictional structures do lead to differences in the integration of non-police partners. For example, upon their creation INSETs rapidly built ties with the Canadian military intelligence service, the customs services, and the CSIS. The RISs only established such ties at a later stage of development, initially with non-police partners within the judicial system (prosecutors) and later, more closely with Revenue Canada (because of their targeting of the proceeds of crime). There are several reasons for this difference in the chronology of non-police partnerships.

Firstly, the RISs were established before the INSETs, and were, in a sense, pilot projects with regard to the use of non-police partners in organized crime investigations. It took some time for investigators to establish partnerships, based on trust and a protocol that enabled the exchange of information regarding active investigations with non-police organizations. Furthermore, the INSETs were three times more likely to rely on non-police organizations than were the RISs. One of the reasons for this difference is public authorities' perceptions of the scope of the threat presented by terrorism and of the vulnerability of national interests. The integration of non-police partners was driven by the mobilization of public resources beyond the economic, political, institutional, communications/technology, and social spheres, itself driven by the threat of terrorism, the presence of exploitable vulnerabilities, and the capabilities of certain terrorist groups. In summary, it appears that the magnitude of the threat, the urgency of the phenomenon, and the political destabilization that may trigger an attack are all factors that encourage the removal of barriers to the sharing of national security-related expertise.

Using two case studies, we have shown how and to what extent social learning was at the heart of the development and refinement of a model of multi-jurisdictional units. We have also examined how the structural adaptations (sometimes imposed) that facilitated police cooperation in the fight against organized crime and terrorism were the result of knowledge transfer (mediated by the transfer of personnel), and changes in social and political environments. We have also established that the convergence of models of police cooperation falls firmly along four axes: organizational, legal, operational, cultural. The similarities among these four axes form the basis for a comparative model that sheds light on the close ties between law-enforcement and national security. According to Sheptycki (2005), policing tends to exhibit convergent organizational and cultural principles, and this convergence is due in large part to the international transfer of technologies. For Reiner (1997: 1007), the convergence of policing models is shaped by the new international regime of expert police technocrats which acts as a source of global knowledge transfer of trends in policing. As these two authors indicate, expertise transfer, the modification of legal frameworks, and political and economical necessities appear to extend the phenomenon of convergence beyond traditional policing to cooperation and anti-terrorism activities.

Notes

1   For more information on open systems see Scott (1987).
2   Bandura (1977) posits three levels or models of social learning: 1) the direct imitation model; 2) the verbal instruction model, which is in some ways learning by description and explanation; and 3) the symbolic model, the basis for learning from the actions of fictional characters in movies, on television, or in literature.
3   The death of a young boy and the attempted murder of two journalists were largely responsible for fanning the flames of public indignation.
4   See Mintzberg (1992) regarding organizational configurations and structures.
5   According to the *Sûreté du Québec*, 16 November 2004: http://www. suretequebec.gouv.qc.ca/accueil/communiques/2004/20041116_01.html
6   In April 2009, the Regional Integrated Squads conducted a similar investigation named SharQc that culminated in the arrest of 158 individuals related to drug trafficking and 22 homicides.
7   Statement by Yvon Gingras, an ex-RCMP agent, during an interview on Radio-Canada's Le Téléjournal, Autumn 1986.
8   For further details, visit http://www.rcmp-grc.gc.ca/security/insets_ f.htm
9   Source: http://www.ctv.ca/servlet/ArticleNews/story/CTVNews/2006 0603/toronto_arrests_060603/20060604?hub=TorontoHome
10 The group also planned to attack a very busy public building. According to police sources, the individuals were to assault a broadcasting centre and the Canadian Parliament. Source: http://www.thestar.com/ NASApp/cs/ContentServer?pagename=thestar/Layout/Article_Type1& c=Article&cid=1149545412024&call_pageid=114932960448
11 Source: http://www.cbc.ca/story/canada/national/2006/06/03/terror-suspects.html
12 For example, the FBI investigation of the attack against the *USS Cole* in Yemen. See Lawrence Wright, A Reporter at Large, 'The Agent,' *The New Yorker*, 10 July 2006, p. 62.

Chapter 8

The France and Europol relationship: explaining shifts in cooperative behaviour

Nadia Gerspacher[1]

Introduction

International police cooperation has been initiated by sub-national actors such as police chiefs and field officers, by state actors such as policy makers, and even above the state by EU ministers at a variety of levels of sophistication, organization and legitimacy. These efforts represent the realization that fighting international crime unilaterally has few promises of success. While there is an undeniable discourse on the necessity of police cooperation, implementation of the political will to share information and engage in joint investigations and strategy design at the operational level tends to lag far behind. If national police services are to increase the risk involved in combating transnational crime, the pooling of resources requires states to revisit the way policing and territorial integrity impacts on their fight against wealthy, borderless and fluid transnational crime actors. So, if police cooperation is so widely deemed desirable by such a variety of actors, why is it still a phenomenon in development? And, if states agree that a multilateral approach is necessary to fight transnational crime and if they devote resources to the formal coordination of police cooperation, why are participation rates still not reflecting a systematic use of this formal coordination? Is the answer in the nature or structure of international organizations, the limitations imposed on international organizations, the pooling of resources, by the respect for the principle of state sovereignty?

The level of participation by member states is not explained only by the structures or mechanisms of international organization. There are a myriad national factors also at play that determine whether a state, via policy making and operational implementation, will utilize the output of international organizations. The mindset and ideology of national governments affect how the discourse of cooperation is translated in collaboration and exchange. The national system of exchange of police information, or information flow system, is also crucial to the ability of a state to collaborate with foreign counterparts. If a state already has channels of communication between local field officers and national offices, going through regional political entities, the national law enforcement apparatus is much more readily organized to allow information from the field to travel all the way to an international framework of communication and be able to receive information that is diffused back again. Resources, training and competences (both technical and knowledge based) are also important factors that will determine the type of participation that one can expect from a particular government. Additionally, in an environment of sheer interdependence, member governments have an interest in inciting cooperation from non-cooperative states as the output of the international organization depends on participation via the sharing of information from all states affected by transnational crimes such as illicit drug trafficking, be it supply, transit or consumer states.

While there are a variety of international police cooperation initiatives that range from informal to formal and bilateral to multi-lateral, I focus on institutionalized organizations formally created by states to serve as the facilitators of cooperation. International police cooperation organizations (e.g. Europol and Interpol) differ from *ad hoc* police cooperation initiatives by the resources they enjoy and the member government commitment that allows them to establish legit-imacy and even a semblance of 'bindingness' (Hallerberg and Weber 2001) and thus opportunities to coerce and enforce. Furthermore, formal international organizations enjoy a unique perspective on the nature of the fight against transnational crime. Their secretariats are staffed with sophisticated law enforcement professionals whose responsibilities include collecting information from national police authorities, analysing this, and then diffusing it back to the membership. This represents an asset that is not attainable by any other actor, either sub-national or national. A collection of police information from the states affected by a particular criminal activity and the compilation of that information give the output of the international organization a big picture perspective that is not attainable on a bilateral or regional basis and difficult to achieve without the sophistication allotted to the systems in place at Europol and Interpol.

The goal of this analysis is to situate the issue of international police cooperation in the growing debate on this phenomenon. In order to better understand the type of actors International Police Cooperation Organizations (IPCOs) are (and can be), we need a better understanding of the nature of the relationship between member states and IPCOs with a focus on participation rates and the motors of change that can incite a utilization of the services offered by these international bodies. By studying the dynamics of a shift in participation by French authorities in the Europol system over time, we can identify the explanatory factors for increased utilization of the Europol output.

When cooperation takes place in instances where it has not done historically, we can learn a great deal about how this shift does take place. In this chapter, I identify the factors and the actors that can stimulate cooperation where it has previously been weak. I suggest some of the factors that affect participation rates and identify which actor(s), processes and dynamics stimulate a utilization of international frameworks of cooperation. The first section sets this debate within both the international organization literature of international relations and the growing scholarship on international police cooperation in order to show specifically that we already have the tools to understand some of the factors that can encourage or inhibit international cooperation. In the second section, I introduce the structure, organization and mission of an international police cooperation organization guided by the case of Europol. The third section offers a presentation of the case in France, specifically the increase in participation that took place early in the new millennium, and highlight the power struggles, interests and political environments among which this increase occurred. In the last section, I provide analysis that contributes to our understanding of the motivations and mechanisms of utilization of international cooperative systems by states and I introduce the idea that the international organization can serve as a backdrop for interstate relations by which cooperation behaviour is encouraged in a complex web of interactions and interest maximizing behaviour.

Theoretical approaches to formal international cooperation

While police cooperation is but one of the issues that require international cooperation and organization, it is also an issue that is set apart because policing, the maintenance of security and safety, is most often perceived as the fundamental role of the state. There is a significant literature on the performance of international organizations (IOs) in general and the roles that they can play to assist states in addressing a range of global issues multilaterally. We know that these organizations can assist states in raising concern, building capacity or solving contracting problems (Keohane *et al*. 1993). A vast literature allows us to better understand why international cooperation is desirable and why states create IOs (Keohane 1984; Keohane and Nye 1997; Martin and Lisa 1992; Stein 1990). And we know what makes them successful, which is fulfilling the mandates given to them by states (Koremenos *et al*. 2001; Wettestad 2001). Further, we have a good understanding of how negotiations take place, both at formal and informal levels (Moravscik 1999), and that the creation of IOs and the commitment to cooperate that is signalled by negotiations and the ratification of conventions yield unintended consequences on the original choices of bargaining outcomes (Wendt 2001). Finally, we know about the impact that IOs have on international cooperation, namely they diffuse norms and have been observed to yield influence over states (Barnett and Finnemore 1999; Finnemore 1993). And we have been shown that the delegation of certain tasks to IOs can be explained by principal agent theories when it comes to the dynamic between IOs and their roles in the international system (Nielson and Tierney 2003).

International organizations are not only 'principles, norms, rules and decision-making procedures' (Krasner 1983: 3), they are also actors that diffuse norms and principles (Keck and Sikkink 1998; Klotz 1995): 'IOs ... increasingly assume a wide range of tasks that their member states lack the competence, will and/or technical expertise to perform' (Cronin 2002). This study shows that norms and the principles that are 'imposed' on the membership can be derived from members with opposing views on cooperation and international organization who debate the place that the output of the IO and consequently the IO itself have. The enhanced knowledge about criminal activity is not that of one state but derived from the output of the police cooperation organization, the finished intelligence derived from a compilation and analysis of voluntarily shared intelligence gathered by national law enforcement authorities. So the analysis, new approaches and recommendations that constitute the output of the IOs establish a new normative environment which becomes crucial to the 'coercive/enforcement' dimension that an IO can then attain. The legal instruments (conventions, ratification) that shape these organizations lend these bodies legitimacy from the government support that *ad hoc* police cooperation efforts cannot attain because they are informal and have relatively fewer resources and support for development.

States will not pull the plug on IOs that are 'not performing', as regime and neo-liberal theories claim. If that were so, when Europol was created would one expect EU member states to cut the support of Interpol and other seemingly redundant arrangements? France gives a significant portion of its budget to Interpol besides housing its headquarters (Bigo 1996) and it is the third largest contributor to Europol. So why create Europol and continue to commit to Interpol and to other cooperative initiatives like the Franco-German Meuse-Rhine agreement? However, as this chapter shows, states do engage in reforming international organizations that do not, or are not able to, fulfill their mandates and serve their interests as intended.

We don't know enough about the nature of the relationship between the state and the IO when this is viewed from a 'service provider to end user' perspective. Specifically, not enough attention is paid to how the rules and principles – essentially the result of international negotiations – affect the operational, focusing on the logistics and motivations of voluntary information exchange. This inquiry strives to contribute to our understanding of how international organizations can coerce, persuade, even bind member governments to utilize their outputs and channels. Paradoxically, states created IOs to assist and coordinate but their competent authorities do not tap its output systematically.

Theoretical explanations of international police cooperation

We must identify the dynamics between concerned actors in police cooperation frameworks and what they contribute to the fight against transnational crime. Specifically, there is a need to identify which actors have the influence, indeed power, to induce change and make IOs more useful/utilized for the membership at large. In many ways the challenges inherent in international bargaining, and even the ratification of agreements, pale in comparison with those imposed by the implementation of those arrangements at an operational level, on the ground. So in gaining a better understanding of the agency's change, we can better identify the means to circumvent obstacles to cooperation and the formulation of policies, agreements and procedures that offer a greater promise of real cooperation on the ground.

The international police cooperation literature can help us to better understand the challenges of joining forces across borders in law enforcement matters. This body of knowledge describes historical developments with a focus on sociological considerations, notably that institutional independence from political centres is most conducive to the internationalization of the police function (Deflem 2002). Historical developments studies offer a comprehensive understanding of the obstacles inherent to international organization in police cooperation, the efforts states make, and the inherent limitations imposed on police cooperation by the principle of sovereignty (Anderson 1989; Bigo 1999; Sabatier 2001).

Internationalization is the most critical challenge for international police cooperation (Den Boer 1999; Sheptycki 2000). Internationalization is a complex task that requires the involvement of both national and sub-national actors and includes the development of information flow systems and the reform of existing policies that are incompatible with that of fellow member governments or the drafting of new ones to categorize specific criminal endeavours as crimes that carry the appropriate impunity. The more integrationist the scenario for police cooperation is, the more conducive to police cooperation it becomes as an international police culture, and a variety of professional exchange and networks of police and customs liaison officers develop (Anderson *et al.* 1995).

Although this growing literature on international police co-operation has made great strides in enhancing our understanding of this phenomenon, the existing studies focus on the dynamics and challenges of police cooperation and mention IOs as forums for states to collaborate, without any real focus on IPCOs with the exception of historical accounts and legal analysis of the conventions. I look at IPCOs as actors engaged in the fight against transnational crime in their own right, with unique contributions from which all concerned actors can stand to benefit. States limit themselves by not participating in the elaborate, sophisticated, demanding instrument of cooperation that they created. This affects participation rates as actors, both national and sub-national, have a limited understanding of how to collaborate and remain frustrated due to the incompatibilities of legal and operational approaches across the memberships of these IOs.

International police cooperation organizations

International police cooperation, according to the Europol Convention, is defined as:

- operational cooperation between competent national authorities in relation to the prevention, detection and investigation of criminal offences;

- the collection, storage, processing, analysis and exchange of relevant information, including information held by law enforcement services on reports on suspicious financial transactions ... subject to appropriate provisions on the protection of personal data;

- cooperation and joint initiatives in training, the exchange of liaison officers, secondments, the use of equipment, and forensic research;

- the common evaluation of particular investigative techniques in relation to the detection of serious forms of organized crime.

International police cooperation organizations serve as clearing houses to collect voluntarily shared police information from all member states, to analyse it and disseminate the 'finished intelligence'. While the conventions of these IOs mandate the facilitation of 'operational cooperation' (the Interpol Constitution), they do not have executive powers, jurisdiction, or their own operational teams and they are strictly bound by the principle of sovereignty and the supremacy of states. While a trend toward the coordination of joint teams and other mutual assistance initiatives has given these bodies, especially in the case of Europol, more influence on the national law enforcement processes, these are still in their infancy and largely dependent on the voluntary cooperation of national police authorities and political actors.

These IOs are intended to promote the exchange of information between foreign police authorities to provide the entire membership with a big picture perspective that is otherwise only possible at the supranational level. This exchange of information is a broad concept in the area of international police cooperation. The reports generated, including threat assessments and trends of criminality, are sophisticated criminal analyses that provide information which transcends borders. The staff, including liaison officers, are composed of highly sophisticated, internationally minded law enforcement professionals (Bigo 1996) whose technological resources and competences are above those commonly found throughout law enforcement communities at the national level.[2] These reports can lead to the undertaking of joint investigations and developing strategies at national and bilateral levels, but most importantly they inform the police authorities about the *modus operandi* of transnational criminal groups. The *ad hoc* sharing of information between foreign counterparts is beneficial to the parties concerned but the more systematized approach of fostering and utilizing finished intelligence allows for a more comprehensive understanding of the enemy, transnational crime and the perpetrators involved even as they cross borders.

To fulfill their mandates and maximize the quality of their output, cooperation rates (the giving *and* receiving of information) must be high. In order to paint a big picture of such transnational criminal activity successfully, which is trans-border in nature, the crime analysis performed by these IOs theoretically must be a collection of information from all those states in which a particular criminal group has operated, whether to seek a safe haven, perpetuate a crime (supply or demand) or hide profits. Consequently the accuracy and completeness, and hence the quality and usability, of the finished intelligence depend on states' willingness and ability to share evidence and any other intelligence gathered by the national police authorities (Gerspacher 2002). All in all, the participation rates of national police services in an international system of cooperation must be of a systematic nature to allow IOs to fulfill their respective, and very similar, mandates of facilitating cooperation at the operational level.

International police cooperation is plagued by the many obstacles inherent to a variety of factors that are largely rooted in the principle of sovereignty and state supremacy. Political systems, culture, *modus operandi*, rules of evidence, work cultures and attitudes on crime and punishment are most often factors that impair police cooperation. They lead to a mistrust of national abilities to handle sensitive information, turf issues, incompatible legal and judicial systems across the membership, language and cultural boundaries, and an unequal ability to participate in a global system of cooperation coupled with widely ranging commitment and recognition of the threats posed by the undertaking of unilateral or bilateral law enforcement. Incompatible law traditions, common law and Roman law, as well as the other law traditions of Islam, China and Japan, lead to misunderstandings to the point that legal proceedings outside borders are hindered (Anderson 1989). Jurisdiction issues are also highly problematic as information always belongs to someone, whether this is suspicion or evidence (Anderson 1989). Also, varying interests and professional experiences yield to disagreements about how to cooperate effectively. And a lack of competence and/or expertise on the part of most police officers in the problems of international crime also play a role in limiting the flow of information exchange.

The internationalization of policing requires integration by member governments that establish institutional channels for information exchange and diffusion at the international level. In order to cooperate effectively and have the ability to receive finished intelligence, to request information or to reply to requests for information, governments have to develop an information flow system at the national level. This type of integration requires varying levels of reform activity depending on the existing system of communication at the national level. Field officers all the way to national police commissioners constitute the source of information, which they acquire through investigations. In order to be diffused to the membership, this information needs channels to the national central point which in turn shares the information with the IPCO and foreign colleagues as an extension.

Europol

Europol, the European Police Office, was created as part of the Maastricht Treaty in 1992 and the European Union intergovernmental Trevi-derived network part of the Third Pillar of EU cooperation. Europol's mandate is to improve the effectiveness and cooperation of member states through their competent authorities in preventing all forms of serious transnational crime, committed by organized crime groups and affecting at least two EU member states. Its mandate is drafted by member states and it implements the political will of the membership. Europol has no formal decision-making power in terms of its approach to international police cooperation. The present structure was adopted by the EU member states to compensate for the suppression of border control that has resulted from cooperative agreements such as Schengen. Europol compensates in opening borders to all except those law enforcement agents for whom they still exist. Europol provides for new police tools of faster, more secure and easier law enforcement cooperation.

On four occasions since the inception of Europol in 1994, the European Council has added various forms of criminality to its original mandate that included the illicit production and trafficking of drugs only. The list includes crimes involving illegal immigration networks, illicit vehicle trafficking, trafficking in human beings, child pornography, the forgery of money and means of payment, illicit trafficking in radioactive and nuclear materials, terrorism and the illegal money-laundering activities that are connected with any of these forms of crime. The Treaty of Amsterdam in October 1997 provided further organization and structure. What counts as crime is broad yet also clearly defined and Europol is prohibited from getting involved in any activity that deals with non-listed crimes.

Besides listing what counts as crime, the mandate specifically defines the 'jurisdictions' that guide the provision of services in Europol. This mandate is restricted by the guiding principle of Europol and the EU at large: the protection of human rights. The Europol Convention clearly addresses, in considerable detail and length (in two of its seven titles), the issue of data protection. In fact there are two types of activities/reports: strategic and operational. Strategic reports might contain personal data, but they will be distributed only to member states and third parties that have a need to know and have signed an 'operational' agreement with Europol that allows the transfer of personal data. Countries and third parties that have signed a 'strategic' agreement only can receive information that contains no personal data whatsoever (technical reports, strategic reports, etc.). Analysis must not contain personal data where general reports on trends are concerned. Personal data, which constitute any characteristic that serves to identify a particular individual, can only be analyzed and reported by specifically authorized Europol personnel and the concerned state(s) through their liaison offices. Strategic reports, for example, must contain data on specific persons suspected of having committed a particular criminal offence or suspected of having the intention to perpetrate a criminal act.[3]

In terms of output, Europol is structured to disseminate 'finished intelligence', derived from the compilation and analysis of voluntarily shared intelligence gathered by national law enforcement authorities. Through this analysis, Europol staff strive to identify current and future trends of criminality and areas of concern both in geographic terms and crime type. Diffusion of information takes place through a sophisticated and secure computerized information exchange (EIE) system which is a part of the Europol Information System (SIS). Besides serving as a means to send information about criminal activity, investigations or other operations to member states, the IE system is available to member states to communicate directly in the event that one would request information from another – e.g. about the criminal record of a perpetrator who originates from one state but conducts criminal activity in the other state.

The finished intelligence, Europol's output, includes strategic products and operational services. There are two types of strategic products: descriptive and predictive.[4] Europol issues the Organized Crime Threat Assessment (OCTA), a descriptive product based on information gathered from member states, and open-source information – derived from in-house research and potentially from third states and/or organizations (e.g. like UNODC or Interpol, or the FBI). This report serves to educate national units and their police forces on the criminality trends, and the main perpetrator groups involved. Predictive strategic products include threat assessment and risk assessment. A threat assessment 'explains the background to a threat in an attempt to understand the causes and predict future events' (Bratz 2001: 3). The analysis in this report evaluates the character, scope and impact of a particular form of criminality, while the information allows member states' law enforcement officials to design a strategy against a particular form of crime and/or criminal group. The risk assessment establishes the vulnerable groups in society that may be targeted by particular criminal trends. This purpose of this report is to develop counter-measures to combat various forms of organized crime.

Operational services include expertise, criminal analysis (analysis work files) and joint investigations and operations (Bratz 2001: 3–4). Experts in various forms of crime provide details of significant cases including the *modus operandi* of transnational criminal groups. The analysis work files are a result of the initiative of member states or experts at Europol. Access to work files is restricted to named experts and analysts to allow analysis to take place in a highly secure environment. Finally, joint operations, usually as a result of analysis work files, are intended to make use of all the information available to Europol and member states to follow up investigations, locate and observe suspects and, once sufficient evidence has been gathered, to lead to their arrest and conviction.

Those reports and services make up the system of information exchange whereby liaison offices (MS LOs at Europol) diffuse information via a sophisticated network of communication with member states and through which member states can communicate directly with each other, which also gets rid of language barriers since

English is the working language of Europol. The Europol system offers several means for member states to give and receive information that will help coordinate investigations. The communication network that links LOs and national units to each other, is the first of these tools. A computerized information system gives member states access to the information sharing system. Liaison officers and national units input the data intended to be shared with other states. Europol inputs data supplied by third party participants – other international bodies, third states, etc. – and analysis and expertise carried out by Europol analysts and experts, organized according to issue areas of crime. The data include information about suspected and convicted criminal offenders.[5]

This network enables member states to communicate on a bilateral basis, to share information with a restricted list of member states or the entire membership – whichever is stipulated by the sharing authority. This information exchange system is especially useful when it is used during existing investigations as its speed solves the traditional problem of a delay in information requests during investigations. The process can be initiated by any state in the membership and constitutes 25 per cent of the information in the Europol database. This system also enables the coordination of investigations, police strategies and operations – within or without the context of Europol. For example, surveillance often has to be taken over from one state to another. In such a case, as a suspect crosses the border, the national authority can take over the surveillance, gather evidence to complete the existing investigation already in progress in another state, and proceed to arrest when enough proper evidence has been obtained for prosecution.

The case of France

Participation rates vary widely even amongst the relatively homogeneous membership of Europol, whereby six out of all the members systematically and regularly send and request information, as indicated during interviews of secretariat officials. One of the non-cooperative states has been France. Respondents pointed out that the French police authorities do request information from other member governments or specific information from crime analysis from Europol from time to time. However, there was a categorical lack of information being sent out, a crucial part of such sharing. So it is surprising that their utilization of Europol has improved dramatically.

In 2002, 174 requests to initiate investigations were sent by the French authorities, which paled in comparison with other member governments and had stagnated since the inception of Europol in 1995. Then, in 2003, 497 requests were made, while in 2004, 667 were initiated. These requests represent a desire to open a crime analysis file or request information on a particular activity and/or specific individual(s) under investigation by French law enforcement.

This type of activity reflects the receiving part of sharing; however, the three-fold increase of request for support in investigations reveals an increase in the legitimization of the Europol output to French authorities. The French authorities have also begun to respond to messages at a significantly higher rate. In 2002, 4000 messages were exchanged between French authorities and Europol and in communication with foreign law enforcement authorities. In 2005, there were 11,000 such exchanges. This increase is so significant that it has placed France in the top three participating members among Europol member governments. In May 2004, the French utilization rate of Europol had grown by 300 per cent in one quarter and had bypassed that of Great Britain, who was the second largest user, and Germany, who was the fifth at that time. This is significant because the UK and Germany have been the leading proponents of police cooperation and ever-increasing institutionalization and the champions of increased operational powers for Europol, as well as the leading users of Europol output and channels of communication.

An unexpected shift

This shift in participation rates by the French authorities is attributed by insiders to a *prise de conscience* in France that resulted from a reaction by national political actors towards a proposal by Denmark (E2064) to modify the Europol Convention to give Europol more powers, especially in the operational realm according to respondents. This finding is a result of interviews of insiders at Europol but also stems from simply comparing the time line of the increase in participation by French authorities and the date of a parliamentary report in 2003 (resolution N 49, French senate 2003–2004 session). The initiative by Denmark to modify the Europol convention (Brussels, 2 July 2002) was aimed at responding to the growing debate at EU level about the powers entrusted in Europol, its role, and the forms of crime that were within its 'jurisdiction'. The proposal represents an effort to give Europol the tools it needs to effectively play the pivotal role that it was intended to play in international police cooperation in Europe and to further its growing involvement in the operational support of national police authorities.

When this initiative was presented to the EU council member governments had varying reactions, ranging from support to the French resistance to the proposed increased 'independence' some member governments were advocating for an ever more operational, even more interventionist, Europol. At issue was the development of Europol's operational capacities and the explosion in communication by Europol with an increasingly wider range of actors. French political actors saw that Europol was gaining power and influence over national policing matters without any of the adequate mechanisms necessary to control its activities. Ultimately, the French position was that the initial project of creating a parliamentary commission to oversee the activities of Europol and that of its director should not be replaced by a directorate that would have increasing influence on the development of Europol and its role as a facilitator of international crime prevention (Rapport N. 58, *session ordinaire du Sénat*, 12 November 2003).

At the same time another factor played a role in the *prise de conscience* of France *vis-à-vis* the operational gains by Europol. The term of the director of Europol was coming to an end. Paradoxically, the opportunity to place a French director at Europol enticed the French to act and as they sought to take a position regarding the future of Europol they opted to pursue a French directorship. In order to lend legitimacy to their efforts, the strategy was to evaluate the French-Europol relationship and implement necessary reforms to make France a significant collaborator. The logic went such that it was deemed difficult to present a successful candidate for the top post of an organization where a failure to participate impaired the legitimacy of that same organization. Besides, due to the new awareness of Europol and its output and the challenges it posed to the sovereignty of the French government, it was also discussed that the $8 million Euros (the third largest contributions to Europol) that France was infusing into the organization should yield some return. As one respondent put it, if it is in the budget you have to do what it takes for it to perform and provide benefits that will serve the national interest.

What impact did these events have on the participation rate by French police authorities? A political change was forced by the proposal to delegate a more active and operational role to Europol. According to respondents, a variety of actors introduced these changes as a response to the factors named above. These actors included political contacts at the EU level of Europol directorate officers, the French parliament, and the general director of the police in France. The French political establishment began to restructure and reform in order to increase efficiency and provide the police authorities with a platform that would be conducive to communicating information, according to respondents. This was the first time since the ratification of the Europol convention that French policy was analysed in the larger context of international policing.

Efforts to enhance participation rates included a combining of the Interpol, Schengen and Europol platforms of communication in order to centralize the information going through these. It should be noted that at the National Bureau, the central office designated to cooperate with foreign authorities, and via international police cooperation organizations and other efforts, contains databases and computers that house separate intranets with the various cooperation initiatives, including one for Europol and a separate one for Interpol. This redundancy makes for lengthy searches in various databases at the expense of speed, a crucial component of successful investigations. Furthermore, the two separate teams of agents that were assigned to the individual cooperation platforms were merged into one (SCCOPOL), essentially doubling the amount of assigned personnel to the overall effort of communication. SCCOPOL allegedly played an important part in precipitating a more active role for France regarding Europol. Again, the reasoning was that one cannot reasonably present a candidate for the directorship of an organization one does not utilize, especially one that is not fed much information. So the reform efforts were an attempt to address the issue of the increasing operational powers of Europol without adequate and increased control mechanisms.

At the operational level, personnel issues were revisited. The French liaison bureau at Europol grew as increasing numbers of police officers, *gendarmes* and customs officers were seconded by France to act as a link between Europol, the membership and the national police authorities, and to promote the analysis and other services offered by Europol. Besides increasing the staff and hence its ability to carry out the intended tasks of the liaison bureau, a new approach on recruiting liaison officers focused on identifying those police officers who wanted to do the job. Police officers are now increasingly selected according to carefully drafted profiles which include an international mindset and the willingness to be an agent of change toward international cooperation, according to respondents.

As a result of these reform efforts, and mostly due to this newly found awareness of Europol, there was an increase in the utilization of Europol early on in the new millennium. In turn, that increase in information sharing impacts on the nature of the analysis that Europol officials are able to conduct because the more information they can obtain, the more complete and the more accurate their output is. An increase in the quality of output brings with it an enhanced value of finished intelligence which provides real gains of productivity in the field. According to respondents, French requests for information and the information they forward to Europol via the liaison bureau are more structured and more specific. The questions are more precise and as a result the answer is that Europol crime analysis or other communications are more targeted and have a real impact on investigations and requests for additional information.

Outside intervention

In this case the national interest is defined by outside factors: transnational crime and the threats it poses and the realization that unilateral action against it is futile. Interest is manifested by taking part in bargaining for an international arrangement to cooperate to fight transnational crime, and the signing and ratification of conventions. It is too great a handicap for national police services to be bound by borders and jurisdictions when criminals can operate with a complete disregard for borders and jurisdictions and thrive on the permissive environments that defection from cooperation creates. Furthermore, there needs to be a pooling of resources across borders, a sort of international coalition so that the resources allotted to international policing initiatives can begin to match the deep pockets of transnational criminal organizations. Multilateral cooperation is thus the answer and organizing to coordinate international policing efforts logically follows on. Formulating interest and signalling a commitment to pursue that interest is one thing. It is another to formulate policies and implement them while considering the collective good, which implies compromises on approaches and procedures.

In this context, the national interest is shaped by the reciprocity that comes from an information sharing framework which, if utilized systematically, can begin to yield real results to national law and order initiatives. There is a need to achieve a level of participation by other states that will translate into serving this national interest. If the finished intelligence offered by Europol, or other like arrangements, is complete and accurate, it will be of much greater benefit to the national police authorities than if several pieces of the big picture of a particular criminal activity are missing. The real challenge arises once states have signed and ratified their agreement to cooperate. They face the enormous task of translating the political commitment to cooperate into policies and developing the systems and tools necessary to implement those policies. In international police co-operation, implementation largely means a reform of policies to reflect a shift toward the internationalization of both processes and mindsets. The main task is to develop a national information flow system which allows police services to forward the result of their investigations all the way to a central location, which in turn will be structured to standardize the information and share it with Europol and Europol's partners or any other similar mechanism. Some states including Germany and the UK have such systems in place already. France is structured with central offices to organize international criminal police initiatives and maintain the Schengen national information system, the Schengen central authority, and the Europol national unit.

Initially, signals were sent that international police cooperation was in France's interest, exhibited by the signing and ratification of the convention. But once implementation of the political commitment became the issue, interest began to waver because information sharing infringed upon the traditionally secret and isolationist police culture in France. Moreover, the French system is a centralized system whereby information can trickle down but few channels are systematically utilized in the field due to a lack of awareness on the part of the police officers who collect information. The result of these conflicting interests was a sort of stagnation at the implementation level whereby police officers did not have the appropriate tools to cooperate, share and request information. Consequently, any output from Europol and attendant benefits were lost to the French authorities in general.

Nevertheless, a shift in cooperative behavior occurred as French political actors were now confronted with what they viewed as an infringement on their territory, which was the supreme power to coerce and enforce their laws. The Danish proposal served as a sort of awareness raising event for the national political establishment in France.

Interestingly, neither Europol nor France was directly responsible for raising this awareness and formulating new interest in Europol. The catalyst of this change was a third party, another state albeit a member of Europol. This is an instance whereby membership in an IO can have an indirect influence by some states over others. This serves the interests of the IO, that of Denmark, and even that of an unsuspecting France. There was a need to reform the French cooperation framework and an outside force stepped in, even if only to serve their own interests which required stimulating a utilization of Europol by the entire membership. This is a sort of norm diffusion that has not been studied in the international organization literature. The norms, principles and policies by which they can be translated are not introduced directly by an IO but because of an existence of an environment that only exists because the IO exists.

Although this is the case, the phenomenon of the influence of one state over another's behaviour would not have been the same if it were not for the environment created by Europol. If there had not been a membership that for a variety of reasons could bind states together, it is likely that France would have not reacted to the initiative by Denmark. This validates the coercive or treaty enforcing power/ability of Europol as its existence provided a backdrop for a cooperation inducement which would not have been likely without the 'threat' that one member posed on another. The catalyst for change in France was an initiative from outside of France, by an actor that was independent of France. Or is there some interdependence? This interdependence should perhaps be scrutinized further since the interest in operational gains by cooperating states is their way of addressing the behaviour of non-cooperating states. If Europol had more operational powers, maybe Denmark would get more information from France, hence enhancing the big picture that Europol can provide with the systematic cooperation of its member governments. Given the fact that France is the third largest contributor to Europol, French political actors, including the national chief of police, wanted to maintain their authority, thereby establishing control mechanisms on Europol's rapid and significant gains in operational activity.

Thus the strategy to control Europol, to make it accountable, is an attempt to maintain control over one's own territory. There is a growing debate about whether international policing can be controlled and how it can be made accountable to the citizens it is ultimately intended to protect (Bruggeman 2002; Den Boer 2002). The question is how much power over national law and order practices and approaches can supranational mechanisms to coordinate and facilitate police cooperation have without foregoing a respect for the principle of sovereignty? We must distinguish between operational powers and executive powers. Operational powers allow Europol or the like to participate actively in strategies and operations, albeit still in a supporting role. The fear on the part of states is that the supporting role will give way to a leading role, as the experts that coordinate joint teams and other operations are often sophisticated police professionals who can teach a thing or two to field officers and the national political establishment.

Conclusion

Commitment to international cooperation signalled by the drafting, signing and ratification of international agreements is one challenge but the implementation of those agreements is even more complex. A framework of cooperation that depends quantitatively and qualitatively on the contributions of its members requires an integration of national policy and operational systems of national law and order infrastructures. This is one of the reasons why some states do not utilize, or have not utilized, the output available from Europol. Because of the interdependence of member governments on each other's police information, defectors become increasingly pressured to share information by colleagues who actively collaborate. Because rates of participation can directly affect the quality of the finished intelligence that results from analysis done by Europol, states that do cooperate want two things: (1) accurate information from which they will benefit, and (2) deeper involvement by Europol in facilitating cooperation (as coordinator, initiator, guide and advisor).

As the case presented here shows, Europol's existence offers an environment in which cooperating states can provoke participation from defecting states by proposing changes (i.e. operational powers) that would exacerbate the reasons as to why defecting states fail to share information. Specifically France, who has always been reluctant to cooperate, especially concerning the sending of information because of the infringement on their sovereignty that Europol can represent, was spurred to begin to participate in order to become an active member of an organization they wanted to control more and in whose growth they wanted to have a say, hence seeking the presidency of Europol. All in all, Europol's existence and proactive stance affect the way states cooperate and the benefits that both cooperating and defecting states can enjoy. Over time and through setting an example and showing the real benefits of participation, cooperating states can persuade non-cooperating states to participate in order to gain the intended benefits of sharing information. Defectors will gain exposure, even if forced to some degree, to the benefits that an IO can offer to the national law enforcement efforts. And the IO gains a legitimacy and scope which are more consistent with the ambitions of the supporters and staff of Europol.

Notes

1 Nadia Gerspacher wrote this article as a post-doctoral fellow at the Center for International Compared Criminology at the University of Montreal, Montreal, Canada.
2 During an interview with a Secretariat official, I asked him where he would go from his present secondment to Interpol. He responded, 'I don't know, there is nowhere to go from here', suggesting that transnational policing is the most sophisticated and advanced and national policing would be a step backwards.
3 This strictly respected standard of data protection, while a part of the fabric of the EU institutional framework, has inhibited cooperation with third states and/or international organizations. Because of the widely differing principles of data protection of the United States, for example, information exchange between Europe and the United States is difficult and rarely occurs. As a result, little cooperation is possible. The perspective on human rights has also inhibited cooperation between Europe and the United States; it is difficult for EU members, and hence Europol, to share information with the United States' authorities because capital punishment is practised in the US. Europol staff and member states have severe (indeed more than severe) reservations about sharing information that will send a perpetrator to his/her death. So while data protection standards set by the Europol Convention have enhanced cooperation, it is worth noting that they contribute to the 'Fortress of Europe' claim. Here I would put it in a different way, since the Europol-US cooperation works and has been a fact since 2001.
4 See Bratz (2001), Group Leader Illegal Immigration, Europol, The Hague, 'Europol's contribution to fight illegal immigration networks'.
5 As a reminder: Europol's mandate to date includes organized crimes in the form of murder, the illicit trade in human organs and tissue, kidnapping and illegal restraint and hostage-taking, racism and xenophobia, organized robbery, illicit trafficking in cultural goods, swindling and fraud, racketeering and extortion, counterfeiting and product piracy, forgery and the trafficking of administrative documents, the forgery of money and means of payment, computer crime and corruption, illegal trading and harm to the environment, illegal immigrant smuggling and traffic in human beings, motor vehicle theft and money laundering activities.

Part III

Special issues on international police cooperation

Chapter 9

Parallel paths and productive partners: the EU and US on counter-terrorism

John D. Occhipinti

Introduction

This chapter takes on the difficult task of examining two different, but related, dimensions of counter terrorism (CT) activity concerning the European Union (EU) and United States (US). The first section of the chapter argues that it is heuristically worthwhile to compare the EU and US on CT. For example, both have engaged in parallel internal initiatives in this area, involving legal change and institutional reform, especially concerning information sharing and leadership. Studying transatlantic similarities and differences in these areas facilitates a better understanding of developments in each place.

The second section of the chapter examines transatlantic relations. This part of the chapter argues that policy convergence best explains the recent pattern of cooperation and agreement in EU-US relations on several internal security issues related to CT. In this regard, the chapter examines cooperation with Europol, judicial cooperation, container security, airline security, and travel documents. The chapter argues that this productive transatlantic partnership on CT can be expected to endure.

Comparing the US and the EU

One major challenge confounding attempts to compare the EU and US on CT is the need to consider the EU as a 'state'. While the EU enjoys many state-like qualities in several policy domains, this is not the case for its handling of CT. Most importantly, EU-level bodies lack the operational authority enjoyed by CT authorities in the EU member states. Related to this, the EU's spending on CT pales in comparison to that of the United States, or indeed that of any true state, regarding internal security. Despite its limited role in these areas, the EU's role on CT has increased steadily since 9/11, especially regarding initiatives that have brought about legal change and institutional reforms aimed at improving information sharing and leadership on CT. These developments can be compared with similar reforms in the US.

Legal change

The fight against terrorism in both the US and the EU has entailed significant legal change. This chapter focuses on notable achievements at the EU level, leaving aside related legal change in its member states (Occhipinti 2008). In general, the attacks on 9/11 in the US created a sense of urgency in the EU that allowed its member states to reach compromises on measures that would have otherwise delayed their passage for months (Kaunert 2007). Just weeks after September 11, 2001, the EU's Justice and Home Affairs Council approved two important framework decisions regarding CT that had been proposed by the EU's Commission. The first was a framework decision on terrorism, defining this crime in its various forms and specifying a range of sanctions for each. The second measure was the framework decision establishing the European Arrest Warrant (EAW), which simplified and hastened extradition on 32 crimes, including terrorism. These measures were followed by a variety of other legal initiatives at the EU level, such as those involving the financing of terrorism, and requirements for telecom companies to store and share data for law enforcement. However, as the sense of urgency faded, the passage of additional legal initiatives, particularly the European Evidence Warrant, became more difficult. Moreover, the implementation of some previously approved measures, such as the terrorism framework decision and the EAW, was also delayed amidst constitutional issues and their impact on civil liberties or concerns for national sovereignty.

There are some parallels here with the experience of legal change in the United States regarding CT. One of the earliest American legal initiatives after 9/11 was the USA Patriot Act ('Uniting and Strengthening America by Providing Appropriate Tools Required to Intercept and Obstruct Terrorism'). As with the terrorism FD and the EAW in the EU, the 'Patriot Act' was enacted with remarkable speed, having been rapidly proposed soon after 9/11, approved by Congress, and signed into law on 26 October 2001.

This new law increased the power of federal law enforcement on CT in the areas of surveillance, information requests, and searches – in some cases by creating novel mechanisms, but in others by simply extending capabilities already permitted in the fight against organized crime to CT. By 2005, as the memory of 9/11 faded, some parts of the Patriot Act had grown increasingly controversial regarding civil liberties. Several of its provisions had 'sunset clauses' and these were set to expire by the end of 2005 – unless Congress re-authorized them. Eventually, changes were made to the most controversial items in the bill, allowing it to be approved in March 2006 and signed into law by the President.

A more recent controversy arose over the Protect America Act that was proposed in 2007 by the Bush administration after it finally agreed to follow the Foreign Intelligence Surveillance Act regarding wire-taps. The new act updates FISA's rules for subpoenas to account for technologies and issues that the original 1978 legislation could not have foreseen, such as foreign email traffic that happens to pass through US-based computer servers. Under pressure to act before a scheduled recess, Congress quickly passed the measure in early August 2007 but included a six-month sunset clause.

When the time came to make the changes to FISA permanent, the contentious issues were whether and how to ease requirements for subpoenas for some wiretaps, and whether to give retroactive immunity to telecommunications companies that faced lawsuits for helping the Bush administration violate FISA before 2007. In June 2008, a deal was finally struck with Congress that included immunity for phone companies. The new legislation permitted the wiretapping of non-US citizens when the phone or internet traffic simply passes through the US. Such surveillance is also allowed regarding US citizens living abroad, but only for seven days and in emergency situations.

Information-sharing

In the US, several initiatives have been aimed at preventing the 'stove-piping' of CT intelligence, whereby security agencies do not share data horizontally with other agencies. The Patriot Act made a significant contribution to this by essentially eliminating the perceived 'wall' that prevented information-sharing between the FBI and CIA.

Unlike its other provisions, this aspect of the new legislation was generally viewed as appropriate in the post-9/11 era.

Another major US innovation to mitigate stove-piping came with the creation of a new institution. In June 2003, President Bush signed an executive order calling for the establishment of a Terrorist Threat Integration Center to bring together and analyse all US intelligence on terrorist threats and use. Following the recommendation of the Commission on Terrorist Attacks upon the United States (known as the '9/11 Commission'), the new centre was soon amalgamated into the newer National Counter Terrorism Center (NCTC) that was first mandated by President Bush via executive order and later specified in the Intelligence Reform and Terrorism Prevention Act of 2004 (the 'Intelligence Reform Act'). The NCTC is staffed by personnel detailed from the CIA, FBI and other parts of the US intelligence community, which formally comprises 16 separate federal entities. The NCTC was later joined by a smaller, parallel body called the National Counter Proliferation Center, which was established in 2005 following a recommendation of the Silberman-Robb Commission on intelligence concerning weapons of mass destruction.

Other key US institutions aimed at information sharing are the Joint Terrorism Task Forces (JTTFs) attached to FBI field offices across the country. These bring local law enforcement officers together with various federal officials from the IC. One aim of the JTTFs is to build the kind of personal familiarity and trust needed to ensure that intelligence data are actually shared effectively and in a timely fashion. Before 9/11, there were 35 JTTFs across the US, but more than 65 were added afterward, including one for each of the FBI's 56 field offices. The work of these bodies is coordinated by a national JTTF attached to FBI headquarters in Washington, DC, bringing together officials from more than 30 federal agencies.

In the EU, the issue of information sharing pertains mainly to the task of promoting the exchange of intelligence data among the CT authorities of the member states. As with the problem of stove-piping in the US, the promotion of information sharing in the EU entails the challenge of using new information technologies to ensure that data are collected, shared and analysed effectively. To be sure, there are information differences within the CT agencies of one country, such as the US, and international sharing via multilateral institutions, such as in the EU. Nevertheless, many of the fundamental issues are quite similar. Just as in the US, where interagency rivalries need to be overcome and trusted partners for information exchange need to be found at multiple levels of government, intelligence officials in the EU member states must become comfortable with exchanging sensitive CT intelligence multi-laterally and not just bilaterally with its most trusted foreign partners. In both the US and the EU, building on new institutions to promote information sharing will not guarantee that quality data are shared in a timely fashion (Walsh 2006).

At the EU level, the international exchange of information for CT is possible through the European Police Office (Europol), which has been fully operational only since 1999. At its heart, Europol is an international liaison network of criminal investigators supported by a criminal intelligence database and a permanent staff of analysts. The overall effectiveness of Europol has been questioned, but there is no doubt that it is being increasingly used by EU member states in their criminal investigations. Its published annual reports describe its rising caseload and increased use by member states (Europol 2008).

However, Europol has not been fully utilized by EU members in the area of CT.[1] In the wake of the terrorist attacks of September 11, 2001, the Director of Europol at that time, Jürgen Storbeck, lamented the fact that his organization could be more effective in the fight against terrorism if only member states would share more intelligence. Later, Storbeck's successor, Max-Peter Ratzel, noted 'We need to combine better our work with other European agencies, such as Eurojust or SitCen [Situation Center]. The flow of information between us must be more structured and more dedicated' (Laitner 2005: 1).

One step in this direction, though not via Europol, has come through changes in the role of the EU's SitCen, housed in the Council's Secretariat and under the direct authority of the EU's Secretary-General of the Council and High Representative for CFSP. Since its inception in 1999, SitCen has brought together foreign intelligence officers from the member states to support the EU's crisis management activities by providing round-the-clock monitoring and analysis of regions and situations of interest. After the terrorist attacks on Madrid in 2004, a CT unit was established in SitCen to provide terrorist threat assessments, drawing on the data supplied by the national representatives from the internal and external security services. In addition, officials from member states' domestic intelligence services have been allowed to join their counterparts from foreign intelligence agencies at SitCen. However, data sharing within SitCen is limited to strategic planning rather than specific CT operations – which is a matter that remains firmly in the hands of the member states. Moreover, only seven EU member states have a formal external intelligence agency.

Along with these institutional reforms, there are a variety of EU-level databases to help collect and share information that could be useful in CT. The Europol Information System (EIS) stores criminal intelligence supplied by member states, as well as so-called analysis work files that are created and continuously updated by Europol staffers on particular cases or types of crime, such as terrorism (Deflem 2006b). Several other databases that might be useful for CT have been created for border management. These include the Schengen Information System (SIS), which entails a watch-list for wanted criminals and weapons at the boundaries of the EU's passport free zone and the new Visa Information System (VIS), which will utilize biometric data to help authenticate travel documents (Occhipinti 2008: 152). There are also new databases in place to help manage asylum applications and customs.

Leadership

In both the US and EU, the development of new institutional structures to prevent the stove-piping of CT intelligences has been bolstered by new leadership positions. In the United States, the Intelligence Reform Act of 2004 prescribed the creation of a Director of National Intelligence to oversee the work of the entire US intelligence community. In principle, the Director of the CIA (DCI) had filled this role, including the related, daily task of being the principal advisor on intelligence to the President of the United States. Yet, the DCI never had much real influence on the work of the intelligence community beyond the CIA itself.

The creation of the Office of the DNI is aimed at changing this situation in several ways. First, the DNI has direct authority over the DCI and CIA as well as the work of the new NCTC, giving him influence over its work and information sharing. Two additional sources of the DNI's power stem from the Bush administration's response in June 2005 to some of the recommendations of the Silberman-Robb Commission. By executive order, the DNI not only has authority over the CIA and its budget, but also most of the FBI's $3 billion annual intelligence budget. Second, President Bush ordered the creation of a 'national security service' within the FBI, to bring together its divisions on CT, counter-intelligence and the proliferation of weapons of mass destruction. The head of this body, which eventually became known as the National Security Branch (NSB), is chosen jointly by the FBI Director, Attorney General, and the DNI. Related to this, the DNI is permitted to communicate directly with FBI field offices through the head of the NSB or its staff. One limit on the DNI is that he does not enjoy much authority over the US military's intelligence budget, which still accounts for more than three quarters of all intelligence spending in the United States. John Negroponte became the first DNI in 2005, to be replaced in February 2007 by Michael McConnell and in 2009 by Dennis Blair.

In the EU, the response to the Madrid bombings not only entailed changes to SitCen, but also included an attempt to provide new 'leadership' on CT. This came in the form of a new position called the Counter-Terrorism Coordinator, a post first held by Gijs de Vries of the Netherlands. Compared with the executive powers of the DNI, the EU's 'Mr Terror', as he became known, has been more of a 'cheerleader' than a powerful administrator. More specifically, de Vries was charged with encouraging member states to exchange more and better intelligence with each other in the fight against terrorism, including the sharing that was done through EU-level institutions. Mr Terror was also tasked with monitoring member states' legal implementation of CT legislation approved at the EU level. To date, any impact by the CT Coordinator on this has been limited, as his influence is largely restricted to 'naming and shaming' laggard member states in periodic reports to the Council.

In March 2007, de Vries resigned for personal reasons and the naming of his successor was delayed for several months as the EU member states reconsidered the nature of the CT coordinator position and who should fill the post. It was not until September 2007 that member states' interior ministers agreed that 'the coordinator should have a largely technical profile and role and be particularly concerned with coordination, and bundling of and pooling resources between member states and other authorities' (Agence France Presse 2007). In the end, member states wanted the CT coordinator to have a lower profile and play a behind-the-scenes role, largely in Brussels via the EU-level institutions rather than in the member states. To this end, the member states agreed on Gilles de Kerchove to fill the new post. He was previously a director for police and customs cooperation in the Council Secretariat's Directorate General. De Kerchove's first report to the Council pointed out several ongoing problems regarding the implementation of EU-level CT legislation, as well as deficiencies in the sharing of information among CT bodies *within* member states, which, in turn, inhibit cooperation at the EU level (European Report 2007a, 2007b).

It is doubtful that the slightly new mandate for the CT coordinator or the attributes of the latest person filling this post will provide the EU with the 'leadership' that it needs to improve its record on the proper and timely implementation of CT legislation. In his first exchange of views with the European Parliament de Kerchove noted his lack of power on CT, including his limited budget. Interestingly, he was also not consulted by the Commission before it presented its new package of CT proposals in November 2007 (European Report 2007c).

Transatlantic relations

In addition to its internal initiatives on CT, the EU has promoted an external dimension of its internal security policy that includes relations with the US (cf Rees 2006: 79–104). Despite the historic low point in transatlantic relations during the Bush administration, this period is actually notable for greater and not lesser EU-US cooperation on internal security, including several measures aimed at counter terrorism (CT). This productive partnership is best explained by a policy convergence between the EU and US.

Europol and information sharing

Once terrorism was thrust on the transatlantic agenda, it was not long before discussions were underway to establish a cooperation agreement between the US and Europol. Although this agreement had already been envisioned for the future and talks had been underway for months, finalizing such a pact with the US was initially not a high priority for Europol. However, in the aftermath of 9/11, forging a transatlantic agreement became much more important for Europol. With this in mind, Europol's then director, Jürgen Storbeck, joined an EU delegation that visited the US soon after the attacks. This meeting eventually led to two separate agreements between the US and Europol (Occhipinti 2003).

The first of these was signed between Europol and the US Department of Justice, allowing the exchange of technical information on terrorist threats, crime patterns, and smuggling routes. This agreement also allowed the establishment of liaison offices in the US and EU, which were opened in the summer of 2002. However, the FBI officers assigned to Europol were withdrawn after just three months. It was not until November 2005 that the US assigned a Secret Service Agent and later an FBI agent to Europol.

A second transatlantic agreement was needed to allow the exchange of criminal and CT intelligence because Europol's rules covering data protection prevented the sharing of specific personal data under the 2001 arrangement and thereby excluded names, addresses, photographs, and criminal records. By this point, Europol had already signed cooperation agreements with the two non-EU members of the Schengen free travel zone (Iceland and Norway) as well as with four of its candidate members at that time (Poland, Hungary, Estonia and Slovenia). In these cases, the EU had first approved these countries' data protection mechanisms before agreeing to intelligence-sharing pacts. The problem was that the US lacked a single authority for data protection, normally a requirement for information exchanges with Europol.

As it already enjoyed bilateral information sharing agreements with most EU member states, the US was not eager to draft new legislation simply to appease Europol's Joint Supervisory Body (JSB) that was charged with its data protection. In the end, the JSB reluctantly relented on the data protection issue, deciding that an agreement with some assurance of data protection by the US was better than the possibility of information from Europol finding its way into the US (via member states) devoid of any restrictions (Mitsilegas *et al.* 2003). The personal information sharing agreement was finally concluded in December 2002 but only after the EU received guarantees about data protection and assurances that its officials would not be liable for civil damages awarded by US courts regarding data supplied by Europol. This second US-Europol agreement permitted the exchange of a variety of personal data but remains underutilized, mainly because the US, and particularly the FBI, has preferred to use its long-standing bilateral channels of information sharing with individual EU member states, especially regarding CT.[2]

Judicial cooperation

While discussions on the second Europol agreement were still underway, transatlantic talks on judicial cooperation had already begun (Mitsilegas *et al.* 2003: 523–533). As with the talks on Europol, the result was two separate agreements – one on mutual legal assistance and the other on extradition. It should be noted that these measures supplemented, but did not totally replace, existing bilateral arrangements, many of which were in need of updating, such as to account for new information technologies. In some cases, however, significant changes have resulted. For example, the extradition of a country's own nationals to the US has been made possible for the first time for Bulgaria, Estonia, Latvia, Malta and Romania. In addition, the new accords not only updated the MLA (mutual legal assistance) accords between the US and several EU members, but also represented the very first MLAs between the US and Bulgaria, Denmark, Finland, Malta, Portugal, Slovakia and Slovenia (Mitsilegas *et al.* 2003).

As was the case with the Europol agreements the scope of judicial cooperation went beyond CT, yet the agreements were framed in this context given that the attacks of 9/11 had only just occurred when formal talks on the two treaties started in May 2002. Negotiations on the two agreements lasted for nearly a year due to the complex issues at hand, as well as the posturing of some member states on the connection between extradition and the death penalty. This was a point that the US was prepared to concede from the outset, but it became an issue because of its controversial treatment of suspected terrorists held without trial at Guantanamo Bay.

The agreement on MLA provides a legal basis for the creation of international joint investigation teams and eases restrictions on banking secrecy to promote the common fight against money laundering and the financing of terrorism. The new agreement also facilitates the sharing of evidence for prosecution, allowing documents to be exchanged more quickly by fax or email and legal testimony to be given by video conferencing. None of these matters proved to be very contentious.

The part of the agreement covering extradition proved to be more divisive, with controversial proposals coming from both sides. For its part, the US demanded that its extradition requests be given equal consideration as claims made by EU member states for the same suspect via the new European Arrest Warrant. The final compromise reached on this point of 'competing claims' leaves the matter up to the member state holding the suspect but lays down several criteria for determining which request to grant, including the location of the offence at hand and the nationality of any victims.

Meanwhile, several EU states, led by France, sought assurances that suspects extradited to the US would not be subject to military tribunals and should face proper criminal trials. In this context, these countries pushed for the inclusion of a reference to such a provision in one of the EU treaties that would bind member states to respect fundamental rights. In the end this was not done, but the (non-binding) preamble of the accord notes that the two sides' legal systems 'provide for the right to a fair trial to an extradited person, including the right to adjudication by an impartial tribunal established pursuant to law'. The extradition agreement also bars the imposition of capital punishment on suspects handed over to American authorities.

Despite rising transatlantic tensions over the war with Iraq at that time, the remaining issues between the two sides were resolved, allowing the accord to be signed on the occasion of the US-EU summit in June 2003. This led to the negotiation and signing of implementation accords between the US and individual EU members, concluding in September 2007 when the last two agreements were reached with Bulgaria and Romania. Only at this point did the US Senate begin to examine the treaties, which easily won ratification in 2008. Ratification took much longer in the EU, however, lasting well into 2009 (European Report 2008). The first bilateral exchange of ratification instruments on the accords state took place between the US and Lithuania in March 2009.

Container security

In January of 2002, US Customs[3] launched the Container Security Initiative (CSI) to help secure cargo and shipping infrastructure (ships, ports, etc.). By this time, over 12 million maritime shipping containers were arriving in the US annually, and less than 2 per cent of these containers were being thoroughly inspected, making them ideal devices for smuggling. In the wake of 9/11, this led to concerns that terrorists could use containers to attack the US with a 'dirty bomb' (Flynn 2002).

Initially, only the world's 20 busiest ports were required to follow the CSI, including 14 ports in eight EU member states, such as Rotterdam, Antwerp, Hamburg, Bremerhaven, Le Havre, Algeciras and Liverpool. To preserve US-bound trade, these ports were required to establish dedicated shipping terminals for US-bound cargo and to allow American customs inspectors to work side-by-side with local officials in screening outbound cargo. On 1 February 2003 a new rule was added, requiring that shippers must share cargo manifests with the American authorities at least 24 hours before a container was to be loaded onto a US-bound ship. Afraid of being cut off from the lucrative American market, the governments of the targeted ports rushed to reach bilateral agreements with the US on the new rules, including those in the EU.

This created friction in transatlantic relations. The European Commission saw the new rules as a violation of an existing EU-US customs cooperation accord and was also irritated that the US had bypassed the EU level where it was the competent authority. The Commission also protested member states' bilateral agreements with the US that essentially violated EU law, which specified a common approach. Eventually, the US expressed its openness to a new agreement with the EU that covered the CSI but also refused to delay its implementation.

In the subsequent negotiations, the Commission opposed the 24 hour rule but relented after observing that most European traders were already in compliance. This facilitated an EU-US agreement in November 2003 that formally approved the accord in the spring of 2004 (Commission of the European Communities 2004; European Report 2004a). The CSI was subsequently expanded beyond the world mega-port to 59 different locations, including 23 ports in ten EU member states.[4]

In 2007, additional US rules for foreign ports were specified in the 'Implementing Recommendations of the 9/11 Commission Act'. This wide-ranging legislation was developed in the US Congress in response to recommendations from the 9/11 Commission and signed into law on 3 August 2007. Among other things, the statute set a five-year deadline for the 100 per cent radiation screening of all US-bound maritime cargo before loading at foreign ports. By 2009, nearly all cargo arriving at US ports was being scanned as it left these ports by trucks or rail, yet less than 3 per cent of cargo was being scanned before it actually arrived at the US in the first place. Early on, the United Kingdom implemented a pilot project at its mega-port in Southampton aimed at 100 per cent screening for bombs/radiation, but by 2009 it was back-tracking on this commitment.

The Department of Homeland Security, even under the Bush administration, was mindful of the tremendous challenges involved in meeting the new scanning rules within the five year deadline, especially given EU opposition and threats of reciprocal rules. In light of these realities and that other modes of transportation were viewed as greater threats (such as non-scheduled flights and small boats), the incoming Obama administration began to consider applying the scanning rules only to those ports posing the greatest risk for the smuggling of bombs to the US, notably those located in Hong Kong, Karachi (Pakistan), Port Busan (South Korea), and Salalah (Oman) (Beary 2009). However, for this, Congressional approval would be needed.

Airline security

Similar to its actions on container security, the US not only unilaterally imposed new guidelines on airline security, but also initially bypassed the EU level while doing so. This once again precipitated additional tensions in transatlantic relations. On the basis of the Aviation and Transportation Security Act of November 2001, the US government instructed airlines operating at US airports to supply passenger data to the DHS authorities before take-off. The information in question was the passenger name record (PNR), which is created when tickets are booked. The DHS intended to filter the data to help identify potential threats before passengers boarded planes.

US airlines were forced to begin data transfers soon after the law took effect, but the European Commission won a series of interim agreements and delays for EU-based carriers, which were governed by the EU's 1995 directive on the protection of personal data. European airlines faced the choice of violating EU law, which could bring sanctions from the Commission, or being fined by the US (at $6,000 per passenger) and possibly denied landing rights. At issue were the types of information to be shared, as well as for how long and for what purpose.

Transatlantic negotiations on PNR data yielded little progress until December 2003, when the US made a few concessions (BBC News 2003; Dombey 2003). For example, the US agreed to hold data for just three-and-half years, to use these only to detect potential terrorists, and to limit their access to specially designated authorities. In keeping with EU demands, the original agreement also precluded the 'bulk-sharing' of PNR data with other federal agencies, meaning, for example, that data could only be transmitted to the FBI on a case-by-case basis. The US also agreed to ask for only 34 PNR data fields to be shared. The EU had wanted just 19 PNR data fields to be included, but conceded on this after receiving American assurances that sensitive data covering ethnicity and religion would be deleted following initial screening.

Over the strong but non-binding objections of the European Parliament (EP), the Commission and the Council of Ministers had taken steps by May 2004 to legalize the agreement with the US. The EP later brought the matter before the ECJ to have the accord overturned, arguing that the accord violated EU data protection rules. In May 2006, the ECJ annulled the pact, though not on substantive grounds. Instead, the court ruled that the Commission had negotiated the treaty on the legal basis of the wrong EU treaty.

This led to new talks, additional demands from Brussels and Washington, another interim agreement, and eventually a new permanent deal by June 2007. Under the new accord, the US agreed to receive just 19 fields of data and to have the airlines 'push' this new data to US authorities (US Customs and Border Protection in the

DHS), rather than be able to 'pull' it from databanks on their own. In exchange, the US won a broader power to share the data with other federal authorities, as well as to store it for 15 years, instead of three-and-a half years. However, in 2008, the US linked additional demands related to airline security to newer EU members' participation in its Visa Waiver Program (see below).[5]

Travel documents

Just when the PNR issue was seemingly resolved in the summer of 2004, another potential crisis emerged when the US VIST programme was implemented and required that newly issued foreign passports would have to contain a biometric identifier for citizens holding these to travel to the US under its Visa Waiver Program (VWP). Of the 15 EU member states at the time, all but Greece's citizens enjoyed visa-free travel, but the timing of the new law threatened this. Among the ten new members state that joined the EU in May 2004, only Slovenia participated in the VWP.[6] The US Congress eventually set 26 October 2004 as the deadline for this biometric passport requirement.

Most EU countries were moving toward biometric passports (containing microchips embedded with facial images or fingerprints), but these were not scheduled for production in most countries until the end of 2005 at the earliest. This situation led to concerns about 'visa war' were the US to maintain its deadline and the EU retaliated with reciprocal demands. It was unclear how consular officials on either side of the Atlantic could handle the millions of extra visa applications that would result annually from such a crisis. In the end, the US Congress was persuaded by the Bush administration to grant the Europeans more time, which allowed all EU members to meet the biometric passport requirements by the end of 2006.

Nevertheless, the issue of expanding the VWP to all EU countries remained, and this also threatened to bring about a visa war. At a high-level meeting held in Brussels in April 2004, both US and EU officials expressed a desire to avoid this (European Report 2004b).[7] Initially, the Bush administration lobbied Congress to bend the normal rules on visa refusal rates and to allow the VWP to be expanded to new member states – many of which were viewed as key American allies. However, by 2007 the US authorities had grown concerned about 'homegrown' terrorism in Europe, which appeared to be responsible for the successful attacks in Madrid and London (2005) and the foiled plots in Germany (2006) and the UK (2006 and

2007). In this regard, the VWP increasingly came to be viewed as a loophole in US border security and CT. Owing to such concerns, additional requirements for the VWP were included in the new homeland security legislation approved in August 2007 (noted above) (Riechmann 2007). This legislation required the implementation of an electronic travel authorization system to pre-clear citizens of the VWP countries 72 hours before their departure for the US.

Later, in early February 2008, the US circulated a draft 'memorandum of understanding' to some EU members, outlining its model for new bilateral agreements that incorporated additional stipulations for the VWP. This came just after DHS Secretary Chertoff linked the growing threat of homegrown terrorism in Europe to a need for greater security measures aimed at European travellers to the US (*BBC News* 2008). The new American plans included not only the electronic pre-clearance programme, but also renewed demands for armed air marshals on some US-bound flights and additional PNR data (Traynor 2008). Almost immediately, the US also began to hold talks on its new plans with some of the EU's newer member states, which had grown tired of waiting for an EU-level solution to its delayed participation on the American VWP.

Reacting to these developments, both the Commission and Slovenian presidency of the EU asked the US to respect the authority of the EU on these matters. In the subsequent months, the American and EU authorities agreed on a twin-track approach, with the US carrying out talks both bilaterally with EU members on one set of issues and with the Commission at the EU level on other matters. The issue of exchanges of DNA and fingerprint data among law enforcement and armed sky marshals on flights was handled bilaterally between the US and individual member states, while talks on travel documents, visas and PNR were handled at the EU level.

By the October of 2008, agreements were reached on both tracks. In addition, the refusal rates for visa applicants from affected EU countries had fallen below the 10 per cent threshold required by the new US legislation of 2007. The VWP was subsequently expanded on 17 November 2008 to include the Czech Republic, Estonia, Hungary, Latvia, Lithuania and the Slovak Republic. On 30 December 2008 Malta was invited into the VWP as well.

To gain participation in the programme, these newer EU members had to complete bilateral deals with US on the exchange of DNA, fingerprints and other personal information for use in criminal or terrorist investigations. These deals were patterned after a similar agreement that the US had previously reached with Germany in

March 2008 (Nakashima 2008). Furthermore, as with the continuing members of the VWP, the new participants were also required to utilize the new pre-clearance programme, which became known as the Electronic System for Travel Authorization (ESTA).[8]

In 2009, the topic of the further widening of the VWP to the remaining EU member states was taken up by a high level EU delegation during its visit to Washington.[9] However, the decision for the Obama administration to admit Poland, Romania, Greece and Cyprus to the VWP coincided with the introduction of new Congressional legislation that would suspend countries from the programme if more than 2 per cent of their citizens overstayed their visits.[10] Indeed, the view that the VWP represented a security loophole was bolstered by the remarks of FBI Director Robert S. Mueller in February 2009 when he warned of homegrown terrorists who might try to enter the US via the VWP (Johnson 2009).

Conclusion

There is much to learn from studying the EU and US regarding counter-terrorism. Comparing the EU and US has its limits, but the juxtaposing of parallel developments in each reveals instructive similarities and differences. The area of legal change provides a good illustration of this. In both the EU and US, the passage of time after 9/11 brought a fading sense of urgency to fight terrorism and a related increase in concerns for civil liberties. Beyond this, comparisons are difficult, mainly because the EU lacks operational power on CT. Though impressive in the historical context of European integration, recent legislation passed at the EU level does not rise to meet the level of change found in recent American initiatives.

In contrast, there is a lot to compare fruitfully regarding the task of institutional change in the EU and US. Regarding information sharing, both the EU and US are trying to move beyond the creation of new formal institutions. In the EU, for example, there have been several initiatives since 2004 aimed at implementing the principle of availability, according to which information for law enforcement purposes needed by the authorities of one member state should be made available by the authorities of another member state. This principle was enshrined in the EU's internal security agenda for 2005–2010 (the Hague Programme), as well as in subsequent initiatives, such as the so-called Swedish framework decision of 2006 and the 'Prüm decision' of 2007. In the US, the main objectives and approaches for improving information sharing in its intelligence community are found the DNI's Information Sharing Strategy of 2008, according to which new institutions, such as the NCTC, are merely the tip of the iceberg. Instead, a change of mindset is required. Indeed, in his foreword to the Strategy, the former DNI, Mike McConnell, argues 'together, we must challenge the status quo of a 'need-to-know' culture and move to one of a responsibility to provide mindset' (Office of the Director of National Intelligence 2008: 2).

In addition, the US and EU are also similar regarding their respective efforts to have created new leadership positions aimed at promoting better information sharing and coordination. However, the EU's position of Counter-Terrorism Coordinator still lacks the kind of power and influence enjoyed by the American Director of National Intelligence. Of course, questions remain in the US about the effectiveness of the DNI position. In a report published in November 2008, the Inspector General of the Office of the DNI (ODNI) identified persistent battles among agencies in the intelligence community and those represented in the ODNI and found that the employees in the intelligence community, as well as within the ODNI itself, were still unclear about the role of the DNI (Maguire 2008).

Nevertheless, the position of the DNI enjoys a greater potential to provide leadership for US efforts in CT compared to the EU's Mr Terror. Much of this stems from the operational activity of US intelligence authorities, which is lacking at the EU level. However, some of this difference stems from the DNI's authority over key intelligence bodies, key personnel decisions, budgets and access to the President. It would be possible to enhance the role of the EU's CT Coordinator by giving him greater influence on the work of SitCen, but this was not included in the revised mandate for the post. Moreover, this position continues to lack any real power to pressure EU member states to implement EU legislation either properly or on time.[11] Thus, for the foreseeable future, a greater role for the EU on counter-terrorism should not be expected, and this is especially evident when juxtaposed with more impressive institutional changes regarding leadership in the US that may nonetheless fall short of expectations.

Regarding transatlantic relations, the second part of this chapter elucidated how policy convergence between the EU and US can explain the productive partnership that has evolved between the EU and US on counter-terrorism since 9/11. More specifically, this chapter made clear that transatlantic relations on CT have not resulted from the US simply dictating undesirable terms to the EU. Instead the post-9/11 pattern of transatlantic agreement and cooperation in this area is best explained by policy convergence (cf Rees 2009).

For example, EU-US relations on Europol have been the product of both sides seeing some value in international liaison relationships and voluntary information sharing arrangements. In fact, in 2009 the EU and the US were in the midst of negotiating an umbrella agreement on data protection that could pave the way for future and more extensive transatlantic information sharing to fight crime and terrorism. In addition, after 9/11 both sides also saw value in enhancing existing agreements on MLA and extradition. Regarding these, transatlantic differences on civil liberties and the death penalty proved inconsequential. Concerning container security, EU-US tensions dissipated once the Commission became directly involved in talks with the US and saw EU ports quickly adapting to the new rules. In fact, the EU subsequently adopted its own rules for container security with its own version of the 24 hour rule, though its implementation was delayed beyond 2009.

Concerning both airline security and travel documents, transatlantic agreements were facilitated when both sides recognized the potential threat of 'homegrown' terrorism in Europe (Rees 2006: 58–60). By 2009, the EU had concluded PNR agreements with Canada and Australia and was developing plans for its own rules on collecting passenger data from airlines. Cooperation on passports and visa waivers can also be explained by the convergence of EU and US approaches to border management, especially after the Commission's announcement in 2008 of initiatives to increase the use of biometrics and to better monitor entries and exits in the Schengen zone.

In conclusion, transatlantic relations on CT will continue to be influenced the most by policy convergence regarding the EU and US. Barring another major terrorist attack on the US or Europe, which could have a different effect on threat perceptions and notions of appropriate responses in each setting, the productive transatlantic partnership on CT can be expected to endure.

Notes

1 Interview by author with Europol Liaison Officer, Washington, DC, 28 May 2009.
2 Interview by author with Europol Liaison Officer, Washington, DC, 28 May 2009. For a broader perspective on transatlantic intelligence cooperation, see Aldrich (2009).

3   This eventually became part of the US Department of Homeland Security (DHS). Within DHS there is now a component for Customs and Border Protection (CBP).

4   In 2006, the Safe Port Act was signed into law in the US. Commonly referred to as the '10+2 rule', the new regulations to be supplied to US Customs and Border Protection of DHS cover before cargo reaches a US port. Importers must supply ten items of data and carry two items of data about their cargo. The new rules have been in effect since January 2009 but will not be enforced until 2010.

5   Throughout the early stages of the PNR dispute, another point of dispute arose in transatlantic relations, namely American demands for armed 'sky marshals' on US-bound flights. The US pressed individual EU member states to employ sky marshals until late April 2004, when it dropped this demand during the course of the first ever US-EU 'dialogue on border and transport security' held in Brussels. See *EUobserver.com*, 'US to back down on air marshals,' 27 April 2004.

6   Regarding the excluded countries, the percentages of their citizens' visa applications for travel to the US that were being refused were still too high for their participation in the VWP.

7   At this same meeting, the US and EU also announced plans to create a stolen passport registry to be administered by Interpol. In addition, the US also confirmed that, starting on 30 September 2004, all EU citizens, not just visa-holders, would be fingerprinted and digitally photographed upon their arrival in the US.

8   ESTA has been mandatory since 12 January 2009 and requires travellers to the US under the VWP to provide information on a web-based system at least 72 hours before their departure to the US. ESTA requires passengers to provide the same data requested by the I-94W cards that have long been completed by travellers on board US-bound aircrafts and cruise ships and then presented to DHS officials upon arrival.

9   The Czech Interior Minister Ivan Langer, representing the Council Presidency, and Jacques Barrot, Vice-president of the European Commission in charge of Justice, Liberty and Security, met with the new US Secretary of DHS, Janet Napolitano, and the new US Attorney General, Eric Holder.

10 The legislation was sponsored by Diane Feinstein (D-California). See Beary (2009).

11 The European Court of Justice will gain new power in this regard when the EU's Lisbon Treaty comes into force.

Chapter 10

Cross-strait police cooperation between Taiwan and China

Yungnane Yang and Frédéric Lemieux

Introduction

Political relations between Taiwan and China have always been fragile. This strained relationship has never been more apparent than during the last 40 years of quarrelling over self-determination issues. Still, a rapprochement between Taiwan and China has shown erratic progress in the past ten years. The Economic Cooperation Framework Agreement (ECFA 2009) put forth by Taiwan's Kuomintang (KMT) administration under President Ma Ying-jeou represents a significant initiative which aims to improve relations between Beijing and Taipei (Cooke 2009). Since the global financial crisis of 2008, both governments are experiencing pressures highlighting the importance of strengthening trade cooperation to safeguard their respective economies. Additionally, recent non-traditional security challenges – such as environmental issues, climate change, energy problems, terrorism, and contagious diseases – call for cooperation between the two countries.

There are strong indicators that the possible development of a Common Market[1] (that includes Taiwan and China) will increase the demand for more effective police cooperation as well, in order to address new security issues, similar to what occurred in other common market zones (Manning 2000; see also Gerspacher and Lemieux in this book). Currently, cross-border criminal activity between Taiwan and China seems to be on the rise in both incidence and significance. The following factors may be contributing to this situation: 1) the exceptional boom in China's economy during the

1990s, which created several illicit lucrative opportunities for both Taiwanese and Chinese people (smuggling and trafficking, white collar crime, etc.); 2) the steady increase of travel between Taiwan and China for cultural, religious and academic purposes since 1987 and the recent authorization of direct flights between the two countries, both amplifying existing problems related to immigration regulations; and finally 3) the communication technology (for instance, the Internet) used to facilitate trade and financial exchanges is also now making it easier to commit fraud and other forms of cybercrime. In western countries, situations such as those mentioned above are considered familiar transborder security problems, but in the existing political context between Taiwan and China, they pose a serious challenge to police cooperation.

Historically, policing functions in both countries are closely tied to politics. Police activities can easily be understood as a component of the national security domain. European police cooperation trends and history of development demonstrate political institutions' dominance on police cooperation, particularly in those countries affected by national security issues threatening the 'status quo' (Deflem 2002). According to North (1990), cross-strait police cooperation (including both formal and informal constraints on it) is controlled by politics or is under the influence of political institutions. Therefore, political concerns related to national security contribute to the inflexibility of cross-strait police cooperation. With such a conception of security governance, it is not surprising that there is limited police cooperation between Taiwan and China.

In the case of Taiwan and China, one can argue that the political 'status quo' is a plausible rationale at the root of the cross-strait police cooperation challenge. On the one hand, police cooperation might not continue if the politics of the 'status quo' is threatened. On the other hand, police cooperation could actually maintain the 'status quo' of a certain political situation.

Because China still considers Taiwan to be part of its territory, bilateral ties between Taipei and Beijing are conducted through semi-official channels in order to circumvent the touchy issue of sovereignty – the Straits Exchange Foundation on the Taiwanese side (SEF) and the Association for Relations Across the Taiwan Strait on the Chinese side (ARATS). Previously, police organizations from both countries were not allowed to have formal contacts with each other. Currently, police cooperation is facilitated through these non-governmental mechanisms created by both governments and aims to handle technical or business matters, including security issues.

This unique political context requires us to adopt an original analytical approach to examine cross-strait police cooperation between Taiwan and China. Since relations between the two countries are complex and sensitive, information or case study examples about police cooperation are not easy to find. However, a few past and more recent initiatives in cross-strait cooperation on security matters can be scrutinized. This chapter outlines how police organizations shape and implement cooperative initiatives dealing with the cross-strait crime between Taiwan and China and points out mechanisms and/or models that can facilitate police cooperation within this complex political environment. To do so, we will use an institutional analysis framework to better understand how informal and formal constraints placed on law enforcement organizations affect police cooperation between Taiwan and China.

Institutional perspectives on cross-strait police cooperation between Taiwan and China

Informal constraints

According to McDavid (1977), informal agreements and/or activities play a more important role than formal agreements when measuring police cooperation in particular. Informal constraints can include values, attitudes, cognitions, perceptions, habits, culture and an interpretation of the rules. North (1990: 36) points out that formal constraints on cooperation, for example, can often originate from informal ones and it is crucial to analyse the development of institutions as well as their performance. In this chapter, informal constraints are considered in regard to information or activities related to cross-strait cooperation, including direct and indirect contacts of police and politicians from both Taiwan and China.

According to information released on China's official website,[2] formal contact between Taiwan and China occurred in May 1986 and was prompted by an international media event. For the first time since 1949, the two governments opened a dialogue to resolve a case involving a Taiwanese commercial flight to China. More precisely, the pilot flew a civil plane to China without the permission and consent of the Taiwanese government or passengers. The case was not only a national security matter but also a crime, according to Taiwanese law. Prior to 1986, the government of Taiwan had utilized the political stance of the 'Three Nos' (no contact, no compromise, no bargaining) in order to avoid any intrusion or destabilization by China into Taiwan's domestic affairs. The cross-strait talks in the flight case broke the habit of the 'Three Nos'. Furthermore, the talks provided both governments and their respective police agencies with a framework for future interaction.

In the 1990s, several transborder criminal incidents required the Taiwanese and Chinese police agencies to establish direct contact. For instance, in March 1994, 32 Taiwanese visitors were burned to death by Chinese thieves at Thousands Lake in Hongzou, China.[3] At the request of the government of Taiwan and under media pressure, Yeou-yi Hou, a high-ranking police officer, was allowed to visit China to help collect criminal evidence in this case. His visit was deemed symbolic because he didn't have the right to investigate formally in China. However, Yeou-yi Hou was able to exchange information with high-ranking police officers in China and his visit had an impact on later cross-strait informal police relationships. The authorization to collaborate, though symbolic, was a precursor for future police cooperation between both countries.

Several other criminal incidents forced cross-strait police cooperation during the 1990s, but have not necessarily led on to successful initiatives. Some of these examples demonstrate how police cooperation is difficult between Taiwan and China and relies heavily on both sides' political attitudes and sensitivity. For example, the smuggling of a specific type of weapon (a 54 model pistol) – which are the guns used by Chinese police officers – was undertaken illegally from China to Taiwan during the 1990s.[4] Many of these pistols were used to commit crimes, influencing the public perception of security (or the lack thereof) in Taiwan. It should be mentioned that the Taiwan government had enacted strict laws regarding gun control and it is forbidden by law for citizens to possess firearms. Trying to put an end to the situation, the Taiwan National Police Agency Commissioner used Interpol channels to ask (in vain) for the Chinese government's assistance in halting these gun shipments to Taiwan. This request had no effect on cross-strait police cooperation since there was a lack of trust between cross-strait politicians. Moreover, China's government was offended by the Taiwan president's defiant speech at Cornell University and cross-strait relations turned sour as the hostility intensified between both countries (Clough 1993).

Another notable example involved a Kaohsiung councillor from Taiwan, Di-Jen Lin, who was kidnapped and killed in August 1998 in Liaolin, China. The Chinese government allowed her relatives and friends to travel to its territory to deal with death-related affairs, but denied entry to officers from the Taiwan Mainland Affairs Council (MAC), the SEF, and DPP members (the Democratic Progressive Party).[5] Also, China's police service was ignorant of many aspects of Di-Jen Lin's history, including her political background, until it was publicized by the Taiwanese media. The Chinese Minister of Public Security ordered the police to try their best to investigate fully the case after learning about the victim's political background. In the meantime, members of the Democratic Progressive Party denounced the government of China for neglecting basic human rights, as the request for a thorough investigation was not acted upon immediately. Responding to such criticism, the Chinese police eventually actively investigated the murder, although there was no obvious progress or influence on cross-strait police cooperation. According to Yang (1999), more informal relationships between the police services of Taiwan and China are needed to deal with trans-border security issues, as the investigative process requires formal communication channels and effective structures to collect a large amount of information and sensitive evidence.

Formal constraints

Cross-strait police cooperation initiatives have also been instigated under formal frameworks or 'formal constraints'. Formal rules can be defined as written agreements and/or laws. According to North (1990: 46–47) 'Formal rules include political (and judicial) rules, economic rules, and contracts.' In fact, there are many laws related to cross-strait relationships in Taiwan, such as the 'Regulation on Citizens' Relationships between Taiwan and Mainland China areas', visiting regulations for Chinese travellers, and regulations on official visits (including those by police). There are also regulations affecting Chinese citizens, politicians and bureaucrats. However, one country's regulations might not be recognized as legitimate by the other, even if the laws are similar.

The Kinmen Agreements are formal rules recognized by both the Chinese and Taiwanese governments. The Kinmen Agreements were signed by officials from Taiwan and China in September 1990 and include five central principles. These principles are concerned mostly with deportations related to illegal Chinese immigrants and Taiwanese fugitives. This framework of agreements was laid down in order to regulate cross-strait government interactions (see Table 10.1) and was prompted by two incidents related to the deportation

Table 10.1 The Kinmen Agreements[6]

The following agreements were set by the representatives of the cross-strait Red Cross Organizations based on information from both sides' governmental departments involved with deportation.

I. The Deportation Principle
To ensure the process of deportation is consistent with principles of humanity, safety, and convenience.

II. The subjects of deportation
i. Those who violate immigration laws must be deported. (An exception is made for fishermen that must enter certain areas for emergency reasons.)

ii. Criminal suspects or fugitives.

III. The place for deportation
Maway ← → Machu is the assigned point of deportation. For reasons of habitation, weather, and marine meteorology, Xiamon ← → Kinmen could be chosen as the deportation point by concession.[7]

IV. The deportation procedure
i. One side should inform the other side about the personal information of deported subjects. The other side should check and respond to one side within 20 days. Both sides have to conduct deportation processes based on the agreed time and point of deportation.

ii. A Red Cross vessel should be used for deportation by each side. Civic ships can be used to arrive at the agreed deportation point for guidance. The deporting ships and piloting ships should fly the Red Cross flag. (Other flags or signs are not allowed in ships.)

iii. Two people representing each side, agreed upon beforehand, must conduct the deportation. They must also sign the witness documents.

V. Others
Both sides have to deal with any technical problems that arise after the agreements are signed in order to implement the deportation immediately. Both sides can negotiate with each other if the agreements are not specific enough for deportation.

---

of illegal Chinese immigrants. During separate deportation processes, a total of 45 people were killed in two separate accidents involving Chinese citizens being returned to China from Taiwan. These accidents involved the victims of human trafficking, a crime under the laws of both countries. Therefore, the two governments had no choice but to interact with each other to deal with the situation. Pressure to engage in talks came from the populace of both countries, though the Taipei government had more pressure than Beijing, owing to the greater freedom of the press in Taiwan.

Formalizing the agreements was largely prompted by the needs of the Taiwanese government and society, but were not considered quite as urgent for China. Deportations did not operate smoothly until the dawn of the new millennium. In fact, the deportation procedures have worked erratically at best due in part to political competition and the ensuing regime changes in Taiwan: from the KMT to the DPP and from the DPP to the KMP throughout the 2000s.[8]

Moreover, for some white collar crime cases, the Chinese government was reluctant to cooperate with the government of Taiwan. China's economic boom is partly influenced by the vitality of Taiwan's economy and close relationships exist between politicians and businessmen in China. Due to political interests (sovereignty) and economic interests, China's public institutions (police) may be reluctant or may refuse to arrest Taiwanese businessmen operating in China, even at the request of Taiwan's government (police). For example, Yuhou Chen was a ruthless businessman who abandoned about US$1.8 billion debt in Taiwan and fled to China in 2004.[9] He was not arrested by the Chinese authorities. Another renowned case involved the Taiwanese business tycoon, Youzeng Wang. He fled to China after declaring bankruptcy in January 2007 leaving behind several debts. The Chinese government refused to arrest him. However, due to Taiwanese media coverage and political pressure, he was expelled from China and subsequently took refuge in the United States.

In fact, there are still many so-called white collar criminals wanted by the Taiwan authorities who are hiding in China. It seems that cases involving homicide and theft are much more straight-forward than white collar crime in terms of cross-strait police cooperation and could constitute a solid common ground for future cross-strait cooperation.

There are several reasons that should be taken into account in explaining the lack of explicit, specified cooperation regarding crime. First, there were more formal and informal cross-strait police contacts during the 2000s than in the 1990s due to a decrease in political hostilities between both governments. Second, as Taiwanese fugitives flocked to China to take advantage of its booming economy in the early 2000s, many of them committed new crimes and/or re-offended, causing several security problems in China. Third, China's government recognized the importance of deportation and its role in earning the respect of Taiwan's citizens. Fourth, cross-strait deportation involves not only technical processes, but also the execution of extensive and complex administrative procedures controlled by each respective government. Consequently, this bureaucratic reality slowed the deportation procedures and extended the training period of the officials involved. Fifth, the agreements were only in principle and more time was needed to negotiate the application of technical procedures pertaining to cross-strait police administration. Sixth, it was only politicians and Red Cross representatives who participated in the drafting and signing of the Kinmen Agreements. Policing concerns were not specifically addressed in the framework. Seventh, more agreements are needed to clarify the earlier stages of the cooperative processes between Taiwan and China. Deportation represents the final stage of cooperation (the outcome) and nothing had been defined regarding the previous stages of investigation and information exchange.

Despite the obstacles, many initiatives in cross-strait deportation took place within this formal framework. According to a statistical report sponsored by both governments, between 1990 and 2006 there were 286 cases of cross-strait deportation between the two countries. A total of 37,790 people were deported using the cooperation process based on the Kinmen Agreements. The report also mentions that 266 illegal Taiwanese immigrants were deported from China to Taiwan.[10] It seems that the Kinmen Agreements did contribute to cross-strait cooperation in this particular matter of deportation, as they had been designed to do. More recently, Taiwan's Minister of Mainland Affairs Council (MAC) stated in November 2008 that 'there should be further talks on cross-strait police cooperation to fight cross-strait crime … And cross-strait police have discussed the cross-strait police cooperation with China.'[11] The Minister implied that formal rules related to police cooperation would be negotiated in 2009. As a matter of fact, in April 2009, a bilateral financial services and direct investments agreement was signed by Taiwan and China. This agreement calls for greater cooperation in the fight against crime, specifically of a financial nature. Again, formal rules do not guarantee its implementation or performance. Managerial procedures, which are the focus of the next section, are needed to facilitate the future of cross-strait police cooperation.

The future of cross-strait police cooperation between Taiwan and China

Despite increasing need on both sides, police cooperation between Taiwan and China remains mostly informal and limited. Police agencies on both sides were not allowed to visit each other without political permission before 2006, except for the purpose of academic exchange or to address important investigative cases. For instance, Taiwan police officials were permitted to visit China in order to arrest and/or deport the 'most wanted' criminals who had escaped from Taiwan and were hiding in China. Since 2006, most Taiwanese police officers have been allowed to visit China without formal permission.

However, the current problem is a lack of planned cross-strait police contacts. According to Anderson (1989: 11) 'the main questions are how this [police cooperation] is to be organized and how should it be supervised and controlled?' These questions certainly apply to the challenges in developing police cooperation strategies between Taiwan and China, since cross-strait politics is still the major concern for the future. In order to better facilitate this process, institutional theories related to inter-organizational cooperation could be applied (North 1990; Ostrom 1990), as well as social networking theory (Scott 1992), organizational theories (Yang 2006), and integrated service theory (Robertson 1998). Following recent agreements signed between Taiwan and China, it has been suggested that both formal and informal strategies could be useful in developing police cooperation. This section emphasizes institutional theories that can be applied to cross-strait police cooperation and facilitates their implementation between Taiwan and China. Our analysis scrutinizes four dimensions related to inter-organizational interactions, including individuals, groups, organizational settings, and environments.

Individuals

Since police visits are now permitted, there are chances for individual police officers to have direct cross-strait links with each other, thereby making it easier to arrange formal and informal contacts for Chinese and Taiwanese law enforcement agencies. There are diverse ways of defining cross-strait cooperation for police officers. 'Formal' contact can be interpreted in different ways. For example, on-site visits, phone calls, and mail (including e-mail) are all possible formal tools for cross-strait cooperation. However, the activation of these tools relies on police officers' attitudes and their motivation toward cooperation and information-sharing. At the individual level, a positive attitude can be generated by organizational incentives such as professional recognition, promotion, or other forms of informal/ formal gratification (Robertson 1998). These can increase motivation as well as change the attitude of police officers in participating in such cross-strait cooperation. It could effectively empower individual members of both sides' police forces to work together on common criminal issues. However, an evaluation of performance in police cooperation can be coloured by cultural differences emanating from peer groups, the organizational culture (symbols and codes), and of course, the environmental 'climate' (China and Taiwan's politics, laws, economy, etc.) in which police officers must function.

Groups

Police officers can be members of formal and informal groups and both types of group play important roles in police cooperation. Group members could be cross-strait police and/or from single-side police organizations. They could contain only police officers or sometimes integrate civilians (non-sworn in officers). In order to ensure cohesiveness and effectiveness, groups must pursue an accepted mission and goals, and their members should be committed to achieving these. Yang (2000) states that non-government relationships are needed to improve the informal cross-strait police cooperation mechanisms to deal with cross-strait crime. According to the Taiwanese Criminal Investigation Bureau, Taiwanese police forces had cracked down on several criminal groups whose membership included both Taiwanese and Chinese citizens.[12] For example, one particular criminal group was investigated by the police in December 2008. The group leader was Chinese and the other group members were performing their criminal activity in Taiwan.

Indeed, cooperation teams are necessary in order to respond effectively to the changes in criminal group activity in Taiwan and China. Forming such high-performance cooperation teams requires the development of common norms, a shared set of values, and the capacity to have a high level of autonomy in accomplishing the objective (Parker 1990: 33). Such an approach is particularly relevant for Taiwan's and China's police agencies in addressing cross-strait crime as cooperation inherently necessitates teams of police officers containing members of both sides' police organizations. Police cooperation teams can also be 'virtual', including, but not necessarily limited to, cooperative groups formed on websites (Duarte and Snyder 1999). In order to overcome the problems of time and space limitations, cross-strait cooperation teams can be structured through the Internet, phone calls, and other technologies which may enhance inter-agency cooperation. The 'virtual team' can be a high-performing team as long as the group members are willing to contribute continuously to the group.

There are some instances in which the Taiwanese and Chinese police will not necessarily agree on an appropriate response to a crime situation. For example, the Chinese police may sometimes not want to arrest escaped Taiwanese fugitives because these fugitives did not violate China's laws. Further, Chinese police may not have organizational or professional incentives to cooperate with the Taiwanese police.

Still, a police group can be formed to deal with specific cases on either side in order to address specific cross-strait crime. For example, a group with all its members coming from Taiwan may be formed to investigate a specific case or to try to arrest Taiwanese suspects who had escaped to China without bothering the Chinese police agencies. However, the performance of such a group depends on the energy and power of the explicit political support.

A police team requires its group members to have investigative competencies, interpersonal skills, and cross-strait affairs knowledge to effectively tackle cross-strait crime. Usually the two first sets of qualities can easily be found in most police organizations. The last one, cross-strait affairs knowledge, is more difficult to find in Taiwanese local police organizations because of their lack of resources, information, and cross-strait work experience. Because the local Taiwanese and Chinese police organizations are still not allowed to initiate cross-strait cooperation, it may be difficult in the immediate future to find cooperation initiatives at the local jurisdiction level. This finding is consistent with Robertson's (1998) general discussion on the ability and capacity of police services to cooperate.

Conversely, the Criminal Investigation Bureau (CIB) (the highest level of Taiwanese investigative organizations) possesses sufficient resources, more hierarchical differentiations, and a better ability to instigate cooperation projects than do local police organizations. Additionally, according to formal rules, the CIB receives comprehensive criminal information. Having said that, the CIB has the capacity, but not as yet the responsibility, to assist and train local police in developing a special team to address transborder crime. Indeed, crime between Taiwan and China represents a major concern for all police organizations nationally. Therefore, developing inter-agency cooperation has become crucial and it is the focus of the following section.

Organizations

Police organizations, especially the investigative divisions or agencies that lie within them, are the key elements in dealing with cross-strait crime. Still, the fight against cross-strait crime will certainly be enhanced if additional organizations (such as non-police agencies involved in the security and safety field) are included as team members or as part of the crime-fighting network. For example, the integration of several branches of government in the fight against cross-strait crime can increase official political support and facilitate inter-agency cooperation. In such a framework, police organizations carry the major responsibility related to crime fighting, but can be greatly aided by other political and security agency allies.

As with the individual and group levels, formal and informal strategies are key components in examining the interaction between organizations. On the formal side, there must be a variety of incentives for Taiwanese as well as Chinese police organizations to participate in this cooperative effort. Like individuals and groups, organizations need to facilitate their own interests in order to cooperate on the cross-strait crime fight. Therefore, incentives or organizational performance outcomes have to be created and recognized for the police services to work on cross-strait crime. In addition, there must be an entity (individual, group, or organization) acting as a facilitator to maintain the motivation to cooperate through assigning tasks, communicating priorities, conveying feedback, and highlighting the operational results and political outcomes. Effective facilitation motivates individuals, groups, and organizations involved in the control of cross-strait crime.

Currently, few departments or offices in China's and Taiwan's police organizations are designated as the entities responsible for cooperation. Those that do exist may possess hotlines on which they can call each other if a high-profile criminal situation is detected. Though they are able to communicate instantly, communication remains restricted due to the involvement of cross-strait political institutions. By using informal communication channels (one-to-one exchange), they are able to utilize such hotlines to work on inter-organizational affairs. Since Taiwanese and Chinese police organizations are so centralized, the most effective way to deal with cross-strait crime is to persuade the national governments on both sides to work together. However, formally creating this kind of incentive to cooperate is not always feasible under the given political conditions.

Naturally, boundaries do exist within and between organizations (Ashkenas *et al.* 1995). To achieve informal cooperation, organizations sometimes need to become 'boundary spanners', defined as agency cooperation based on leaders having formal and/or informal contacts with each other. These leaders must possess the power and credibility to influence their own organizations and lead the way toward cooperation initiatives. Of course, cross-strait cooperation between Taiwan and China cannot only rely on high-placed organizational leaders. Based on the known premises of organizational development theory, leaders have to organize teams or units in order to formalize a culture of cooperation within the police institution. To achieve a full and effective implementation of teams dedicated to cooperation activity, leaders must rely on individuals and/or groups possessing a certain level of knowledge on cross-strait affairs as well as a broad access to internal and external resources (for example social networks).

Environments

Organizations are surrounded by diverse and dynamic environments which can create incentives or barriers for inter-agency cooperation. Due to several cross-border crime incidents, the need for police cooperation between Taiwan and China did exist prior to 1986. However, it is only since the beginning of this century that we can clearly observe changes in several domains (including policing) between the two countries. An organization's surrounding environment constitutes a critical variable that can greatly impact on police cooperation. Key environmental impacts include the political arena, the social composition, and the economic situation (or institutions), and these are scrutinized in turn in the following sections.

Political factors

Political factors are probably the most important issues influencing police cooperation. According to Anderson (1989: 4) 'contact between police forces of different states is always a delicate matter because it touches on sensitivities concerning sovereignty and the territorial principle'. One powerful example of political influence related to police cooperation that comes to mind is the decision made by China to replace Taiwan's Interpol membership with Chinese membership instead (Anderson 1989: 46–47). Moe (1990) indicates that organizational structures are determined by the political power and authority. In the case of Taiwan and China, this rule definitely applies. Police cooperation cannot occur without prudent political guidance and detailed calculations from both governments.

Accordingly, ARATS and SEF were created to handle all cross-strait affairs, including criminality issues. Both organizations claim to be non-governmental and they insist that their contacts happen in an informal setting. In fact, both the Taiwanese and Chinese governments control the respective agencies and their interactions are inevitably influenced by cross-strait political issues. However, it should be noted that ARATS and SEF do not specialize in cross-strait crime *per se* and they may not have the ability and capacity to work on this issue. Therefore, cross-strait police cooperation is not yet fully operational. Ways to address such limitations could be 1) the recruitment of a team of retired police officers who can join ARATS and SEF, or 2) the creation of a police unit under these two agencies, inevitably subject to political influence.

In other words, current cross-strait political situations create constraints which ban formal contact and influence police cooperation. One way to circumvent such political barriers is to enhance the informal relationships or create activities that are not politically sensitive. However, the most efficient way to improve inter-organizational cooperation is to create formal relationships on both sides. Given the current political situation, ongoing development of both formal and informal constraints is critical in facilitating cross-strait police cooperation and remains an important possibility for the future. Government-sponsored cross-strait police conferences and meetings are two things that may encourage cooperation and reduce political distrust.

Social factors

Another aspect that should be taken into account is social interaction. Despite the fact that politics ban formal contacts between the Taiwanese and Chinese governments, citizens have a greater opportunity for social exchange than before. This increase in social interaction coincides with an augmentation of cross-strait crime activities. Social exchanges between Taiwan and China are dynamic and have been constantly evolving over many years, requiring the two governments to create ways to improve formal cross-strait relationships. China is more open to the world than ever before.

In order to understand and better adjust to an evolving social environment, governmental agencies need to adopt an open organizational system possessing an organic design (highly adaptive) rather than a closed system with a mechanistic setting (heavy bureaucracy) (Burns and Stalker 1961; Katz and Kahn 1966). This is especially true in the case of interrelations between Taiwan and China, where the politics is rigid and the formal constraints are difficult to change. In other words, Taiwanese and Chinese cooperative structures need to possess flexible organizational settings to circumvent restrictive politics and improve inter-governmental relations, and must be able to utilize the developing social environment as a reason to do so.

Moreover, creating other non-governmental organizations to enhance police cooperation on both sides might be necessary when formal or governmental organizations are not able to respond to environmental needs. For example, there is an organization called the Criminal Investigation Association, which was founded by a retired Commissioner of the National Police Administration in Taiwan. The association promoted cooperation between the police organizations from both countries, despite the sensitivities related to that role. Even if just a few cross-strait activities are facilitated, the non-governmental organization may be a wise choice for implementing inter-agency cooperation in dealing with cross-strait crime.

Economic factors

As with social factors, economic factors constitute an important force in inter-agency cooperation. Economic institutions create incentives and opportunities to fight cross-strait crime. The increase in economic activities and exchanges between Taiwan and China naturally led to more financial-related conflicts and disputes. Many of these have resulted in criminal cases. For example, the motive behind the murder of the Taiwanese councillor or mentioned earlier stemmed from cross-strait business conflicts. In recent decades, there have been several cases involving Taiwanese businessmen being killed, kidnapped, and injured in relation to business conflicts. For example, in June 2009, two Taiwanese businessmen were killed by their Chinese employees due to disagreements over compensation.[13]

Due to cultural differences and misunderstandings, Taiwanese victims and/or their relatives may not trust the Chinese police. They are often dissatisfied by the way investigations are handled. Influential businessmen might ask the Taiwanese police to intercede in these criminal cases. All the above-mentioned situations have increased the demand for cross-strait police cooperation and clearly political, social, and economic factors may either help or hinder inter-agency cooperation in dealing with cross-strait crime.

Effective cooperation also means a reciprocity in information exchange and investigative processes. In reality, Taiwanese police organizations seem to need more help from China than China's police need from the Taiwan authorities. This is related to the number of Taiwanese fugitives who are hiding in China versus the number of illegal Chinese immigrants living in Taiwan. Given this context, the Taiwanese governmental police authority has more incentive to work on combating cross-strait crime than does the Chinese police authority. It is therefore logical for the Taiwanese police to make the first move in police cooperation initiatives. Still, as the number of Chinese victims of cross-strait crime grows, so will the interest for Chinese police to cooperate with their Taiwanese counterparts.

Conclusion

Police cooperation is quite unique in the Taiwan-China relationship, since there were no official police and government contacts prior to 1986. Cross-strait government cooperative structures formed because of inter-agency problems that were made public (and therefore influenced by public pressure and perception) and the increasing crime rate between Taiwan and China. Despite this introduction of formal and informal contact between both governments, cross-strait police direct contact did not begin until 1994. In fact, the Kinmen Agreements signed by both governments in 1990 were not effectively implemented before the new millennium. Politics was the main factor influencing cross-strait police cooperation during that period. Our analysis of inter-agency initiatives points out that informal rules play a crucial role in improving cross-strait police cooperation between Taiwanese and Chinese police. Indeed, formal constraints such as the Kinmen Agreements have had a critical impact on police cooperation, with more than 37,000 people deported based on the agreements since these were implemented. Also, more formal articulation agreements should not be overlooked and are needed to facilitate ongoing and effective police cooperation.

To ensure the future of cross-strait police cooperation between Taiwan and China, it is proposed that inter-organizational police cooperation strategies should be developed. A four-level strategy, including individuals, groups, organizations and environments, needs to be considered within an inter-agency framework in order to implement efficient and effective police cooperation structures. Moreover, four factors proposed by Robertson (1998), including incentives, willingness, ability and capacity, should be promoted within police institutions to develop and sustain cross-strait police cooperation. The creation of special police teams is suggested as a specific cooperative structure to fight cross-strait crime, with a close monitoring of their configuration, operations and accountability mechanisms in order to ensure their efficacy.

Notes

1 According to Cooke (2009), there are several antecedents pointing in that direction: '1) the creation in 2000 of the Cross-Strait Common Market Foundation by the current Taiwanese vice-president, Vincent Siew, following his loss in Taiwan's 2000 Presidential election to Chen Shui-bian; 2) the formal accession of China and Taiwan to the World Trade Organization in December 2001; and 3) the signing of the China and Hong Kong closer economic partnership arrangement (CEPA) in June 2003.'

2 Source:
http://www.taihainet.com/news/intercoastal/lasthw/lastwx/2008-06-11/260040.shtml accessed on 27 January 2009.

3 Source:
http://zh.wikipedia.org/wiki%E5%8D%83%E5%B2%9B%E6%B9%96%E4%BA%8B%E4%BB%B6 accessed on 28 January 2009.

4 Source:
http//www.hudong.com/wiki%E9%BB%91%E6%98%9F%E6%89%8B%E6%9E%AA accessed on 28 January 2009.

5 Source:
http://zh.wikipedia.org/wiki/%E6%9E%97%E6%BB%B4%E5%A8%9F accessed on 28 January 2009.

6 Sources: http://www.mac.gov.tw/big5/negociat/negociate/gd.htm translated by the author and accessed on 26 January 2009.
7 Maway ← → Machu means from Maway in China to Machu in Taiwan and/or from Machu to Maway; Xiamon ← → Kinmen means from Xiamon in China to Kinmen in Taiwan and/or from Kinmen to Xiamon.
8 The KMT returned to power in 2008 after the DPP won the presidential election in 2000. The KMT was in power from 1949 to 2000.
9 Source: http://www.epochtimes.com/b5/4/2/12/n465145.htm accessed on 31 January 2009.
10 Source: http://www.cns.hk:89/tw/lajl/news/2007/01-31/864900.shtml accessed on 28 January 2009.
11 Source: http://www.chinareviewnews.com/doc/1007/9/8/9/100798969_2.html?coluid=7&kindid=0&docid=100798969&mdate=1113084810 accessed on 29 January 2009.
12 Source: http://www.cib.gov.tw/index.aspx accessed on 30 January 2009.
13 Source: http://www.chinanews.com.cn/tw/tw-mswx/news/2009/06-17/1737353.shtml accessed on 6 July 2009.

Chapter 11

Police cooperation in the context of peacebuilding: observations from African quarters[1]

Elrena van der Spuy

Introduction

Keeping the peace in foreign countries is not a role that has come easily to police officers in South Africa and elsewhere on the continent. Prior to the end of apartheid, for example, the South African Police (the SAP, now the SAPS) were heavily involved in counter-insurgency operations on the Zambezi border between 1967 and 1975. Special units with a clandestine police status were regularly involved in cross-border incidents of assassination and the like. One break in this pattern which was significant was the policing of the 1989 Namibian elections, with Pretoria at least strongly in the background of ostensibly local forces. Since 1994, and the formal end of the apartheid state, hostility has made way for at least a superficial amity and a professed role for the SAPS (in conjunction with elements of the South African army) in supporting peace initiatives in African areas of open conflict.

New patterns of police cooperation have been shaped by the regional dynamics of a broader socio-political and specific police organizational nature. Despite inhibiting political and organizational legacies, the current picture regarding police cooperation is not altogether bleak. Over the past decade and a half, cooperation between police agencies has evolved around a number of cardinal issues. In the case of Southern Africa, for example, the critical areas of police cooperation range from attempts to curb the flows of illegal weapons, to containing forms of 'organized crime', and the war on terror. More recently peacekeeping and post-conflict reconstruction have also come to provide a space within which the security agencies, including civilian police agencies, have new roles to fulfil. In this discussion we turn to a more detailed examination of the prospects and challenges which the peacekeeping agenda poses to police agencies and to cooperation amongst them in the continent. With that purpose in mind we draw on observations made at a couple of recent African policy workshops, on international policy and scholarly literature on 'police building'[2] in the context of peacekeeping operations, and on five interviews with South African law enforcement officers involved in peacekeeping training.[3]

Recent discussions on the role of the police in the context of African peacekeeping

In October 2008 a Police Dimension, Training and Rostering Workshop took place in Algiers, at the opposite end of the continent to South Africa. Organized under the auspices of the African Union's Peace Support Operations Division, the workshop brought together 60 delegates from various security structures across Africa as well as a smattering of international delegates. The flags of member states of the African Union provided a colourful background to the discussions. Pomp and ceremony marked the opening and closure of the proceedings. Translators relayed the three-day deliberations in English, French and Arabic. Not all, however, were equally satisfied with the way the proceedings evolved. A delegate from the North African Regional Economic Community (NARC) objected to the policy documents not having been translated into Arabic. An Angolan colleague lamented the absence of Portuguese interpreters. Both agreed that Africans had to come to terms with the linguistic diversity of the continent. With hindsight one could have added that discussions on peacekeeping had also to engage with divergent colonial legacies and the consequent diversity in police systems in Africa.

The objective of this policy engagement in Algiers was to finalize the policy framework for the police component of the proposed African Standby Force. Agreement was reached, and a round of applause was rightly called for. Now other structures within the African Union would have to take responsibility for translating the agreed-upon-policy into purposeful action. Many difficulties lay ahead – difficulties to which the discussions in Algiers made only fleeting reference. However, for those interested in the prospects for, and dynamics of, police reform at the national and regional level, the discussions in Algiers opened up new vistas. The focus on the role of police challenged the dominance of the military in the business of peacekeeping. In itself this was no small achievement given the long-standing supremacy of the military and the marginalization of the police within African security sectors. The policy discussions also seemed bent on a radical expansion of the role of the police in peace enforcement (and building) clearly informed by recent developments in UN peacekeeping further afield (in places such as Haiti, Timor, Kosovo and Croatia.) How would these proposals pan out in the context of Africa? But issues of implementation aside, the workshop provided symbolic proof of a newfound willingness in African political circles to create Africa's 'own' capacity to resolve its 'own' conflicts.

As already stated, the policy engagement in Algiers did not engage with the actual realities of police peacekeeping. It was not meant to do so. In search of a pragmatic assessment of the challenges on the ground one had to look elsewhere. A contrasting case in point was to be found in a workshop organized under the African Peace Support Trainers Association (APSTA) which took place in Nairobi a mere two months later (December 2008). This structure, which was established in 2002, is a continental chapter of the International Association of Peace Keeping Training Centres (IAPTC).[4] The event brought together 20 delegates from APSTA member institutions and with representation from regional organizations[5] and two leading experts on the Somalian conflict. Billed as an attempt to explore 'policy research on current developments in peacekeeping to inform doctrine and to shape training', the focus at this workshop fell on Somalia.[6] Predictably, the deliberations on peacekeeping in Somalia stood in sharp contrast to the much more abstract conversations on the doctrine, functions and roles of the police within the African Standby Force which took place in Algiers.

Any engagement with the (elusive) quest for peace in Somalia brought home the extraordinary challenges for peacekeeping in 'hostile' environments. The discussions were both broad – aimed at mapping the social legacies which shaped political conflict – and specific – in scrutinizing past efforts aimed at forging a rudimentary peace in Somalia.[7] Twenty years of largely *ad hoc* international efforts at peacemaking were put in an historical context. Presentations dealt with the specific history of colonial conquest in Somalia; the carving up of the territory into imperial enclaves; the entrenchment of social inequalities over time; the clan-based dynamics of political conflict; and the continuing allure of clan loyalties. The roles of adjacent states (Eritrea and Ethiopia) and of the Somalia diaspora in the conflict were considered. So too were the exponential growth of warlord-ism and the consequent militarization inside Somalia. The phenomenon of Somalian piracy – which has gripped the attention of the international community – as one delegate argued, was indicative of the extent to which domestic disorder can spill over into international havoc. Mogadishu was a place awash with guns of all shapes and sizes. There were one million guns in a population of one and a half million, said one delegate. Somalia was a 'country' where the 'state' had long since imploded.

An examination of various AU Mission(s) to Somalia provided a more descriptive view of the range of external and internal challenges confronting the containment of conflict. 'Windows of opportunity' in the recent past were identified but were also said to have been squandered. Beyond the broader structural issues discussions turned to a consideration of the kinds of factors which have affected peace enforcement at an operational level: low force generation capacity amongst African states and the UN; a lack of operational equipment in the 'theatre' itself; the politicization of peace efforts; and a political environment characterized by endemic instability. What indeed could peacekeeping amount to when there was 'no peace to keep', as one contributor put it. This rhetorical question hovered for a long while over the discussions. What indeed were the pre-conditions and pre-requisites for peacekeeping, including a police presence, to render a modicum of peaceful dividends?

What sense then is to be made of the policy discussions in Algiers regarding the police component of the African Standby Force and the multiple constraints which peace interventions routinely confront in difficult situations? More particularly, what conclusions can be drawn about the prospects for police building and cooperation amongst police agencies in the context of post-conflict reconstruction in Africa? It is to these questions that we now turn in more detail. But before doing so the very genesis of the idea of an African Standby Force needs to be briefly outlined.

The concept and envisaged practice of an African Standby Force

The guiding principles for peacekeeping adopted by the United Nations in 1992 are set out in a key policy document, *An Agenda for*

Peace (United Nations 1992). The latter placed particular emphasis on the role of regional organizations in managing conflict. It also opted for a decentralization of the responsibility for managing conflict. The decision to establish a continental peacekeeping capability in Africa is linked to the UN Protocol on Peace and Security which required regional economic communities to have peacekeeping forces.[8] A 15-member Peace and Security Council (PSC) was established in July 2004 and given responsibility for making decisions on conflict prevention (Gomes 2008). The Peace and Security Council was to be complemented by an African Standby Force consisting of five brigades for each of the five regional economic communities (RECs). The development of peacekeeping capacities at each of the regional levels was a prerequisite for building continental capacity (Gamba 2008). Once established, the African Standby Force (ASF) was to provide the African Union with the capabilities for a rapid deployment of a wide range of peace support operations.[9] The force was to consist of 'standby multi-disciplinary contingents, with civilian, police and military components located in their countries of origin and ready for rapid deployment' if and when the need should arise.[10] This conceptualization of the ASF was informed by state of the art strategic analysis as contained in the Brahimi Panel Report[11] and Capstone Doctrine developed by the UN in 2008. Over the past couple of years a number of workshops have been held, roadmaps designed, and policy frameworks crafted to expedite matters relating to the establishment of the ASF. So, for example, the ASF Policy Framework Document and the ASF Training Policy (2006) jointly aim at establishing common doctrines, integrating logistics, and standardizing training across the five sub-regions. Such deliberations suggest that progress towards the Africanization of peacekeeping has indeed been underway.

The ASF is looked upon as the key mechanism for undertaking future peace support operations on the continent (Adebajo 2008). Creating a continental peacekeeping capacity, however, is no small undertaking in a continent where the regularity and scale of conflict far outstrip other parts of the world. Consider the recent cases of Liberia, the Côte d'Ivoire, Sudan, Ethiopia/Eritrea, the Congo, and the Western Sahara for example. The demand for peacekeeping in Africa has shown no signs of abating. Since 1948, Pan (2005) has calculated there have been 54 UN peacekeeping missions in Africa. Between 2002 and 2007 the need for peacekeepers in Africa had grown from 31,000 to 60,000. A record number of peacekeeping forces are currently deployed, from West Africa to the Horn of Africa, from the

Western Sahara to the Great Lakes. Or to look at it from a different angle, by 2005 peacekeepers in Africa made up nearly 50,000 of the 65,000 UN peacekeepers deployed worldwide (Pan 2005: 2). All of these figures illustrate a demand for peacekeeping in the continent. But what is known about the capacity for, and dynamics of, a supply from within the continent?

Major constraints confront the realization of an African peacemaking capacity. The very idea of an African Standby Force is an ambitious one. The capacity of force-generating countries to adhere to the entry requirements of the UN cannot be taken for granted.[12] In addition, the time frames for the operationalization of the ASF are extremely tight. More debilitating still are the resource constraints. Africa cannot foot the bill on its own for continental peacekeeping. Without international financial backing the ASF will founder long before it has gone into actual 'theatre'. To this list of obstacles, Adebajo (2008: 132) adds two more: 'the relative weakness of regional security actors', on the one hand, and 'the lack of political consensus among African leaders on collective security norms and practices' on the other. Lastly, the relationship between key structures such as the UN, the AU and regional economic communities is characterized by a certain tension. In combination, such factors will also impact on the prospects for generating an African police capacity within the broader peacekeeping structures.

Inserting the police into the African Standby Force

As envisaged on paper, each of the five brigade-level forces of the African Standby Force will be supported by police and other civilian capacities. For the purposes of this discussion we are particularly interested in the police component. The concept of police formations within peacekeeping structures as currently advocated in African discussions needs to be understood against international developments in peacekeeping. In 'first generation' operations the role of peace enforcers focused on the monitoring of peace agreements in a non-partisan fashion. In recent decades the nature of peacekeeping has changed significantly. Mandates have shifted and roles have changed. 'Second' and 'third' generation peacekeeping has become much more complex and sophisticated (Day and Freeman 2003). Roles traditionally associated with peacekeeping have now expanded to also include more ambitious 'peace building' objectives. The latter, argued the Brahimi Panel Report (2000), required a 'doctrinal shift' in support of the use of police in UN operations (Levine 2008: 1). Peacekeeping operations in the contemporary era are, as a leading peacekeeping think-tank put it:

> Multidimensional, multifaceted and multifunctional. They are characterised by a mix of military, police, and civilians who are often deployed to hostile situations where there is no peace to keep. They involve a range of organizations including the UN, regional organizations, NGOs and other non-state actors. Finally, they incorporate political, economic, social and/or cultural elements as well as military security components and cover a multitude of tasks including monitoring, enforcement, protection of civilians, security, governance, rule of law, human rights, humanitarian assistance, and elections. (Pearson Peacekeeping Centre 2008: 1)

International efforts towards peace building in a post-Cold War environment have given rise to an industry of policy templates, operational guidelines, and practical assessments. Policy and academic literature on the topic have grown accordingly. Lessons from Bosnia, and more recently from Iraq and Afghanistan, have emphasized the extent to which *order maintenance* is a critical component of peace interventions. In order to address public security deficits, as Perito (2004) argues, appropriate mechanisms such as constabulary and civilian police units need to be deployed. Building the domestic capacity to help establish stability within the framework of human rights has thus become a core objective. In such jurisdictions the establishment of internal order through what Day and Freeman (2003) prefer to call 'police keeping' has moved centre stage as military formations are considered ill-equipped for this role (Perito 2004). To the traditional role of police keeping there are added the objectives of police building too, i.e. the reform of local police capacity under the tutelage of international police contingents attached to the peace keeping formations. As Celador, drawing on experiments in Bosnia and Herzegovina (BiH), puts it:

> ... it is now an accepted idea and policy goal – within the international community – that the post-conflict reconstruction and rehabilitation of war-torn societies must entail from an early stage the reform and restructuring, or even the complete re-establishment, of local police forces according to the norms of 'democratic policing'. (2005: 364)

It is here that the role of police and civilian formations in more complex peace building missions has been inserted into the political agenda. Developments within the UN are indicative of the growing importance of such formations. In recent years the UN Police Division has been elevated to a new status in response to the 'deepening and broadening' of policing activities (Greener 2009). An expansion of the roles of UNCIVPOL has prompted re-assessments of mandates, doctrines and training needs. In pursuit of 'interoperability' the need for common standards to regulate the work of such units has been identified. Furthermore, conformity is also required in terms of structure, organization and equipment. This in turn will require the development of appropriate training modules informed by particular policing models. The conversations in Algiers focused on the policy terms of reference for the envisaged structures and functions of police components of the ASF and thus left the operational details for others to contend with.

Building capacity: the importance of training and ever more training

A critical structure in the quest for building capacity within the African Standby Force is that of APSTA. A Training Support and Coordination Workshop held in Ethiopia in April 2007 and organized by APSTA revealed enormous challenges for an effective collaboration amongst institutions.[13] There was reference to the need for streamlining the collaboration between the AU and APSTA, and of the urgency to strengthen APSTA. Participating training institutions had to be accredited and training standards standardized. APSTA's capacity will itself be dependent on the contributing capacities of a number of peacekeeping institutions situated with the region. Of particular importance here are regional peacekeeping training centres such as the Kofi Annan International Peacekeeping Centre (KAIPTC) in Accra, Ghana; the Peacekeeping School in Koulikoro, Mali; the Peace Support Training Centre (PSTC) in Karen, Kenya; the African Centre for Strategic Research and Studies (ACSRS) in Abuja, and the Regional Peacekeeping Training Centre (RCTC) in Harare. Furthermore the contribution of policy and research centres such as the Institute for Security Studies (ISS) and the African Centre for the Constructive Resolution of Disputes (ACCORD) also needs to be acknowledged. Overall APSTA's endeavours will be critically reliant on international assistance.

In the terrain of peacekeeping, both technical and financial assistance have been forthcoming from international quarters. Training in various aspects of peacekeeping in Africa has become the focus of a number of international institutions and development agencies. For example, the Training for Peace (TfP) programme is funded by the Norwegian Institute for International Affairs (NUPI). This programme has brought two competent NGOs, the ISS and ACCORD, squarely into continental training efforts. The building of capacity through training is further advanced by US assistance[14] through its African Contingency Operations Training and Assistance Programme (ACOTA). This programme has been integrated into the Global Peace Operations Initiative (GPOI) which provides support to peace operation centres of excellence (Boucher and Holt 2007). Furthermore, French assistance has been forthcoming through the Reinforcement of African Peacekeeping Capabilities (RECAMO). Since 2005 the European Union has also committed itself to supporting the building of a peacekeeping capacity in Africa in line with the AU's African Peace and Security Agenda (Martinelli 2006). The quest of building Africa's capacity for peacekeeping has allowed for extensive networking and cooperation amongst various constituencies situated within and beyond the continent.

On paper at least it would thus appear that training for peace-keeping in Africa provides opportunities for advocating common values for police deployment in peacekeeping missions, for standard-izing curricula and operational strategies. Such prospects are likely to be constrained by an uneven capacity at national levels to provide training for peacekeeping which conforms to the envisaged UN standards.

The role of African police in peacekeeping operations: recent developments

The deployment of police in African-led peace operations is a very recent development. None of the Economic Community of West African States (ECOWAS)-led missions included a police component. In contrast, by March 2008, 1,486 civilian police were being deployed in Darfur. The number of African police deployed in peacekeeping operations (both internationally and within Africa) has increased dramatically over the past four years (Levine 2008). Between 2003 and 2007 African contributions to UNPOL have grown from 348 personnel to 2,406 personnel. This represents an increase from 7.4

per cent to 25.2 per cent of the total number of UNPOL personnel deployed (Levine 2008: 2). The top police contributing countries (PCC) to UN missions in Africa have been Cameroon, Ghana, Niger, Nigeria and Senegal. Newcomers on the scene are: Rwanda, South Africa, Uganda and Zimbabwe (Boucher and Holt 2007). African police increasingly play roles at all levels of peacekeeping missions. Nigeria and Senegal in particular make critical contributions to specialist police divisions, such as Formed Police Units. But Africa's homegrown policekeeping capacity continues to be constrained by weak structures at the national level (Levine 2008). Limited capacity at the national level to deploy and manage police outside the countries impacts negatively on regional capacities to generate peacekeepers.

Despite debilitating constraints, however, progress has been made over the past few years. As Levine argues:

> African police capacity has improved dramatically over the past few years, with more contributions to international missions; significant progress on the ASF and regional brigades, and the deployment of a full-scale African-led police component in AMIS. But serious challenges remain, and African police capacity for peacekeeping still lags behind the continent's military capabilities. (2008: 35)

Mainstreaming the reform and development of national police through international policekeeping

The conversations that came about in Algiers brought home the fact that peacekeeping deliberations hold some potential for opening up political spaces and opportunities for defining the role of police in peace operations, and for clarifying both the principles and standards to which they should adhere. The deliberations in Algiers, for example, created opportunities for reiterating the ethical and professional rules of police components attached to the ASF. Time was spent on clarifying the doctrine for police components attached to the ASF. Furthermore the discussions revisited the 'principles', 'operational standards', and 'rules of engagement' for police within the 'theatre of peacekeeping'. In this regard there was reference to the principles concerning the 'use of force' proportionate to the threat encountered and the necessity of adhering to the principles of 'human rights'. Issues relating to staffing the police component of the

ASF meant that the standards for recruitment, selection, composition and training were made explicit.

Peacekeeping deliberations can also provide opportunities for various actors to become involved. The discussion on the role of the police in Algiers was one that was shared by regional economic communities, security networks, training institutions across the region, and a variety of NGOs involved in security sector reform and conflict resolution. To this proposed 'collaborative' approach there was one curious exception – a point to which the discussion returns below.

In recent years significant progress has been made towards the 'Africanization' of peacekeeping. Progress has also been made with regard to the clarification of roles and responsibilities to be played by civilian police in future peace missions in Africa. Field experiments – such as the deployment of police as peacekeepers in Darfur in the African Union Mission in Sudan (AMIS) – are bound to yield important lessons for aligning practices on the ground to policies currently existing on paper. Evaluative assessments of the selection, training and deployment of police in foreign missions, the demands for in-mission support, and the challenges for a re-integration of police-keepers upon their return to national bases are likely to provide insights for bridging the gap between theory and praxis.[15]

The successful deployment of police in support of future peace missions in Africa, however, will depend on a range of factors. For the purposes of this discussion four observations will suffice. Such observations relate, in turn, to the institutional identity of the evolving African Standby Force; the scope of the police's role in African peacekeeping; the inter-relationship between regional police capacity and capacities at the national level; and the need to adapt policy to pan-African realities.

The prospects for developing professional and civilian police capacity for peacekeeping will in large part depend on the space provided by the ASF itself. Recently concerns have been expressed about the evolution of the ASF as a deeply militarized endeavour. Such concerns have led to calls for a 'civilianizing' of the African Standby Force in terms of policy tools and structures so that it may evolve into a 'truly multidimensional body' (Dersso 2009: 2). The prospects for developing civilian police capacity will be shaped by the institutional identity of the ASF and the extent to which the military elite (currently in charge) will open up space for police colleagues to pursue their particular objectives. The Brahimi Panel Report of 2000 argued in favour of a 'doctrinal' shift in order to utilize police more forcefully in future peace operations. There is no guarantee that this doctrinal shift will be embraced by military elites in a continent where the police have long been viewed as second cousins within the security establishment. In fact, the nature of the inter-relationship between police and military within the broader institutional context of the ASF is likely to be a contested one. To illustrate the point: organized police networks were absent from the policy discussions in Algiers. Some would argue that their absence could be taken as indicative of the fact that discussion on the African Standby Force – including its police component – continues to be dominated by military personnel. Consultation with police chiefs and regional police bodies around the proposed policy framework stitched together in Algiers was envisaged at 'some later stage', or so said the conference organizers. Clearly, a direct engagement with police networks should be a strategic priority if support for the ASF as a truly 'multi-dimensional' and 'multi-agency' endeavour is to be galvanized amongst police forces within the continent. On this score some progress has been forthcoming.

The Technical Workshop on Formed Police Units which was held in Senegal in mid-April 2009, however, brought international police and a smattering of continental police experts together to consider the Draft Concept of the Formed Police Units of the AUPOL and its Standard Operating Procedures.[15] This discussion seemed to have paved the way for finalizing policy documents which need to be adopted at some later stage by African Chiefs of Police and Heads of Gendarmerie.

A second note of caution touches on the envisaged scope of the police's role in peace interventions in Africa. We noted earlier that contemporary peace building conversations impute increasingly ambitious agendas for civilian police missions. As Wisler puts it:

> Restructuring is a new, non-classical task, of international civilian police missions. Traditional, civilian police missions have focused on micro-level activities such as training, monitoring and vetting. What has changed … is the nature of the international interventions themselves. Originally limited to peacekeeping, they involve today a peacebuilding or a nation-building agenda. (2007: 266)

The discourse on complex peace operations now routinely includes references to activities aimed at 'stabilization' and 'reconstruction'. The sheer scope of such activities necessitates more 'integrated approaches'. 'Mission coherence' is regarded as a prerequisite so as to bind a variety of players into 'cooperative networks'. Police building objectives require sophisticated skills and capacities amongst police contingents. In recognition thereof leading Western nations have opted for an increasing specialization of the police function in foreign peace missions. Developments within the Australian Federal Police (AFP) are instructive. The formation of an International Police Deployment Group and a Peace and Assistance Operations Unit allows for a mobilization of skills in support of executive and developmental functions in the context of peace operations (Peake and Studdard Brown 2005). Within US circles too, persuasive arguments in favour of establishing civilian 'stability forces' consisting of constabulary and police personnel with specialized skills for addressing civil disorder and crime have been forthcoming (see Perito 2004, 2008). Such specialized skills, however, are likely to be in short supply in the African context. As a consequence, modesty and pragmatism should shape the priorities for the ASF and, by implication, for its police contingents (Serafini 2006).

The realization of a regional police capacity to partake in continental peace operations will depend – in part at least – on national capacities to provide suitable personnel who can benefit from transnational training programmes. Such programmes can go some way towards moulding regional police formations according to 'cosmopolitan' scripts. The difficulties underlying such processes which aim at instilling democratic habits should again not be underestimated. Africa's police remain very much tied to the apron strings of their political masters (Hills 2007). Efforts aimed at police building will have to contend with the politics evoked in the process.

In the turbulent 'theatre' of peacekeeping, transnational efforts to develop police capacity in line with the principles of democratic policing can easily become derailed. Ongoing human rights violations by peacekeeping forces operating under the mandate of the UN provide ample proof of the scope for deviation from the rules in everyday operational practices. The involvement of peacekeepers in sexual harassment and exploitation has been a feature of many peace missions. The complicity of African peacekeepers in such practices has provoked public condemnation as in the case of Liberia and the DRC. The African Standby Force will have to grapple with the need for both external monitoring and effective internal disciplinary procedures to rein in abusive practices amongst Africa's blue helmets.

The last note of caution relates to the fit between international policy and local context. The discussion in Algiers took its cues from UN policy frameworks, terminology and operational practices. One illustrative example concerns the policy framework for community policing in peace operations as defined by the UN Department of Peacekeeping Operations.[17] This policy 'describes a methodology to conduct a standardized practice of community policing for the United Nations police officers in their capacities as advisors, mentors, trainers and monitors in peace operations as they assist in the reform, restructuring and rebuilding of local law enforcement agencies'. It goes on to note that building the community policing function of national police forces is 'integral' to the reform, and restructuring, of the national police. Drawing on the experience of developed countries, community policing aims at ensuring 'the trust of the public in law enforcement agencies' by both strengthening the bond between law enforcement agencies and the community and building effectiveness within police organizations. It advances a 'partnership approach' which is considered vital to the 'resuscitation of community confidence' through building impartiality in law enforcement and being 'responsive' to local needs through a 'preventative problem-solving approach'.

There was very little discussion at the Algiers workshop about the appropriateness of the state-centred community policing philosophy, as outlined in UN documents, in the African continent. Francophones could have made a simple point: that the concept of community policing does not exist in police systems which have been shaped by French colonial traditions of policing. This dependency on Anglophone understandings of police and police building was brought into sharp relief when the discussions turned to the appropriate policing model to inform public order maintenance. In terms of the policy vision this task is meant to be undertaken by specialist Formed Police Units. These units – a new concept in UN policies – will be responsible for 'stabilizing' situations. They are 'robust, armed police units' expected to fulfil specialized law enforcement and public order functions (Dziedzic and Stark 2006). FPUs have executive missions and are thus granted executive powers – much like the military. They are considered critical components for watching over local police and building the local police capacity.[18] Some engagement with divergent models of public order policing in Africa seems necessary in order to align policies to pan-African heterogeneity. Clarification of the model and operational strategies of Formed Police Units would be a good starting point.

Recent discussions held in Dakar (April 2009) at which the generic concept of the ASF AUPOL Formed Police Units was finalized have gone some way towards a clarification of mandates, core functions (with specific reference to functions relating to public order management, VIP protection, and the contribution to the capacity building of local police agencies), and the organizational structure of Formed Police Units. In this particular document one finds explicit recognition of the need for internationally accepted professional standards to guide the conduct of FPUs in Africa given the 'diversity of cultural and legal backgrounds' for police contributing countries.[19]

At one level the rhetorical incantation of a policy script for police contingents according to UN understanding is problematic. In Algiers only passing reference was made to the need to adapt UN policy to the African context, so as to instill some pan-African sensibilities. The prospects for a straightforward transfer of policy templates and operational strategies from New York to Algiers, Kinshasa and Maputo are dim. Those actually involved in peacekeeping on the ground are quick to point out the lack of rudimentary skills (English language skills, driving licences and some basic computer literacy) amongst police in the region and the consequent failure of PCCs to meet the UN entry qualifications.[20] Coming to terms with the implications of the institutional underdevelopment of police agencies in large parts of Africa is critical for developing a pan-African police peacekeeping capacity. The African Union will have to engage with the contextual realities within which Africa's peacekeeping capacity needs to be forged.[21]

Conclusion

For those interested in the fortunes of Africa's state police agencies, recent efforts towards the expansion of peacekeeping capacity provide new opportunities for cooperation and interaction between police agencies. Over such deliberations the international community hovers as a benevolent bearer of advice, support, expertise and financial resources. The quest for peacekeeping capacity within the continent has put security structures in an ever closer interaction with their international counterparts. As this review of recent policy engagements relating to the future role of the police within the African Standby Force illustrates, the international rules, principles and operational strategies relating to peacekeeping provide the template for African developments. At a rhetorical level there is much commitment to the building of pockets of professional police conversant with human rights and due process and geared to the demands of peace missions. The extent to which this commitment is institutionalized in routine practices on the ground will depend on a variety of factors – political, economic and institutional. Only time will tell if the African Union and its regional subsidiaries will be able to rise to the challenges which confront the institutionalization of good and effective governance of the police's role in Africa's peacekeeping initiatives. Regardless of the outcome, what is clear at this stage is that peacekeeping has forged a regional space within which Africa's police do have a role to play. This is a regional role – good, bad or mediocre – which is likely to affect the predisposition of police institutions located at the national level.

Notes

1 Thanks to Lynsey Bourke for the research assistance and to Jeffrey Lever for commenting on earlier drafts.

2 The concepts 'policekeeping' (Day and Freeman 2003) and 'police building' have recently cropped up in the work of policing scholars interesting in peacekeeping deliberations and refer explicitly to the police's role within the broader political contexts of peacekeeping and peacebuilding. See Peake and Studdard Brown (2005) as well as Goldsmith and Dinnen (2007).

3 Interview with AR, SAPS Training division; XX, SAPS HQ; JB SAPS HQ; CK SAPS HQ; AR II, Pretoria.

4 Source: http://www.apsta-africa.org retrieved 4 March 2009.

5 Representatives of regional organizations included the African Union (AU), the Intergovernmental Authority for Development (IGAD), the Eastern African Standby Brigade Coordination (EASBRICOM) mechanism, and the UN Political Office for Somalia (UNPOL).

6 Concept Paper for APSTA seminar, December 2008, on the theme of *Somalia: The quest for peacemaking and peacekeeping*.

7 African Peace Support Trainers Association (2008) *Somalia: The quest for peacemaking and peacekeeping*. Research Seminar Report.

8 See Zambia Mwananwasa: Launch of the SADC Brigade at http://www.polity.org.za/article.php?a-id=115536 retrieved 10 February 2008.

9 Such functions would include – at least on paper – preventive deployment, peacekeeping, peace building, post conflict disarmament, demobilization, re-integration and humanitarian assistance (Cilliers 2008: 1).

10 The African Standby Force: Police Dimension Staffing, Training and Rostering Workshop, Background Discussion Paper, 18–20 October 2008, p. 6.

11 The Brahimi Report is named after Lakhdar Brahimi, the Minister of Algeria, who chaired the Panel on United States Peace Operations. This

panel undertook a five month-long review of UN peacekeeping in 2000. It formulated wide ranging recommendations for strategic direction, decision making, rapid deployment, operational planning and so on. The report has been influential in shaping peacekeeping operations after 2000.

12 Personal communication, Peacekeeping Trainer attached to IPCS, Tanzania, Nairobi, 10 December 2008.

13 See in this regard: Aboagye, F.B. (2007) *Report of the African Standby Training Support and Coordination Workshop* (Pretoria: Institute for Security Studies) p. 7.

14 For a discussion of US peacekeeping policy and training interventions see Bah and Aning (2008).

15 See in this regard Mokhine (2008).

16 Details are contained in a short in-house report (nd) compiled by the ISS conference facilitators.

17 United Nations: Department of Peacekeeping Operations (2006) *Community Policing in Peace Operations.*

18 United Nations: Department of Peacekeeping Operations Police Division (2006) *Guidelines for Formed Police Units on Assignment with Peace Operations.*

19 ASF Generic Concept of the ASF AUPOL Formed Police Units. Draft document, Version 3, April 2009, as discussed at the ASF AUPOL FPU Workshop, Dakar, Senegal, 14–17 April 2009.

20 Personal communication, SAPS official involved in regional training, Pretoria, 11 November 2008.

21 See Background (Discussion) Paper on the African Standby Force tabled at the Police Dimension Staffing Training and Rostering Workshop which was held in Algiers, Algeria, from 18–20 October 2008 and coordinated by the Training for Peace programme at the Institute for Security Studies.

Chapter 12

Police–military cooperation in foreign interventions: Timor-Leste and the Solomon Islands

Andrew Goldsmith and Vandra Harris[1]

Introduction

Police–military cooperation within and between Western countries has tended to be limited in nature and, with some exceptions, rarely practised. In this regard, the picture is quite different from military-military cooperation in war-fighting and peacekeeping (Soeters and Manigart 2008). In the latter role, until recently, policing *per se* has tended to be performed by the military, largely for the reason that they have been 'present, capable and well-resourced' (Hills 2009: 43). The United Kingdom's experience in Northern Ireland during the 1970s, 1980s and 1990s is one exception (Brewer *et al.* 1988). For most of the past two centuries, the separate role of the military and police institutions in the life of nation-states has been a shibboleth of constitutional government (Critchley 1967: 51ff). It was, however, acknowledged that there would be situations that might now be characterized as domestic 'enforcement gaps' where the military, whose task was essentially to focus on external threats, might provide 'aid to the civil power', for example in the face of riots, major breakdowns of law and order, or threats to the integrity or indeed survival of governments. As its name suggests, the doctrine of military aid to the civil power (MACP) is intended to limit the involvement of military personnel in internal affairs to very restricted circumstances, basically to those when the civilian authorities (including the police) were unable to deal with civil unrest threatening public safety and the continuity of democratic government.

More cooperation, and indeed the blurring of functions, has been visible in a variety of other settings, both domestic and foreign. In the United States, since the end of the Cold War the cases of border protection and drug trafficking have provided occasions for police–military cooperation (see Dunn 1999; Kraska 2001). Such perceived (re-)militarization of policing in democratic countries has its critics (see Ericson and Haggerty 1997; Kraska 2001). Western nations, during the colonization period in particular, often practised a more 'integrated' approach to security in their foreign territories (Anderson and Killingray 1992). More recently, there has been disquiet about the blurring of these roles in many authoritarian states, as well as in so-called weak and fragile states (Fitz-Gerald 2003; Goldsmith 2003). In the fight against communism, and latterly in the 'wars' against illicit drugs and terrorism, the militarization of policing has been facilitated in many developing countries under the auspices of technical assistance provided to police by Western nations (Gill 2004; Goldsmith *et al.* 2007).

Since the 11 September 2001 terrorist attacks on the USA, the international demand for nation-building and greater cooperation in tackling humanitarian disasters and the threat posed by Islamist terrorism has provided its own impetus for greater, and more effective, police–military cooperation (Fitz-Gerald 2003; Greener 2009). The United Nations in this century has actively sought the greater involvement of police alongside military peacekeepers in a variety of unstable situations (United Nations 2000). Despite ceasefires and political settlements of one kind or another, the potential for further conflict and civil violence during such operations is often very real and obvious. In 2006, there were two reversions to significant levels of violence and civil disorder in the context of international operations involving Australian police officers: in the Solomon Islands in April, and in Timor-Leste from April to December (Operation Serene).[2] In such zones of 'anything but normal' policing (Goldsmith 2009), police may suddenly need to rely upon military forces, or may feel it necessary to employ military-style techniques and equipment themselves for reasons and under conditions that would rarely, if ever, arise in their home environments, and for which they would therefore generally not be well prepared for through training or experience. Similarly, in such situations the military may not have 'orders or nonlethal capability to interfere' in circumstances that are nonetheless critical to ongoing stability, as in the case of the looting in Baghdad following the arrival of the US army there in 2003 (Perito 2007: 2).

The involvement of both the police and military in such volatile settings in recent years has seen the emergence of a policy focus upon police–military interoperability,[3] reflecting some of the experiences in these engagements. Interoperability is widely viewed as being a key factor in the success of complex peace operations (Goldsmith and Harris 2009). Police–military interoperability is therefore a critical component for creating and sustaining a stable and secure environment in which the long-term goals of peace operations, including nation-building and the promotion of democracy, can flourish. In this regard, the Australian Federal Police's International Deployment Group (IDG) has worked extensively since 2006 to further formalize cooperation with the military, including the appointment of former military personnel to work in IDG on peace operations and doctrine. Such developments point to growing attempts within Australian policing and military circles to achieve greater police–military cooperation in overseas deployments.

In this chapter, we draw upon interview data with Australian police personnel involved in peace operations in Timor-Leste and the Solomon Islands. The data relate to a larger research project, Policing the Neighbourhood, which looks at Australian involvement in police capacity-building and peacekeeping activities in three countries (Timor-Leste, the Solomon Islands and Papua New Guinea). We will look at the kinds of experiences disclosed by our interviewees in relation to their dealings with the military forces, revealing quite varied experiences in the two countries. Many Australian police who participated in Operation Serene in Timor-Leste in 2006 also worked alongside military personnel from Malaysia, New Zealand and Portugal (Goldsmith and Harris 2009). In the Solomon Islands, during the early stages of the Regional Assistance Mission to the Solomon Islands (RAMSI) from 2003 until the civil disturbances in 2006, police personnel potentially worked in conjunction with military personnel from New Zealand and/ or a number of other Pacific Island countries (Dinnen 2008). In these interviews, the questions relating to this theme were open in nature, such that we have tried to group the discussion that follows in terms of the themes that emerged relatively naturally in our interviews.

Key conceptual issues

The enforcement gap challenge

Unstable societies quite commonly – and often quite quickly and dramatically – can present police and military peacekeepers with a dilemma known in the literature as the enforcement gap: 'Precisely when and where military enforcement shades into policing tends to be relative and controversial, especially in PSOs [peace support operations] where tactical actions may have strategic consequences' (Hills 2001: 94–5). Military force is often necessary in support of rule of law restoration, particularly since the label 'post-conflict society' conceals the reality that while violence may be reduced, the conflict in question may be far from resolved. At the same time, military force is necessarily limited in peacekeeping contexts by how far it can go and the forms it can take. Caution must be exercised not to prolong or distort the conflict, for as Rupert Smith has noted, the 'more the measures to impose order involve terrorizing the population the more the position of the opponent as their defender is enhanced' (2005: 380). While the mere presence of the military can establish a deterrent effect sufficient to allow civilian policing to occur, maintaining this level of stability is typically complex. There may be a return to disorder that requires the re-insertion of military might to re-establish order and protect the civilian authorities, including the police.

In short, police and military personnel frequently co-exist in challenging and unstable milieux, described by Paddy Ashdown as 'this *demi-monde* between hot war and a stable peace' (Ashdown 2007: 75). From an operational as well as a planning point of view, the difficulty lies not just in the *timing* of the shift from one modality to another (police to military, military to police), but also in the *respective contributions of each* that are required in particular settings. Furthermore, as both the police and military are typically challenged by their environments to adapt their methods and practices, the traditional role distinction is subjected to a greater challenge, raising the chances that it may be eroded, with the police becoming more militarized while the military move into law enforcement (Greener-Barcham 2007: 97). This can further complicate the negotiation of the shift between modalities, added to which, as Smith's comment above suggests, there are *legitimacy* as well as *effectiveness* outcomes at stake for both forces in how this balance works in practice.

Commenting on the Australian police and military response to the breakdown of law and order in Timor-Leste in 2006, one Australian police officer interviewed observed:

I think it's very difficult to go from a totally military environment and progress through to a police environment. I think the military find it more difficult than we do because they seem to operate in *either* green *or* blue and there seems to be this bit in the middle where it's green *and* blue where they do find it difficult to operate, which makes it extraordinarily difficult because 90 per cent of the time it is actually in that zone and in Timor, and particularly for six months, we were in that zone the whole way through except for the first month. (R96)

This officer's comment echoes Smith's reflection on the difficulty that both military and police can have in 'finding their feet' in these situations, noting that in many complex operations military 'practitioners have in the main been trained for a war they are not fighting' (Smith 2005: 380).

Mortlock (2005: 209) is one of few commentators to advocate that the military are well placed to perform the full spectrum of tasks required in peacekeeping, stating that the capabilities 'important to the various forms of peace intervention ... all stem from training for war'. A more common position on this training is that 'military forces were trained to fight and win wars, working together in large groups, using violence or the threat of violence to kill or deter opponents. Police forces, in contrast, were trained to patrol individually or in pairs, to work closely with the population to deter crime and detain criminals' (Marten 2007: 242). Both of these approaches are important in realizing the transition from conflict to peace, but each is particularly well suited to a specific point in the transition. With this in mind, we include in our data analysis a consideration of which tasks police and military respectively appear better suited for in peace operation contexts, as well as the difficulties of establishing these roles and coordinating the different components responsible for them in the field.

A note on the nature of cooperation

In analyzing the data for this chapter, we needed to be clear about the scope and meaning of cooperation. At first glance this seems straightforward: military and police are pursuing the same goals by different (or even not so different) means, in what might be termed *integrative cooperation*. Stopping the looting in a post-conflict urban environment might be one example of such a shared objective. There is another form of cooperation, namely cooperation between the police and military in order to achieve their distinct, respective goals – what could be called *complementary cooperation*. Ideally such cooperation should not only retain the distinctiveness of each party's role, but also be *enabling* of the other's achievement of its role performance.

Conceivably, of course, this might not occur in practice, in which case such formal cooperation in effect might be *disabling*.

Each kind of cooperation potentially raises questions of a legal and ethical, as well as a practical, nature. For instance, as well as potentially breaching legal and ethical constraints, international police effectiveness and legitimacy over the medium to long term in foreign deployments are likely to be undercut by an overt commitment to war-fighting and major disorder suppression, and the actual or potential use of lethal force that is commonly associated with such functions. Preserving police professionalism within peacekeeping implies imposing limits on cooperation to the extent that any advancement of military objectives would be at the expense of police objectives. Our data show that during the less stable points in peace operation trajectories, the police are more likely to play a subsidiary, integrative role with the military, whereas during times of greater stability a more complementary form of cooperation emerges.

Exploring the data

While Australian police are relative newcomers to serving in overseas locations, this is far less true of military personnel. For the latter, operating outside the home country is common practice, whether it be for training, peacekeeping or combat purposes. Inevitably, this has meant that military forces come to peace operations with certain capacities that are not shared by police that can be of critical importance to restoring basic order and ensuring that the police as well as the military can perform their tasks. At the same time, the police and military are trained for somewhat different purposes, so it is to be expected that they will encounter a range of differences when they collaborate.

In this section, we look at a range of operational areas in which differences of approach emerged from our data analysis, including planning, the use of force, civil-military affairs, and joint patrols. We also discuss areas in which capacities and resources differed, including logistical capacities and intelligence. The section concludes with a reflection on the preparation for cooperation on these deployments.

Joint patrols

Joint military/police patrols are quite common in peace and stability operations, especially in the early stages of an intervention. Unless they had served previously in other international peacekeeping type missions, Australian police personnel were unlikely to have experienced working closely with or alongside military personnel in this kind of integrative cooperation.[4] As might be predicted, this lack of familiarity with each other's modes of operation under challenging conditions led to some interesting observations about those differences among the police we interviewed.

In Timor-Leste during the 2006 intervention and in the Solomon Islands during the first phase of the RAMSI intervention in 2003, the confirmed presence of heavily armed militias and renegade members of the local security forces resulted in the operation of joint military/police patrols until the areas in question had been calmed, key rogue elements were detained, and weapons were seized. In both cases, the role of the military was clearly in part a deterrent one, through their visible, heavily armed presence on the streets and in the conduct of specific operations to seize arms and arrest particular persons believed to be coordinating or provoking disorder. R61 explained the benefits of the joint patrols, saying that 'in the case of RAMSI in particular, going in there with the military was a significant bonus. It gave us force protection. It gave us some sort of military authority. It gave us the ability to move swiftly and quickly to areas. It was well thought out.'

Planning and approach

One theme arising in several of our interviews was the perception that the military were very formal in planning and executing street patrols, which was clearly a surprise to many of the police interviewed. Some officers articulated the differences between police and military approaches as an issue of flexibility and responsiveness, with eight officers viewing the military as 'rigid' in their approach compared to a 'flexible' police force. One officer who served in Timor-Leste contrasted the police and military approaches during the period when the army was in charge of Operation Serene, noting that the police were free to vary their patrols spontaneously while the approach of the army was 'We're going to go down this road, then we'll turn down this road, then we'll turn down that road, and we'll stop there for five minutes and then we'll have a break. Then we'll go down that road' (R10).

Differences regarding the best tactics or intervention styles in particular situations also drew comment. As R61 explained, 'In a policing environment we have to be quite reactive. A spontaneous situation happens so we need to deploy. We manage risk appropriately for police, but in terms of military they wanted to plan things out for three days prior, rehearse it for another two, call in a billion dollars worth of resources and then go.' These differences clearly reflect the distinct contexts for which police and military are trained, including the level and type of danger.

Divergent approaches were also revealed in relation to arresting people, where the 'Military tend to be straight down the line following procedures rigidly, whereas I think police tend to adapt and flow and change their – their tack as the situation changes' (R51). This highlights a fundamental difference between the two organizations: where discretion is key to the policing role, it is not part of the sanctioned toolkit of military personnel. This is a clear example of integrative cooperation, where methods were not necessarily complementary. Interestingly, while Australian police officers often expressed annoyance at the different approaches of police from other nations on these missions (see Goldsmith and Harris 2009), they were less likely to be irritated by the divergent practices of the Australian military. Although they were at times frustrated, the Australian police officers were more likely to speak positively about the professionalism and effectiveness of the Australian Defence Force (ADF), with comments such as 'I actually enjoyed the experience because you know, it just really – really highlighted the differences here between the way we operate and the way they operated' (R51).

Significant differences of approach to conducting searches largely reflected the *criminal-evidential* focus of the police, compared to the *war-fighting/tactical victory* orientation of the military. This was clearly shown in the following account from Timor-Leste:

> There was no getting warrants, we *were* the warrants. So if we so decided there was enough evidence on that house we would enter and it was basically suspect. If you suspected there was a weapon in there, we had the power of entry. [It was] very different in the beginning and it was literally, the military would stand in the middle of the door and kick the door in and go in (inaudible) helicopters and everything at our beck and call if we decided. The military commander would come '[Respondent's name], this bloke said this is in there' and we said okay in the first week we could go straight in on one person and the military kicked 15 doors in somewhere and the government came down on them. (R84)

In these complex and volatile environments, such differences of tactical approach can have a significant impact. R84 explained that while watching the military tactics just described, 'We thought oh my God we are going to get shot here'. In this instance, ongoing collaboration led to the police collaborating with the military on strategies for entering premises in a policing context: 'We said why not just try the door handle and we said if you try the door handle you got a little bit of surprise on your side too because they don't hear you coming'. According to R84, this collaboration was well received all around ('The Major loved it'), and this meant that the Australian police and military were better able to complement each other's skills and resources.

Use of force

Related to this, a key distinction between the police and military that can arise in patrol contexts is their respective doctrines and practices related to the use of force. While 'Military doctrine has forces moving on a target by fire and maneuver with a view toward destroying the target', on the other hand the police 'have to exercise the studied restraint' that goes with gathering evidence and arresting citizens who must be assumed innocent until proven guilty (Dunlap 2001: 35). The military are thus accustomed to dealing forcefully and quickly with 'enemies', while Western police are more used to notions of graduated force and, in particular, to using lethal force as a last resort. Indeed this difference is the logical and pragmatic reason for the deployment of *both* the military and police on these operations: different levels of force are necessary for both legitimacy and effectiveness at different points of the stabilization and peace-building process.

The impact of differences in the police and military approach to the use of force was evident in the field. One police officer who served in Timor-Leste noted:

The military had, obviously, different rules of engagement – they were straight up on lethal force really, whereas we were obviously scale responsive, you know physical presence, verbal, open hand, baton strike, weapons, and then obviously weapon force, whereas with the military it was straight to weapon force in reality because that's what they were there for and that's what their training covers. (R21)

This officer described developing a clear understanding of roles and of role demarcation, such that 'A consideration when I was calling the military to assist me in whatever duties I needed them to assist me in, was that those guys were trained to do a different role than policing' (R21).

The greater level of force available to military units and to gendarmeries such as the Portuguese Guarda Nacional Republicana (GNR) (deployed in Timor-Leste) was in fact greatly appreciated by some Australian police. This stood in marked contrast to the use of significant levels of force by other national police forces, which was viewed as transgressing notions of 'good policing' and positive role modelling and capacity building for local police forces (Goldsmith and Harris 2009). The Australian police in Timor recounted incidents where the greater range of force options available to militaries and gendarmeries meant they had better control over volatile situations – and that the population knew which nations would and would not use force and acted accordingly.

Logistical capacities

Police operating outside their 'normal' (i.e. home) jurisdictions are presented with some fundamental challenges of a logistical nature. In many foreign interventions, the capacity of police personnel to move around the territory of the mission has depended upon the availability of military transport. This has been the case in both the Solomon Islands and Timor-Leste. A key example of this was the Australian navy's provision of boats for use in policing operations throughout the nearly 1,000 islands that make up the Solomon Islands. R29 describes the collaboration (or complementary cooperation) between the Royal Solomon Islands Police (RSIP), the ADF, and the Australian police:

> the RSIP drove the boats and the – the [Australian] navy effectively or defence force provided the boats and funded them and their fuel and resources, the [Australian] police had to direct them. So it was a three way, sometimes very challenging role to – well all agreed on how the resources would be used, so we had to work very closely. (R29)

Criminal investigation provides another clear example of the logistical challenges faced by the police. In Timor-Leste in 2006, Australian police were involved in the exhumation of bodies of those killed in the conflict, and conducting the post-mortems. The resources available in the country were meagre, as might be anticipated in a country with the lowest human development ranking in the Asia-Pacific (UNDP 2007: 229–232). One Australian police officer described intensive cooperation with the Australian army to perform this task:

> with the exhumations we used one of their trucks, so they provided a driver and support staff for that vehicle and also had, we used their personnel and x-ray equipment for x-raying bodies in the mortuary because the mortuary only had access to the hospital equipment which was being used on other patients, so we couldn't use it for any extended period of time. We had contact with the army in relation to cataloguing all the confiscated firearms which was a forensics responsibility. We had our ballistic experts working with them in the mortuary and also worked with the army in cataloguing all (inaudible). (R108)

Under such difficult conditions, the army had the capacity to meet several logistical deficits encountered by police, providing another example of complementary cooperation.

Intelligence

Adequate country briefings and the provision of local intelligence can often be crucial to police operations within complex peace operations. R70 reflected that the Australian police who 'had been there previously were able to give us a pretty good run down on how things worked', but several officers interviewed expressed the view that intelligence and country briefings provided by the military prior to deployment and on arrival in the country were superior to those provided by their police commanders or external consultants due to the extensive local knowledge gathered by the military. Obviously, serving police officers with prior experience in a particular setting can complement such briefings provided by military personnel, by focusing on appropriate police responses.

Intelligence capacity on the part of the military reflects their relative proficiency in operating outside home borders, which can include access to superior technologies and staff capacities in the field of intelligence collection. In Timor-Leste, for example, the ADF has used Uninhabited Aerial Vehicles (UAVs) as part of its surveillance and intelligence collection apparatus (Hutcheson 2007). One Australian

231

police investigator serving in Timor-Leste commented that 'we relied heavily on the Army because they [had] done a lot of groundwork in establishing who was who in areas that they were overseeing' (R79). Collaboration like this streamlines stability operations and enables police to move more quickly into the practice of community policing.

Both Timor-Leste and the Solomon Islands experienced fluctuating security conditions during the period of these deployments. Intelligence-sharing was considered critical once police were deployed in-country. One of the challenges that police and military faced in Timor-Leste early on in the 2006 intervention was the presence of gangs on the streets, engaged in looting and various forms of destruction. Gaining intelligence on their ring-leaders became critical for any degree of effectiveness in containing and defusing outbreaks of disorder. A few police interviewed thought that military cooperation in this regard was not as good as it should have been. One of those officers stated:

> The second time around, we would go to the local chiefs and, perhaps because it's different in the city to rural [areas], the chiefs had no power. The power was actually with the gang leaders. The army, from my understanding, had identified who all the gang leaders [were] but kept that intelligence to themselves and didn't pass it to the AFP [Australian Federal Police], so we were struggling a bit. (R9)

While speculating that this was due to military concerns about security clearances, several police stated that it was critical to their own safety that these concerns be fully addressed at the appropriate level in order that the information could be communicated to the police on the ground. Information silos and turf protection between different agencies are hardly unique to peace operations, but in these contexts it can be more than just un-collegial: it could pose significant risks to operational effectiveness or even result in loss of life.

Local relationships

Our data suggest that operational differences can impact not just on these police/military forces and their relationships with each other, but, in some ways more significantly, also upon local perceptions. The Australian army has had considerable experience in civil–military relations, including the building of links between army personnel and local populations in foreign settings. Its involvement in Somalia in 1992–93 is one early example (Patman 1997), while East Timor ('Timor-Leste' since 2002) is another example (Smith 2003). Skills in communicating with local populations are not exclusive to military personnel – indeed this is a key function of policing in Australia – however, the Australian police saw it as highly beneficial to be able to utilize relationships already established by the military, to build this rapport rapidly in international situations.

Once more, the Australian police reported a range of experiences in this regard, some of which were contradictory. R84 (Timor-Leste) discussed problems for the police in terms of approaching members of the public, saying that 'People really didn't come near us because they were still pretty frightened of the military, and after about a week they started seeing the blue shirts and they started coming about a bit more, the kids started coming closer'.[5] In contrast to this, and demonstrating once again the breadth of experiences on such missions, several interviewees commented positively on the community relations skills shown by the Australian military in both Timor-Leste and the Solomon Islands and that these relationships were extended to the Australian police. As one officer who served in the Solomon Islands noted, 'I'm not in the defence force, nor sort of want to be, but I admire what they do and that they fit in to communities and help them out' (R99).

The military's development of relevant language skills within their numbers was also greatly appreciated by the Australian police, who recognized that without such skills they were at a significant disadvantage in terms of building relationships, gathering intelligence, and performing normal policing functions. Aptitude for local languages is an area where, historically, the military have been better prepared for such missions than Australian policing contingents (Kilcullen 2009).

Preparation for cooperation

While the police were positive about the experience of working with the Australian military, some interviewees nonetheless suggested that the police could be better trained in the ways in which the military operate in these settings. While much of the international deployment was novel for the police, this close collaboration was new for both police and military, and thus such training could be relevant to both forces. This is powerfully conveyed in an interview with an officer who served in Timor-Leste:

Understanding issues with education, understanding [the military] role and that transitional role, and their supporting role, wasn't covered particularly well [in training]. I think police in terms of selection having a bit of an understanding of the way the military system works, if people had that … it would be very useful in terms of how the military run and how they patrol, and being aware of discipline in terms of night and noise because we would be patrolling at night time and they were patrolling with night vision gear quite quietly to apprehend people and the police would have no concept of discipline with light and they would turn a torch on, or they'd start talking and that's – I guess that there's an assumed knowledge from the police that the army would know about what they were doing and that went both ways, and that was difficult. That wasn't always beneficial to understanding and appreciating your particular roles we had because of the … [shortcomings – AG] of communication. But the Defence Force did an exceptional job. (R23)

An interesting discovery arising from our data was the fact that a considerable number of the police interviewed in relation to these two country engagements had had previous experience as full-time or reserve members of the military. This group felt that they were better equipped than other police to work with the military and in this environment generally. They also shared a view that they were already familiar with much of what was taught in the police pre-deployment training. R81 reflected that military service was one of a range of experiences that, together with pre-deployment training, helped to prepare police officers to be generally adaptive enough to operate effectively in environments in which police–military interactions are required. He said that 'Everybody's got a unique experience base, but there's generally a reduction in people having had military experience, school cadets or scouting and that, so there were a lot of people who had never been in the field or had communal living … [or] that really haven't been in the outdoors'. Such experiences, he felt, not only gave police experience in the intense proximity and communal living that characterize international deployments such as these, but they also benefited police officers through 'just having those social interaction skills and dealing with your own – own self and discomfort, plus the shock of cultural clash and all those other things' (R81).

One police officer with previous military experience serving in RAMSI pointed out the relevance of prior military service for some of the more extreme risks such settings can provide. R87 stated that 'At some stage in the [future], I can see our people getting taken, captured, and if they don't have that resistance to interrogation training, or that resistance to capture training or at least some basic understanding of it, I think that's an area where they should possibly do a little bit more'. While no Australian police officer has yet been captured on an international mission and thus exposed to hostile interrogation, one police officer was shot and killed in the Solomon Islands during a night patrol in 2004. Police officers from other nations have been captured on international missions to countries including Colombia, Mexico and Iraq, and have been subjected to harsh interrogation, prolonged detention, torture and execution. In an unstable world, there is certainly some basis for police planners to anticipate this possibility in contemplating future overseas police deployments.

Conclusion

Despite its increased frequency in the past decade or so, the issue of police–military relations within peacekeeping and state-building exercises has received relatively little sustained scholarly or policy attention. The need for doctrine in this area is well-recognized and is particularly necessary if *complementary cooperation* remains the principal orientation within these exercises. The volatile, changeable nature of the security deficit in many post-conflict situations, as noted previously, can make the preservation of a clear differentiation of roles difficult at best. Our study offers an operations-level window into this little understood but highly important aspect of international peace operations. Despite the fact that this study looked mainly at relations between *Australian* police and military personnel (thus not addressing the likely more vexed relationships across national as well as service lines), it enabled the identification of some differences in perspective about how these delicate security situations should be approached. It also revealed just how difficult effective cooperation can be even without international differences, though overall the Australian police personnel interviewed were generally positive about their collaboration with the military.

Given the short history of such cooperation in peace operations and nation-building, it should come as no surprise that our data reveal that some areas remain for improved training, communication and coordination. Intelligence needs to be better shared, both for the purpose of pre-deployment training and briefings, and during the conduct of operations. The military need to accept that in such zones they will often possess superior intelligence, but that such an advantage needs to be shared with their operational partners for overall effectiveness and safety. While the ADF was very effective in enhancing the safety of Australian police on these missions, several of the police felt that they would have been both safer and more effective had they had greater access to the intelligence that the ADF had gathered. Where this information and the ADF's links with communities were shared, it was viewed positively by the police. Another area in which better reciprocal understanding would benefit future operations is respective approaches to patrolling during periods of ongoing instability. Police officers need to appreciate the reasons for the military's way of operating, and the two forces need to be clear with each other about how and when force will be applied.

Not all forms of cooperation should be *integrative* in the sense suggested earlier, and differences in the application of force should remain an important marker of the respective roles in these operations. Indeed failures to ensure that such a difference is achieved routinely in practice are likely to prejudice the operations themselves. A further advancement of doctrine in this area would assist this kind of cross-service understanding. The impact that each approach has on relations with the local populations is an area in which further research could prove helpful in terms of minimizing the harms to those relationships that can arise from such engagements. Our data suggest quite strongly that each service can potentially learn a lot from the other. Some military personnel were clearly held in high regard by Australian police officers in terms of their civil–military relations. Equally, there were instances (such as searches) in which a more 'softly softly' approach was favoured by the police over the more direct, robust military approach. Such *complementary* forms of cooperation are likely to temper any negative consequences from differences in approach or actions. They may also signal to the local communities, despite often quite negative and contrary previous experiences by those communities, that it is possible to establish and maintain demarcations between the police and military even under situations of volatility and stress. Given the histories of many of the settings in which peace operations are taking place, such a lesson cannot be valued highly enough.

Notes

1 This chapter forms part of work done under an ARC Linkage grant (LP0560643), *Policing the Neighbourhood*. The authors gratefully acknowledge the support of the ARC and the Industry Partner, the Australian Federal Police International Deployment Group, as well as helpful comments on the paper from Beth Greener and Frédéric Lemieux. Author contact: andrew_goldsmith@uow.edu.au

2 Operation Serene is the name of the Australian police mission deployed in response to this crisis, while the concurrent military mission led by the Australian Defence Force was code-named Operation Astute.

3 While the term is used more narrowly in some areas of security studies, Rubinstein *et al.* (2008: 540) define interoperability in the context of integrated UN missions as 'The ability to work with others in the mission and to work with local populations [which] is essential to the mission working smoothly'. In this article, we apply this broader understanding of interoperability, specifically using the term to describe the degree to which police and military work together rather than at cross purposes (see also Goldsmith and Harris 2009).

4 Seventeen of the 122 officers in this research had previous international policing experience (in Jordan, Nauru, Cyprus, Mozambique and/or Haiti), followed by police service in Timor-Leste and/or the Solomon Islands.

5 B.K. Greener notes that the opposite effect has been reported to her, namely that green shirts are more comforting than blue shirts in the Solomon Islands, which is perhaps unsurprising given the problems that the community there experienced with the Royal Solomon Islands Police prior to the commencement of RAMSI (pers. comm. 2009).

Part IV

Accountability and effectiveness in police cooperation

Chapter 13

International police organizations: the missing link to effective cooperation

Nadia Gerspacher[1] and Véronique Pujas

Introduction

The demand for international cooperation between national police services has become very clear in an environment ridden with anxiety about security challenges such as terrorism, arms and drug-trafficking, cyber crime or corruption. The globalization process that opened up so many channels for transnational criminal activity and the recent terrorist attacks in the US, Spain and Bali, to name the most recent, exacerbated the perception that the threats are numerous, varied and destabilizing. The various treaties adopted to fight transnational crime (TC) stipulate the adaptation of law enforcement apparatus as the best way to increase the risk of conducting criminal activity. The demand for enhanced cooperation, information exchange on the personal data files of suspected individuals and the build-up of new surveillance technology is continually reaffirmed, and states increasingly see the international collaboration of police services as the answer to the internationalization of crime. However, national law enforcement authorities are traditionally reluctant to share information and delegate the analysis of intelligence outside the state.

As systematic cooperation becomes desirable, international police cooperation organizations (IPCOs) are being formed to facilitate such cooperation between the national services concerned by these security issues. Interpol was established at the beginning of the last century to facilitate the collaboration of national police services all around the world. Europol began full operations in 1998 to ensure the security of European member states. However, the widely differing resources and often incompatible legal and procedural systems among the membership translate into a less than continuous and systematic cooperation. Both IOs were given mandates that were strictly limited to the facilitation of information exchange, a sort of clearing house function through which information flows, is collected, analysed, and then diffused back to states as finished intelligence.

In light of the demand for cooperation to address the threat posed by transnational crime, what prevents states and their national law enforcement agencies from benefiting from the IPCO they deem desirable? We provide an explanation that identifies a missing link. This chapter suggests a need for managing institutional pluralism, for the enhancement of coordination, for fostering communication and ensuring that information is shared. We suggest that IPCOs have introduced capacity building initiatives to be able to fulfil their missions and establish legitimacy in the expanding security market, even though capacity building is not mandated.

Guided by *rational choice analysis*, we illustrate the increasing needs of cooperation emerging from how national leading actors perceive their ability to fight transborder crime when so many reasons suggest defection is often the most predictable issue. The *neo-functionalist view* is useful to explain why member states prefer the option of creating international organizations to enhance cooperation. But we show that paradoxically, and contrary to neo-functionalist predictions that the mere recognition of the problem will produce cooperation, states are often unable to participate in and benefit from the output of IPCOs. Because we find that while states define preferences around cooperation mechanisms but are unprepared to use them, we show how Interpol's and Europol's efforts to build capacity in defecting states give them a supranational dimension. We exploit the concept of 'informal supranational entrepreneurship' (Moravcsik 1999) to demonstrate further how these IOs have assumed a capacity building role to socialize political leaders and national services whose participation they need to be legitimate and to ensure their role (Haas *et al.* 1993).

Context and approaches to explain the development of cooperation supranational agencies to fight transnational crime

The recognition that international cooperation may be the answer to international crime was first sparked by the theft of the imperial jewels in Vienna, Austria, in 1913. After several weeks, the jewels were located in another European capital. When the Austrian government requested restitution of the jewels and the extradition of the perpetrator, no one knew how to proceed as no procedure to do so existed. Dr Schroder and Prince Albert of Monaco called the first International Criminal Congress in 1914, organized as a meeting of police chiefs. This led to the creation of Interpol.

Even if the perception of transborder crime is not new, the rising attention paid to it in the last decade is the result of different contextual trends. Since the 2001 G8 summit, many forms of crime have been recognized as 'international crimes'. Perceiving crime as an international phenomenon has led to the belief that it can only be countered multilaterally. The level of sophistication of transnational criminal organizations has far reaching consequences as the shift from maritime piracy to software piracy exemplifies (Williams 1995). According to the UN,[2] TC includes any 'offense(s) whose inception, proportion and/or direct or indirect effects involved more than one country' (United Nations 1995). For example, a reported 40 per cent (total seizures of 9.5 tons) increase in ATS (Amphetamine-type stimulants) seizures in seven years, or a 68 per cent in Ecstasy, leads to the assumption that drug trafficking is on the rise (UNFDC 2004).

Based on the assumption that there is a growing and urgent demand for security and inherent pressure on member states to commit sufficient resources and adopt harmonized legal frameworks, we look at the two principal mechanisms that states have formed to coordinate the multilateral fight against TC – Interpol and Europol. The focus of this chapter is the give-and-take relationship between the state and the IPCO. Based on evidence from interviews of Interpol and Europol officials, we highlight the importance of the human factor and demonstrate how capacity building has become a role that both IOs have been forced to assume.

Rational choice analysis is useful to explain the development of these IOs to facilitate cooperation as states address the threat posed by TC, specifically to overcome the permissive environments that arise from non-cooperation. States and sub-national actors will support the idea of cooperation if they believe they will derive benefits (i.e. more apprehension of perpetrators, enhanced prosecutorial performance). The desirability of these benefits of cooperation remains linked to the positive outcome of costs-benefits analysis. Some state actors articulate the need for a multilateral response, suggesting a 'demand driven' explanation of the creation of these police cooperation organizations. When policy makers realize that a unilateral response is inappropriate and creates safe havens for criminals, and when competence, expertise and/or resources are insufficient, states are more likely to support cooperation.

The costs of such cooperation should not be underestimated. Cooperation comes at a high cost due to the inevitable loss of autonomy (Keohane 1983). The fight against crime is managed by justice and police departments strictly defined around the principle of national sovereignty. As a consequence, states can lose their initiator role and some autonomy once they delegate to an international organization (IO), even if they attempt to retain control by limiting the mandates. For instance, an IO may eventually initiate specific policies and the mediation and mobilization of domestic supports and resources and develop a sense of their own self-interest and identity. Moreover, if just one state defects, the rest lose the benefit of cooperation in a specific case. The risks of this happening are very high due to the interdependence created by the need for cooperation (Keohane 1984). As Nash shows, a bargaining solution among actors will most probably be defined outside cooperation.

While the demand-driven explanation for the formation of IPCOs leads us to expect that these international actors will be the logical response to transnational crime, their mere existence does not support expectations of effective organizations. Deception can be very profitable. The implementation as well as the enforcement process involved in cooperation are costly in terms of the aggregation of domestic interests, for instance. Very often, implementation and enforcement are the missing links in cooperation. Moreover, to keep information secret fits better with a national police culture tradition rather than to share it. Non-cooperative behaviour consequently leads to an IO that will have difficulty gaining the political and symbolic legitimacy necessary to significantly contribute to the fight against TC. Our question is how can we explain the large gap between what states define as their interest (e.g. the high demand for cooperation) and their helplessness in reaching a functional outcome (e.g. the systematic sharing of information, harmonizing national policy)?

The neo-functionalist view is helpful in explaining why these IPCOs were formed by states, partly addressing our question by identifying the incentives for cooperation. National political officials who decided to pursue international cooperation as an approach to the fight against transnational crime are at the heart of these IOs. The distributive outcomes expected from these organizations are considered to be more valuable than the isolation of national services in the fight against TC, even in situations of asymmetrical interdependence. As a consequence, states will formulate a limited mandate, scopes and resources, expecting that this will facilitate the mobilization of interstate resources and promote the benefits of cooperation to national competent authorities. Thus, the IO is considered to be a unique way of overcoming interstate bargaining problems and the most able to represent the 'general interest', which is fighting TC as effectively as possible.

Any effectiveness in facilitating cooperation is constrained by the participation of the national services. So without the active participation of members' national services, the IO cannot fulfil the mandate with which it was entrusted. States' efforts to minimize the costs of cooperation illustrate the reasons for guarded cooperation. And the reservations of national police authorities about cooperating via the Europol or Interpol frameworks are due to 1) fear that information shared will fall into the wrong hands; 2) nationalist ideals; and/or 3) the reality that national authorities are not adequately informed/trained/educated on how information can be sent and received and generally on how to benefit from the output of the IO. Therefore the interests as defined by states do not translate into the ability to participate in an international system of cooperation (Gerspacher 2002) as the consequences of such shortcomings illustrate. So we would argue that the gap between demand and its fulfilment lies in the capacity building efforts that IOs have initiated due to a sort of incapacity of participants to benefit from the added-value of the IO. The neo-functionalist approach does not explain why IOs are so slow to institutionalize, to gain legitimacy in front of their formal participants, who remain sceptical and defiant toward what they consider to be 'black holes'.

The IO persuades member states to reform their legal and operational approaches to fighting crime with harmonization and compatibility as the overarching goals. From this point of view, the IO is 'supply driven' (Finnemore 1996). Interpol and Europol set the tone for cooperation by establishing cooperative mechanisms that incite states to cooperate in specific ways (the format for reporting info, encryption, following specific methods for wire tapping, etc.). By introducing capacity building initiatives, the IO makes an imprint on participation rates and methods. And by thriving to establish itself as legitimate, the IO also establishes standards for operation and rules for conduct and operation, promotes norms for stimulating cooperation and even brings attention to new forms of TC.

We suggest that a type of 'informal supranational entrepreneurship' takes place to explain that IOs have to develop informal capacities, mobilizing and influencing the domestic actors they negotiate with in order to go beyond their narrow mandate. Such a phenomenon is largely confirmed in the case of Europol especially when compared with Interpol. We show that the development of a political and operational ability reinforces the influence of IOs as shown by the stronger influence of a younger Europol compared with a long-established Interpol.

Cost-benefit analysis to explain the demand for cooperation by specific state actors

The argument that fighting TC is rent-seeking for political actors is supported by three observations. An increasing focus on TC suggests that it cannot be controlled at the state level. A climate of insecurity means that unexpected events will damage the interests of a limited number of actors. The fear generated by the belief that a threat is imminent will feed conservative political attitudes aimed at securing the environment, such as focusing on the identity of the enemy (often different and exterior to the community) but also accumulating weaponry and other resources, controls on communications and self-protection techniques (Müller 2003). The second observation is that the fear of TC can help to promote a globalized governance that is embodied by specific IOs (Pujas 2004). Indeed, the perception of the phenomenon, escaping the control of national institutions, gives the opportunity for national governments to escape accountability for the development of criminality. The IO then can be made the scapegoat in case of failure in the fight against TC (Pujas 2003). Finally, the consequent idea is that the perception of crime as international enhances the idea that the police and judicial cooperation are the most appropriate tools to fight it. The outcome is a strong interest in forming cooperative institutions that are intended to play a strong supportive role in the development of national, regional and international security policies.

Reaching a common agreement on the creation of Interpol and Europol was not a spontaneous outcome. They resulted from the voluntary associations of states with common goals facing common struggles and are structured as semi-autonomous bodies. Interpol was initially more an association of national police services than of states but quickly required an oversight by national governments, at least to pay the membership dues (Lebrun 1997: 103). Since its creation in 1914, Interpol has embodied a forum where confrontations and diplomatic struggles between the most powerful member states played out. The strategic choice of the leader of the Secretary General as well as the members of the Executive Committee, the working language, the agenda-setting of specific security matters like terrorism result from subtle struggles between self-interested actors.

Without covering the wide range of tensions since the creation of Interpol, one main point of tension has been the Franco-American competition for the leadership of the organisation (Lebrun 1997). For example, in 1974–75, the United States used the fight against drug trafficking to settle liaison officers (under the authority of Interpol) in South America and Southeast Asia where they were losing influence. At the beginning of the 1980s, they decided to involve themselves more actively within the organization in order to increasingly influence a body that was traditionally under the direction of French officials. In this they will succeed by invoking the issue of international terrorism using their traditional allies for such scope.

The situation with Europol is not any easier because its scope largely infringes on the basic functions of the state, which is to provide safety, security and stability within territories. However, the challenges raised by the creation of Europol are of a different nature. Indeed, they reflect the tension between two options for European integration within a specific area of influence: a relative homogeneity of its membership, in terms of human and capital resources, and adhesion to a common West European democratic tradition. The idea of Europol was introduced during negotiations for the Maastricht Treaty at the beginning of the 1990s and was modelled around the idea of a European FBI. Some member states had become rather dissatisfied with the extended but very fragmented and disorganized system of intergovernmental cooperation which had emerged since 1986 (Mitsilegas *et al.* 2003: 31). This was particularly true of the German authorities, who felt highly exposed to the immigration problems created by the new permeability of borders in Central and Eastern Europe. They wanted to improve cooperation at the European level to fight evermore powerful illicit networks.

As a consequence the German government played a key role in improving the inadequacies within the existing structures of cooperation (the European Drug Unit, extradition treaties) and bringing the mounting external challenges to member states' internal security onto the agenda of the 1990/91 Intergovernmental Conference which set the stage for the future Maastricht Treaty. One group composed of Germany, Belgium, Italy, the Netherlands and Spain advocated a wide range of justice and home affairs matters as part of the Third Pillar of the Maastricht Treaty when the United Kingdom and Denmark defended the idea of a limited range of JHA areas to be brought into the treaty. One of the outcomes of this bargaining process was the adoption of measures in the area of border control in criminal matters and police cooperation for the purposes of combating TC and terrorism, as well as the final establishment of Europol as the desirable institutional design to reach these goals. However, as a result of many compromises, a rather passive role that was largely limited to information exchange was assigned to Europol in the first half of the 1990s.

The intended role of these IOs, as mandated via their conventions, is to provide technical assistance to states to upgrade their ability to deal with TC at the operational level (i.e. national police departments). So the challenge for a member state is the necessity of police cooperation initiatives to rely on existing police structures at the national levels of various participating agencies. However, within national enforcement bureaucracies not all services benefit from the 'cooperation trend'. In other words, some traditional domestic services can show a strong resistance to the globalization of border control. Indeed, the changes introduced by the internationalization of the fight against TC stimulated struggles within national enforcement institutions. For example, with regard to the integration of security matters within the JHA pillar, 'those most favourable to (it) are inside ministerial cabinets or in the formal co-ordination structures between major services, their role gives them power over the services which they co-ordinate, and they have their own correspondents, interests and political outlook' (Bigo 1994: 172).

As a result domestic agencies that are disconnected from national elites or not involved in intra-agency collaboration and absent from the European wide collaboration (such as the French Gendarmerie, Guardia Civil, British HM Customs and Excise, and HM Immigration Service) tend to be opposed to common EU internal security policies (Bigo 1994). Nevertheless, the redistribution of resources from the agencies that have become obsolete because of the erosion of borders to new agencies that 'fit' with the new security environment in Europe created a lot of conflict. Thus, cooperation becomes essential to the survival of domestic services that otherwise run the risk of being removed from the law enforcement landscape.

Finally, cooperation at the EU level offered administrative elites a new level of independence from political interference from party leaders and parliamentary scrutiny. As a consequence, we have shown that while Nash's assumption remains true so many national actors can also have a self-interest in involving themselves within international cooperation, which gives them the opportunity to develop new strategies of empowerment within their area of influence.

However, the complexity and multiplicity of interests of domestic agencies that are automatically pulled within the cooperation spill-over effect (that are neither functional nor political but operational) lead to an unintended effect on domestic services. The following section will concentrate on the impact of the work of Interpol and Europol on domestic actors, showing that paradoxically and despite the fact that national preferences are oriented towards 'cooperative ways of working', national services will often demonstrate a limited capacity to benefit from the added-value of information exchange provided by these IOs.

The ability of national police to cooperate: Germany and France

The ability of a state to cooperate largely depends on the adequacy of the information flow of police information. In order to participate in a system of cooperation, field officers from national law enforcement agencies must have the ability to forward the information they gather during investigations to a central collection point (besides a willingness due to mistrust and nationalist mindsets). They also have to have channels to send this information to their national liaison/national bureau to be analysed by the IO. Alternatively, a national central agency must have the procedures/ability to diffuse rapidly produced intelligence (trend reports, and the like) back to their localities however they are organized. As is the case in most law enforcement efforts, time is of the essence as are accuracy and clarity.

Based on that mechanism of cooperation, we can identify three groups of states. Those that defect – who do not send or receive information systematically. Those that defect *vis-à-vis* their commitment – who do not send but request information. Those that cooperate – who both send and receive information. Such asymmetry in the participation rate is explained by varying levels of capacity to cooperate. Adequate capacity is the result of a legal and practical compliance with the agreement for most states. A few have national systems that lend themselves well to participating in a cooperative framework. But most states have nationalistic and culturally distinct bases for procedures in law enforcement which are not outward looking. After all, legal and judicial systems are the sediment of national legal history with little regard as to how others in the international system were structured. The capacity to participate depends on the ability of domestic services to integrate rules that are compatible with the information exchange system maintained by the IO. The level of integration depends on how adequately organized and informed a state and its sub-national actors are, which will determine the level of participation that a state will engage in or its level of capacity to cooperate. Europol and Interpol developed very similar information exchange systems, which facilitates a comparison in terms of the integration of national services.

The integration of national law enforcement infrastructures requires 1) a shift from a nationalistic, secretive police mindset, and 2) the development of a national information flow system that enables local police authorities to forward intelligence to the national authorities who in turn will have a system to centralize and forward that information to Europol/Interpol. Furthermore, an adequate information flow system must accommodate the diffusion of finished intelligence, the output of the IOs, back to the border patrols, the criminal police or order police where the information can enhance investigative efforts and strategy development, and 3) all concerned authorities, those who come across information that could be useful to the entire membership of the IO, are aware of the existence of the IO and its services and are competent in the utilization of the trends or assessment reports. Once this process has taken place, the capacity to benefit from the services of the IO is significantly enhanced and collaboration benefits the whole of the membership, thereby making defection more costly and raising the advantages associated with cooperative behaviour. Because these conditions are not often met cooperation is not systematic, that is, part of procedures in investigations. The distinct cases of Germany and France illustrate this point.

Initially, two states cooperated systematically by sending and receiving information as intended by the Europol and Interpol frameworks: Germany and the UK. Both states had an established national information flow system as part of their law enforcement infrastructure prior to the implementation of a cooperation initiative. So the established channels for domestic cooperation among the local authorities but especially the regional and national agencies did not have to be created in order to allow compliance with the convention.

Here we can point out a few factors that explain why Germany has traditionally exhibited cooperative behaviour. Germany first proposed the idea of Europol via an official in 1974 in the *Bund Deutscher Kriminalbeamter*, the Federation of German Criminal Police, and then by Helmut Kohl in 1988, leading to the adoption of the Europol convention (Busch 2002). Coincidentally, Germany has an adequate information flow system and relatively little compliance work was necessary to systematically share intelligence gathered during investigations, making police cooperation less problematic in terms of both mindsets and operational ability. Although the German authorities have resisted the shift from relative autonomy to a structure in which a hierarchy is dictated by the need to share information with the membership, those same authorities have also enjoyed a legitimacy in the interfacing of a new system because it addressed the much deplored pre-eminence of the *Bundeskrimilant*, the national and traditionally all powerful police in Germany respectively (Hartmut 2003). The case of the UK is very similar as are their participation rates (interview, Europol officials, 2001).

This fragmented approach to policing, whereby various police services are engaged in law enforcement and have a significant amount of leeway in terms of judgement (an interpretation of laws and actions based on moral judgements), is coordinated by an already existing National Criminal Intelligence Service in the UK (now Serious Organized Crime Agency (SOCA)) and the *Bundeskrimilant* in Germany. Thus, an information flow system is in place whereby information gathered from the four corners of the territory will follow established channels toward one national clearing house for collection – making participation at the international level via Europol and/or Interpol more likely. Generally speaking, the North-European and Anglo-Saxon police culture fits better with the concept of a clearing house because it is based on the accumulation and processing of data conceived as the main pillar of intelligence and operational resources in comparison with the southern police tradition where intelligence and investigations are separated (interview, July 2004, Europol official).

France, on the other hand, has a centralized law enforcement infrastructure that is based on a need-to-know basis. Various forms of crime fall under the jurisdiction of agencies that are not connected to each other or to a centralized national collection point. For example, border controls are the responsibility of the *Police Nationale* but when it comes to money laundering the Ministry of Finance has been designated as the enforcer (Levy and Monjardet 2003). The highly hierarchical French system is not necessarily structured to be in a position to collect and share the information gathered during investigations by its various police services because these are not connected to each other, they are not necessarily part of a larger system where components can interact. As a result, the communication that comes from the 'state' does not comprise evidence gathered by all concerned authorities. And the French national units responsible for interaction with other states within a cooperative framework have more of a diplomatic outlook than the necessary operational focus (interviews, Europol officials, 2003).

France has also resisted standardizing its investigative techniques and methods (Deflem 2002). Intelligence gathering methods and information have been regarded as a propriety by states which is still very much the case for France (interview, Europol official, 2001). This reluctance to harmonize the legal and procedural infrastructure, thereby looking outward for reform direction, has proven difficult because French political culture stresses formality and politics that come from inside the state. And there is a different perspective in terms of what constitutes intelligence and how it is gathered. The prevailing method in the international community based on the English approach is the collection of intelligence via surveillance and wire tapping. The French system depends more on infiltration by informants and other more operational (in the purest sense of the word) methods. There is also a lack of training and even awareness of the threats posed by TC and the channels that have been established via Europol, all contributing significantly to the incompetence/inability of the national authorities to share information (interview, Europol Official, 2001, and French Liaison Officer at Europol, 2004).

Such non-cooperative behaviour as exhibited by the French case results in investigations that cannot be completed due to the perpetrators fleeing to neighbouring states and a mediocre prosecutorial record (interview, Europol Official, 2003). Many police officers don't even know that the ICPO exists (interview, Secretariat, Europol, 2003 and Liaison Office, 2004). As a result, states will go to Europol when they have exhausted all other options and when the national agencies have been contacted by foreign counterparts to bring in reinforcements for an investigation. The French case shows that in the absence of targeted comprehensive training programmes, law enforcement professionals will not know how to practise international law enforcement and nor will they know the resources available to them.

The French case also shows that national debates on how to address the threats posed by TC fail to include Europol and that other IOs are important to the internationalization of counter crime efforts (Pujas 2000). Magistrates have earned a reputation for ignoring Europol and the role that they play in the collection of admissible information, thereby perpetuating an ignorance about the benefits that these organizations can bring to law enforcement efforts (interview, Europol, 2001). Furthermore, most of the relevant international instruments, like Schengen, do not make reference to the IO even though it would serve as a significant partner in the guarding of borders (interview, Europol, 2003).

Non-cooperative behaviour leads to a large amount of information that could be diffused by Europol to all member states never making it beyond the local police databank. As a result the wider picture of criminal activity is never presented. In such a case the distributive outcome provided by the IO is substantially weakened. Given that national governments are investing significant human and financial resources for the functioning of IOs and believe that this will stimulate positive issues for transnational investigations, how can we explain why they are not able to use it in order to obtain proportional benefits? This is exactly what happened in April 2003 when a parliamentary report pointed out that France contributed 16 per cent of the Europol budget but only benefited from 8 per cent of the information because of a lack of knowledge of the Europol mechanism.[3] The traditional limits mentioned above cannot be overcome within the functionalist framework which focuses on the dependence of the IO on domestic actors. Alternatively, the constructivist approach focuses on the diffusion of norms by supranational actors guiding the discussion towards the missing link to potentially enhanced cooperation.

Capacity building toward a maximization of IO output

In order to further their aims of facilitating cooperation between member states, an IO 'need[s] the constant and active cooperation of its members, who should do all within their power that is compatible with legislation to participate diligently in its activities'.[4] So if the entire membership does not send and receive information, the output of these bodies suffers from inaccuracy due to its incompleteness.[5] Thus, in order to legitimize itself, or to 'survive', officials of both IOs have implemented new initiatives as they have realized that states were not systematically cooperating because the know-how to integrate international cooperative mechanisms in their national infrastructures was consistently lacking (interviews, Interpol and Europol secretariat officials, 2001).

While the mandates of these IOs are intended to facilitate communication, if the members do not implement adequate information flow systems for information to be sent and received and do not provide training/education to their practitioners, cooperation will remain *ad hoc* and hinder the network put in place. Thus, Interpol and Europol officials have engaged in capacity building initiatives to assist states in the development of the respective national information flow systems in a sort of informal supranational entrepreneurship.[6] Some of these initiatives were born out of ideas about officials lacking the intelligence for analysis and others came from feedback they received from national authorities. If information does not trickle down to the IO, the IO will decide to persuade sub-national actors to cooperate. We will see what sort of institutional tools they designed to fulfil this, bypassing the limits imposed on them via their respective mandates.

Interpol and Europol maintain a highly secure communication network to collect information from national competent authorities of the membership and to diffuse a variety of crime analyses which will be based on the voluntarily shared information that states send them. The information is channelled through national offices designated by states as the go-betweens for the IO and individual member states, the National Central Bureaux at Interpol and the Liaison Offices at Europol. Few main strategic products and operational services have been designed to lead new investigations and to further existing ones (interview, Europol Officials, 2001). These tools are evidence of the 'supply driven' approach to explaining how Europol and Interpol will gradually become supranational actors in their own right.

Initiatives for building capacity include information diffusion, training and education, as well as awareness raising programmes. Europol issues *The General Situation Report*, a descriptive product based on information gathered from member states and from open-source information – derived from in-house research, and potentially from third states and/or organizations (e.g. like the Office of Drug Control and Crime Prevention, or Interpol, or the FBI). This report serves to educate national units and their police forces on criminality trends, and the main perpetrator groups involved. Predictive strategic products include the *Threat Assessment* and *Risk Assessment*, which explain the background to a threat in an attempt to understand the causes and predict future events (Bratz 2001). The analysis in this report evaluates the character, scope and impact of a particular form of criminality and allows national authorities to design a strategy against a particular form of crime and/or criminal group (interview, Europol official, 2001).

Operational services include the *Information Bulletin, Analysis Work Files*, and joint investigations and operations. These discuss the details of significant cases including the *modus operandi* of transnational criminal groups. Finally, *joint operations*, usually as a result of *Analysis Work Files*, are intended to use all the information output available to Europol and member states to follow up investigations, locate and observe suspects and, once sufficient evidence has been gathered, to arrest and convict these suspects (interview, Europol official, 2001).[7] Interpol maintains a system of notices to communicate an effort to locate a suspect.

Similarly, Interpol officials introduced a Regional Modernization Programme to help states set up national central bureaux. They coordinate the opening of an office as a sort of local empowerment approach, giving the government in question the necessary technology and training to participate in the network of communication at Interpol. As an Interpol official said 'We buy them a car, we give them driving lessons, put gas in it, and ask them to drive'. In 2000, the Interpol General Assembly approved the Model Cooperation Agreement that the legal department had proposed in response to the observation that state policies needed to be compatible to be shared and utilized as admissible evidence in foreign judicial proceedings. This tool offers states a guide to agreeing on specific investigative techniques and is meant to harmonize national policies as a result of states utilizing these compatible legal guidelines.

Europol officials also quickly realized that a lack of cooperation by member states resulted from an inadequacy in national systems *vis-à-vis* the international network of cooperation these embody. The drug expertise department started to offer training in drug lab raids, including on how to identify an illegal facility that is producing illegal drugs, how to arrest the perpetrators, and how to gather evidence in the hopes of harmonizing practices across the membership. Europol has also issued recommendations on judicial and investigative procedures. Victim protection, for example, had been an obstacle to testimony in courts across the membership. So Europol proposed a victim protection programme whereby victims would testify without being identified, thereby enhancing the prosecutorial ability of states. These recommendations and other diffusions of expertise and general awareness-raising activity take place during conferences hosted by Europol.

Even if the need for collaboration is the impetus for the creation of an international mechanism to share information, the post-agreement development of these IOs can at best be described as norm diffusion. Early on in the development process a transformation of the role of the IO occurs from passive bystander to intervener. The capacity building initiatives undertaken by each IO show a process of self-determination by the IO whereby they quickly fulfil a demand which they themselves identify based on the source of a defection of member states. In the case of Europol, we can observe an after-the-fact legalization of practices already in place. The institutionalization process of Europol followed that *post-factum* legalization path. Europol was organized four years before its ratification in 1999 which is the official date of the formation of Europol – suggesting that the officials leading it are going ahead with self-determination with or without member states (Busch 2002).

In order to increase the participation of states and the quality of the output, the IO engages in a sort of intervention when it trains, educates, raises awareness and recommends information flow systems and outward-looking policies to enhance the participation rate among the membership. This is where 'informal supranational entrepreneurship' takes place in a sort of behind-the-scenes reconciliation of the political commitment to cooperate and operational autonomy. Europol's case illustrates how policy initiation can take place via the introduction of tools that are outside the scope of the mandate and that eventually become formalized as they are legitimized by the national authorities that benefit from them. The adoption of the Mutual Legal Assistance Treaty by the Europol membership is a case in point.

The 2002 Convention on Mutual Legal Assistance in Criminal Matters adopted the results from proposals by the directorate of Europol to address obstacles to police cooperation which they encountered regularly. This treaty was a significant step towards executive powers that would make Europol a supranational organization. According to the convention, Europol could coordinate joint teams whereby surveillance, interrogation and pursuit can span across borders by including police officials in the various affected states. The convention also requires the sharing of satellite tracking data and the transfer of evidence via Europol for analysis and diffusion to the membership. In addition, a scoreboard mechanism was put in place whereby Europol could assign a team to evaluate the information flow systems of states and issue recommendations. And finally, the convention gives Europol the right to initiate investigations.

These provisions allow Europol to shape the way that states fight TC, teaching them to cooperate by sharing information and collaborating in investigations and strategy. The proposal to give these 'powers' came from inside Europol, which is why we categorize the IO as entrepreneurial, informal and supranational. Europol, as part of the EU's institutions, and with a directorate which have been able to make themselves heard in policy-making circles at the EU level (and national levels in some cases), has been able to gain significant ground and establish itself as *the* EU institution to fight TC. This does not mean that all states will cooperate, but that is the goal. However, it is obvious that moves at EU level to enhance police and judicial cooperation in criminal matters have been based since the 1999 Tampere European Council on the principle of recognition, which is premised on all member states trusting in one anothers' criminal justice systems. One main measure to implement this principle was the European Arrest Warrant, adopted hastily after 9-11 after a difficult bargaining process due to the resistance of the Italian Prime Minister (Pujas 2004).

On the other hand Interpol, which remains blocked within the complex power relationships of a wider range of heterogeneous states, is also careful to retain its apolitical character. It has not made such significant changes in its status as an IO. Although capacity building initiatives have been formalized, as has been shown above, Interpol has very much stayed in the background, settling for providing tools that will build capacity and not establishing the legal grounds to gain executive powers.

Capacity building is then the vehicle for the development of a partnership between the state and the IO, but there are significant factors that will limit a further exploitation of the potential of the system and the processes that it comprises. Indeed, political and legal accountability as well as the reluctance of some states to develop towards communitarization within European justice and home affairs embody a main hurdle to the supranationalist approach.

Contemporary limits to the expansion of IPCO

As we have shown, Europol has gained executive powers since its creation. However, none of these new parameters can function without a field compliance concerning data protection and respect for civil liberties in the case of prosecutions resulting from police cooperation. An absence of adequate minimum standards in this field will result in the application of variable and insufficient levels of protection to those required by Europol. This is actually the main obstacle for deepening such empowerment processes. In the absence of adequate and enforceable EU-wide safeguards, there is a danger that the rights of those accused will suffer as a consequence of greater cooperation between member states. Only such confidence in the criminal justice systems of all the member states which in turn will lead to more efficient judicial co-operation in a climate of mutual trust[8] could create a spillover effect enhancing cooperation. Indeed, the rights of those affected by EU police and judicial cooperation in criminal matters need to be protected. If met, this requirement would genuinely substantiate the trust that underlies the principle of mutual recognition.

Cooperation at a supranational level offered administrative elites a new level of independence from political interference by party leaders and parliamentary scrutiny. The lack of a democratic oversight for supranational officials which insulates them from interest group pressure and national controls is problematic (Pujas and Benoît 2003). An increase in cooperation by the French services since the report by the French parliament reacting to the proposal of Denmark granting more powers to fighting all kinds of 'serious crime' is seen by French representatives as producing an increasingly difficult organization to control and render accountable to the membership. This development shows how the impact of Europol's efforts to build capacity, raise awareness and coordinate investigations and strategies shapes the normative behaviour of the state.[9]

Finally, we have to keep in mind that by promoting the development of police cooperation, national representatives have clearly induced the realization of a much bigger project as this includes the construction of a single judicial area at a regional and/or global level. The concept of police cooperation has reached a crossroads between political strategic views, both national and supranational. But at this stage of development, it enhances the control paradigm more than the freedom and liberties of the world's citizens. The risk would be to forget freedom and democracy by focusing on enemies who are necessary for the expansion of police services.

Notes

1 Nadia Gerspacher wrote this chapter as a visiting fellow at the CNRS/ Department of International Relations, in Grenoble, France.
2 While the list is not exhaustive, the UN has identified money laundering, terrorist activities, thefts of art and cultural objects, theft of intellectual property, illicit traffic in arms, aircraft/land hijacking, sea piracy, computer crime, insurance fraud, trafficking in persons, environmental crime, illicit drug trafficking, trade in human body parts, infiltration of legal business, fraudulent bankruptcy and corruption as the categories of TC (UNCJS 1975).
3 *Rapport d'information déposé par la délégation de l'Assemblée Nationale pour l'Union Européenne sur l'avenir d'Europol*, No 819 (29 Avril 2003).
4 Interpol Convention, Article 31.
5 Output will be inherently incomplete if the criminal activity that takes place in one state is not communicated to the membership via the international network and the analysis will not include that information.
6 Moravcsik discusses informal supranational entrepreneurs as it relates to negotiations but it is also a useful concept to describe the initiation of programmes that are outside the scope of the formal agreements on which these IOs are structured.
7 This information exchange system is especially useful when it is used during existing investigations as its speed solves the traditional problem of a delay in information requests during investigations (EUROPOL official, 2001). For example, surveillance often has to be taken from one state to another. In such a case, as a suspect flees across a border, the national authority can take over the surveillance, gather evidence to complete the existing investigation already in progress in another state, and proceed to an arrest when enough proper evidence is gathered for prosecution.
8 European Commission, Green Paper, February 2003.
9 *Rapport du Sénat du Parlement Français, session ordinaire de 2003–2004.*

Chapter 14

Tackling transnational drug trafficking effectively: assessing the outcomes of the Drug Enforcement Administration's international cooperation initiatives

Frédéric Lemieux

Introduction

International police cooperation is an increasingly crucial approach to fighting transnational crime, particularly in light of the growing threats to national and international security posed by transnational organized crime. While data, information and resources are abundant in these areas, analysis of law enforcement practices is much less common, specifically as it pertains to collaboration between foreign law enforcement agencies. One way of identifying the limits of existing law enforcement approaches to combating transnational crime is to scrutinize criminal investigations that span two or more countries, commonly known as international task force cases. Following this logic, there are three sets of factors that can guide the evaluation of existing police cooperation mechanisms.

First, we can identify the constraints on police cooperation by scrutinizing environmental contingencies including international legal frameworks and the economic and political relations between states afflicted by transnational criminal activity (production, transportation or distribution). Second, certain characteristics of law enforcement agencies, including weakened inter-organizational ties, structural asymmetries and inherent incompatibilities, a lack of competence in cross-border information sharing, nationalistic mindsets and practices, cultural diversity, and technological incompatibility highlight the existing challenges that police cooperation infrastructures face. Finally, we can factor in the effect that a police understanding of supply chains can have on the early stages of an investigation, then throughout its progression, and ending with the conclusion of the case. This difference between the early and final stages of a case can reflect the adequacy (or lack thereof) of the manner in which police agencies conceptualize international drug trafficking structures.

This chapter aims to assess the outcomes of major international investigations initiated by the US Drug Enforcement Administration (DEA). More precisely, this study examines the relation between 1) the estimated operational outcomes of the DEA's international cooperation projects and 2) the intensity of these joint operations as well as the nature of interactions among the involved agencies (nil, bilateral, multilateral). The assessment of police cooperation allows an opportunity to measure the effectiveness of the DEA's international joint investigations and helps to gauge, indirectly, a fundamental aspect of international police cooperation: criminal intelligence sharing. The results of this study are based on a quantitative and qualitative analysis of major investigations initiated by the DEA related to international drug trafficking (cocaine, heroin, marijuana). This study offers an original assessment approach of international police cooperation and criminal intelligence sharing outcomes.

Transnational drug trafficking

The illegal movement of psychoactive substances across national borders is one of the most typical forms of transnational crime. The trafficking of illicit drugs between producer and consumer countries along drug supply chains has been taking place for over a century (Chawla and Pietschmann 2005: 160). Recent studies point out that 'criminal rings' have access to the latest technology and are able to conduct sophisticated counter-intelligence operations against police forces (Van Meter 2002). Earlier research has pointed out that traffickers will segment the supply chain to maximize the use of human resources by recruiting experts and professionals in many domains in different countries (Gregory 1998; Williams and Savona 1995). It is interesting to note that the growth rate for drug trafficking started to decline in the early twenty-first century and had significantly decelerated in the 1990s (United Nations Report on Global Seizures of Cocaine and Opiates between 1980–2002, 2003). While this apparent decline could be explained by, among other factors, either a shift in demand in terms of product or in demand stemming from a rise in consumer countries, we would still ask whether an apparent drop in drug trafficking activity could be attributed to the proliferation of international agreements. A variety of arrangements have led to the creation of international police cooperation forums in order to lend police investigations the international dimension necessary to apprehend suspects who cross borders (Deflem 2000, 2002; Joutsen 2005; Koenig and Das 2001; Sheptycki 2000). The existing research on drug supply chains and police cooperation does not take into account the international conditions and organizational constraints already in place. Rather than assuming the vision of either body of literature, we develop a wider approach which focuses on studies that build on the idea of an international drug market structure and describe the international control mechanisms that have been established.

Early studies on organized crime depict criminal monopolies that are hierarchical and rigid in structure and authoritative in their grasp of the supply of illegal goods and services (Cressey 1969). Although this view often represents the dominant framework in law enforcement responses to organizational crime (Beare and Naylor 1999; Kelly 1978; Morselli et al. 2003; Naylor 1997), this traditional approach has been challenged by the research of the past three decades. Whether in illegal drug trafficking, import settings or specific geographical settings, the idea of a criminal bureaucracy has largely been seen as a myth (Block and Chambliss 1981; Beare 1996; Desroches 1999; Dorn et al. 1992; Haller 1990; Ianni 1972, 1974; Krebs et al. 2003; Lupsha 1983; Potter 1994; Reuter 1983; Reuter and Haaga 1989; Williams 1998). Conventional perspectives view transnational organized crime as all-powerful cartels, or pax mafiosa, who control the global distribution of psychoactive substances (Raufer 1993; Sterling 1994). Although it is likely that structured criminal enterprises exist in the Andean region, in the Golden Triangle and the Golden Crescent, we must ask how and why they can survive under the crime control policies of western countries. In this light, it seems more suited to conceive of drug trafficking structures in terms of market rather than organization (Tremblay and Cusson 1995).

The basic structures embedded in ongoing international drug trafficking activities are more accurately represented by an inherent flexibility and autonomous supply chains than by authoritative and powerful criminal organizations. Supply chains channel drugs into the international market by moving the psychoactive substances from a starting point (producer countries) to a final destination (consumer countries) through 'relay countries'. The supply chain represents both a path travelled by an illicit product and a network of traffickers who move illicit substances from production to consumption points. A supply chain is transnational when it spans the borders of two or more countries and its geographical impact is determined by the number of countries through which it passes. Cocaine, heroin and hashish are predominant in the trafficking of drugs while marijuana and synthetic drugs are often produced at the local, sometimes regional, level due to ease of production (laboratories, hydroponics installations, etc.).

According to past studies (Reuter 1996; Reuter and Greenfield 2001; Reuter et al. 1988), the structure (length and complexity) of supply chains may be shaped by several influential attributes. On one hand, the degree of specialization required to produce psychoactive substances and the varieties of specific activities required at each point of relay (transformation, storage, transit) account for the complexity of the supply chain. On the other hand, the funding and social capital of police services and the strength of repressive measures against a particular type of drug (cocaine or heroin) can account for the length of a drug supply chain. A drug supply chain can be controlled by the actors that take it from the point of origin to delivery. Alternatively, a supply chain can be autonomous, meaning that no one can entirely control the path it will take. The latter is more vulnerable because it is not supported by a network that can ensure continuity in the chain (due to the absence of relational redundancies between concerned actors). Supply chains that have a centralized power base are seemingly less current than autonomous ones because of the additional costs incurred in circumventing logistical obstacles (Reuter 1983; Tremblay et al. 1998).

Drug supply chains often exhibit structural characteristics influenced by conditions that present themselves along hemispheric lines. The North-South polarization of drug supply chains can be explained by four factors: 1) favourable climatic conditions for the production of psychotropic substances; 2) the prevalent economic conditions of the countries along the chain's path (this can have a significant effect on the profit margins and prices – see Kopp 1997); 3) political situations that ignore the production of drugs, particularly in countries with weak government institutions and a limited capacity to eradicate and dismantle production installations (Labrousse 1995); and 4) the intensity of police repression (more important and systematic in developed countries) and the inherent increase of a risk of arrest at the end of the supply chain rather than at its beginning. While it would be expected that the risks would lessen the further a drug shipment travels from its point of production, the risk of arrest and seizure is actually higher when the shipment nears its destination.

Controlling international drug trafficking

Given that the span and complexity of international supply chains are determined by the intensity of the application of certain social controls, the development of common economic markets has forced states to formulate new security interests in order to combat transnational crime. This demand for security has promoted the explosion of judicial cooperation treaties and has required a greater commitment to collaboration between foreign police services (Haas 1972; Occhipinti 2003). The implications of this spillover of assistance are demonstrated by the emergence of international police cooperation structures and/or organizations, as well as the extension of national police powers through instruments such as mutual legal assistance treaties (Benyon *et al.* 1993; Fijnaut 1993; Nadelmann 1993). The resulting 'common security spaces' encourage national police services to share their intelligence and expertise with foreign colleagues (Manning 2000) resulting in an increase in police socialization. In concrete terms, we can observe a significant progression of police and judicial cooperation inside occidental free market zones. In North America, we can notice a proliferation of police initiatives since the late 1990s that hinges on bilateral agreements between the US and Canada as well as between the US and Mexico (Deflem 2001). Police cooperation has been in practice for even longer in Europe, as the implementation of a common European space has significantly contributed to the development of legislation to enhance and structure collaboration between foreign police services.

International police cooperation is the dynamic through which criminal intelligence is shared across borders (Robertson 1994). It allows police services to tap the information sources that can be available to them in other countries in order to better understand the *modus operandi* of their suspects. It enables them to identify specific criminal activity within specific criminal groups and to develop a knowledge base about actual or potential criminal activity not necessarily because it took place within their jurisdiction, but because it has occurred in another country which has made investigation results available to foreign colleagues. Exchanging information gathered during criminal investigations establishes networks and links between police professionals (Bigo 1996), but it also goes a long way to building trust (with reciprocity and communication) (Anderson 2002). In addition, sharing information provides opportunities to develop strategies and set priorities to determine the resources necessary for conducting multi-layered operations that often require the establishment of a team of foreign colleagues. International police cooperation also allows investigators to organize their plan of attack more accurately since they have more knowledge of the activities of a group/perpetrator being investigated as a result of the 'big picture' perspective that arises when bits of information are compiled. Since transnational crime displays a complete disregard for national boundaries, the police services must be able to counter this behaviour with a softening of the concept of national jurisdiction. International police cooperation allows police operations to disregard national boundaries somewhat, to operate on an international scale, and to develop a more informed approach which can guide the prioritizing and targeting of criminal groups (e.g. vulnerabilities, threats, etc.). Finally, international cooperation allows police agencies to develop a network of foreign investigators, a common characteristic of criminal groups and one that is so often credited for many successes.

However, like transnational drug supply chains, international police cooperation takes place under difficult, and at times hostile, environmental conditions. The national agency that participates in a system of police cooperation faces numerous obstacles due to incompatible structures, cultures, technologies, judicial procedures, and policies which limit the impact of cooperative behaviour in the fight against transnational crime. Asymmetry in the structure of national police organizations (centralized and decentralized) results in a proliferation of agencies involved in the cooperation process and thus encourages the convergence of communication channels (formal and informal) and the explosion of information sources (Den Boer 2002). Furthermore, the cultural heterogeneity inherent in international cooperation introduces the potential to aggravate the lack of trust that is ever present in police subcultures (Skolnick 1996). There are also myriad problems linked to the integration of information technology as incompatibilities in systems considerably complicate the establishment of informational bridges between police services (Sheptycki 2004). This phenomenon is particularly relevant in North-South cooperation efforts where the use of technology is often disproportionate.

Despite the existence of official initiatives, systematic police co-operation remains encumbered by obstacles inside common economic spaces and a variety of recourses are necessary to achieve adequate levels of cooperation. According to Nadelmann's (1992) work, a path-finding study in the fight against drug trafficking, agents from the US Drug Enforcement Administration (DEA) assigned to Latin America employed four tactics to avoid dealing with corrupt police organizations in the region: 1) collaboration with the least corrupt police departments and/or an alternating between police services; 2) the establishment of relationships based on trust and friendship with local officers; 3) exploitation of the competition between different national law enforcement agencies; and 4) the carrying out of large operations during regime changes, when the spread of corruption is typically at its lowest point. The goal of these tactics was and is to improve the performances of international police cooperation in order to obtain better operational results (arrests and seizures).

Assessing police cooperation effectiveness

In the United States, several hundreds of millions of dollars have been allocated to governmental initiatives intended to encourage inter-agency cooperation and thereby reduce the isolationism of police agencies (Hayeslip and Russell-Einhorn 2003).[1] In light of this, joint police structures designed to successfully conduct complex investigations beyond the capabilities of a single police force have been established. This strategy also allows investigations to draw upon more extensive and diversified resources, especially by pooling professional expertise (Chaiken et al. 1990; Levine and Martin 1992). Other arguments in support of a cooperative inter-agency strategy include improved management of police resources, a decreased duration of investigations, and fewer issues related to arrests and convictions (Perras 2006).

Nevertheless, there are few rigorous, empirical evaluations of the performance of multi-jurisdictional teams (Jeffries et al. 1998; Sherman 1997). The only studies that have examined these teams are descriptive, and their results are ambiguous at best (Coldren et al. 1993; Schlegel and McGarrell 1991). In theory, the coordination of resources should allow police forces to surpass their individual capacities by improving the efficiency of operations and reducing the cost of managing investigations.

Smith et al. (2000) analysed the performance of multi-jurisdictional investigative teams. More specifically, they compared organizations participating in multi-jurisdictional teams both with each other and with organizations that did not participate in such teams. Performance was measured in terms of three factors: the extent of inter- and intra-agency communication, the number of drug-related arrests, and the 'quality' of drug-related arrests. Their results suggest that members of multi-jurisdictional teams feel more effective in their work and recognize the opportunities for inter- and intra-organizational exchanges of information, expertise, etc. On the other hand, the establishment of multi-jurisdictional teams did not have any influence on objective measures such as the quantity or quality of arrests.

However, it appears that the results were a function of the teams' geographical contexts. For example, United States agencies participating in national multi-jurisdictional investigative teams are seemingly more effective than stand-alone teams, as measured by both arrests and the quality of intra- and inter-organizational relations. These results strongly suggest that the effectiveness with which multi-jurisdictional investigative teams fight organized crime can be better assessed by taking into account each team's unique characteristics.

Past and recent studies on international police cooperation focused on trans-border areas and used qualitative analysis to examine the capacity of national police services to initiate joint operations. Results show that international police cooperation is significantly influenced by national cultural differences such as language or terminology. Moreover, political agendas can 1) affect the quality and the fluency of interactions between national police services; 2) pressure public safety priorities and law enforcement's tasks; and 3) influence strategic orientations and the focus of international police cooperation. Also, the compatibility of national legal frameworks and criminal justice systems represents a significant challenge and inevitably shapes the scope of police cooperation as well as the nature of joint initiatives (information exchanges, joint investigation, co-prosecution, etc.) (Sabatier 2001). Finally, two other factors that deeply influence police cooperation performance should also be mentioned: an individual motivation to work with foreign colleagues and mutual confidence (Anderson 2002; Bigo 2000; Block 2008; Brady 2008; De Kerchove 2005). However, none of these studies has scrutinized or measured the performance of international police cooperation.

Analytical design and methodology

This chapter focuses on the analysis of international drug trafficking, the disruption of which represents a high priority for most governments and police agencies around the world. More precisely, this study proposes an in-depth examination of major international operations initiated by the Drug Enforcement Administration (DEA) between 2000–2008. The DEA was chosen for its strong leadership and influence in the national and international fight against drug trafficking. In fact, this US federal agency possesses an extended network of international liaison officers (500 agents) dispersed in 75 countries and had a budget estimated at $2.3 billion in 2007. The functioning of the DEA at the international level was previously studied by Nadelmann (1992, 1993) who examined how the DEA's methods have contributed to the modernization of the European justice system regarding international cooperation. Nadelmann also analysed the circumstances/contexts in which the DEA was able to accomplish its mission at the international level, more precisely in Latin America and the Caribbean region, despite rampant corruption and political instability. Finally, the author looked at the progress made by the DEA under international agreements related to criminal evidence collection and exchange. Nadelmann concluded that despite the fact that a police agency like the DEA seems to be more effective in capturing high-profile drug traffickers, it remains difficult to measure the impact of anti-drug policy and strategic priority at the international level.

In order to evaluate the operational outcomes of international police cooperation, this study includes a total of 61 major investigations initiated by the DEA during the period between 2000 and 2008. Among these cases, only the ones related to natural drugs have been selected (cocaine, heroin and marijuana). Investigations related to synthetic drugs have not been included in the analytical design because the production and distribution of these substances are usually based at the local level or limited to specific trans-border areas. According to that criterion, 47 major investigations involving cooperation with foreign police agencies and 14 investigations related to international drug smuggling into the US without international partnership have been identified. Within these investigative cases, several key factors have been selected to design a measure of operational performance: a) operation duration (number of months); b) the number of police agencies involved in each investigation; c) the volume of seizures (kilograms); d) the number of arrests; e) the value of the proceeds of crime; and f) the nature of the assistance provided to the DEA by foreign police agencies.

The analytical framework of this study is based on the examination of two research propositions. The first part of the analysis section scrutinizes the existence of a correlation between the intensity of international police cooperation and the outcomes of the DEA's international investigations (arrests and seizures). The intensity of international police cooperation is measured by two proxy variables:

1) the duration of each investigation (in months) which refers to the capacity of police agencies to invest resources (human, material and financial) over a certain period of time; and 2) the number of police agencies involved in each investigation case which relates to law enforcement mobilization capacity to target a specific drug supply chain or criminal group. It is important to remember that the literature suggests that police cooperation aims to pool and coordinate law enforcement resources to address a security problem that a single police agency cannot tackle alone. In other words, for the purpose of this research, the intensity of international police cooperation translates into the capacity of national law enforcement agencies to put a collective and continuous pressure on drug trafficking over a certain period of time. The second part of the analysis section examines how the diversity of national police services within each international investigation initiated by the DEA can affect operational outcomes (arrests and seizures). Indeed, the quality and diversity of the interactions between national law enforcement agencies can deepen investigators' knowledge on several dimensions related to cooperation practices and investigation expertise (criminal analysis, investigative techniques, development of investigation strategies, etc.). Moreover, the diversity of inter-agency cooperation, as well as the frequency of interaction, increases the chance of overcoming jurisdictional barriers and competition among national police services highly concerned about international drug trafficking.

Finally, in order to have a better understanding of and to enrich the interpretation of the information gathered in some of the most important investigation cases, several interviews have been conducted with investigators coming from the DEA and the national police services of several countries (Canada, Colombia, the Netherlands, the United Kingdom and Venezuela). The semi-directed interviews were structured around two main dimensions: 1) the sharing of criminal intelligence with foreign police services involved in an investigation; and 2) the organizational learning outcomes from inter-agency cooperation or, more precisely, the diffusion of innovative procedures and techniques related to investigative practices.

Assessing the performance of the DEA's international investigations

Between 2000 and 2008, the DEA made 3,264 arrests related to international drug trafficking. This represents 1.3 per cent of arrests made by the organization at the domestic level during the same period (246,671 arrests). Regarding drug seizures, international investigations can account for 8 per cent of the total volume of seized drugs made by the DEA during the period of reference (240 tons *vs.* 3,000 tons). More precisely, 21 per cent of the overall cocaine seized by the DEA comes from international investigations: 41 per cent for heroin and 4 per cent for marijuana (Drug Enforcement Administration 2008). These preliminary results show that some trafficked substances, such as cocaine and heroin, possess more of an international profile than other substances, like marijuana.

During this time period, anti-drug trafficking policies usually focused on 'hard' drugs and the targeting of cocaine/heroin international supply chains. The consequences of these policies impact on international investigations and, at times, undermine them. During an interview, an investigator from the Royal Canadian Mounted Police (RCMP), in charge of the coordination of a joint investigation on marijuana smuggling with the DEA, mentioned that some major inconsistency in priority occurred with a partner agency from the United Kingdom. According to the interviewee, international investigations related to marijuana smuggling were not a main concern for the UK's police services and also not a priority in the Home Office's strategic objectives. This lack of assistance from the UK authorities provoked an urgent need for physical surveillance in order to gather intelligence on high-profile marijuana smugglers travelling to London to do 'business'. The situation was eventually resolved outside of the traditional chain of command and the RCMP/ DEA joint investigation received a minimal amount of operational support from the UK for a limited period of time. Nevertheless, in that case, the UK's anti-drug policy considerably affected the portion of the joint investigation responsible for gathering more intelligence on a potential connection with European traffickers.

Intensity of international police cooperation

The previous example underlines the need to scrutinize the relationship between the intensity of international police cooperation initiatives and the operational outcomes. In this analysis, the concept of 'intensity of police cooperation' is measured by using two variables: 1) the duration of the international investigation in months; and 2) the number of agencies that invest resources in order to support the international investigation. Table 14.1 presents the results of correlation analysis between investigation duration, the number of

Table 14.1 Correlation analysis between intensity of the DEA's international investigations and operational outcomes (n=36)

	Drug total Average 6 858 kg	Cocaine Average 4 026 kg	Heroin Average 70 kg	Marijuana Average 6 041 kg	Arrests Average 99 indiv.	Proceeds Average $3,574,391
Duration Average 16.4 months	r= 0.23**	r= 0.27**	r= 0.04	r= 0.01	r= 0.01	r= 0.02
Number of police agencies Average 2.3 agencies	r= 0.547**	r= 0.69**	r= 0.03	r=- 0.02	r= 0.07*	r= 0.12*

*p<0.05 **p<0.01

countries involved, and operational outcomes. The results show a positive and moderate correlation between operation duration and total drug seizures. It's also interesting to note that the strength of the correlation coefficient increases slightly for cocaine seizures. However, the relation between investigation duration and operational outcomes disappears completely when we look at the number of arrests, other drugs seizures (heroin and marijuana) and the proceeds of crime (money and other valuables assets).

The strong relationship between investigation duration and cocaine seizures is interesting and its implication should be nuanced. It is highly probable that these particular results reflect the DEA's international strategic priority that primarily targets cocaine supply chains. Nevertheless, the existing correlation between investigation duration and drug seizures is not counter-intuitive and the bias resulting from law enforcement strategic prioritization remains an inevitable reality of police work. Moreover, strategic priority can explain the reason why the number of arrests is not correlated with the duration of investigation. During the interviews, several investigators mentioned that most of the time the investigation strategy was founded on the targeting of high-profile individuals who were deeply involved in international drug trafficking (intelligence-led policing). Consequently, it is not surprising to observe that the number of arrests is not correlated with the investigation duration because most of the criminals involved were already identified at the beginning of the operation. However, this rationale does not apply to drug seizures or the proceeds of crime, since the time devoted to the investigation reflects the difficulties related to infiltrating, monitoring and intercepting large-scale drug shipments or several smaller drug delivery operations.

Secondly, regarding the relation between the number of police agencies involved in the DEA's international investigations and the operational outcomes, the results show clearly that when more foreign police services are involved, the more likely it is that the volume of drug seizures (especially cocaine), arrests and seized proceeds of crime will increase. In other words, the number of foreign law enforcement agencies with which the DEA interacts by exchanging intelligence and/or providing judicial assistance is strongly and significantly correlated to the operational success of joint international drug investigations. These results indicate that the intensity of police international cooperation or, more precisely, the mobilization capacity of several law enforcement agencies to target a specific drug supply chain or criminal group, can produce tangible outcomes.

Moreover, it seems that the number of law enforcement agencies involved in DEA international investigations presents stronger correlation coefficients than does investigation duration. Consequently, the results may suggest that the number of police partners constitutes a better predictor when assessing the possible outcomes of law enforcement efforts to dismantle international drug supply chains. At first glance this assumption can appear trivial, but its operational application is not insignificant at all. In reality, it could mean that investigation duration (which refers to the capacity of police agencies to invest resources – human, material, and financial – over a certain period of time) can be less important than the diversity of interactions among police services. Consequently, it is essential to examine if a relationship exists between the diversity of interaction among foreign national law enforcement agencies and the operational outcomes of international investigations. The rationale behind this proposition is based on the assumption that the diversity of interactions with foreign police services could provide the DEA with an enlarged network of expertise and intelligence sources, significantly affecting the way that international investigations are conducted.

Diversity of international police cooperation

Table 14.2 displays the results of the average distribution of specific operational outcomes (total drug seizures and arrests) as regards

Table 14.2 Arrests and drug seizures per operation according to three levels of police cooperation diversity (2000–2008)

Level of Diversity in Police Cooperation	Average Arrests (total arrests) (total seizures)	Average Drug Seizure
(1) **Nil** – No foreign police service involved (n=14) (average investigation duration=17 months)	93 (1,306)	3,332 kg (46,659 kg)
(2) **Limited** – Coop. with police from developing countries (n= 29) (average investigation duration=15 months)	87 (2,448)	3,548 kg (102,900 kg)
(3) **Extended** – Coop. with several foreign police services (n=18) (average investigation duration=17 months)	273 (4,924)	24,411 kg (439,400 kg)

three levels of diversity of interaction in international investigations initiated by the DEA. The first level refers to major operations targeting international drug trafficking rings initiated by the DEA without any assistance from foreign police services (Diversity=Nil). These types of investigations usually take place when the DEA receives privileged information related to imminent drug shipments bound for the United States or on transit vessels located in international waters near US shores. During the period 2000–2008, the DEA conducted at least 14 investigations of this type, lasting an average of 17 months. This duration may seem long, considering that these investigations were based on first-hand intelligence. However, one must consider the fact that in these operations the investigative work begins after the crackdown in order to backtrack through the criminal network of connections and identify key individuals involved in a specific drug smuggling endeavour. Over an eight-year period, the DEA's solo operations generated a total of 1,306 arrests and the seizure of 46,659 kilograms of drugs, which represent an average of 93 arrests and 3,332 kilograms per operation.

The second level refers to international police cooperation initiatives exclusively involving bilateral partnerships between the DEA and law enforcement agencies coming from 'developing countries' or weak states. According to the documents provided by the DEA, most of these investigations were done in cooperation with police services from Colombia and Mexico, though there were a few joint investigations with security forces located in Honduras and the Caribbean as well. The importance given to Colombia and Mexico at this level highlights the DEA's strategic objectives regarding the targeting of cocaine production and transportation in 'transit countries' located in Central America.

During the period between 2000–2008, the DEA conducted at least 29 major international joint investigations with police partners coming from 'developing countries'. On average, these bilateral operations lasted 15 months, generating 87 arrests and seizures of 3,548 kilograms per operation (for a total of 2,448 arrests and 102,900 kg seized). These results are particularly interesting for the reason that bilateral police cooperation limited to developing countries shows no differences in terms of operational outcomes when compared with the DEA's 'solo international investigations' (an average of arrests and seizure by operation). This observation seems to be counterintuitive especially when police cooperation is with law enforcement agencies situated in countries where cocaine is produced or transported. One should expect that this type of partnership increases the availability and exchanges of first-hand criminal intelligence and generates better operational outcomes since national police forces have a direct access to primary sources of information in the criminal milieu. However, this lack of difference between the DEA's solo operations and bilateral investigations can be explained by political, economic and legal issues.

Firstly, it's essential to point out that countries like Colombia and Mexico are states in which the police apparatus is weakened considerably by domestic tensions provoked by the presence of revolutionary groups and powerful drug cartels. In other words, police agencies face several difficulties and an incapacity to maintain order and enforce laws. Moreover, there is also considerable political pressure from the US on the Colombian and Mexican governments to maintain, and accelerate, the 'war against drugs' in order to significantly reduce cocaine production and drug smuggling (Merida Initiative 2007; Plan Colombia 1999). This internal pressure translates into an increase in US federal law enforcement leadership regarding the management and execution of numerous major investigations targeting cocaine trafficking rings in Colombia and Mexico. More precisely, these conditions directly affect the work of the DEA and cooperating agencies as regards: 1) the recruitment process for

Colombian police officers who will work on major investigations with US investigators (*vetted team*) in order to minimize the risk of corruption; 2) a redefinition of standards and norms related to training; and 3) the management of key human sources.

Information gathered in interviews with police officers from the national police and the *Departamento Administrativo de Seguridad* in Colombia has highlighted the US influence on anti-drug operations. For instance, the DEA is actively involved in the recruitment and remuneration of police informants with the assistance of the local US embassy and the Colombian authorities. This situation, which is similar to operations in Mexico, helps us to understand better the small differences in operational outcomes that exist between Levels 1 and 2 (see Table 14.2). In fact, similarities in operational outcomes reflect, to some extent, the replication and imitation of the DEA's investigative techniques and know-how by 'junior police services' coming from in-transition countries. This explanation emphasizes a certain form of 'colonialism' when bilateral cooperation operations are led by the DEA. Consequently, the potential contribution of international police cooperation methods seems to be diluted by the political and resource dominance of one police organization over another.

Secondly, it should also be mentioned that legal processes remain a primary concern of the DEA, especially judicial procedures regarding criminal investigations. Since a portion of an international investigation will take place in a foreign country, the DEA's investigators will want to ensure that evidence gathered abroad will be accepted by a US court of law. In fact, a large number of investigation cases used in this study contained several extradition orders for traffickers arrested in Colombia and Mexico. Therefore, it is not surprising to observe that the DEA's investigative and intelligence collection techniques (recognized by the US criminal justice system) are replicated in international investigations taking place in 'weaker' foreign countries, especially when these countries do not have the capacity or willingness to protect their sovereignty in such security matters.

However, it appear that the DEA's extended international operations require a greater degree of diversity in police cooperation (Table 14.2 Level 3) as these generate far more arrests and seizures when compared with 'solo operations' and/or those only involving police agencies from developing countries. During 2000–2008, the DEA led at least 18 multilateral cooperation initiatives with an average duration of 17 months and utilized several national law enforcement agencies from both developed and developing countries

275

(mixed international cooperation). These investigations generated approximately a total of 4,924 arrests and 439,400 kilograms in drug seizures, which represents an average of 273 arrests and 24,411 kilograms per operation. One might think that the inflation of arrests and seizures is disproportionately affected by a few outliers in the data set. However, a close examination of the cases presented in Level 3 shows that the characteristics common to all 18 investigations are precisely the large number of arrests and massive seizures.

Information gathered in interviews with investigators from the United Kingdom, France, the Netherlands, and Canada shows that highly diversified international cooperation initiatives offer four types of advantages: 1) sharing and pooling knowledge acquired on several drug supply chains using different routes across continents generates a better understanding of criminal network structures and the nature of connections among key traffickers; 2) a diversification of investigative and intelligence collection techniques offers investigators more legal options when they press criminal charges; 3) a diversification of information sources and police informants offers better chances to penetrate or infiltrate criminal groups targeted by the investigation; and 4) benefits from loose or different legal environments in other countries allow investigators to collect intelligence that may be less valuable in court, but is still essential to the success of an investigation. Therefore, it seems that when the DEA initiates multilateral investigations at the international level, the gains in terms of outcome and expertise enhancement (output) increase sharply.

Still, according to the information gathered in the interviews, one of the main downsides of increased diversity in international police cooperation is the competition for arrests and seizures among northern hemisphere-based law enforcement agencies. In principle, all police services participating in an international investigation will pursue the same objective which is the dismantling of a given drug supply chain. When bilateral cooperation is established between police services situated in the North-South axis, any merit associated with a successful investigation is generally self-proclaimed by the law enforcement agency coming from the northern hemisphere. Indeed it is the northern-based agency that usually initiates the investigation. It is not surprising to observe this sort of interaction between Colombian or Mexican police services and the DEA when considering the importance of the investment made by the latter in terms of technology and human and financial resources. Yet, when international investigations are conducted using a multilateral approach and include interactions between law enforcement agencies in a North-North alliance, the management of the partnership becomes more delicate and the redistribution of expected operational outcomes can be subject to intense negotiations, leading at times to profound disagreements. Among the most common disagreements mentioned by the investigator interviewees are: 1) the location of seizures (country); 2) the individuals who should be arrested and those who should remain free for further investigations; and 3) a country's right to extradite and the priority of extraditions when an individual is facing several arrest warrants from multiple countries.

Conclusion

This study does contribute to the existing body of research on police cooperation assessment in the US at the local and regional levels. The work of Smith *et al.* (2001) indicates that partnerships between police services increase operational performances (arrests) and improve professional relations internally and externally (organizational sociability) when compared with law enforcement agencies acting alone. In this vein, our results recall the importance of considering numerous implicit components of international investigations related to the level of diversity in police cooperation – a diversity that cannot be measured using a quantitative methodology. Therefore, to better assess the effectiveness of international police cooperation initiatives, it will be critical to pay closer attention to the nature of exchanges between partnering police services by scrutinizing the quality of criminal intelligence, the type of information sources, and the sophistication of investigative techniques. At the strategic level, it would be important to examine how legal, organizational and political dimensions can affect partnerships between foreign police services and the way they share intelligence.

A central challenge in police cooperation is to overcome both reactive policing and the complex bureaucratization of police work. In order to cope with these organizational obstacles and implement successful cooperation initiatives, police officers and law enforcement agencies usually adopt specific strategies which must be in accordance with environmental characteristics and the purpose of their mission. Continental divides regarding international cooperation strategies between North America and Europe are not new. In fact, a similar contrast has been made by Kagan (2002: 3), positioning Europe and the US at two diametrically opposed strategic poles in international relations in general. According to the author, America is from Mars and Europe is from Venus, meaning that the first is more inclined to use force and the latter is more diplomacy-oriented when dealing with international security issues (e.g. the war in Iraq, a response to terrorism). This premise of opposing approaches has been increasingly criticized (Kohring 2007) and challenged, in light of recent EU policies indicating an intention to develop a European military capacity in the near future.

Nevertheless, when it comes to international police cooperation, national police agencies in North America and Europe are clearly operating differently. In the EU, cooperative modes appear to be oriented toward the development of a means of interaction (international structures and systems). In North America, cooperation amongst police agencies seems to be strongly influenced by operational outcomes. This differentiation indicates that a development of police cooperation strategies could fall under two paradigms: economic and political. However, it should be mentioned that, in both paradigms, police cooperation follows opportunistic motives.

In the first paradigm, police agencies function with an economic rationale led by drivers such as efficiency, performance, effective resource allocation, and operational outcomes. Under such a paradigm, the main postulate specifies that police cooperation or interagency assistance should only occur with the involvement of key actors who can positively affect the results of a given international investigation. This paradigm considers police agencies as rational entities that want to maximize their gains (operational outcomes) and minimize their costs (resource investment). In this context, leadership of the cooperative initiative generally falls to those agencies that have access to more resources and usually possess excellent 'records' in terms of operational outcomes. In other words, effectiveness and cooperation are legitimated by the expected results in terms of arrests, seizures and convictions. Operational objectives represent a central factor in determining the amount of resources needed and the scope of the police agencies' networks ('police net') required for the undertaking (Nadelmann 1993). This performance-based approach to several police functions has been described and studied in recent years, especially in North America or Anglo-Saxon countries (for example, see the works of Maguire 2000; O'Connell and Straub 2007; Sherman 1997, 1998).

The second paradigm is political: international police cooperation operates under political leadership that shapes structures and systems. In such a paradigm, the police cooperation drivers are related to past and current diplomatic relations, consensual collaboration amongst states actors, a common legal framework, and shared security issues. The outcomes do not necessarily focus on operational results but are also geared towards implementing effective strategies, structures and systems that can increase information sharing among national police agencies without provoking political or legal outrage. In this context, international police cooperation is based on consensus and the establishment of collective processes (multi-governmental cooperation structures). In the EU, this particular paradigm creates the situation in which national police agencies primarily compete not for results and resources, but rather for exercising political influence and imposing professional standards (best practices) on the rest of the European police agencies (see Gerspacher and Lemieux, this book).

It is interesting to see how the domestic cooperation background of national police agencies in North America differs from that of Europe. We can easily observe the existence of several multilateral cooperation initiatives among North American police agencies, taking the form of regional integrated units, joint task forces or multi-jurisdictional task forces (especially in the United States). Usually, these initiatives are oriented toward specific criminal problems and aim to avoid a duplication of investigations at the regional level, as well as integrate all jurisdictions and key actors concerned with a particular security problem (local, regional and federal agencies; prosecutors; non police agencies; etc.). This strategy gained popularity during the 1990s and spread rapidly after 9/11 in order to deal more effectively with terrorism, organized crime and repeat offenders (see Perras and Lemieux, this book). Currently, a convergence of the judicial and extra-judicial with the aim of addressing security issues represents a strong trend in domestic law enforcement cooperation, encouraging the creation of numerous fusion centres and integrated structures across America. The aptitude of North American law-enforcement agencies to engage in multilateral investigations at the domestic level contrasts sharply with the trend observed at the international level, where bilateral cooperation initiatives are the main focus (Deflem 2001).

The distinction between EU and North American police cooperation practices can be explained by the historical foundations and the sources of legitimacy of police systems. As noted by Deflem (2002, 2005), most of the European police apparatus was based on certain administrative and bureaucratic approaches, influencing the way agencies cooperate today. Moreover, in continental Europe, police legitimacy is granted by the government and the police mission is generally oriented more toward administrative tasks and aligned with the particular country's security issues (Bayley 1985). In contrast, North American law enforcement agencies are held accountable to private citizens as well as governments and they are predisposed to provide measurable performance achievement based on crime rates and public satisfaction surveys. These organizational performance measures are published in annual reports and weekly press releases. Differences in political and legitimacy concerns between police systems in Europe and North America can help to explain disparities in international police cooperation approaches and practices.

Note

1 At the end of the 1980s, the US Department of Justice established the Edward M. Byrne Foundation, whose mandate is to support and promote the implementation of multi-jurisdictional investigation teams by local (city), regional (county) and state police agencies. This initiative has provided funding of $200–300 million in support of police partnerships.

Chapter 15

Challenges of governance and accountability for transnational private policing

Les Johnston and Philip C. Stenning

Introduction

The last two decades of the twentieth century and the first decade of the twenty-first have witnessed four developments, all of which have significantly affected the provision of policing and security. First, there has been a growing diversity of policing provision. At the domestic level – and increasingly at the international level too – the newly emerging 'policing family' is being made up of a multiplicity of partners, including both 'public' (state-sponsored) policing agencies and a host of 'private' and civil society bodies which, collectively, pose major challenges for effective and coherent regimes of governance and public accountability. Second, policing and security, both at the domestic and international level, have been subject to significant degrees of 'marketization' or 'commodification'. By and large, this has been built upon programmes of neoliberal reform that have come to dominate contemporary governance. A third factor, globalization, is closely connected to these processes. Globalization is a complex phenomenon. On the one hand, it tends to homogenize and integrate national and local differences. On the other hand, just as global forces impact on the local, so local actions will impact, reciprocally, on the global. This paradox is captured in what has become a mantra for transnational corporations, in general, and for transnational commercial security (TCS) in particular: 'Think globally, act locally'.[1]

A fourth theme, concerning the changing character of governance, connects with the previous three. A quarter of a century ago it was taken for granted that the state bore responsibility for governance, in general, and for the governance of security, in particular. Today, it is widely accepted that both have become 'multilateralized', 'pluralized' or 'polycentric'; the prerogative and responsibility of multiple auspices and providers (Bayley and Shearing 1996; Berg and Shearing 2008). Some of the factors contributing to these developments are, by now, well-rehearsed. Neo-liberal theories have tried to demarcate the 'steering' and 'rowing' functions of governance (Osborne and Gaebler 1993), employing policies of privatization, outsourcing and contracting-out to devolve what had, previously, been state functions to the non-state sector. Previously, under the traditional 'Westphalian model', governance – both domestic and international – was conceived according to hierarchically ordered, state-centric principles. Westphalian governance was also predicated upon a series of relatively clear distinctions being maintained: between 'the public' (the state) and 'the private' (the market and civil society); between 'internal' and 'external' security; and between 'the military' and 'the police'. Nowadays, these distinctions are increasingly undermined. Organized and cross-border crime has spawned transnational policing initiatives, such as Europol. The problem of weak and failing states has sanctioned police and military intervention by outside states and peacekeeping initiatives by supra-state bodies. Private security companies sell their services to multinational corporations and to weak states unable to maintain order within their territories. Soldiers, police officers and commercial security guards are employed as peace-keepers in war-torn regions.

One consequence of these developments is that the challenges to governance and accountability associated with domestic policing pluralization are replicated internationally in arenas which are beyond the reach of effective national regulation. In this chapter we examine some of these developments, explore the challenges they pose for effective governance and accountability, and consider some of the possibilities for meeting these challenges.

The chapter consists of four sections. In the first, we discuss some conceptual aspects of governance and accountability. Two points are emphasized: that governance is almost always multiplex, typically involving a plurality of institutions and mechanisms; and that the distinction between 'public' and 'private' governance is particularly difficult to apply to the governance of commercial security. This is especially so in respect of transnational commercial security (TCS). The second section examines the structural and functional complexity of TCS, focusing on the 'peace and stability operations' sector, since this encapsulates many of the governance issues that arise regarding relations between TCS organizations, states and non-state bodies. The third section considers the 'tangled web' of governance and accountability sources arising in respect of TCS. These include the widespread lack of transparency in financial relations between contractors and companies, the opacity of transnational subcontracting arrangements and the ambiguous legal status enjoyed by those working in TCS companies. A further, and particularly significant problem, involves the complex jurisdictional issues that arise from the plurality of legal regimes impacting on TCS, something which we outline in a number of 'scenarios'. The concluding section of the chapter reviews the preceding argument and explores further how multiplex regimes might be applied to the governance and accountability of TCS.

Governance and accountability: key concepts

Governance is a broad concept which refers to a set of relations between those who govern and those who are governed. It is generally understood to involve two key elements – control (or regulation) and accountability. Control involves institutions and mechanisms through which those who govern seek to direct or limit the activities of those whom they govern. Accountability refers to an obligation on the part of the governed to render accounts of their activities and so on to those who govern. Referring to the particular situation of the governance of public statutory authorities, Goldring and Wettenhall (1980: 136) have nicely captured the relationship between these two elements of governance:

> When we speak of the responsibility of statutory authorities, we are referring to two parallel and interlocking mechanisms. The first is the mechanism of control, which extends from the controlling person or institution to the controlled statutory authority. The second is the mechanism of answerability or accountability. The control mechanism provides a means for ensuring that the statutory authority acts, or refrains from acting, in certain ways. The answerability mechanism provides information to the controller, and may indicate the occasions in which the control mechanism is to be brought into play.

For a variety of reasons, however, the right to insist on the accountability of the governed is not always accompanied by the unfettered authority of governors to exercise control over them. So, for instance, the concept of 'political independence' is sometimes employed to insulate decision makers from unwanted (and especially partisan) political control, while at the same time ensuring that they remain politically accountable. These situations may be regarded as important exceptions to the general rule that control and accountability typically go hand in hand.

Governance is almost always multiplex (Mashaw 2006), which is to say that both control and the accountability of any person or body are typically achieved through a multiplicity of institutions and mechanisms. So, for instance, control over an institution may be vested in a number of different governing authorities, each with a different governing mandate, and institutions will typically be accountable to different authorities for different aspects of their operations. It therefore makes sense to think of controls and accountabilities (Day and Klein 1987) in the plural when considering the governance of a particular institution or set of institutions.

We may distinguish between 'public' and 'private' governance, although for reasons previously mentioned – and to be explored further below – such a clear distinction is becoming increasingly difficult to sustain. Broadly, however, institutions and agents of the state, as well as non-state institutions that are in receipt of public funding or whose activities are considered to have significant 'public interest' implications, are expected in a democracy to be the subjects of public governance while other 'private' institutions are, for the most part, not.[2] Public governance is typically enacted through constitutional provision, laws and various other forms of state regulation,[3] with four principal 'modes' of governance being political, legal (i.e. via courts and tribunals), administrative[4] and direct public governance.[5] Private governance (Macaulay 1986), on the other hand, is most typically enacted through the institutions of private contract (Fried 1981; Buckley 1999)[6] and/or trust (Bachmann and Zaheer 2008; Brinig 2000), albeit supported and facilitated by institutions for dispute resolution (such as civil courts and various tribunals) provided by the state at public expense. The principal 'modes' of private governance are thus legal governance and governance through negotiation and consent (e.g. through markets); property and privacy laws ensure that private corporations and institutions are subject to only limited political or direct public governance.

Such relatively straightforward concepts are not easily applied to the governance of private security companies and providers for three principal reasons. In the first place, they frequently provide security services under contract to governments or public institutions; such contractual arrangements inevitably render them susceptible to some level of public governance (Davies 2001). Secondly, even when they are operating on private property under private contract, if that property is of a kind that has come to be described as 'mass private property' (Jones and Newburn 1999; Kempa *et al.* 2004; Shearing and Stenning 1981, 1983) – that is, property, such as a shopping centre, which, although privately owned, can be considered a public place to which the general public are routinely invited and admitted – their activities will inevitably attract some measure of public governance 'in the public interest'. And thirdly, to the extent that 'security' is regarded as a public (or collective) as well as a private good (Crawford 2006; Hope 2000 and forthcoming; Loader and Walker 2001), there will inevitably be pressures to subject its provision, even by private providers, to some degree of public governance.[7]

These pressures towards public governance of private security pose major challenges at the domestic national level (Loader 2000; Stenning 2000, 2009). For reasons which we will elaborate in the following section, these challenges are multiplied and rendered greatly more complex when private security providers operate transnationally (Sheptycki 2002).

The transnational policing and security complex

Background

The changes to policing, security and insecurity just described have coincided with increased international collaboration between state security organizations and between the state and non-state security sectors. Examples include information and intelligence exchange in connection with offenders and offences; the exchange of investigative knowledge; the coordination of police operations across jurisdictions; the development of common programmes and strategies; the facilitation of 'hot pursuits' across borders; and the development of specialist investigative and other teams.

Several authors have tried to capture the complexity of these developments in a typological form. Benyon *et al.* (1993) differentiate between 'micro', 'meso' and 'macro' levels of cooperation, while

Loader and Walker (2007) distinguish between security practices operating 'below', 'above' and 'beyond' the state. Bowling and Foster's (2002) typology is particularly useful, drawing a four-fold distinction in which national policing agencies (such as MI5, MI6, Special Branch, the CIA, the DEA or the FBI), are operated 'by government'; transnational and cross-border police arrangements, such as Schengen, TREVI and Europol, operate 'between governments'; international policing agencies, such as the UN Security Police, the UN's Civil Police Units and Interpol, operate 'above government'; and private transnational policing bodies, such as Securitas and MPRI, operate 'beyond government'.

It is the last of these categories – what we shall term 'transnational commercial security' (TCS) – that provides the subject matter for the remainder of this chapter. The first and most important thing to say is that a consideration of the various bodies that make up TCS reveals this to be far from homogeneous. On the contrary, TCS is made up of six distinct, though by no means mutually exclusive, organizational types (Johnston forthcoming).

1 In-house security departments within transnational corporations. Many, if not most, global companies maintain in-house security departments though neoliberalism has coincided with security functions being increasingly outsourced to contract companies (see 2-6 below).

2 TCS companies offering specialist services (e.g. SECOM in respect of the provision of electronic surveillance).

3 Transnational service companies which, despite having little or no prior history in the security field, have now entered it due to the opportunities offered by the outsourcing of public services (e.g. Sodexho and Serco in the domain of private corrections).

4 Companies, such as Blackwater and MPRI, which are involved in the provision of armed defensive security services (sometimes called 'private military companies', though preferring to regard themselves as members of the 'peace and stability operations industry').

5 Multi-service security companies, such as G4S and Securitas, the largest players in the security market.

6 Security consultancies, such as Kroll and Control Risks, primarily concerned with the minimization of client risk.

The industry's functions are correspondingly wide, ranging from conventional ones (such as guarding, cash handling, alarm services, electronic security, and the provision of integrated security systems) to more specialized ones linked to transnational governance (such as airline security, drugs-testing, surveillance, executive protection, facility hardening and the monitoring of populations engaged in travelling, tourism and migration). A particularly important area of work is the anticipation of business risks and the minimization of losses arising from them. A critical factor in this has been the commodification of information, with Manning (2000) having noted some years ago that the US government – though the same is true for others – in cooperation with large corporations had broadened its definition of 'the national interest' to include industrial ideas with R&D potential (see most recently 'Running the world' 2009).

The 'peace and stability operations industry'

Clearly, TCS is both functionally and organizationally complex. Yet, while heuristically useful, the six-fold categorization is also porous, with companies sometimes operating across categorical boundaries.[8] This makes the task of analysing governance and accountability issues in respect of TCS all the more challenging. In order to simplify the task slightly we shall focus here on only one of the six categories just described: the 'peace and stability operations industry' (Category 4). Our reason for doing so is that this category encapsulates many of the problems that need to be addressed both across TCS as a whole, and in respect of relations between TCS organizations, states and non-state bodies.

Messner and Gracielli's recent (2007) survey on behalf of the Peace Operations Institute[9] provides important information about what these companies do; about where they do it; and about their clients and employees. They undertake a variety of functions including security services (e.g. armed or non-armed, static or mobile protection of 'nouns')[10]; training and security sector reform services (e.g. disarmament, demobilization and reintegration; training on cultural sensitivity and the history of regions/conflicts); information analysis and consultancy services (e.g. risk analysis/security audit); logistics and operational support services (e.g. participation in humanitarian action, counter-intelligence measures); IED/mine action services; and development services (e.g. institution building, humanitarian aid) (Messner and Gracielli 2007).

Their clients include government departments (such the US Department of Defense and the UK Ministry of Defence), NGOs (such as Christian Aid and Oxfam), international organizations (such as the UN and the African Union), private sector companies (such as those involved in the extractive industries in Nigeria and elsewhere) and private individuals. Their employees comprise three categories: expatriates who are usually from the same country as the employing company; local nationals or host country nationals who are from the country where the operation is taking place; and third country nationals who are from neither of these. Different categories of employee may pose different problems. For example, as we suggest in a moment, expatriates may be able to claim immunity from local laws; local nationals may contribute to the local economy but may bring problems of their own (e.g. the expedient hiring of armed local militias in Afghanistan has done little for disarmament, demobilization and reintegration; see Spearin 2008); and third country nationals may have dubious operational histories (e.g. the employment of Chileans, trained by the Pinochet regime, as guards at Baghdad Airport).

Finally, these companies operate simultaneously across several geographical spheres. Messner and Gracielli (2007) differentiate between three such levels: operational activities focus on a particular contract 'in-venue' (e.g. the provision of security in Iraq); support activities are provided in a venue outside the arena of operation (e.g. using Kuwait as a staging post for the provision of security services in Iraq); and administrative activities are usually centred on where a company has its headquarters. However, they also note that 'activities in any country can potentially encompass multiple activity categories' (Messner and Gracielli 2007: 22), a factor which may, potentially, raise complex legal and jurisdictional issues.

Sources of governance and accountability of TCS – a tangled web

Identifying possible sources of governance and accountability in respect of TCS is aided by having access to information, such as that just described: information about who companies are working for; about what relationships pertain between those they are working for, those they employ, and those they are policing; about where they are working; and about what they are doing. On that basis it is useful to distinguish between the following kinds of scenarios:

1 A TCS company based in Country A is providing policing/security services under contract to the government of Country B, in Country B.

2 A TCS company based in Country A contracts with the government of Country A to provide policing/security services to the government of Country B under the terms of an inter-governmental foreign assistance agreement.[11]

3 A TCS company based in Country A has contracted with Country A's government to provide policing services to its personnel working in Country B (e.g. providing protection for Country A's diplomats working in Country B).

4 A TCS company based in Country A contracts with an international organization (such as the United Nations or NATO) to provide policing/security services in Country B.

5 A TCS company based in Country A has contracted with a private transnational corporation or a charitable NGO, to provide protection for its property and/or personnel working in Country B.[12]

In each of these situations, the TCS company is potentially subject to the laws and judicial system of Country B while operating in that country, although in some cases immunity from Country B's laws and legal system may have been given as a condition of the contract under which the TCS operates in Country B (as was the case until very recently, for instance, for US TCSs working in Iraq under contract to the US government after the invasion of that country in 2003).[13] Private corporations, as well as governments, may sometimes be able to negotiate such immunity as a condition of operating/investing in a foreign country.

In each of these situations, too, the TCS company may also be subject to the laws of Country A while working in Country B. But this will depend on whether Country A's laws have applicable extra-territorial effect.[14]

When Country B is in a situation of war or insurgency, International Human Rights Law (IHL) will also come into play, and the TCS's liability to governance and accountability under IHL will depend on who its personnel are working for or with, and what services they are providing. Specifically, if TCS personnel are working for or with military units, they may be classed as 'combatants' or 'civilians accompanying military forces' (CAFs) depending on whether, and to what extent, their activities could be considered to involve active engagement in, or support of, combat. Such distinctions, unfortunately, are not always as clear cut, or subject to universal agreement, as one might wish.

Related to this, what domestic law (i.e. laws of Country A) the TCS and its employees may be subject to in situations 2 and 3 above may depend on which part of the government of Country A they have contracted with. In the United States, for instance, TCSs that contract with the Defense Department become subject to the US's Code of Military Justice (UCMJ), whereas those who contract, for instance, with the US State Department to protect US diplomats overseas do not.

In situation 4, where a TCS company contracts with an international body to, for instance, assist in peacekeeping activities, it will also be subject to the international body's own rules and guidelines (in the case of the United Nations, the United Nations Peacekeeping Operations: Principles and Guidelines 2008), which may include accountability requirements. In many such cases, only the countries of origin of the company and its employees (which will often not be the same) have the authority to take action against misconduct, and in the case of UN peacekeeping missions Country B will typically have entered into a Status of Forces Agreement in which it surrenders jurisdiction over peacekeeping personnel for violations of its own laws (Allred 2006).

Finally, since the promulgation of the Treaty of Rome in 1998, personnel employed by TCSs may find themselves liable to the jurisdiction of the International Criminal Court if they are involved in crimes against humanity (such as genocide) or war crimes.

So far, we have considered a variety of formal-legal-jurisdictional issues that impact on sources of governance and accountability in respect of TCS. However, it is also worth noting a number of other factors that affect these issues.

First, limited knowledge makes the pursuit of accountability difficult. The situation in Afghanistan illustrates this problem. The private military and security budget is projected to reach $210 billion in 2010 (Perrin 2008: 5). Yet, a recent Canadian report on human security in Afghanistan (Independent Panel 2008) makes no reference at all to the industry (Spearin 2008: 8). This is indicative of widespread ignorance about this industry. As Bearpark (2008) points out, the current regulatory debate is hampered by a general lack of knowledge. For instance, we have no reliable figures on the number of security operators on the ground in Iraq and Afghanistan and, more often than not, we do not know the nationality of individual contractors.

A second problem concerns the widespread lack of transparency in financial relations between contractors and companies. A report from the US Congressional Budget Office recently stated that $100 billion had been spent on contractors in Iraq since the invasion of 2003. Yet, critics suggest that lack of adequate auditing in the first years of the war renders such estimates highly problematical (Risen 2008). These criticisms are likely to be true, given the fact that many contracts were awarded on a 'cost plus' basis, an approach that has led to allegations of dubious practice.[15] Lack of accounting transparency has also coincided with what Joras and Schuster (2008: 1) call 'an overall lack of transparency regarding [private security companies] with respect to hiring practices, mandates, identification [of personnel], accountability and supervision'.

Third, these issues are exacerbated by the opaque transnational subcontracting arrangements that underpin service delivery in arenas like Iraq. In one alleged instance, a TCS contractor first added a 36 per cent mark-up, plus its overhead costs, to an invoice. The invoice then went, first to a Kuwaiti hotel (sic) company which added on its costs for buying vehicles and weapons plus a profit element; then to a German company that cooked meals for the troops, which added on its costs and profit; then to the primary contractor, which added further overheads and profit before sending the bill to the Pentagon (Neff and Price 2004). In another case a TCS contractor was unable to document 42 per cent of a $4 billion invoice submitted to the Pentagon, much of it for subcontracted services about which the contractor refused to communicate on grounds of commercial confidentiality (Johnston 2006).

A fourth issue, to which we alluded earlier, concerns the ambiguous legal status of many employees working in this sector and the implications of that ambiguity for their human rights. Gomez del Prado (2008), Chairperson of the UN Working Group on the Use of Mercenaries, notes that most of the guards recruited by these companies perform military or quasi-military tasks in low intensity conflicts or in post-conflict situations. They operate with little oversight or army control and many are neither nationals of one of the parties to the conflict nor residents of the country in conflict. Most have taken direct part in conflicts, though they are not trained to do so, and many (e.g. Chileans, Nepalese, Fijians) have not been officially sent by their respective states. From a legal point of view, as long as they do not participate in hostilities they remain civilians with the right to protection under international humanitarian law. Once they participate in hostilities, however, they lose that right. Overall, their status is both ambiguous and problematic for international law:

> The fact ... that they are neither civilians nor combatants; that they are operating in a grey area; and that they may be easily assimilated to mercenaries, paramilitaries, irregular fighters or 'unlawful combatants', is undermining the international humanitarian law and the Geneva Conventions. (Gomez del Prado 2008: 10)

The situation is particularly difficult for third-country nationals, the majority of whom come from poor socio-economic environments. Frequently, they will sign contracts of employment which call upon them to waive certain rights (e.g. the right to sue an employing company when that company has contributed to personal damage, injury or death). Once employed, many face excessively long hours, poor working conditions, partial or non-payment of salaries, and a lack of access to medical and other services.

A hypothetical example

To illustrate these complexities, let us consider an hypothetical example. PrisonOps is a TCS company that provides services to governments for managing detention facilities. The company contracts with the Defence Department of the fictional state of Auberon, which has recently invaded, and now occupies, the 'failed' state of Zebron, which is now under the administration of a transitional government appointed by Auberon and its invading allies pending 'stabilization' and the holding of free elections. The contract is to manage a detention centre for persons who were taken into custody by the coalition forces during and after the invasion, and insurgents ordered to be detained by the transitional government. Auberon and Zebron, prior to its invasion, were signatories to the UN Convention Against Torture and Other Cruel, Inhuman or Degrading Punishment, and Zebron, but not Auberon, was a signatory to the Rome Statute of the International Criminal Court. The contract between PrisonOps specifies that the company must comply with the laws of Auberon, the military Code of Conduct of the Auberon Defence Forces, and with the terms of the UN Convention, in operating the detention centre in Zebron, but that its employees will enjoy immunity from the laws of Zebron while operating in that country. This immunity is confirmed by the transitional administration in Zebron.

To staff the detention centre, PrisonOps advertised internationally for staff, and many of those it employs are not citizens either of Auberon or of Zebron. It is discovered that employees on one shift of workers at the facility have engaged in treatment of the detainees which can be considered to be in violation of the UN Convention, as well as of the laws of Auberon and Zebron, and consequently of the terms of PrisonOps' contract. Staff on this shift who are implicated in these allegations include citizens of Auberon, citizens of Zebron, and citizens of third countries. Most of the detainees involved are citizens of Zebron, but some are citizens of neighbouring countries who had entered Zebron illegally in support of the insurgency.

Without going into great detail, it will be evident that holding individual PrisonOps employees accountable for their alleged offending will involve a lot of difficulties and complexity, especially if the state of Auberon, for whatever reasons, is disinclined to do so. The status of the particular detainees concerned (were they prisoners of war under international law?), the status of the staff involved (their citizenship), and the nature of the alleged offences (did they amount to torture or other 'crimes against humanity' or war crimes?) will all be relevant to whether, and in which courts, if any, PrisonOps executives or any of its employees directly or indirectly implicated in the alleged offending can be brought to justice. In such circumstances, the risk of impunity may sometimes be as high as the probability of effective accountability and justice for the victims of the abuses, particularly if the employees concerned have since left Zebron and/ or their employment with PrisonOps.

Conclusion: multiplex governance and TCS

In the first section of this chapter we discussed some key conceptual issues in respect of governance and accountability. Two points were emphasized: that governance is almost always multiplex, typically being enacted through a multiplicity of institutions and mechanisms; and that the distinction between 'public' and 'private' governance is particularly difficult to apply to the governance of commercial security. This is particularly so in respect of TCS, the structural and functional complexity of which was explored in the second section. In order to simplify this task, our analysis focused on the 'peace and stability operations' sector, taking this to encapsulate many of the problems that arise across TCS as a whole, and in respect of relations between TCS organizations, states and non-state bodies.

Drawing on that analysis, the third section considered the 'tangled web' of governance and accountability sources arising in respect of TCS. These included the widespread lack of transparency in financial relations between contractors and companies, the opacity of transnational subcontracting arrangements, and the ambiguous legal status enjoyed by those working in TCS companies. A particularly significant problem – as indicated in our five scenarios – concerned the complex jurisdictional matters arising from the plurality of legal regimes impacting on TCS. In Iraq, for example, TCS is governed by at least seven different types of legal regime, including the Military Extraterritorial Jurisdiction Act (MEJA), the Uniform Code of Military Justice, and licensing systems run, respectively, by the Iraqi government and Iraqi Kurds ('Whose law must mercenaries obey?' 2008). Inevitably, legal plurality generates jurisdictional contestation. Thus, the decision of the US authorities to indict Blackwater personnel in connection with their alleged involvement in the shooting dead of 17 Iraqi civilians (see note 14) was the culmination of a long dispute in which Blackwater lawyers had claimed that MEJA could only be applied to contractors working for the Defense Department, not the State Department (Wilber and de Young 2008).

This analysis suggests that once security ceases to be the exclusive prerogative of the state and becomes, instead, the product of multiple auspices and providers, the limits of conventional ('Westphalian') solutions to security governance are exposed. Despite this, debate about the governance and accountability of TCS remains dominated by formal-legal discourse. According to this, 'good governance' is the product of formal-legal interventions by states, either individually or in collaboration with one another. Undoubtedly, legal intervention does have a vital role to play in governance. Yet, it also has limitations. Thus, attempts to outlaw mercenaries in international law have foundered because of the problem of defining the term 'mercenary' (Ghebali 2006); governance of TCS is problematic because companies, faced with harsher regulation, simply move their headquarters from one jurisdiction to another (Caparini 2006: 272); calls for the harmonization of international law face multiple obstacles (Grabosky 2000); and even when formal regulation is actually implemented, political expediency may undermine its more laudable aims; the mobilization of TCS as a vehicle of US foreign policy has led to what

Caparini (2006: 272) aptly terms 'regulatory capture'. Last, but not least, state-commercial partnership is not a 'one-way street'. When commercial organizations carry out functions on behalf of the state they remain subject to its legal authority; but, crucially, the parameters of state action will be conditioned by the organizational practices of the companies involved.[16]

Despite these obstacles, state meta-regulation over plural security nodes – what Loader and Walker (2007) term 'state anchored pluralism' – is commonly regarded as the *sine qua non* of good security governance. Yet, while meta-regulation may be a desirable objective in respect of TCS, there is 'much discretionary space between the principles that meta-regulators use to direct governance and the way in which their directions are applied in practice' (Shearing 2007: 262–3). What we may find in reality, then, is less a single anchor empowered to steer governance, than 'multiple actors, each contesting to realize competing governing agendas' (Shearing 2007: 263). That is not to dismiss formal-legal regulation, of course; it is merely to suggest that pluralised security demands pluralistic modes of governance and accountability.

Though writing, primarily, about the private military sector, Cockayne's (2008) image of the future is applicable both to commercial security in general and – in light of the difficulties of constructing transnational legal solutions – to TCS in particular. In it, he suggests that particular attention should be paid to the construction of hybrid – or what we earlier called multiplex – forms of regulation. These forms, combining state, market and normative regulatory power:

> ... will only come about through multiple forms of regulatory activity – not only through state-based legislation and judicial action, but also through transnational political mobilization and direct interaction with the industry to foster changes in values, views and practices. Law alone will not be enough ... we need to think about ways of treating non-state actors ... not only as objects of governance, but as sources of normativity and legitimacy. This will require a highly creative approach to global governance, going well beyond state-centric international legal approaches, emphasizing non-territorial and non-hierarchical aspects of global 'public' citizenship, and ... 'democratic' control ... through transnational action combining civil society, industry and state-based action. (Cockayne 2008: 21, 30–31)

Under such multiplex regimes, many different actors would be required to play a governance role including state bodies, professional associations, industry associations, accreditation bodies, labour unions, banks and other businesses, insurance companies, NGOs, and international organizations, such as the IMF, the World Bank and the EU (Caparini 2008). Their role would be to offer a plurality of interventions in respect of governance: from compliance and standard-setting to the inculcation of professional norms; and from the application of formal-legal rules to the development of self-regulatory regimes. Of course, hybridity cannot guarantee efficacy and it would be naïve to ignore its limitations. Formal regulation may have its limits but so does self-regulation, and the normative benefits of professionalization are lost if it becomes a mere 'occupational strategy' supporting sectional interests (Johnson 1972). Nevertheless, in circumstances where security governance is beyond the reach of effective national regulation, multiplex solutions are both inevitable and essential.

Notes

1 Significantly, one of the earliest versions of this mantra came from a security company, the former Securicor Group Plc having once headed its web page with the slogan 'Global expertise, local understanding'.
2 Of course, the criminal law and other branches of public law (e.g. immigration law) ensure that all of us are to some extent the subjects of public governance.
3 And in some cases custom or 'constitutional convention' (Marshall 1984).
4 Which is typically internal (i.e. administrative arrangements within the governed institution) and external (i.e. control by, and accountability to, external administrative bodies such as government departments, auditors, etc.).
5 Direct public control is rare; direct public accountability is most notably achieved through so-called 'freedom of information' laws.
6 Although, as Crawford (2003) and others have pointed out, in some circumstances public governance is now being enacted through a form of 'contractual governance'.
7 E.g. public licensing and regulation of private contract security companies and their employees.
8 Examples would be the acquisitions of Pinkerton and ArmorGroup (Category 6) respectively by Securitas and G4S (Category 5); and the role of security consultancies (Category 6) in the provision of private military services in Iraq and Afghanistan (Category 4).

9 The POI was established in 2006 by the IPOA, a lobbying organization for the industry, to educate the public about peace and stability operations: see http://peaceops.org/poi/

10 Industry parlance for 'people, places and things'.

11 A variant of this would be where a TCS based in Country C contracts with the government of Country A to provide policing/security services in Country B.

12 Private corporations may also, of course, employ their own in-house security personnel to protect their property and workers in foreign countries.

13 Under Coalition Provisional Authority (CPA) Order #17 (28 June 2004). TCS companies operating in Iraq were required to obtain a licence to operate there from the Iraqi government. In January 2009 the immunity of TCS personnel from Iraqi law was removed (Pallister 2008), and later in the same month the Iraqi government refused to renew the licence of a US TCS company in light of its alleged involvement in an incident in central Baghdad which resulted in 17 Iraqi civilians being shot dead (Chulov and Tran 2009 – and see note 14).

14. Private security personnel employed by the TCS company Blackwater (since renamed Xe Services), under a contract with the US State Department to provide protection for US personnel working in Iraq, were indicted in the US for activities there resulting in the deaths of 17 Iraqi civilians. The prosecution, however, collapsed as a result of violations of the accuseds' rights, following which the company offered financial compensation to the survivors of the incident and victims' relatives, by way of settlement of several civil lawsuits. The Iraqi government has now indicated its intention to initiate civil proceedings against the company in the U.S. courts. In early 2010 two former security guards with this company were arrested in the U.S. on murder charges arising out of a shooting in Afghanistan which left two Afghans dead (Risen, 2010).

15 Under 'cost plus' the company is paid a fee ('cost-plus 2%') above the cost of the service. Since contracts are demand-led their value is open-ended and, as a result, there is neither an incentive for good nor a disincentive for bad service. Allegations include claims that KBR ran empty fuel convoys in order to benefit from 'cost-plus' contractual arrangements; and that Custer Battles which, despite having no relevant experience, gained a $16 billion contract for guarding the Iraq International Airport, set up shell companies in the Cayman Islands to rack up profits from false receipts. Overall, it has been estimated that the total sum 'stolen, missing and not properly accounted for' in Iraq amounts to $23 billion (*BBC Panorama Special* 2008).

16 See Abrahamson and Williams (2005) on the role of TCS in Nigeria; and Johnston *et al*. (2008) on state policing and the Private Finance Initiative in Britain. For further discussion of the issue of 'conditionality' in governance see Johnston (forthcoming).

Chapter 16

The constabulary ethic reconsidered

James Sheptycki[1]

> *He who fights with monsters might take care lest he thereby become a monster. And if you gaze for long into an abyss, the abyss gazes also into you.*
>
> Friedrich Nietzsche

Introduction

The starting point here is a previous essay in which I introduced the notion of a 'constabulary ethic' to the literature on transnational policing and tied it to the nascent rubric of 'human security'. The reason for choosing to write about the 'Constabulary Ethic and the Transnational Condition' (Goldsmith and Sheptycki 2007: 31–71) was a perceived gap in the literature. There has been sustained examination of what is wrong with the institutions of social ordering and the best of this work is global in its intellectual and practical reach. This interdisciplinary socio-legal scholarship has frequently paid considerable attention to processes of reconciliation and restorative justice; it has done remarkable things in terms of exposing the abuses of police power around the world; and this academic work has dove-tailed very well with human-rights activists and the nexus of NGOs in which these actors are embedded (Downes *et al.* 2007). The cue for this work was 'a triple loyalty: first an overriding obligation to honest intellectual enquiry itself ... second, a political commitment to social justice; and third (and potentially conflicting with both), the pressing and immediate demands for short-term help' (Cohen 1998: 122). The watchwords for this intellectual project could have been taken from ancient Roman statecraft's *si vis pacem, para iustitiam* (loosely translated 'if you want peace, prepare justice'; cf. Reiner 2007: 418).

This type of engaged scholarship is quite rightly concerned with describing accurately the array of institutions – and the structural forces at play between them – that sustain the manifest and manifold injustices of the global system as it is. Such work is often equally concerned with transition states where there is the hope of making things better (see the special edition of *Policing and Society* 2004). Scholars working in this vein have also been quite directly involved in pressing and immediate issues, for example concerning matters of surveillance, detention and torture. Scholarship to date has, quite rightly, been concerned with both the *is* and the *ought*. The gap I perceive in the literature concerns the theorizing of a constructive role for policing in the transformation of the emergent global social order. It seems necessary to argue that the 'people involved in policing, transnational and otherwise, must be positively involved in the project of global governance; either they are part of the solution or they are part of the problem, there is no middle way' (Sheptycki 2004: 32). At present a variety of policing agents have acquired positions of considerable responsibility in the complex system of governance globally and they are guided by rather different watchwords from Roman statecraft: *si vis pacem, para bellum* (if you want peace, prepare for war). The development of a vocabulary of constabulary ethics is one way to help move the conversation from *para bellum* to *para iustitium. Nil desperandum, cedant arma iustia* (never despair, let arms yield to justice) (Sheptycki 2007: 62).

Previous criticism of the constabulary ethic idea

Some criticisms of the original formulation of the constabulary ethic have been suggested and these have taken several forms. The first observes that, as it was expressed, the constabulary ethic idea lacked practical specificity as a guide to police action. In other words, my initial attempt did not formulate the constabulary ethic in terms of precise rules. In response I can only say at the outset that my perspective does not allow that ethics can be demonstrated in the manner of a mathematical proof. Perhaps ethics teachers in police training colleges desire a geometric model in which axioms and propositions follow each other with strict logical necessity. There are lots of reasons to adopt this view and good examples in the policing literature of this axiomatic approach (Bayley 2001; Neyroud 2001). However, and as police working in operational settings will attest, once reduced to formulae ethics seldom survive the first point of contact with reality.

Ethics – and certainly something like a constabulary ethic – are ultimately about practical action to change the circumstances that give rise to moral dilemmas in the first instance. In such contexts that involve policing there cannot be a pre-established ethical calculus because constabulary action inherently concerns provisional solutions to contingent situations involving social harm, conflict, injustice and disorder that cannot be fully specified in advance. There can be no meaningful discussion of a constabulary ethic which seeks to reduce the idea to a strictly logical schema, a set of axioms, or a list of rules. As I have argued throughout my earlier work, in the era of transnationalization – where the very grounds of knowledge are uncertain – human beings *really* do have to make political choices and they have to do so with regard to circumstances which exhibit many urgencies. Albeit in the absence of certain grounds for knowledge, efforts to change the transnational condition will, I have argued, hopefully result in the rediscovery of the possibilities of freedom, rights, responsibilities and human creativity; but none of this can be specified with mathematical precision and no list of do's and don'ts will suffice either.

What is consistently useful in shaping ethical police behaviour, whether of a parochial or global nature, is that constabulary activity is opened up to constant scrutiny by critically informed outside observers: 'It doesn't take long for experienced people to determine whether community policing programs are real, abuses of authority minimal, patrol officers responsive, the public cooperative, management open, operational decisions based on adequate information, and police activities open to public inspection' (Bayley 2001: 76). This applies equally to all manner of human security issues. The effects of such scrutiny are not necessarily enhanced by being blinkered (some would say 'guided') by lists of auditable criteria; it is enhanced by cooperative and open discussions between both independent observers and involved practitioners, neither of whom should act in what Jean-Paul Sartre called 'bad faith'.

Other criticisms have been levelled. These focus on actually existing transnational policing missions. Fieldwork reveals the incommensurability of cultural norms surrounding the police use of force in different regions of the world and in different policing institutions (Hills 2009). Examining extensive evidence concerning transnational police missions, Hills avers that there is no evidence of an actually existing police craft and accompanying value set that could be characterized as a constabulary ethic and that it is extremely difficult to move from case studies, project assessments and anecdotal accounts to universal first principles. Moreover, she also suggests that globally traditions of totalitarian policing are in the ascendant. This is nowhere more obvious than in the Global South. Observing the distinction between 'force' and 'violence' (PUOF 2008) she argues that cultural differences influence the use of force in everyday policing – that policing is therefore fundamentally different in Ohio and Nigeria.[2] It follows that it is difficult to inductively derive from existing practice a universal transnational ethic for policing that can integrate the full range of practices and values that constitute the term 'police'.

Professor Hills and I agree that the present offers a laboratory in which to investigate the many practical obstacles to good policing and that it is essential to document the many 'natural experiments' taking place as policing standards habituated at the local and sub-state level cross-pollinate under conditions of transnationalization. The ominous signs are that the results of that cross-pollination are contributing towards an authoritarian drift in global governance (Goldsmith and Sheptycki 2007: 44–46). It is the case that current modes of transnational policing are not primarily intended as a means for ensuring a just and equitable world order – indeed all too often things seem opposite. That is why it is all the more important to articulate a language of good policing as a bulwark against repressive policing. Philosophical reflection is not, by itself, a guarantee against totalitarian tendencies in transnational policing, but when the action heats up and the 'red mist' descends (Waddington 1991), it is one important resource against the psychological pressures than can turn authoritative force into repression and irrational violence.

Another criticism of the constabulary ethic idea is that, insofar as it has been linked to the notion of 'human security', it has been linked to a policy term that is past its historical moment. The concept was first introduced – some would say it was stillborn – not long prior to 9/11, that symbolic watershed date that facilitated the subsequent launch of the so-called global 'war on terror'. The phrase 'war on terror' is no longer *de rigueur*, but as long as the state of affairs it purportedly described remains, so the argument seems to go, national security will continue to trump human security and the world system will inevitably remain trapped in a cycle of violence and preparation for violence. Perhaps the term 'human security' may quietly drop out of the vocabulary of the diplomatic corps, the international civil service and the transnational non-governmental organizational sector, or there may still be some life in the term (Bohle 2007). But the myriad agencies and institutions that are involved in defining and governing the transnational condition are always in such organizational flux that it is scarcely surprising when the preferred terminology also changes.

While the word itself may or may not be *passé*, problems still remain. Underlying the emergent so-called 'doctrine' of human security was the simple thought that an essential precondition for a durable global peace is that human beings should all live equally free from fear and from want. In my earlier work I argued that a huge variety of policing-type agencies counted among the multiple governmental organizations of the transnational system, and that the personnel in those institutions might all reasonably choose to contribute to such ends in the name of a global Commonwealth. That view, it seems to me, remains reasonable because its opposite is not: national security thinking demonstrably leads to global insecurity (Held 2004). Given the variety of manifestations of apparent ungovernability that confront humanity as a whole – terrorism and organized crime to be sure, but also, it needs to be emphasized, disease pandemics, climate change, food and water shortages, etc. – 'national security' is the term which should be consigned to the dustbin of history.

Let us not quibble over the term 'security', what it is and what it is not. What I propose to do here is to explore further some philosophical thoughts that inform the idea of a constabulary ethic. This discussion is not entirely original; indeed it is an *hommage* to the (1972) work of William Ker Muir Jr – a sociologist of policing who was himself influenced by earlier thinkers, among whom were Max Weber and Alexis de Tocqueville. I aim to develop Muir's insights concerning 'street corner politicians' and the role of coercion in the practical ethics of policing; and I want to do so with specific reference to the transnational condition. What follows is a deliberately abstract and philosophical approach to talking about policing the global polity. A fundamental paradox is that the deployment of coercion creates problems coercion is then invoked to solve. It is also more than this, as shall be demonstrated, because transnationally speaking coercive social ordering is being orchestrated in the context of uncertain human knowledge (Ericson 2007). The uncertainty of the transnational condition makes a confrontation with the paradoxical *modus operandi* of liberal democratic policing – that it curtails freedom through its activities in order to promote conditions in which freedom can flourish – all the more compelling.

Foreshadowing my conclusion, Muir strongly argued that policing had, inevitably, to work through many contradictions and that, ultimately, the good police officer had to face up to using 'coercion for the general welfare in the face of personal danger without becoming radically Machiavellian' (p. 279). He suggested that the key to doing so was fourfold:

> ... what must be counted on to reinvigorate the souls of individuals depleted by the exercise of coercive power is a passion for freedom, made articulate in constant social discussion, interpreted within a tragic perspective which presupposes free will, reflected on by a government of political mentors and institutionalized by law. (p. 282)

A major thrust of my earlier discussion was that, under conditions of transnationalization, the rule of law is, at best, partial and the apparatus of global governance is not a good incubator for political wisdom on matters involving liberal democratic policing. This concentrates responsibility for practical action, and hence ethical decisions, in the hands of the would-be constables themselves and so this is precisely where philosophical attention should be directed.

The paradox of coercion

Police agents are not politicians in the conventional sense and yet the deadly sanctions that members of a national security council may invoke are different only in a degree to that of the humble constable. Muir observed that 'pacifying a dispute between husbands and wives involves much the same techniques statesmen use to contain outbreaks between embittered nations' (1972: 271). Coercion is understood to be a core tactic for the would-be peacekeeper and peacemaker, and any answer to the philosophical question 'What is good policing?' extends from this. There are some who insist that – in a variety of circumstances characterized by the potential for conflict, danger and disorder – what is required is 'security first' and 'boots on the ground'; terms that are, in fact, euphemisms for coercion (or at least its threat). And yet, coercion seems to be cruel, if not barbaric, and hence incompatible with any notion of the civilized or the good. For this reason, if for no other, constabulary ethics are elusive.

'Great men are almost always bad men', Lord Acton famously observed, while 'Power tends to corrupt and absolute power corrupts absolutely'. Acton's dictum stands as a powerful warning against glibly asserting that the law and official strictures can successfully underwrite the constabulary ethic. Wielding coercive power invites the abuse of power and thus democratic policing ideas have emphasized the value of oversight and insisted that police are 'citizens in uniform' whose ultimate interests are no different from those of the people and communities they serve. However, even when Acton's dictum can be modulated – for example, by improving the 'governance of governance' and tipping the balance in favour of 'socially weak actors' (Wood and Shearing 2007: 101–112) – the problem of coercion remains. Coercion lies at the core of the policing function, Muir observed, and this fact necessitates the full integration of thought, ethics and action, thus making individual philosophical reflection crucial if moral breakdown is to be avoided. Paraphrasing Muir, if those who practise coercion in pursuit of social order do not fully realize what they take upon themselves, the consequence can only be bitterness, banal self-acceptance or flight (Muir 1972: 128).

Muir, in common with virtually every other serious sociologist or philosopher of policing, put coercion at the very heart of the problem (Reiner 1985). Here coercion means controlling the conduct of others through the threat or use of force. Social life both tolerates and makes possible many uses of coercion. In civilized societies formally specified individuals are delegated official licence to use coercion within a framework of law in order to uphold the general and specific social order. We call this 'authority' in order to distinguish it from those forms of coercion which we call 'tyranny', 'blackmail' and 'criminal extortion'. In either its formal and socially sanctioned aspect, or its unauthorized and extra-legal form, the practice of coercion in complex and has troublesome consequences. Muir observed that, when we consider the coercive relation, one thing immediately stands out: it is antagonistic. The person who would coerce is always a potential victim of counter-threats. Both parties in a coercive relation are preoccupied with self-defence. Coercion is a symmetrical relation. It can amplify itself. It must be tamed in order to make social life possible.

Briefly, Muir identified four paradoxes of coercive power that make the prospect of its taming difficult: the *paradox of dispossession* (as Bob Dylan put it: 'If you ain't got nothin', you got nothin' to lose'); the *paradox of detachment* (of which the suicide bomber is a manifestation);

the *paradox of face* (the nastier one's reputation, the less nasty one has to be); and the *paradox of irrationality* (summed up this way: the more delirious the threatener, the more serious the threat; the more delirious the victim of would-be coercion, the less serious the threat). In the following sections these paradoxes will be fleshed out and examined with reference to policing and the transnational condition.

The paradox of coercion and dispossession

Muir's discussion of policing and the paradox of dispossession is grounded in considerations about 'skid row', an urban space characterized by a disorganized ecology of violence intertwined in an illicit night-time economy. On the basis of his own ethnographic observations Muir reports that a 'sense of mutual obligation between skid row denizens and the world which shunned them was nonexistent' (1972: 62). Muir's descriptions of a somewhat generalized and archetypal American urban setting are strikingly similar to those pertaining to so-called 'broken', 'failed', or 'failing' states. He observes a place that 'is close to anarchy' in which 'the strong-arm, the bully, the vicious' seek their profits: 'when the rebels against authority knew they were in control, skid row went to hell in a hand basket'. The losers in this scenario were 'good people – old-folks, sick folks, hardworking poor, recent immigrants to the city, minorities, small businessmen – struggling to maintain the margin of survival' (quotes taken from Muir 1972: 63–67). Muir saw that the police were outsiders in this world and, by virtue of their relatively small numbers, able to enforce the law only intermittently. When police actually did deploy their powers of coercion in attempts to quell volatile situations the results were difficult to predict, save for the likelihood that people would get hurt.

Marxian analysis tends to emphasize the point that historically the principal role of modern police was to control the 'dangerous classes' (Reiner 2000: 15–47). According to this perspective, liberal policing contains the poor and disadvantaged and maintains class privileges: it 'keeps the lid on'. As long as grave social disparities exist there can be no policing solutions to situations of social conflict, since the function of the police is to maintain the circumstances that give rise to the conflict in the first instance. With this in mind, it is interesting to ponder the words of General Smedley D. Butler – the most decorated marine of his generation – contemplating the failure of American policy in Latin America over the years of his career:

I helped make Haiti and Cuba a decent place for the National City Bank boys to collect revenues in. I helped in the raping of half a dozen Central American republics for the benefit of Wall Street. The record of racketeering is long. I helped purify Nicaragua for the international banking house of Brown Brothers in 1909–1912. I brought light to the Dominican Republic for American sugar interests in 1916. I helped make Honduras 'right' for American fruit companies in 1903 ... Looking back on it, I feel I might have given Al Capone a few hints. The best he could do was to operate his racket in three city districts. We marines operated on three continents. (Ferguson 2004: 58–59)

The policy that failed was, and continues to be, the paradoxical one of 'dictating democracy, of enforcing freedom, of extorting emancipation' (Ferguson 2004: 54). The American imposition of 'international policing power' – an idea first articulated by Theodore Roosevelt in his 4th annual message to Congress in 1904 (Goldsmith and Sheptycki 2007: 6–7) – turned, on the paradox of dispossession, into a transnational organized crime racket.

Whatever linguistic attributes might be ascribed to a transnational constabulary ethic, martial metaphors are not among them. Muir describes an officer who handled the challenges of policing skid row well, a man who 'enjoyed what Tocqueville referred to as "that respectable power which men willingly grant to the remembrance of a life spent in doing good before their eyes" (Muir 1972: 79). This exemplary officer had put many years into policing his beat and his 'development of skid row had transformed the dispossessed of that community into "good citizens," into people who had something to lose and therefore something to protect' (Muir 1972: 79). This suggests that the key to unlocking the paradox of dispossession lies in closing the gap of 'social exclusion' (Young 1999). The gap has actually been widening, increasing the 'vertigo of late modernity' (Young 2007). Globally, the paradox of coercion and dispossession has intensified this effect. Rather than 'a life spent doing good before their eyes', the exertion of policing power – parochially and transnationally – has tended towards the posture of Leviathan (Goldsmith and Sheptycki 2007). This is evident in the intensified militarization of policing (Kraska 2001) tied to a growing surveillant assemblage (Haggerty and Ericson 2000). Rather than doing good before their eyes, policing is increasingly 'planting time bombs of resentment set to go off in the future' (Sheptycki 2007: 61).

The paradox of coercion and detachment

The paradox of dispossession presents the problem of how to equalize the stakes in social order. The paradox of detachment presents us with its corollary: what happens when the players have become detached from that social order? Muir digs in to his rich ethnographic material for an illustration of the paradox of detachment and coercion, and the archetypal scenario he chooses to make his case is 'the Family Beef'. He begins this discussion with a profile of the stereotypically detached police officer based on 'unquestionably the worst officer in the sample' (Muir 1972: 85) and shows how the defensive pattern of avoidance developed in repeatedly (non)responding to domestic disputes eventually tainted the entirety of this officer's professional self-image with disastrous results. The consequences of his non-fulfillment of duty, erratic behaviour, and increasing avoidance of police-work were that he became 'an individual without identity, a man who played no worthwhile part, a wastrel of himself' (Muir 1972: 87). Paraphrasing Muir, considering the consequences of a detached citizenry policed by detached officers, when the violence does not abate the weak get hurt but, having no recourse to law, those yet strong enough to tear down civilization when they themselves have come unglued encounter no effective resistance to brutishness: 'The values of family life, love, growth and responsibility died in the devastation' (Muir 1972: 88).

Feminist analysis of domestic violence has long emphasized the interactive nature of the public and private realms in the maintenance of patriarchal power and they have done so with special reference to domestic violence (Hester *et al.* 1996; Radford *et al.* 2000). The detached police officer's response to 'the family beef' is inactivity. The inactivity of public power – of police authority – reinforces the private power of the domestic tyrant which, continuing unabated, eventually destroys the family unit in one way or another. The story of battered Michigan housewife Francine Hughes who, after 13 years of domestic abuse, set her husband aflame while he slept is one possibility (McNulty 1980). The 'burning bed' has its gender opposite in the so-called 'family annihilator' – who kills himself and his entire family in his psychological desperation to assert patriarchal dominance under conditions of acute social and psychological detachment (Gresswell and Hollin 1994). Both are pathological manifestations of domestic violence that arise when detached people are policed by detached officers. When a cycle of violence gets out of hand and the responsible authority stands idly by or, just as bad, enacts inappropriate enforcement responses, the expected result can only be tragic.

With the example of the family beef and the paradox of detachment in mind, it is interesting to consider the phenomenon of suicide bombing which so exercises contemporary transnational policing. This is obviously a pathological social form of coercion. It is usually found in conditions of asymmetrical warfare, where some individual members of the weaker party, detached and forlorn of any hope of constabulary protection and despairing because of their evident weakness of sovereignty, nevertheless resist by turning their own bodies into bomb delivery systems (Ignatieff 2004). Might it be that the personal sovereignty of the individual in situations of family violence is analogous to that of group sovereignty in territorial conflicts? In which case, the suicide bomber is a manifestation of an asymmetrical geo-political system in the same way that the burning bed is a manifestation of patriarchy in the private realm of the family.

Muir further illustrated his thoughts on coercion and the paradox of detachment by reference to Plutarch's account of the career of Cleon. It was the detached Cleon who distinguished himself in 427 BC with his proposal to put to death the whole male population of Mytilene on the island of Lesbos after the city revolted against Athenian power during the Peloponnesian war. His proposal was accepted and quickly rescinded but not before one thousand prominent men of the city were executed. Cleon's career was marked by military success, notably his participation two years later in the capture of the Spartan garrison at the Battle of Sphacteria in 425 BC. Aristophanes derided him as a warmonger and demagogue. In his *History of the Peloponnesian War* Thucydides remarks that Cleon had been one of the principal opponents of peace because 'his crimes would be more open to detection and his slanders less credited'. If Cleon had lived in the contemporary period, it might be argued, he would be a war criminal.

Thinking historically reminds us that the notion of virtuous policing is contextual. Local cultural standards create different perspectives on what little acts of public good might look like and what counts as social attachment. It is not the case that policing agents can find answers to complicated questions that pervade cultural difference by referencing the legally prescribed rules of human rights. They can, however, be quite certain that doing injustice harms the doer, whereas doing justice benefits the doer, just as doing justice is fairer and more honourable than suffering injustice. At any rate, that is what Plato has Socrates suggest in *The Gorgias*. By the very facts of multi-culturalism and cultural relativism, however, it is only to the extent that the constabulary has the knowledge and understanding to be able to connect across such divides with common humanity that an ethical approach to the paradox of detachment can be tried. To what degree must a constabulary ethic accommodate action to local cultural values? The answer depends on the recognition that there are two kinds of governance: that which makes people better and that which only confirms them in their prejudices.

Even if poor governance is too often the result of a self-serving but nonetheless professed desire to do good, it remains obvious that to do justice is better than to suffer injustice and that both qualities are self-evident because what is pain, suffering and indignity, or pleasure, growth and untroubled self-worth for one is the same for the other. It is precisely when perspectives that do not allow this humanising viewpoint come into detached interaction that the need for an idea of good policing is most acutely felt. Transcending the paradox of detachment is to move from the particularity of injustice towards the generality of common humanity and constabulary ethics aim to facilitate this. That is why teaching little girls to read in places where women have never had the chance to develop literacy is an apt undertaking. It may be upsetting of a particular traditional cultural order, but at the same time it is a validation of the general humanity denied to females by that particular order.

Extreme manifestations of coercion under the conditions of social detachment are monstrously paradoxical: the family annihilator, the suicide bomber, the 'genocidal' war criminal. This paradox exposes the simplistic nostrum of 'security first' to its surest test; when coercive power simply 'keeps the lid on' eventually the worst consequences of the paradox of detachment will surely be manifest. In situations of conflict, disruption and violence, by avoiding brutish coercive action but nonetheless authoritatively facilitating strategies that aim at the reattachment of friendships and relationships; that justify present sacrifice and forbearance by attaching self-interest to the future reward of pride and dignity for all; that use unpretentious opportunities to strengthen a general sense of social solidarity; then policing may stand the best chance of helping to create the conditions for social peace.

The paradox of coercion and face

The paradox of coercion and face – the nastier one's reputation, the less nasty one has to be – is inescapable for those who practise the extortionate transaction. The successful management of the paradox of face preserves future opportunities to employ purposeful threats. Such a reputation confers a future entitlement to control others through intimidation. Working with the paradox of coercion and face demands grace under pressure. It wreaks the greatest havoc with the phonies. What makes this so is that the paradox of coercion and face affects the future. Not only does the would-be diplomat or street corner politician have to win the war, it must be won with honour. To gain a momentary objective only to sacrifice credibility is to win a Pyrrhic victory.

Muir made his points concerning the paradox of face by looking at the way different police officers handled the 'crowd scene' which he exemplified by ethnographic reference to the archetypal 'neighbourhood beef'. He understood that police professionals confer a high degree of respect on colleagues who have the ability to handle such scenes. The neighbourhood beef is complicated because it is played out on more than one level. The first concerns the two (or more) parties to a dispute – the flashpoint. The second concerns the potentially explosive relationship involving the on-looking crowd and the protagonists. A third level would be the relationship between all of these actors and the intervening policing agents. In order to be successful in managing the crowd scene, police must be able to make appropriate judgments about the factors operating at all of these levels and then engage with them in order to successfully change the psychology of the situation.

Muir observes the actions of a 'soft-spoken irrepressible and multilingual' officer – one of three ethnic minority members in his sample – whose athletic abilities and personal warmth had earned him wide respect within the department (Muir 1972: 111). This officer 'understood, as some never did, that men must never show weakness in the presence of bullies', but nevertheless had imposed strict limits on the means he would personally deploy (Muir 1972: 114). Simultaneously brave and committed to the non-violent resolution of conflict this officer typified what might be thought of as 'the negotiator'. When negotiating the crowd scene this type of officer was dependent on an established reputation and knowledge of the local ecology in order to discover the natural stabilizing agents of the neighbourhood and activate them: 'Because his neighbourhood recognized him, he was not the symbol of the enemy, to be fought as evidence of respectability' (Muir 1972: 117).

However, if and when non-violent strategies work in controlling the crowd scene itself, what happens to the problem that provoked the beef in the first instance? In other words, what happened at the primary level? In such situations, for those who perceive themselves to be victims, the patience non-violence requires can be upsetting. It is one thing for a person to practise non-violence in the face of personal peril; it is something else when the safety of others is involved and especially when there is a putative 'duty to protect'. Conflict-ridden situations can be worsened in the event that a self-perceiving victim feels deserted enough to undertake self-defence. Paradoxically, and in spite of good intentions, an unwavering commitment to non-violence can bring about conditions where violence escalates out of control. Despairing and unable to successfully overcome this paradox, police agents wholly dedicated to non-violent means may be inclined to withdraw from the field. Muir observed a tendency for this type of officer to gravitate towards less trying niches inside the police organization with the result that the streets are turned over to more coercively inclined individuals (Muir 1972: 118).

The non-violent response is naturally contrasted with the 'enforcer-type': 'He was unafraid to do things that made other policemen quail or that embarrassed them. He pulled his gun earlier than most officers, and he was not afraid to use it. Moreover, he was tireless. He tackled any job. He was not a phony. He was brave, and he was fearless to the point of craziness' (Muir 1972: 108). Confronting antagonists in a crowd situation the enforcer would 'put 'em up against a wall'. He would 'lay it down bluntly'. He would 'buffalo' them with his knowledge of the criminal code and his capacity to classify all their behaviour in terms of it. And he was prepared to 'call in 500 cops' to back up his ultimatums. Muir characterized the 'pre-emptive and terrorist methods' of the enforcer-type as often being 'extra-legal and abusive' (Muir 1972: 109). The enforcer-type 'depended on making the public feel impotent to resist, and a beat that felt that downtrodden was a woeful place to live' (Muir 1972: 111).

Bittersweet is the officer who, in the crux of the paradox of coercion and face, recurrently enforces. Muir observes that the enforcer's beat was 'unhappy with the oppression he inflicted on it' (Muir 1972: 111). Not being able to be merciful, having to build an unblemished reputation for nastiness, the enforcer type tends to make harsh examples not only of the deserving bad, but of the exemplary good as well. Obvious is the Aristotelian 'golden mean' that blends aspects of the negotiator and the enforcer, but policing is the accomplishment of a complex division of labour as well as an individual feat. Therefore striking the balance often seems to be a matter of practical sociological impossibility.

Muir's study focused on street-level police who were subjects of democratic and legal principles set against demagoguery and intimidation. In that context, he observed, the pure enforcer-type operates at considerable psychological cost:

> The outlook they [the enforcers] developed to justify their extralegal terror was shared only by fellow terrorists; when they were with other officers, they had to watch their step, for they were out of step. The brotherhood was divided; they had to be careful about what they said, always checking against the spontaneous reaction; and they had to be cunning about covering up their innermost thoughts from those they suspected might divulge them to the administration. (Muir 1972: 110)

Isolated amongst themselves, the enforcer-types begin to hate – first the policies that uphold civil and/or human rights and transparency values, then fellow officers who adapt to such policies, 'and finally their job, which estranged them from all but each other' (Muir 1972: 110). Under conditions of adequate democratic oversight, the pure enforcer-type may ultimately be neutralized within an aggressive cynicism no less limiting than the negotiator-type's retreat to the administrative backwaters of headquarters. But it needs to be emphasized, Muir's example of the police 'enforcer' character is one who was at least somewhat subject to democratic and rule-of-law constraints, constraints which are much less sure under transnational conditions. Indeed, under those conditions for the enforcer there are no brakes that are not self-imposed.

When it comes to the paradox of coercion and face, the parallel dilemmas of street corner politicians and transnational policing are nicely alluded to with Muir's choice of an illustrative quote from John F. Kennedy: 'We dare not tempt our adversaries with weakness. For only when our arms are sufficient beyond doubt can we be certain beyond doubt that they will never be employed' (Muir 1972: 101). In other words, *si vis pacem, para bellum*. History records that on more than one occasion Kennedy attempted to parlay the paradox of coercion and face in the geo-political context, a domain scarcely under the purview of law. The Bay of Pigs fiasco, the Cuban Missile Crisis, the secret escalation of US involvement in Vietnam, are just a few examples of his administration's geo-political forays. Kennedy's administration was Janus-faced, as revealed in his inaugural address in which he asserted: 'Let us never negotiate out of fear. But let us never fear to negotiate.' It is one of the most memorable speeches in history, calling for an active citizenry – 'Ask not what your country can do for you; ask what you can do for your country' – and internationalism, to fight 'the common enemies of man: tyranny, poverty, disease, and war itself' because, 'world peace, like community peace, does not require that each man love his neighbour – it requires only that they live together with mutual tolerance, submitting their disputes to a just and peaceful settlement'. 'The hardest tumble any politician can take', Muir remarks, 'is the fall over his own bluff' (1972: 101).

The paradox of coercion and irrationality

Irrational adversaries are no less formidable than courageous ones. Perhaps they are more so. The irrational are like none other. Different from the dispossessed, who become prudent when they are invested with something to lose. Different from the detached who, re-inspired with hope, may become careful. Different from those who become either remorseless or withdrawn in their confrontation with the paradox of coercion and face. In such cases it is at least possible to look at things over the longer term, to aim to change the psychology of the situation by 'talking it down' and, if coercive power needs to be employed, by always striving for the minimal use of force while deliberately aiming to limit the harm done. With the paradox of coercion and irrationality – where the seriousness of the threat increases in proportion to the deliriousness of the threatener even while it decreases in proportion to the deliriousness of the would-be victim of coercion – nothing is certain.

Muir illustrates these points with ethnographic material relating the stereotypical police street corner encounter with 'the juvenile caper'. On the face of it, he admits, such an example may seem trivial, juveniles after all are not 'fiends or zealots'. In his observation, 'the young simply foresaw their actions' having consequences different from those which adults anticipated' (1972: 127). Yet the juvenile caper perfectly embodies the paradox of coercion and irrationality: the more delirious the threatener the more serious the threat, the more delirious the threatened the less serious the threat. Street-level police officers face irrational persons of many kinds everyday – the drug addled and drink sodden, the deranged and enraged, persons so single-minded, so one-dimensional in their perceptions of the world, so selective in what they hear and what they comprehend that normal communications break down. The ultimatum 'Stop or I'll shoot' means nothing to a methamphetamine addict too high to hear. The assassin whose ideology requires a martyr's death and the hooligan who seeks affirmation of a violent hyper-masculine identity through riot and disorder are both implacable and terrible. The irrational actor seemingly lacks the self-concerned prudence on which threats may work effectively (Muir 1972: 127).

Muir discerns a pattern in successful encounters of this kind (1972: 131). Successful policing encounters with the irrational begin by anticipating miscalculation. The potentially or conceivably irrational actor must be given psychological room, time to adjust, and clear signals about what is required. Good policing uses the 'edge of fear' with subtlety, leaving enough slack to absorb any surprises due to miscalculation. The thoughtful and wise constable purposefully uses time to dispel irrationality. First is a clear understanding and statement of objectives. This is followed by a considered increase in pressure evidencing the determination to prevail. This determination is helped by cultivating the presence of fear yet not hastily deployed. Instead, the insistent reminder by word and deed is that the ultimate responsibility for any coercive act lies not with the police agent, but with the other actors on the scene. All this to give the potentially or actually irrational actor time to recalculate and take stock of prospects. Such deliberate rational tactics may cause the irrational to start thinking of themselves as identifiable, responsible individuals. By reminding such persons about the broader issues at stake and reinstalling proper regard for the prospective and real dangers faced by all, such individuals may be restored to rationality.

What helps the police officer to ensure that this approach might actually work, Muir tells us, is the cultivation of the 'tragic perspective' which provides a sense of meaning about human conduct – a comprehension of the suffering of each inhabitant on earth, a sensitivity for human dignity, and the belief that no individual is worthless. From a tragic perspective it is possible to avoid Machiavellian distortions which only make the world appear hateful, thereby justifying the violence being used against it. Developing a tragic sensibility, ethical equanimity and compassion create the possibility of resolving the contradictions of trying to achieve just ends with coercive means.

Lest this seem overly idealistic, the pattern described above should be contrasted with its less deliberate and irrational opposite. Any policing response that can be construed as turbulent, impulsive, impatient, or temperamental in effect meets irrationality with irrationality and the resultant coercive encounter can quickly spiral out of control. Dealing with extremely complicated problems of human motivation on the simple-minded presumption that everything is grounded in irrational and unchanging malevolence feeds the expectancies of the worst elements in a community. The irrational is not the same as the diabolical, yet non-rational police action frequently treats it as if it were so. Irrational and compulsive acts of coercion performed by policing agents without fostering an adequate communicative basis for comprehending their moral justification reinforce the assumption that the constabulary is simply savage, malevolent, self-interested and power-hungry. Meeting irrationality with irrationality can only bring out the worst in everybody.

The policing paradox vortex

Irrationality abounds. The constable, whether operating at the transnational or domestic level, is positioned at the centre of relations wracked by conflict, coloured by antagonism, and shaped by the irrational impulses of pride, covetousness, lust, anger, greed and envy. At the vortex of this lies what the police do and what the police do is, among other things, terrifying. In order to best cope with such frightening circumstances, it is useful to have given some thought in advance to the contradictions and potential consequences that the threat or use of force implies. Being able to think philosophically may help to forestall the worst and may even tip the balance in favour of a positive outcome. The dilemmas posed by the invitational edge to corruption that coercive power excites – together with the paradoxes of dispossession, detachment, face and irrationality – do not mean that the practice of coercive force is forever beyond the bounds of civilized behaviour. In fact, sometimes the opposite is the case. The office of the constable, or something like it, is a societal necessity for securing provisional solutions to the unpredictable situational exigencies that are born of social conflict and natural emergency and this is so at every level of governance.

Policing is essential to the craft of governance; it is a way of authoritatively securing provisional solutions to problematic situations that are not specifiable in advance. Coercion is indispensible, it is the *sine qua non* of authority but, as the preceding discussion suggests, successful policing is about being able to minimize the use of force. After several decades of sociological scrutiny, it has been shown that the craft of good policing consists of the ability to use the background possibility of legitimate coercion so skilfully that it never needs to be foregrounded (Reiner 2000: 112). What then of the constabulary ethic?

Considering three ethical elements for the constabulary

Philosophy treats ethics in three ways. For Aristotle, ethics focuses on the character of the agent. This is 'virtue ethics' which are concerned with the internalized habits of thinking that shape how one lives one's life. Similar to Aristotle, contemporary virtue ethicists (MacIntyre 1990) argue that the judgements of virtuous and wise persons in determining what is good or bad, right or wrong, positive or negative are more important than formal rules. What is important is that the moral agent cultivates a life of virtue generally and in all aspects. We can perhaps all agree that it is generally a good thing when public acts are based on sound private ethics; that is why hypocrisy is not a virtue. When personal conduct characteristically demonstrates a tragic sensibility, ethical equanimity and compassion, for example, this aspect of public ethics is fulfilled.

The second approach to ethics is associated with Kant. It is the deontological approach which focuses not on the qualities of the person, but rather on the qualities of the act. Kant argued that it was not the consequences of actions that make them right or wrong but the nature of the act itself. There are several commonly expressed ethical invocations that bear a degree of similarity to Kant's 'categorical imperative': 'What if everybody did that?', or 'Do unto others as you would have them do unto you' being two examples. One of Kant's own formulations was: 'Act in such a way that you always treat humanity, whether in your own person or in the person of any other, never simply as a means, but always at the same time as an end'. Other ideas, such as the Hippocratic oath's 'Do no harm', or 'Act so as to minimize harm' are examples of practical ethics of this type.

A third type of moral thinking is consequentialism, which looks neither to the actor nor the act, but rather to the outcome of the act. Bentham's utilitarianism aims at consequences: to maximize pleasure and minimize pain. The popular aphorism that 'the needs of the many outweigh the needs of the few' is an example of consequentialism. In general, consequentialist ethics are moral theories which assign weight to consequences in evaluating the rightness and wrongness of actions (see also MacIntyre 1998). In democratic societies the evaluation of the consequences of policing is generally a public matter and, also bearing in mind the ever-present possibility of unintended consequences, such an evaluation should provide occasion for reflection about the nature of the enterprise, its goals and the actors involved and the ends thereby achieved.

The philosophy of ethics distinguishes between actors, acts and the consequences of acts. It also makes distinctions between intended and unintended consequences. Of course these are ideal types and, when it comes to sociological questions of practical ethics, they inevitably co-mingle in the hurly-burly of real life. Since *The Republic* and *The Laws* of Plato, philosophy has often bent to imagining a constitution of rules that could bring the end of history, that is to imagining a perfectly functioning society of law, justice and virtue. History flows like a river and sometimes the rapids are rough. Contemporary conditions invite nihilism which, if that is to be avoided, require a responsible, compassionate and tragic perspective to lay the foundation for good self-government, the key to good governance generally. This might seem to leave everything up to the individual. Under conditions of globalization we are alone in this together and there is no Other. Virtue ethics, deontology and consequentialism are only separable in an analytic sense and not practically. The constabulary ethic is nothing if not a practical humanist ethic which simultaneously involves thinking at all three levels. The resemblances found between the dilemmas faced by the street cop and the commander-in-chief show lessons about the paradoxical nature of policing (in)security. These strongly suggest that the language of national security – with its endless cycle of violence and preparation for violence – needs to be broken in order make room for the language of human security, just as vigilantism needs to give way to restorative justice, in order for a lasting peace to be secured.

Conclusion

The inherent unpredictably of the life-world and the confounding paradoxes of coercion are two good reasons why constabulary ethics cannot be reduced to an easy recipe. More than that, since the paradoxical nature of coercive power means that – even in instances where an evidently unimpeachably virtuous actor undertaking an apparently unambiguously justifiable application of coercive power for what appears at the time to be a demonstrably good end is not guaranteed a positive outcome – things do not necessarily turn out as planned. The sociologist Max Weber put it this way: 'He who lets himself in for politics, that is, for power and force as means, contracts with diabolical powers and for his action it is *not* true that good can follow only from good and evil only from evil, but that often the opposite is true' (1946, quoted in Reiner 2000).

Policing solutions for social ills can easily be harnessed to invidious ends. Philosophical reflection is crucial if the balance of thinking in policing is to be shifted from *si vis pacem, para bellum* to *si vis pacem, para iustitium*, thereby avoiding the worst of all possibilities – *Bellum omnium contra omnes*, the war of all against all. The security function is dramatically present in the contingent solutions to problems encountered *in situ* by street-level police and these sociological pictures can be extrapolated to yield lessons about transnational policing. Institutions of governance, from the street-corner cops described by Muir right up to the higher national and transnational levels, form a family of resemblance. They resemble each other because of the connections of coercion and social ordering. Generally speaking, good governance is a political and social skill, a moral action to achieve specified ends serving the greater good but, when it comes to the application of policing power, there are never sure results. The fragmentation and incommensurability of our moral discourses – and, indeed perhaps even knowledge claims more generally – seem inescapable in the contemporary period and authority is contestable as a result. What millennia of human history, from the 'pristine civilizations' of ancient times (Mann 1986) until now, have shown is that it is sometimes possible to shift the balance in favour of social peace. In spite of uncertain knowledge, it does not therefore seem entirely unreasonable to hold on audaciously to the hope that police craft can be part of the solution to transnational social injustice instead of being one of its mechanisms.

In closing, I wish to return to a thought that wove throughout my earlier essay 'The Constabulary Ethic and the Transnational Condition', a steady allusion to the nautical metaphor of governance. The metaphor was once popular in neo-liberal discourse and is apt since the etymological root of the word governance is the Greek word *'kybernan'* which means helmsman. Under conditions of transnationalisation, there are 'many boats floating rudderless on the sea of (in)security, with many hands bent hard to the tasks of rowing and steering. The winds of history are blowing upon that sea and all the signs indicate a drift towards authoritarianism' (Goldsmith and Sheptycki 2007: 46). The rhetoric may have been windy, but it emphasized the fact that the huge variety of security and governmental logics that inform the equally numerous institutions and personnel that make up the transnational condition have resulted in a condition of practical ungovernability and growing feelings of insecurity. In other words, when it comes to global governance, the steadying power of the rule of law and the governance of wise political council from on high are in very short supply. The absence of a 'nocturnal council', what Plato referred to in *The Laws* as the *nukterinos syllogos*, both empowers and responsibilizes all human actors advocating actions that aim to achieve amiable consequences.

Normative and ethical questions cannot be postponed. It is not enough to simply critique the logics of security, the mechanisms of governance or the institutional arrangements of the constabulary. The ethicist Peter Singer (2004) has put the challenge most succinctly, arguing that the task of the twenty-first century is to develop a suitable form of government for one world: 'it is a daunting moral and intellectual challenge, but one we cannot refuse to take up [since] the future of the world depends on how well we meet it' (Singer 2004: 200–201). Propounding an ethic of good policing will be integral to that challenge. The alternative is more than just dire straits. Extending the nautical metaphor once more, the global system has subsumed virtually all preceding societies – it is like a great ship steaming ahead into an uncertain future without the benefit of maps, compass bearings or astral navigation and only the strength of character, skill and safety record of her crew left to ensure that the vessel does not become like Théodore Géricault's *Raft of the Medusa*.[3]

Notes

1 The author would like to thank William 'Sandy' Muir for his helpful comments on a previous draft of this chapter, and for his warm encouragement, as well as the participants (especially Alice Hills) in the workshop on the *Rise of the Rescue Industry* held at Bristol University in May of 2009. Thanks are also due to Frédéric Lemieux, whose comments helped to tighten and focus the argument, and to Ronnie Lippens, whose last minute poke in the eye removed a small logjam.

2 The force-violence distinction is a difficult but important one to make. Force is the authoritative use of physical intervention for reasons justifiable for the general interest, even when it extends to particular matters such as the need to defend life or bring a law-violator to justice. Violence is coercion for personal, private, gain without the justification of more general interests.

3 http://www.historyhouse.com/in_history/medusa/

References

Abrahamson, R. and Williams, M.C. (2005) *The Globalisation of Private Security: Country Report: Nigeria*. Aberystwyth: University of Aberystwyth/Swindon: ESRC.

Adebajo, A. (2008) 'The Peacekeeping Travails of the AU and the Regional Economic Communities', in Akokpan, J., Ndinga-Muvumba, A. and Murithi, T. (eds), *The African Union and its Institution*. Johannesburg: Fanele, pp. 135–162.

Agence France Presse (2007) *EU seeks to name low profile technocrat as new 'anti-terror' chief*, 18 September.

Aldrich, R.J. (2009) 'US-European Intelligence Co-operation on Counter-Terrorism: Low Politics and Compulsion', *The British Journal of Politics and International Relations*, 11 (1): 122–139.

Allred, K. (2006) 'Peacekeepers and Prostitutes: how deployed forces fuel the demand for trafficked women and new hope for stopping it', *Armed Forces & Society*, 33 (1): 5-23.

Anderson, M. (1989) *Policing the World: Interpol and the Politics of International Police Co-operation*. Oxford: Oxford University Press.

Anderson, M. (2002) 'Trust and Police Co-operation' in Anderson, M. and Apap, J. (eds), *Police and Justice Co-operation and the New European Borders*. The Hague: Kluwer Law International, pp. 35–46.

Anderson, M. (2003) 'Les Répercussions du Traité d'Amsterdam et de la Déclaration de Tampere sur les Institutions de Police' in *De Tampere à Séville : bilan de la sécurité européenne. Cultures et Conflits*, 45 (1): 115–123.

Anderson, M., Den Boer, M., Cullen, P., Gilmore, W.C., Raab, C. and Walker, N. (1995) *Policing the European Union*. Oxford: Clarendon.

Andreas, P. and Nadelmann, E.A. (2006) *Policing the Globe: Criminalization and Crime Control in International Relations*. Oxford: Oxford University Press.

Appiah-Mensah, S. (2006) 'The African Mission in Sudan: Darfur Dilemmas', *African Security Review*, 15 (1): 2–19.

ASEAN (2002) *Agreement on Information Exchange and Establishment of Communication Procedures*. Putrajaya, Malaysia, 7 May.

ASEAN (2004) *Treaty on Mutual Legal Assistance in Criminal Matters*. Kuala Lumpur, Malaysia, 29 November.

Ashdown, P. (2007) *Swords and Ploughshares: Bringing Peace to the 21st Century*. London: Weidenfeld and Nicolson.

Ashkenas, R., Ulrich, D., Jick, T., and Kerr, S. (1995) *The Boundaryless Organization: Breaking The Chains of Organizational Structure*. San Francisco, CA: Jossey-Bass.

Ashraf, M.A. (2007) 'The Lessons of Policing in Iraq – a Personal Perspective,' *Policing*, 1 (1): 102–110.

Bachmann, R. and Zaheer, A. (eds) (2008) *Landmark Papers on Trust*. Cheltenham: Edward Elgar.

Bah, A.S. and Aning, K. (2008) 'US Peace Operations Policy in Africa: From ACRI to AFRICOM', *International Peacekeeping*, 15 (1): 118–132.

Bandura, A. (1977) *Social Learning Theory*. New York: General Learning.

Barnett, J.R. (1985) 'Extradition Treaty Improvements to Combat Drug Trafficking', *Georgia Journal of International and Comparative Law*, 15 (2): 285–315.

Barnett, M. and Coleman, L. (2005) 'Designing Police: Interpol and the Study of Change in International Organizations', *International Studies Quarterly*, 49 (4): 593–619.

Barnett, M. and Finnemore, M. (1999) 'The Politics, Power, and Pathologies of International Organizations', *International Organization*, 53 (4): 699–732.

Batley, R. and Larbi, G.A. (2004) *The Changing Role of Government: The Reform of Public Services in Developing Countries*. Palgrave: MacMillan.

Bayley, D.H. (1985) *Patterns of Policing: A Comparative International Perspective*. Piscataway, NJ: Rutgers University Press.

Bayley, D.H. (1995) 'A Foreign Policy for Democratic Policing', *Policing and Society*, 5 (2): 79–93.

Bayley, D.H. (2001) *Democratizing Police Abroad: What To Do and How To Do It*. Washington DC: National Institute of Justice.

Bayley, D.H. (2005) *Changing the Guard: Developing Democratic Police Abroad*. New York: Oxford University Press.

Bayley, D.H. and Shearing, C. (1996) 'The Future of Policing', *Law and Society Review*, 30 (3): 585–606.

BBC News (2003) *US gets access to airline details*. 17 December, <news.bbc.co.uk>

BBC News (2008) *US fears Europe-based terrorism*. 15 January, <news.bbc.co.uk>

BBC Panorama Special (2008) *Daylight robbery*. Broadcast BBC 1, 10 June.

Beare, M. (1996) *Criminal Conspiracies: Organized Crime in Canada*. Toronto: Nelson Canada.

Bearpark, A. (2008) *Why private security companies are essential in post-conflict Iraq*. Retrieved on 16 November 2008 from http://www.bi-me.com/main.php?id=17863&t=1&c=34&cg=4

Beary, B. (2009) 'EU/US Washington may relent on 100% container scanning rule', *Europolitics*, 3 April.

Bellanova, R. (2008) 'The "Prüm Process:" The Way Forward for EU Police Cooperation and Data Exchange?', in Guild, E. and Geyer, F. (eds), *Security Versus Justice, Police and Judicial Cooperation in the European Union*. Aldershot: Ashgate, pp. 203–221.

Benyon, J. (1992) *Issues in European Police Co-operation*. Department of Politics, University of Leicester.

Benyon, J. (1994) 'Policing the European Union: The Changing Basis of Cooperation on Law Enforcement', *International Affairs*, 70 (3): 497–517.

Benyon, J. (1996) 'The Politics of Police Co-operation in the European Union International', *Journal of the Sociology of Law*, 24 (4): 353–379.

Benyon, J., Turnbull, L., Willis, A., Woodward, R. and Beck, A. (1993) *Police Cooperation in Europe: An Investigation*. Leicester: Centre for the Study of Public Order, University of Leicester.

Berg, J. and Shearing, C. (2008) 'Integrated Security: Assembling Knowledges and Capacities', in Williamson, T. (ed.), *The Handbook of Knowledge Based Policing: Current Conceptions and Future Directions*. Chichester: Wiley pp. 389–404.

Berthelet, P. (2005) 'Le programme de La Haye: quelles avancées en matière de coopération policière?', *Journée d'étude portant sur Genèse et institutionnalisation de l'espace européen de justice et de sécurité*. Strasbourg: GPSE, Université R. Schuman.

Bie de E., Ferwerda, H. and van Leiden I. (2004) *Op de grens, evaluatie van het A-team*. Arnhem: Advies- en onderzoeksgroep Beke.

Bigo, D. (1994) 'The European Internal Security Field: stakes and rivalries in a newly developing area of police intervention', in Anderson, M. and den Boer, M. (eds), *Policing Across National Boundaries*. London: Pinter, pp. 161–173.

Bigo, D. (1996) *Polices en Réseaux: L'expérience Européenne*. Paris: Presse de science Po.

Bigo, D. (2000) 'Liaison Officers in Europe: new officers in the European security field', in Sheptycki, J.E.W. (ed.), *Issues in Transnational Policing*. London: Routledge, pp. 67–99.

Bigo, D. (2002) 'Border Regimes and Security in an Enlarged European Community', in Zielonka, J. (ed.) *Europe Unbound: Enlarging and Reshaping the Boundaries of the European Union*. New York: Routledge, pp. 213–239.

Bigo, D. (2003) 'Les archipels des professionnels de l'(in)sécurité', in Fortmann, M., Macleod, A. and Roussel, S. (eds), *Vers des périmètres de sécurité? La Gestion des Espaces Continentaux en Amérique du Nord et en Europe*. Outremont : Athéna Éditions, pp. 169–184.

Bigo, D. and Guild, E. (2003) 'De Tampere à Séville, vers une ultra gouvernementalisation de la domination transnationale?', *Cultures et Conflits*, 45 (1): 5–18.

Birrer, S. and Ribaux, O. (2008) 'La statistique policière de la criminalité en Suisse peut-elle s'envisager dans le cadre du renseignement criminel?' *Revue Suisse de Criminologie*, 2: 3–19.

Block, A. and Chambliss, W.J. (1981) *Organizing Crime*. New York: Elsevier.

Block, L. (2008a) 'Combating Organized Crime in Europe: practicalities of police cooperation', *Policing*, 2 (1): 74–81.

Block, L. (2008b) 'Cross-Border Liaison and Intelligence: Practicalities and Issues' in Harfield, C. MacVean, A., Grieve, J. and Phillips, D. (eds), *The Handbook of Intelligent Policing: Consilience, Crime Control, and Community Safety*. Oxford: Oxford University Press, pp. 183–194.

Boekhout van Solinge, T. (2005) *Dealing with Drugs in Europe: An Investigation of European Drug Control Experiences: France, the Netherlands and Sweden*. The Hague: BJu Legal.

Bohle, H-G. (2007) *Living with Vulnerability; Livelihoods and Human Security in Risky Environments*. Bonn: United Nations University, Institute for Environment and Human Security.

Bouchard, M. and Leduc, M. (2007) 'Dissuasion et contre-dissuasion', in Cusson, M., Dupont, B. and Lemieux, F. (eds), *Traité de sécurité intérieure*. Montréal: Hurtubise, pp. 517–529.

Boucher, A.J. and Holt, V.K. (2007) *African Perspectives on African Security Challenges and Modern Peace Operations*. Washingto,n DC: The Henry L. Stimson Center. Available at http://www.bi-me.com/main.php?id=17863 &t=1&c=34&cg=4.

Bowling, B. and Foster, J. (2002) 'Policing and the Police', in Maguire, M., Morgan, R. and Reiner, R. (eds), *The Oxford Handbook of Criminology*. Oxford: Oxford University Press, pp. 980–1033.

Brady, H. (2008) 'Europol and the Criminal Intelligence Model: A Non-State Response to Organized Crime', *Policing*, 2 (1): 103–109.

Brammertz, S. (1999) *Grenzüberschreitende polizeiliche Zusammenarbeit am Beispiel der Euregio Maas-Rhein*. Freiburg: Max Planck Institut für ausländisches und internationales Strafrecht.

Brammertz, S., de Vreese, S. and Thys, J. (1993) *Internationale Politiesamenwerking: Onderzoek naar de modaliteiten voor Belgische participatie in internationale politiesamenwerkingsprojecten van regionale omvang*. Politeia, Brussels: Ministerie van Binnenlandse Zaken.

Bratz, C. (2001) *EUROPOL's contribution to fight illegal immigration networks*. Presentation in The Hague, 19 June.

Bressler, F. (1992) *Interpol*. Paris: Presses de la Cité.

Brewer, J., Guelke, A., Hume, I., Moxon-Browne, E. and Wilford, R. (1988) *The Police, Public Order and the State: Policing in Great Britain, Northern Ireland, the Irish Republic, the USA, Israel, South Africa and China*. Basingstoke: Macmillan.

Brinig, M. (2000) *From Contract to Covenant: Beyond the Law and Economics of the Family*. Cambridge, MA.: Harvard University Press.

Brodeur, J.-P. (1983) 'High Policing and Low Policing: Remarks About the Policing of Political Activities', *Social Problems*, 30 (5): 507–520.

Brodeur, J.-P. and Dupont, B. (2006) 'Knowledge Workers or "Knowledge" Workers?', *Policing and Society*, 16 (1): 7–26.

Bruggeman, W. (2002) 'Policing and Accountability in a Dynamic European Context', *Policing and Society*, 12 (4): 259–273.

Buckley, F. (ed.) (1999) *The Fall and Rise of Freedom of Contract*. Durham, NC: Duke University Press.

Burns, T. and Stalker, G.M. (1961) *The Management of Innovation*. London: Tavistock.

Busch, H. (1988) 'Von Interpol zu TREVI: Polizeiliche Zusammenarbeit in Europa', *Bürgerrechte und Polizei/CILIP*, 30: 38–55.

Busch, H. (2002) 'Le piège légaliste: La coopération policière après Tampere', *Cultures et Conflits*, 45 (1): 125–132.

Call, C.T. and William, S. (2001) 'Protecting the People: public security choices after civil wars', *Global Governance*, 6 (2): 151–172.

Caparini, M. (2006) 'Applying a Security Governance Perspective to the Privatisation of Security', in Bryden, A. and Caparini, M. (eds) *Private Actors and Security Governance*. Vienna: LIT, pp. 263–282.

Caparini, M. and Marenin, O. (eds) (2004) *Transforming the Police in Central and Eastern Europe*. New York: Transaction.

Cascio, W. (2000) 'Managing a Virtual Workplace', *Academy of Management Executive*, 14 (3): 81–90.

Celador, G.C. (2005) 'Police Reform: peacebuilding through "Democratic Policing?" *International Peacekeeping*, 12 (3): 364–376.

CEPOL (2008) *Annual Report*. Bramshill Hook, UK: CEPOL House.

Chaiken, J., Chaiken, M. and Karchmer, C. (1990) *Multijurisdictional Drug Law Enforcement Strategies: Reducing Supply and Demand*. Cambridge, MA: Abt Associates.

Chandler, D. (2005) 'How 'State-building' Weakens States: the new focus on the international community's "responsibility to protect" failing states is external meddling by another name' Retrieved on 4 March, 2009: http://www.spiked-online.com/Articles/0000000CADDB.htm.

Chappell, D. and Evans, J. (1999) 'The Role, Preparation and Performance of Civilian Police in United Nations Peacekeeping Operations', *Criminal Law Forum*, 10 (2): 171–271.

Chawala, S. and Pietschmann, T. (2005) 'Drug Trafficking as a Transnational Crime' in Reichell, P. (ed.), *Handbook of Transnational Crime & Justice*. Thousand Oaks, CA: Sage, pp. 160–180.

Chulov, M. and Tran, M. (2009) 'US Security Firm Loses Licence to Work in Iraq', *The Guardian*, 30 January, p. 27.

Cilliers, J. (2008) *The African Standby Force: An Update on Progress*. Johannesburg: Institute of Security Studies. ISS Paper 160.

Cilliers, J. and Malan, M. (2005) *Progress with the African Standby Force*. Johannesburg: Institute of Security Studies. ISS Paper 98.

Clapham, C., Herbst, J. and Mills, G. (eds) (2006) *Big African States*. Johannesburg: Wits University Press.

Cleary, S., Cross, S. and Ntsimi, M. (2006) *Developmental Support by South Africa to the African Continent: assessment and recommendations on policies and procedure*. Unpublished report prepared for the TEA-Cegos Consortium.

Clough, R. (1993) *Reaching Across the Taiwan Strait: People-to-People Diplomacy*. Boulder, CO: Westview.

Cockayne, J. (2008) 'Taming the dogs of war: the strategic logic of the professionalization of private military and security companies'. Paper presented to conference on *The Privatization of Security and Human Rights in the Americas: Perspectives from the Global South*, University of Wisconsin-Madison, 31 January – 2 February. Available at http://www.havenscenter. org/privatemilitaryconference2008

Cockburn, A. and Highsmith, J. (2001) 'Agile Software Development: The people factor', *Computer*, 11: 131–133.

Cohen, S. (1998) 'Intellectual Scepticism and Political Commitment: the case of radical criminology', in Walton, P. and Young, J. (eds), *The New Criminology Revisited*. London: Macmillan, pp. 98–129.

Coldren, J.R., McGarell, E., Sabath, M., Schlegel, K. and Stolzenberg, L. (1993) *Multijurisdictional Drug Task Force Operations: Results of a Nationwide Survey of Task Force Commanders*. Washington, DC: Criminal Justice Statistics Association.

Coldren, J.R., and Sabath, M. (1992) *Multijurisdictional Drug Control Task Forces 1988–1990: Critical Components of State Drug Control Strategies*. Special Analysis Report of the Consortium for Drug Strategy Impact Assessment for the Bureau of Justice Assistance.

Commission of the European Communities (2004) 'Customs – commission welcomes signature of agreement with the United States on expanding cooperation to trade security', in *Convention Based on Article K.3 of the Treaty on European Union, on the Establishment of a European Police Office* (Europol Convention). Brussels: European Parliament.

Cook, C.W., Rush, R.G. and Seelke, C.R. (2008) *Merida Initiative: Proposed U.S. Anticrime and Counterdrug Assistance for Mexico and Central America*. Washington DC: US Congress – Library of Congress.

Cooke, T. (2009) 'Cross-Strait Matrix: The Economic Cooperation Framework Agreement', *China Brief*, 9 (11): 7–9.

Corstens, G. and Pradel, J. (2002) *European Criminal Law*. The Hague/ London/New York: Kluwer.

Corten, M. and Martens, P. (2006) *Succesvolle samenwerking in internationaal samengestelde (politie)teams*. Leergang Internationale Politie Oriëntatie – 4 (www.spl.politieacademie.nl).

Council of the European Union (2005) *Evaluation Report of the European Judicial Network 2002–2004*. Document 6724/1/05 REV 1, 9 March.

Crawford, A. (2003) 'Contractual Governance of Deviant Behaviour', *Journal of Law and Society*, 30 (4): 479–505.

Crawford, A. (2006) 'Policing and Security as "Club Goods": the new enclosures?', in Wood, J. and Dupont, B. (eds), *Democracy, Society and Governance of Security*. Cambridge: Cambridge University Press, pp. 111–138.

Cressey, D.R. (1969) *Theft of the Nation*. New York: Harper & Row.

Critchley, T. (1967) *A History of Police in England and Wales*. London: Constable.

Cronin, B. (2002) 'The Two Faces of the United Nations: the tension between intergovernmentalism and transnationalism', *Global Governance*, 8 (1): 53–72.

Cummings, T.G., and Worley, C.G. (2001) *Organizational Development and Change*. (7th edn). Cincinnati: South-Western College Publishing.

Daele D. van and Geebergen G. van (2007) *Criminaliteit en rechtshandhaving in de Euregio Maas-Rijn deel 2*. Antwerp/Oxford: Intersentia.

Daele D. van, Spapens, T., and Fijnaut, C. (2008) *De strafrechtelijke rechtshulpverlening van België, Duitsland en Frankrijk aan Nederland*. Antwerp/Oxford: Intersentia.

Dallaire, R. (2003) *Shake Hands with the Devil: The Failure of Humanity in Rwanda*. Toronto: Knopf.

Davies, A. (2001) *Accountability: A Public Law Analysis of Government by Contract*. Oxford: Oxford University Press.

Day, G. and Freeman, C. (2003) 'Policekeeping is the Key: Rebuilding the Internal Security Architecture of Postwar Iraq', *International Affairs*, 79 (2): 299–313.

Day, P. and Klein, R. (1987) *Accountabilities: Five Public Services*. London/New York: Tavistock.

De Kerchove, G. (2005) *La confiance mutuelle dans l'espace européen*. Brussels: L'Université de Bruxelles.

Deflem, M. (2000) 'Bureaucratization and Social Control: historical foundations of international police cooperation' *Law & Society Review*, 34 (3):601–640.

Deflem, M. (2001) 'International Police Cooperation in Northern America: a review of practices, strategies, and goals in the United States, Mexico, and Canada', in Koenig, D.J. and Das, D.K. (eds), *International Police Cooperation: A World Perspective*. Lanham, MD: Lexington, pp. 71–98.

Deflem, M. (2002) *Policing World Society: Historical Foundations of International Police Cooperation*. Oxford: Oxford University Press.

Deflem, M. (2004) 'The Boundaries of International Cooperation: problems and prospects of U.S.-Mexican Policing', in Menachem, A. and Stanley, E. (eds), *Police Corruption: Challenges for Developed Countries – Comparative Issues and Commissions of Inquiry*. Huntsville, TX: Office on International Criminal Justice, pp. 93–112.

Deflem, M. (2006a) 'Global Rule of Law or Global Rule of Law Enforcement? International police cooperation and counter-terrorism', *The Annals of the American Academy of Political and Social Science*, 603: 240–251.

Deflem, M. (2006b) 'Europol and the Policing of International Terrorism: counter-terrorism in a global perspective', *Justice Quarterly*, 23 (3): 336–359.

Den Boer, M. (1997) *Undercover Policing and Accountability from an International Perspective*. Maastricht: EIPA.

Den Boer, M. (2001) 'From Networks to Institutions … or Vice Versa? Opportunities for "good governance" in EU police cooperation', in *Collegium on Integrated Security in Europe: A Democratic Perspective*. Bruges: College of Europe, pp. 36–43.

Den Boer, M. (2001) 'The Fight Against Organised Crime in Europe: A Comparative Perspective', *European Journal on Criminal Policy and Research*, 9 (3).

Den Boer, M. (2002a) 'Intelligence Exchange and the Control of Organised Crime: from Europeanisation via centralisation to dehydration?', in Anderson, M. and Apap, J. (eds), *Police and Justice Co-operation and the New European Borders*. The Hague, The Netherlands: Kluwer Law International, pp. 151–163.

Den Boer, M. (2002b) 'Internationalization: a challenge to police organizations', in Mawby, R.I. (ed.), *Europe in Policing Across the World: Issues for the Twenty-first Century*. London: UCL Press, pp. 59–74.

Den Boer, M. (2002c) 'Law-Enforcement Cooperation and Transnational Organized Crime in Europe', in Berdal, M. and Serrano, M. (eds), *Transnational Organized Crime & International Security*. London: Rienner, pp. 103–116.

Den Boer, M. (2002d) 'Towards an accountability regime for an emerging European policing governance', *Policing and Society*, 12(4): 275–289.

Den Boer, M. (2003) 'The EU Counter-Terrorism Wave: window of opportunity or profound policy transformation?', in Leeuwen, M.V. (ed.), *Confronting Terrorism: European Experiences, Threat Perceptions and Policies*. London: Kluwer Law International, pp. 185–206.

Den Boer, M. (2005) 'Copweb Europe: venues, virtues and vexations of transnational policing', in Kaiser, W. and Starie, P. (eds), *Transnational European Union: Towards a Common Political Space*. London: Routledge, pp. 191–209.

Den Boer, M. (2008) 'Governing Transnational Law Enforcement in the EU: accountability after the fuse between internal and external security', in Den Boer, M. and Wilde, J. (eds), *The Viability of Human Security*. Amsterdam: Amsterdam University Press, pp. 63–78.

Den Boer, M. and Bruggeman, W. (2007) 'Shifting Gear: Europol in the contemporary policing era', *Politique européenne*, 23 (3): 77–91.

Den Boer, M. and Doelle, P. (2000) *Controlling Organized Crime: Organizational Changes in the Law Enforcement and Prosecution Services of the EU Member States*. Maastricht: European Institute of Public Administration.

Den Boer, M., Hillebrand, C. and Noelke, A. (2008) 'Legitimacy Under Pressure: the European web of counter-terrorism networks', *Journal of Common Market Studies*, 46 (1): 101–124.

Dersso, S.A. (2009) 'The Need for Civilianising the African Standby Force', *Peacekeeping This Month*, 26 March. Retrieved on 5 April. http://www.apsta-africa.org/news/article260309.php.

Desroches, F. (1999) *Drug Trafficking and Organized Crime in Canada: A Study of High-Level Drug Networks.* Report prepared for the Nathanson Centre for the Study of Organized Crime and Corruption, Toronto, Canada.

Diehl, P.F. (1998) 'Peacekeeping Operations and the Quest for Peace', *Political Science Quarterly*, 103(3): 485–507.

Dinnen, S. (2008) 'Dilemmas of Intervention and the Building of State and Nation', in Dinnen, S. and Firth, S. (eds), *Politics and State Building in Solomon Islands.* Canberra: Asia Pacific Press ANU, pp. 1–38.

Dombey, D. (2003) 'EU agrees to give US information on airline passengers', *Financial Times* (London), 17 December.

Dorn, N., Murji, K. and South, N. (1992) *Traffickers: Drug Markets and Law Enforcement.* London: Routledge.

Dorn, N. (1996) 'The EU, Home Affairs and 1996: Intergovernmental Convergence or Federal Diversity?' in Dorn, N., Jepsen, J. and Savona, E. (eds), *European Drug Policies and Enforcement.* New York: St. Martin's Press, pp. 153–170.

Downes, D., Rock, P., Chinken, C. and Gearty, C. (2007) *Crime, Social Control and Human Rights: From Moral Panics to States of Denial, Essays in Honour of Stanley Cohen.* Cullompton: Willan.

Drug Enforcement Administration (2008) *The National Drug Assessment.* Washington DC: Department of Justice.

Duarte, D.L. and Snyder, N.T. (1999) *Mastering Virtual Teams.* San Francisco, CA: Jossey-Bass.

Dunlap, C.J. (2001) 'The Thick Green Line: the growing involvement of military forces in domestic law enforcement', in Kraska, P. (ed.), *Militarizing the American Criminal Justice System: The Changing Roles of the Armed Forces and the Police.* Boston, MA: Northeastern University Press, pp. 29–42.

Dunn, T. (1999) 'Military Collaboration with the Border Patrol in the U.S.-Mexico Border Region: inter-organizational relations and human rights implications', *Journal of Political and Military Sociology*, 27: 257–277.

Dupont, B. and Pérez, E. (2006) *Les Polices du Québec, Que sais-je?* Paris: PUF.

Dziedzic, M. and Stark, C. (2006) *Bridging the Public Security Gap: The Role of the Center of Excellence for Stability Police Units (CoESPU) in Contemporary Peace Operations.* US Institute for Peace: Washington DC.

Eising, R. and Kohler-Koch, B. (1999) 'Introduction: Network governance in the European Union', in Kohler-Koch, B. and Eising, R. (eds), *The Transformation of Governance in the European Union.* London: Routledge, pp. 3–13.

Ekengren, M. *et al.* (2006) 'Solidarity or Sovereignty? EU cooperation in civil protection', *Journal of European Integration*, 28 (5): 457–476.

Elsen, C. (2007) 'From Maastricht to The Hague: the politics of judicial and police cooperation'. Paper delivered at ERA's summer course in Trier, 3–7 July 2006. *ERA Forum*, 8: 13–26.

Ericson, R.V. (1981) *Making Crime: A Study of Detective Work*. Toronto: Butterworth.

Ericson, R.V. (2007) *Crime in an Insecure World*. Cambridge: Polity.

Ericson, R.V. and Haggerty, K. (1997) *Policing the Risk Society*. Toronto: University of Toronto Press.

European Parliament (2008) *La coopération policière et douanière*. Brussels: Parlement Européen.

European Report (2004a) *EU/US: Council Rubber-Stamps Pact to Boost Container Security*, 31 March.

European Report (2004b) *EU/US: Visa Waivers and Passport Security Dominate First High-level Meeting*, 28 April.

European Report (2007a) *Justice and Home Affairs: "De Kerchove to spell out his concern to ministers"*, 6 December.

European Report (2007b) *Justice and Home Affairs "De Kerchove calls on Ministers to stick to their commitments"*, 7 December.

European Report (2007c) *Counter-Terrorism: EU Coordinator highlights poor implementation of measures*, 8 November.

European Report (2008) *Justice and Home Affairs Council: pressure on for ratification of extradition agreements with US*, 24 October.

Europol (2003) *Annual Report*. The Hague: European Police Office.

Europol (2006) *Drugs 2006* (Europol, The Hague). Available at http://www.europol.europa.eu/publications/Serious_Crime_Overviews/drugs2005.pdf (accessed 24 May 2009).

Europol (2008) *Annual Report 2007*. The Hague: European Police Office.

Federal Bureau of Investigation (2008) *Today's FBI Facts and Figures*. Washington DC: Department of Justice.

Federale Politie (2007) *De aanpak van rondtrekkende dadergroeperingen: een actualisatie*. Brussels: Federal Politie.

Fijnaut, C. (1987) 'De internationalisering van de opsporing in westelijk Europa', *Panopticon*, 8(4): 300–320.

Fijnaut, C. (1992) 'Naar een Gemeenschappelijke Regeling van de Politiële Samenwerking en de Justitiële Rechtshulp', in Fijnaut, C., Stuyck, J. and Wytinck, P. (eds), *Schengen: Proeftuin voor de Europese Gemeenschap?* Arnhem: Gouda Quint, pp. 89–118.

Fijnaut, C. (1993a) 'The Communitization of Police Cooperation in Western Europe' in Schermers, H. *et al.* (eds), *Free Movement of Persons in Europe: Legal Problems and Experiences*. Dordrecht: Martinus Nijhoff, pp. 75–92.

Fijnaut, C. (1993b) *The Internationalisation of Criminal Investigation in Western Europe*. Boston, MA: Kluwer Law.

Fijnaut, C. (2004) 'Police Co-operation and the Area of Freedom, Security and Justice' in Walker, N. (ed.), *Europe's Area of Freedom, Security and Justice*. Oxford: Oxford University Press, pp. 241–282.

Fijnaut, C. (2006) 'The Hague Programme and Police cooperation between the Member States of the EU', in de Zwaan, J. and Goudappel, F. (eds), *Freedom, Security and Justice in the European Union: Implementation of the Hague Programme*. The Hague: TMC Asser Press, pp. 233–248.

Fijnaut, C. and De Ruyver, B. (2008) *Voor een gezamenlijke beheersing van de drugscriminaliteit in de Euregio Maas-Rijn*. Maastricht: Meuse-Rhine Euroregion.

Fijnaut, C. and Van Gestel, G. (1992) 'De Politiële Samenwerking in het Belgisch-Nederlandse Grensgebied', in Fijnaut, C. (ed.), *De Reguliere Politiediensten van België en Nederland: hun Reorganisatie en Onderlinge Samenwerking*. Arnhem: Gouda Quint, pp. 175–200.

Finnemore, M. (1993) 'International Organizations as Teachers of Norms: the United Nations educational, scientific, and cultural organization and Science Policy', *International Organization*, 47 (4): 567–7.

Finnemore, M. (1996) *National Interests in International Society*. Ithaca, NY: Cornell University Press.

Fisher-Thompson, J. (2007) 'U.S. Military Training Program Benefits African Peacekeepers' *UnInfo*, US Department of State. Available at http://www.globalsecurity.org/military/library/news/2007/03/mil-070320-usia04.htm.

Fitz-Gerald, A. (2003) 'Security Sector Reform – Streamlining National Military Forces to Respond to the Wider Security Needs', *Journal of Security Sector Management*, 1: 1–21.

Fitzsimmons, T. (2005) 'The Postconflict Postscript: gender and policing in peace operations', in Mazurana, D., Raven-Roberts, A. and Parpart, J. (eds) *Gender, Conflict, and Peacekeeping*. New York: Rowman & Littlefield, pp. 185–201.

Flynn, S. (2002) 'America the Vulnerable', Foreign Affairs, 81, 1. Retrieved on 15 June 2009 at http://www.foreignaffairs.com/articles/57620/stephen-e-flynn/america-the-vulnerable

Fooner, M. (1989) *Interpol: Issues in World Crime and International Justice*. New York: Plenum.

Fried, C. (1981) *Contract as Promise: A Theory of Contractual Obligation*. Cambridge, MA: Harvard University Press.

Frontex (2008) *General Report*. European Agency for the Management of Operational Cooperation at the External Borders of the Member States of the European Union. Warsaw.

Frost, T.B. (1996) 'The Case for International Police Cooperation on Training Issues', in Pageon, M. (ed.), *Policing in Central Europe: Combining Firsthand Knowledge With Experience From the West*. Slovenia: College of Police and Security Studies, pp. 151–162.

Fukuyama, F. (2004) *State Building: Governance and World Order in the Twenty-first Century*. London: Profile.

Gallagher, D.F. (1998) *European Police Co-operation: Its Development and Impact Between 1967–1997 in an Anglo/French Trans-Frontier Setting*. Unpublished thesis, University of Southampton.

Gamba, V. (2008) *SADC Security Cooperation and Progress with the SADC Brigade*. Unpublished paper. Pretoria: SaferAfrica. Available at http://www.army.mil.za/vision2020ver2008/Doccies/abstracts/Abs-Virginia%20Gamba.doc Retrieved 4 April 2009.

Gambetta, D. (1993) *The Sicilian Mafia*. Cambridge, MA: Harvard University Press.

Gambetta, D. and Reuter, R. (1995) 'Conspiracy Among the Many: the Mafia in legitimate industries', in Fiorentini, G. and Peltzman, S. (eds), *The Economics of Organized Crime*. Cambridge: Cambridge University Press, pp. 116–139.

Gerspacher, N. (2002) *International Police Cooperation as a Response to Transnational Crime: A Study of Effectiveness*. Unpublished doctoral dissertation, The University of Illinois at Chicago.

Gerspacher, N. (2005) 'The Roles of International Police Cooperation Organizations: beyond mandates, toward unintended roles', *European Journal of Crime, Criminal Law and Criminal Justice*, 13 (3): 413–434.

Gerspacher, N. and Dupont, B. (2007) 'The Nodal Structure of International Police Cooperation: an exploration of transnational security networks', *Global Governance*, 13 (3): 347–364.

Gerspacher, N. and Lemieux, F. (2005) 'Coopération policière, marché de l'information et expansion des acteurs internationaux: le cas d'Europol', *Revue internationale de criminologie et de police technique et scientifique*, 4: 461–478.

Ghebali, V-Y, (2006) 'The United Nations and the Dilemma of Outsourcing Peacekeeping Operations', in Bryden, A. and Caparini, M. (eds), *Private Actors and Security Governance*. Vienna: LIT, pp. 313–330.

Gill, L. (2004) *The School of the Americas*. Durham, NC: Duke UP.

GNIM (2005) *Guidance on the National Intelligence Model*. London: Home Office.

Goldring, J. and Wettenhall, R. (1980) 'Three Perspectives on the Responsibility of Statutory Authorities', in Weller, P. and D. Jaensch (eds), *Responsible Government in Australia*. Richmond, Vic.: Drummond pp. 136–150.

Goldsmith, A. (2003) 'Policing Weak States: citizen safety and state responsibility', *Policing & Society*, 13 (1): 3–21.

Goldsmith, A. (2009) 'It Wasn't Like Normal Policing: Voices of Australian Police Peace-Keepers in Operation Serene, Timor 2006', *Policing and Society*, 19(2): 119–133.

Goldsmith, A. and Dinnen, S. (2007) 'Transnational Police Building: critical lessons from Timor-Leste and Solomon Islands', *Third World Quarterly*, 28 (6): 1091–1109.

Goldsmith, A. and Harris, V. (2009) 'Out of Step: multilateral police missions, culture and nation-building in Timor-Leste', *Conflict Security and Development*, 9 (2): 189–211.

Goldsmith, A. and Sheptycki, J.W.E. (eds) (2007) *Crafting Transnational Policing: Police Capacity-building and Global Policing Reform*. Oxford: Hart.

Goldsmith, A., Llorente, M.V., and Rivas, A. (2007) 'Making Sense of Transnational Police-Building: Foreign Assistance in Colombian Policing', in Goldsmith, A. and Sheptycki, J.W.E. (eds) *Crafting Transnational Policing: Police Capacity-building and Global Policing Reform.* Oxford: Hart, pp. 73–109.

Goldstein, H. (1990) *Problem Oriented Policing.* Philadelphia, PA: Temple University Press.

Gomes, S. (2008) 'The Peacemaking Role of the OAU and the AU: a comparative analysis', in Akokpan, J., Ndinga-Muvumba, A. and Murithi, T. (eds), *The African Union and its Institutions.* Cape Town: Fanele, pp. 113–130.

Gomez del Prado, J.L. (2008) 'Private military and security companies and challenges to the UN Working Group on the Use of Mercenaries'. Paper presented to conference on *The Privatization of Security and Human Rights in the Americas: Perspectives from the Global South,* University of Wisconsin-Madison, 31 January to 2 February. Retrieved on 17 November from http://www.havenscenter.org/privatemilitaryconference2008

Grabosky, P. (2000) 'Computer Crime in a World Without Borders', *Platypus Magazine: The Journal of the Australian Federal Police,* June. Retrieved on 30 November 2007 from http://www.afp.gov.au/about/publications/platypus_magazine/june_2000/compcri

Greener, B.K. (2009) 'UNPOL: UN police as peacekeepers', *Policing and Society,* 19 (2):106–118.

Greener, B.K. (2009) *The New International Policing.* Basingstoke: Palgrave Macmillan.

Greener-Barcham, B.K. (2007) 'Crossing the Green or Blue Line? Exploring the military-police divide', *Small Wars and Insurgencies,* 18: 90–112.

Gregory, F. (1998) 'There is a Global Crime Problem', *International Journal of Risk, Security and Crime Prevention,* 3 (2): 133–137.

Gresswell, D.M., and Holin, C.R. (1994) 'Multiple Murder; a review', *British Journal of Criminology,* 34 (1): 1–14.

Grewe, C. (2001) 'La convention Europol: l'émergence d'une police européenne', *Acte du colloque de l'Institut de recherches Carré de Malberg.* Strasbourg: Presses universitaires de Strasbourg.

Guille, L. (2009) *Police and Judicial Cooperation in Europe: Europol, Eurojust and the European Judicial Network: Master Pieces of the European Union's Puzzle in Justice and Home Affairs.* Unpublished thesis, University of Sheffield.

Guyomarch, A. (1995) 'Problems and prospects for European police cooperation after Maastricht', *Policing and Society,* 5(3): 249–261.

Haas, E. (1972) 'International integration: the European and the Universal Process', in Hodges, M. (ed.), *European Integration: Selected Readings.* London: Penguin, pp. 91–97.

Haas, E.B., Butterworth, R.L. and Nye, J.S. (1972) *Conflict Management by International Organizations.* New York: General Learning Press.

Haas, P.M. (ed.) (1997) *Knowledge, Power, and International Policy Coordination Studies in International Relations*. Columbia: University of South Carolina Press.

Haas, P., Keohane, R. and Levy, M. (1993) *Institutions for the Earth: Sources and Effective International Environmental Protection*. Cambridge, MA: MIT Press.

Haggerty, K.D. and Ericson, R.V. (2000) 'The Surveillant Assemblage', *The British Journal of Sociology*, 51(4): 605–622.

Hall, B. and Bhatt, A. (1999) *Policing Europe: EU Justice and Home Affairs Co-operation*. London: Centre for European Reform.

Haller, M.H. (1990) 'Illegal Enterprise: a theoretical and historical interpretation', *Criminology*, 28: 207–235.

Hallerberg, M. and Weber, K. (2001) 'Explaining Variation in Institutional Integration in the European Union: why firms may prefer European solutions', *Journal of European Public Policy*, 8 (2): 171–191.

Hartmut, A. (2003) 'La coopération internationale des polices', *Cultures et Conflits*, 48–1:15–34.

Hartz, H. (1999) 'CIVPOL – the UN instrument for police reform', *International Peacekeeping*, 6 (4): 27–43.

Hayseliph, D. and Russell-Einhorn, M. (2003) 'Evaluating Multijurisdictional Drug Enforcement Task Forces', *National Institute of Justice Journal*, 250: 40–42.

Hebenton, B. and Thomas, T. (eds) (1995) *Policing Europe: Cooperation, Conflict and Control*. New York: St. Martin's Press.

Held, D. (2004) *Global Covenant: The Social Democratic Alternative to the Washington Consensus*. Cambridge: Polity.

Hermans, L., Claes, W., Schmitz, P., Soete, L., Toonen, T. and Kuijers, F. (2007) *De toekomst van Limburg ligt over de grens*. Maastricht: Provincie Limburg.

Hester, M., Kelly, L. and Radford, J. (eds) (1996) *Women, Violence and Male Power*. Milton Keynes: Open University Press.

High Level Advisory Group on the Future of European Home Affairs Policy (2008a) *Freedom, Security, Privacy: European Home Affairs in an Open World*. Brussels: European Parliament.

High Level Advisory Group on the Future of European Justice Policy (2008b) *Proposed Solutions for the Future EU Justice Programme*. Brussels: European Parliament.

Hills, A. (2001) 'The Inherent Limits of Military Forces in Policing Peace Operations', *International Peacekeeping*, 8 (3): 79–98.

Hills, A. (2007) 'Police Commissioners, Presidents and the Governance of Security', *Journal of Modern African Studies*, 45(3): 403–424.

Hills, A. (2009) *Policing Post-Conflict Cities*. London: Zed.

Hills, A. (2009) 'The Possibility of Transnational Policing', in *Policing and Society*, 19(3): 300–317.

Hoffman, J. (1998) *Sovereignty*. Buckingham: Open University Press.

Hofmann, H., Pfeifer, R. and Vinkhuyzen, E. (1993) *Situated Software Design*. Zurich: University of Zurich, ifi-93.18.

Hofstede, G. and Faure, M. (1993) *Grensoverschrijdende politiesamenwerking tussen België, Duitsland en Nederland met speciale aandacht voor de Euregio Maas-Rijn*. Maastricht: Maastricht University Press.

Holm, T. and Eide, E. (eds) (2000) *Peacebuilding and Police Reform*. London: Portland.

Hooghe, L. and Marks, G. (2001) *Multi-Level Governance and European Integration*. Lanham: Rowman and Littlefield.

Hope, T. (2000) 'Inequality and the clubbing of private security' in Hope, T. and Sparks, R. (eds), *Crime, Risk and Insecurity*. London: Routledge, pp. 83–106.

Hope, T. (forthcoming) 'The Economy of Private Security'. Paper presented to the European Society of Criminology, Bologna, September 2007.

Hutcheson, J. (2007) 'The Lessons of 2006: Australian Army Operations in East Timor' in *Institutions for the Earth: Sources of Effective International Environmental Protection*, Haas, P.M., Keohane, R.O., Levy, M.A., (eds). Cambridge, MA: MIT Press.

Ianni, F.J. (1972) *A Family Business*. New York: Russell Sage Foundation.

Ianni, F.J. (1974) *Black Mafia*. New York: Simon and Schuster.

ICPO (1989) *Interpol Constitution and General Regulations*, 15 January.

Ignatieff, M. (2004) *The Lesser Evil: Political Ethics in an Age of Terror*. Princeton: Princeton University Press.

Independent Panel (2008) Independent Panel on Canada's Future Role in Afghanistan (Chair Hon. John Manley), Minister of Public Works and Government Services, Canada. Retrieved on 16 November 2008 from http://dsp-psd.pwgsc.gc.ca/collection_2008/dfait-maeci/FR5-20-1-2008E.pdf

Innes, M. (2005) 'Why "Soft" Policing is Hard: on the curious development of reassurance policing, how it became neighbourhood policing and what this signifies about the politics of police reform', *Journal of Community & Applied Social Psychology*, 15 (3): 156–169.

Interpol (2009) *Annual Report*. Lyon: Interpol General Secretariat.

Jackson, A. and Lyon, A. (2001) 'Policing after ethnic conflict: culture, democratic policing, politics and the public', *Policing: An International Journal of Police Strategies & Management*, 24 (4): 563–584.

Jefferis, E.S., Frank, J., Smith, B.W., Novak, K.J. and Travis, L.F. (1998) 'An Examination of the Productivity and Perceived Effectiveness of Drug Task Forces', *Police Quarterly*, 1 (3): 85–107.

Johnson, C. (2009) 'FBI Director Warns of Terror Attacks on U.S. Cities', *The Washington Post*, 23 February, http://www.washingtonpost.com/wp-dyn/content/article/2009/02/23/AR2009022301850.html

Johnson, T. (1972) *Professions and Power*. London: Macmillan.

Johnston, L. (2006) 'Transnational Security Governance', in Wood, J. and Dupont, B. (eds), *Democracy, Society and the Governance of Security*. Cambridge: Cambridge University Press, pp. 33–51.

Johnston, L. (forthcoming) 'Glocal Heroes: transnational commercial security companies in the 21st century', in Loader, I. and Percy, S. (eds), *Reconfiguring Security: Contemporary Insecurities and the Pluralisation of Coercive Force.*

Johnston, L. and Shearing, C. (2003) *Governing Security. Explorations in Policing and Justice.* London: Routledge.

Johnston, L., Button, M. and Williamson, T. (2008) 'Police, Governance and the Private Finance Initiative', *Policing & Society,* 18 (3): 225–244.

Jones, T. and Newburn, T. (1999) 'Urban Change and Policing: mass private property reconsidered', *European Journal on Criminal Policy and Research,* 7 (2): 225–244.

Jones, T. and Newburn, T. (2002) 'The Transformation of Policing? Understanding current trends in policing systems', *British Journal of Criminology,* 42 (1): 129–146.

Joras, U. and Schuster, A. (eds) (2008) *Private Security Companies and Local Populations: An Exploratory Study of Afghanistan and Angola.* Bern: Swisspeace. Retrieved on 16 November from http://www.swisspeace.ch/typo3/fileadmin/user_upload/pdf/Working_Paper/WP_1_2008.pdf

Joutsen, M. (2005) 'International Instruments on Cooperation in Responding to Transnational Crime', in Reichel, P. (ed.), *Handbook of Transnational Crime & Justice.* Thousand Oaks, CA: Sage, pp. 255–274.

Kagan, R. (2002) 'Power and Weakness: why the United States and Europe see the world differently', *Policy Review,* 113: 1–22.

Katz, D. and Kahn, R.L. (1966) *The Social Psychology of Organizations.* New York: Wiley.

Kaunert, C. (2007) 'Without the Power of Purse or Sword? The European arrest warrant and the role of the commission', *Journal of European Integration,* 29 (4): 387–404.

Kean, T.H. and Hamilton, L.H. (2004) *The 9/11 Report: The National Commission on Terrorist Attacks Upon the United States.* New York: St. Martin's Press.

Keating, M. (1998) *The New Regionalism in Western Europe: Territorial Restructuring and Political Change.* Cheltenham: Edward Elgar.

Keck, M. and Sikkink, K. (1998) *Activists Beyond Borders: Advocacy Networks in International Politics.* Ithaca, NY: Cornell University Press.

Kelly, R.B. (1978) *Organized Crime: A Study in the Production of Knowledge by Law-Enforcement Specialists.* Unpublished doctoral dissertation, University of New York.

Kempa, M., Stenning, P. and Wood, J. (2004) 'Policing Communal Spaces: a reconfiguration of the "mass private property" hypothesis', *British Journal of Criminology,* 44 (4): 562–581.

Keohane, R. (1983) 'The Demand for International Regimes', in Krasner, S. (ed.), *International Regimes.* Ithaca, NY: Cornell University Press, pp. 325–355.

Keohane, R. (1984) *After Hegemony: Cooperation and Discord in the World Political Economy.* New Jersey: Princeton University Press.

Keohane, R. and Levy, M. (1996) *Institutions for Environmental Aid: Pitfalls and Promises.* Cambridge, MA: MIT Press.

Keohane, R. and Nye, J. (1997) *Power and Interdependence: World Politics in Transition.* Boston: Little Brown.

Kersbergen, K. van and Waarden, F. van (2001) *Shifts in Governance: Problems of Legitimacy and Accountability.* Paper as part of Strategic Plan 2002–2005, Netherlands Organisation for Scientific Research, July.

Kersbergen, K. van and Waarden, F. van (2004) 'Governance as a Bridge Between Disciplines: cross-disciplinary inspiration regarding shifts in governance and problems of governability, accountability and legitimacy', *European Journal of Political Research*, 43: 143–171.

Kettl, D.F. (2000) 'The Transformation of Governance: globalization, devolution, and the role of government', *Public Administration Review*, 60 (6): 488–497.

Kilcullen, D. (2009) *The Accidental Guerrilla: Fighting Small Wars in the Midst of a Big One.* Melbourne: Scribe.

Klotz, A. (1995) *Norms in International Relations: The Struggle against Apartheid.* Ithaca, NY: Cornell University Press.

Koenig, D.J. and Das, D.K. (2001) *International Police Cooperation: A World Perspective.* Lanham, MD: Lexington.

Kohler-Koch, B. (2000) 'Beyond Amsterdam: regional integration as social process', in Neunreither, K. and Wiener, A. (eds), *European Integration After Amsterdam: Institutional Dynamics and Prospects for Democracy.* Oxford: Oxford University Press, pp. 68–92.

Köhring, M.K. (2007) *Beyond 'Venus and Mars': Comparing Transatlantic Approaches to Democracy Promotion.* Bruges, Belgium: College of Europe.

Kopp, P. (1997) *L'économie de la drogue.* Paris: Éditions de la découverte.

Koremenos, B., Lipson, C. and Snidal, D. (2001) 'The Rational Design of International Institutions', *International Organization*, 55 (4): 761–799.

Korps Landelijke Politiediensten (2005) *Eindrapportage van het Project Polaris.* Driebergen: Dienst Nationale Recherche.

Kraska, P.B. (ed.) (2001) *Militarizing the American Criminal Justice System: The Changing Roles of the Armed Forces and Police.* Boston, MA: Northeastern University Press.

Krasner, S. (1983) *International Regimes.* Ithaca, NY: Cornell University Press.

Krebs, C.P., Costelloe, M. and Jenks, D. (2003) 'Drug Control Policy and Smuggling Innovation: a game-theoretic analysis', *Journal of Drug Issues*, 33: 133–160.

Kube, E. and Kuckuck, W. (1992) 'Research and Technological Development in the Police: Requirements from the Western European point of view', *Policing: An International Journal of Police Strategies & Management*, 4: 15–24.

L'Heuillet, H. (2001) *Basse politique, haute police: une approche historique et philosophique de la police.* Paris: Fayard.

Labrousse, A. (1995) *The Geopolitics of Drugs.* Boston, MA: North-Eastern University Press.

Laitner, S. (2005) 'Practical Hurdles Slow Europe's Joint Effort to Tackle Terrorism', *Financial Times* (London), 1 August.

Lake, D. and Powell, R. (1999) *Strategic Choice in International Relations*. Princeton: Princeton University Press.

Latham, E.J. (2001) 'Civpol Certification: a model for recruitment and training of civilian police monitors', *World Affairs*. Highbeam Encyclopedia. Available at http://www.encyclopedia.com/printable.aspx?id=1G1:78729188

Lave, J. and Wenger, E. (1990) *Situated Learning: Legitimate Peripheral Participation*. Cambridge: Cambridge University Press.

Le Jeune, P. (1992) *La coopération policière européenne contre le terrorisme*. Brussels: Bruylant.

Leamy, W.J. (1983) 'International Co-operation Through the Interpol System to Counter Illicit Drug Trafficking', *Bull Narcotics*, 35 (4): 55–60.

Lebrun, M. (1997) *INTERPOL*. Paris: Presses Universitaires de France.

Lemieux, F. (2006) *Normes et pratiques en matière de renseignements criminels: une comparaison internationale*. Ste-Foy: Presses Université Laval.

Lemieux, F. (2008) 'A Cross Cultural Comparison of Intelligence Led Policing', in Williamson, T. (ed.), *The Handbook of Knowledge Based Policing: Current Conceptions and Future Directions*. London: Wiley, pp. 221–240.

Lemieux, V. (2003) *Criminal Networks*. Report prepared for the Royal Canadian Mounted Police, Ottawa: Research and Evaluation Branch.

Lester, N. (1998) *Enquêtes sur les services secrets*. Montréal: Les éditions de l'Homme.

Levine, D.H. (2008) *African Civilian Police Capacity for International Peacekeeping Operations*. Washington, DC: The Henry L. Stimson Center.

Levine, M. and Martin, D. (1992) 'Drug Deals Have No Boundaries: multijurisdictional narcotics task forces', *Law Enforcement Technology*, 34: 37.

Levy, R. and Monjardet, D. (2003) 'Les polices nationales et l'unification européenne, enjeux et interactions', *Cultures et Conflits*, 48 (1): 5–14.

Loader, I. (2000) 'Plural Policing and Democratic Governance', *Social and Legal Studies*, 9 (3): 323–345.

Loader, I. and Walker, N. (2001) 'Policing as a public good: reconstituting the connections between policing and the state' *Theoretical Criminology* 5, 1: 9–35.

Loader, I. and Walker, N. (2007) *Civilizing Security*. Cambridge: Cambridge University Press.

Luphsa, P.A. (1983) 'Network Versus Networking: analysis of an organized crime group', in Waldo, P. (ed.), *Career Criminals*. Beverly Hills, CA: Sage, pp. 43–87.

Macaulay, S. (1986) 'Private Government', in Lipson, L. and Wheeler, S. (eds), *Law and the Social Sciences*. New York: Russell Sage Foundation, pp. 445–518.

MacIntyre, A. (1990) *Three Rival Versions of Moral Enquiry: The Gifford Lectures*. Notre Dame, IN: University of Notre Dame Press.

MacIntyre, A. (1998) *A Short History of Ethics* (2nd edn). New York: Macmillan.

Maguer, A. (2004) *Les frontières intérieures Schengen: Dilemmes et stratégies de la coopération policière et douanière franco-allemande*. Freiburg: Edition Iuscrim.

Maguire, E. (2008) *Critical Intelligence Community Management Challenges*. Washington, DC: Inspector General, Office of the Director of National Intelligence.

Maguire, M. (2000) 'Policing by Risks and Targets: some dimensions and implications of intelligence control', *Policing and Society*, 9 (4): 315–336.

Malan, M. (1998) 'Peacekeeping in the New Millennium: towards "fourth generation" peace operations?', *African Security Review*, 7 (3): 13–20.

Mann, M. (1986) *The Sources of Social Power: A History of Power from the Beginning to A.D. 1760* (Vol 1). Cambridge: Cambridge University Press.

Manning, P.K. (1980) *The Narc's Game: Organizational and Informational Limits on Drug Law Enforcement*. Cambridge, MA: MIT Press.

Manning, P.K. (2000) 'Policing New Social Spaces', in Sheptycki, J.W.E. (ed.), *Issues in Transnational Policing*. London: Routledge, pp. 177–200.

Marenin, O. (2005) 'Building a Global Police Studies Community', *Police Quarterly*, 8 (10): 99–136.

Marshall, G. (1984) *Constitutional Conventions: The Rules and Forms of Political Accountability*. Oxford: Clarendon.

Marten, K. (2007) 'Statebuilding and Force: the proper role of foreign militaries', *Journal of Intervention and Statebuilding*, 1: 231–247.

Martin, L. (1992) *Coercive Cooperation Explaining Multilateral Economic Sanctions*. Princeton: Princeton University Press.

Martinelli, M. (2006) 'Helping Transition: the EU police mission in the Democratic Republic of Congo (EUPOL Kinshasa) in the framework of EU policies in the Great Lakes', *European Foreign Affairs Review*, 11 (3): 379–399.

Mashaw, J. (2006) 'Accountability and Institutional Design: some thoughts on the grammar of governance', in Dowdle, M. (ed.), *Public Accountability: Designs, Dilemmas and Experiences*. Cambridge: Cambridge University Press, pp. 115–156.

McCasky, M.B. (1974) 'An introduction to organizational design', *California Management Review*, 17: 13–20.

McDavid, J.C. (1977) 'The Effects of Interjurisdictional Cooperation on Police Performance in the St. Louis Metropolitan Area', *Publius*, 7 (2): 3–30.

McDonald, D.C. (1981) *Commission d'enquête sur certaines activités de la Gendarmerie royale du Canada*. Ottawa: Approvisionnements et Services Canada.

McNulty, F. (1980) *The Burning Bed*. New York: Harcourt.

Merlingen, M. and Ostrauskaite, R. (2005) 'Power/Knowledge in International Peacebuilding: the case of the EU police mission in Bosnia', *Alternatives*, 30 (3): 297–323.

Messner, J. and Gracielli, Y. (2007) *State of the Peace and Stability Operations Industry. Second Annual Survey 2007*. Washington, DC: Peace Operations

Institute. Retrieved on 30 October 2008 from http://peaceops.org/poi/images/stories/poi_rp_industrysurvey2007.pdf

Mintzberg, H. (1992) *Structure in Fives: Designing Effective Organizations*. New York: Prentice Hall.

Mitsilegas, V. (2003) 'The New EU-USA Cooperation on Extradition, Mutual Legal Assistance and the Exchange of Police Data', *European Foreign Affairs Review*, 8 (4): 516–519.

Mitsilegas, V., Monar, J. and Rees, W. (2003) *The European Union and Internal Security*. London: Palgrave Macmillan.

Moe, T. (1990) 'The Politics of Structural Choice: Toward a Theory of Public Bureaucracy', in O. Williamson (ed.), *Organizational Theory*. New York: Oxford University Press, pp.116–153.

Mokhine, N.S. (2008) *South African Police Service Deployed its First Peacekeepers to Darfur, Sudan: A Descriptive Study on the Deployment Preparations and the Role of the South African Police Peacekeepers in African Union Mission in Sudan (AMIS)*. Unpublished MPhil thesis, Nelson Mandela Metropolitan University.

Moravcsik, A. (1999) 'A New Statecraft? Supranational entrepreneurs and international cooperation', *International Organization*, 53 (2): 267–306.

Morselli, C., Turcotte, M. and Petit, K. (2003) 'Des éléments du crime organisé et son contrôle au Québec', in LeBlanc, M., Ouimet, M. and Szabo, D. (eds), *Traité de criminologie, 3ᵉ édition*. Montréal: Presses de l'Université de Montréal, pp. 161–192.

Mortlock, R. (2005) 'The Role of the Military', in Henderson, J. and Watson, G. (eds), *Securing a Peaceful Pacific*. Christchurch: Canterbury University Press, pp. 35–42.

Muir, W.K. (1972) *Police, Street Corner Politicians*. Chicago: Chicago University Press.

Müller, H. (2003) *Terrorism, Proliferation: A European Threat Assessment*. Institute For Security Studies, Chaillot Paper, No. 58.

Murray, J. (2003) 'Who will Police the Peace-Builders? The failure to establish accountability for the participation of United Nations civilian police in the trafficking of women in post-conflict Bosnia and Herzegovina', *Human Rights Law Review*, 34 (2): 475–527.

Murray, T. (2007) 'Police-Building in Afghanistan: a case study of civil security reform', *International Peacekeeping*, 14 (1): 108–126.

Nadelmann, E.A. (1988) 'U.S. Drug Policy: a bad export', *Foreign Policy*, 70: 3–108.

Nadelmann, E.A. (1992) 'The DEA in Latin America: Dealing with institutionalized corruption', *Journal of Inter-American Studies and World Affairs*, 29 (4): 1–39.

Nadelmann, E.A. (1993) *Cops Across Borders: The Internationalization of U.S. Criminal Law Enforcement*. University Park: Pennsylvania State University Press.

Nakashima, E. (2008) 'U.S. Seeks Data Exchange', *Washington Post*, 8 July.

Natarajan, M. (2000) 'Understanding the Structure of a Drug Trafficking Organization', *Crime Prevention Studies*, 11 (2): 273–298.

Naylor, R.T. (1997) 'Mafias, Myths, and Markets: on the theory and practice of organized crime', *Transnational Organized Crime*, 3 (1): 1–45.

Naylor, T. (2002) *Wages of Crime: Black Markets, Illegal Finance, and the Underworld Economy*. Ithaca, NY: Cornell University Press.

Neff, J. and Price, J. (2004) 'Contractors in Iraq Make Costs Balloon', *The News & Observer*, 24 October. Retrieved on 17 November 2008 from http://www.newsobserver.com/511/story/241329.html

Neild, R. (2001) 'Democratic Police Reforms in War-torn Societies', *Conflict, Security and Development*, 1 (1): 21–44.

Nelken, D. (1991) *Some Problems with the Impersonal Rule of Law in Italy*. Paper presented and distributed at the International Conference of the Law and Society Association, Amsterdam, 28 June.

Nelken, D. (1994) 'Whom Can You Trust? The future of comparative criminology', in Nelken, D. (ed.), *The Futures of Criminology*. London: Sage, pp. 220–243.

Neyroud, P. (2001) *Policing, Ethics and Human Rights*. Cullompton: Willan.

Nielson, D. and Tierney, M. (2003) 'Delegation to International Organizations: agency theory and World Bank Environmental Reform', *International Organization*, 57 (2): 241–276.

Nogala, D.E. (2001) 'Policing Across a Dimorphous Border: challenge and innovation at the French-German Border', *European Journal of Crime, Criminal Law and Criminal Justice*, 9 (2): 130–143.

Nomden, K. (2001–2) 'De europeanisering van provincies en gemeenten', *Openbaar Bestuur*: 17–20.

North, D. (1990) *Institutions, Institutional Change and Economic Performance*. New York: Cambridge University Press.

O'Connell, P. and Straub, F. (2007) *Performance-Based Management for Police Organizations*. Long Gove, IL: Waveland.

Occhipinti, J.D. (2003) *The Politics of EU Police Cooperation: Toward a European FBI?* Boulder, CO: Lynne Rienner.

Occhipinti, J.D. (2008) 'A Secure Europe? Internal security policies', in Bomberg, E. and Stubb, A. (eds), *The European Union: How Does it Work?* New York: Oxford University Press, pp. 139–158.

Office of Criminal Justice Services (OCJS) (1994) *Ohio 1994 State Annual Report: Byrne Memorial State and Local Law Enforcement Assistance Act*. Colombus, OH: Office of Criminal Justice Services.

Office of the Director of National Intelligence (2008) *United States Intelligence Community Information Sharing Strategy*. Washington, DC.

O'Malley, P. (1997) 'Policing, Politics and Postmodernity', *Social and Legal Studies*, 6 (3): 363–381.

Osborne, D. and Gaebler, T. (1993) *Reinventing Government*. New York: Plume.

Ostrom, E. (1990) *Governing the Commons: The Evolution of Institutions for Collective Action*. New York: Cambridge University Press.

Pallister, D. (2008) 'Foreign Security Teams to Lose Immunity from Prosecution in Iraq', *The Guardian*, 27 December, p. 7.

Pan, E. (2005) *African Peacekeeping Operations*. Washington, DC: Council on Foreign Relations. http://www.cfr.org/publication/9333/african_peacekeeping_operations.html retrieved on 14 February, 2009.

Paris, R. (2002) 'International Peacebuilding and the "Mission Civilisatrice", *Review of International Studies*, 28 (4): 637–656.

Parker, G.M. (1990) *Team Players and Teamwork: The New Competitive Business Strategy*. San Francisco, CA: Jossey-Bass.

Parlementaire Enquêtecommissie (1996) *Inzake opsporing*. The Hague: SDU.

Patman, R. (1997) 'Disarming Somalia: the contrasting fortunes of United States and Australian peacekeepers during United Nations intervention, 1992–1993', *African Affairs*, 96 (384): 509–533.

Peake, G. and Marenin, O. (2008) 'Their Reports are Not Read and Their Recommendations are Resisted: the challenge for the global police policy community', *Police Practice and Research*, 9 (1): 59–70.

Peake, G. and Studdard Brown, K. (2005) 'Policebuilding: the International Deployment Group in the Solomon Islands', *International Peacekeeping*, 12 (4): 520–532.

Pearson Peacekeeping Centre (2008) *Then and Now: Understanding the Spectrum of Complex Peace Operations*. Ottawa: Pearson Peacekeeping Centre.

Peers, S. (2000) *EU Justice and Home Affairs Law*. Harlow: Pearson Education Limited.

Perito, R.M. (2004) *Where is the Lone Ranger When We Need Him? America's Search for a Postconflict Stability Force*. Washington, DC: United States Institute of Peace Press.

Perito, R.M. (2007) *U.S. Police in Peace and Stability Operations*. Special Report 191. Washington, DC: United States Institute of Peace.

Perito, R.M. (2008) 'Police in Peace and Stability Operations: Evolving US Policy and Practice', *International Peacekeeping*, 15 (1): 51–66.

Perras, C. (2006) *Innovations, transformations et adaptations structurelles dans la lutte au crime organisé au Québec: une analyse de l'Opération Printemps 2001*. Unpublished Master's thesis, École de criminologie, Université de Montréal.

Perrin, B. (2008) 'Guns For Hire – with Canadian taxpayer dollars', *Human Security Bulletin*, 6 (3): 5–7. Retrieved on 30 October 2008 from http://www.humansecurity.info/#/securityprivatization/4527756237

Perrow, C. (1987) *Complex Organizations: A Critical Essay*. Glenview, IL: Scott & Foresman.

Peterson, J. (2004) 'Policy Networks', in Wiener, A. and Diez, T. (eds), *European Integration Theory*. Oxford: Oxford University Press, pp. 117–135.

Peterson, J. and Bomberg, E. (1999) *Decision-Making in the European Union*. New York: St. Martin's Press.

Pitcher, B. (2008) 'CIVPOL Diary: from the classroom to the field', Royal Canadian Mounted Police http://www.rcmp-grc.gc.ca/po-mp/civpol-field-terr-eng.htm retrieved on 2 February 2009.

Policing and Society (2004) Special Issue on the Governance of Security. Shearing, C. *et al.* (eds), 14(1): 1043–9463.

Politieregio Limburg-Zuid, (2005) *Jaarverslag.* Maastricht: Politieregio Limburg-Zuid.

Potter, G.W. (1994) *Criminal Organizations.* Prospect Heights: Waveland.

Programme de la Haye, Le (2004) *Renforcer la Liberté la Securité et la Justice dans l'Union Européenne.* Brussels: Le Conseil de l'Union Européenne.

Pujas, V. (2000) 'Les pouvoirs judiciaires en France, en Espagne et en Italie dans la lutte contre la corruption politique', *Droit et Société*, 44/45: 41–60.

Pujas, V. (2003) 'The European Anti-Fraud Office: a European policy to fight against economic and financial fraud?', *Journal of European Public Policy,* 10 (5): 778–797.

Pujas, V. (2004a) 'Immunity and Extradition: obstacles to justice', *Global Corruption Report,* Transparency International, pp. 89–93.

Pujas, V. (2004b) 'International Organisations and the Emergence of Anti-Corruption Policies', *Working Group on International Organisation and Policy Implementation.* Uppsala: European Consortium of Political Research.

Pujas, V. and Benoît, A.-M. (2003) 'Les nouvelles exigences de la responsabilité politique', in Perrineau, P. (ed.), *Le désenchantement démocratique.* Paris: L'Aube, pp. 89–103.

PUOF (2008) *A Joint Transnational Research on Justification of Use of Force by Police.* Available at http://www.policeuseofforce.org/background_information.htm

Pushpanathan, S. (1999) 'Combatting transnational crime in ASEAN', 7th ACPF World Conference on Crime Prevention and Criminal Justice, New Delhi, India, 23–26 November.

Radford, J., Friedverg, M. and Harne, L. (2000) *Women, Violence and Strategies for Action.* Milton Keynes: Open University Press.

Ramraj, V. V. and Roach, K. (2005) *Global Anti-Terrorism Law and Policy.* Cambridge: Cambridge University Press.

Ratcliffe, J. (2008) *Intelligence-Led Policing.* Cullompton: Willan.

Ratle, F., Gagné, C., Terrettaz-Zufferey, A.-L., Khanevski, M., Esseiva, P. and Ribaux, O. (2007) 'Advanced Clustering Methods for Mining Chemical Databases in Forensic Science', *Chemometrics and Intelligent Laboratory Systems*, 90: 122–131.

Ratle, F., Terrettaz-Zufferey, A.-L., Khanevski, M., Esseiva, P. and Ribaux, O. (2006) 'Learning Manifolds in Forensic Data', *International Conference on Artificial Neural Networks.* Berlin: Springer.

Raufer, X. (1993) *Les Super Puissances du Crime, Enquête sur le Narco Terrorisme.* Paris: Plon.

Reaves, B.A. (1992) *Drug Enforcement by Police and Sheriffs' Departments, 1990.* Washington, DC: US Department of Justice.

Reenen, P.V. (1989) 'Policing Europe after 1992: co-operation and competition', *European Affairs*, 3 (2): 45–53.

Rees, W. (2006) *Transatlantic Counter-Terrorism Cooperation: The New Imperative.* New York: Routledge.

Rees, W. (2009) 'Securing the Homelands: transatlantic co-operation after Bush', *The British Journal of Politics and International Relations*, 11 (1): 108–21.

Reiner, R. (1985) *The Politics of the Police*. Oxford: Oxford University Press.

Reiner, R. (1997) 'Policing and the Police', in Maguire, M., Morgan, R. and Reiner, R. *The Oxford Handbook of Criminology*. Oxford: Clarendon, pp. 997–1034.

Reiner, R. (2000) *The Politics of the Police* (2nd edn). Oxford: Oxford University Press.

Reiner, R. (2007) 'Criminology as a Vocation', in Downes, D., Rock, P., Chinken, C. and Gearty, C. (eds), *Crime, Social Control and Human Rights: From Moral Panics to States of Denial, Essays in Honour of Stanley Cohen.* Cullompton: Willan, pp. 407–421.

Reuss-Ianni, E. and Ianni, F.A.J. (1983) 'Street Cops and Management Cops: the two cultures of policing', in Punch, M. (ed.), *Control in the Police Organization*. Cambridge, MA: MIT Press, pp. 251–274.

Reuter, P. (1983) *Disorganized Crime: The Economics of the Invisible Hand.* Cambridge, MA: MIT Press.

Reuter, P. (1996) 'The Mismeasurement of Illegal Drug Markets: the implications of its irrelevance', in Upjohn, W.E. (ed.), *Exploring the Underground Economy*. Institute for Employment Research, pp. 63–80.

Reuter, P. and Greenfield, V. (2001) 'Measuring Global Drug Markets', *World Economics*, 2 (4): 159–173.

Reuter, P. and Haaga, J. (1989) *The Organization of High-Level Drug Markets.* Santa Monica, CA: Rand.

Reuter, P., Crawford, G. and Cave, J. (1988) *Sealing the Borders: The Effects of Increased Military Participation in Drug Interdiction.* Santa Monica, CA: Rand.

Rhodes, R.A.W. (1981) *Control and Power in Central-Local Government Relations.* Aldershot: Ashgate.

Rhodes, R.A.W. (1997) *Understanding Governance: Policy Networks, Governance, Reflexivity and Accountability*. Buckingham/Philadelphia: Open University Press.

Ribaux, O., Girod, A., Walsh, S., Margot, P., Mizrahi S., and Clivaz, V. (2003) 'Forensic Intelligence and Crime Analysis', *Probability, Law and Risk*, 2 (2): 47–60.

Ribaux, O. and Margot, P. (1999) 'Inference Structures for Crime Analysis and Intelligence using forensic science data: the example of burglary', *Forensic Science International*, 100: 193–210.

Ribaux, O. and Margot, P. (2003) 'Case-Based Reasoning in Criminal Intelligence using Forensic Case Data', *Science & Justice*, 43 (3): 135–143.

Ribaux, O., Walsh, S. J. and Margot, P. (2006) 'The Contribution of Forensic Science to Crime Analysis and Investigation: forensic intelligence', *Forensic Science International*, 156: 171–181.

Riechmann, D. (2007) 'Bush Signs Homeland Security Bill', *Washington Post*, 3 August.

Risen, J. (2008) 'Use of Iraq Contractors Costs Billions, Report Says', *New York Times*, 18 August. Retrieved on 16 November 2008 from http://www.nytimes.com/2008/08/12/washington/12contractors.html

Risen, J. (2010) 'Former Blackwater Guards Charged with Murder', *New York Times*, 7 January 2010.

Robertson, K.G. (1994) 'Practical Police Cooperation in Europe: the intelligence dimension' in Anderson, M. and Den Boer, M. (eds), *Policing Across National Boundaries*. London: Pinter, pp. 106–118.

Robertson, P.J. (1998) 'Interorganizational Relationships: key issues for integrated services', in McCroskey, J. and Einbinder, S.D. (eds) *Universities and Communities: Remaking Professional and Interprofessional Education for the Next Century*, Westport, CT: Praeger, pp. 67–87.

Royal Canadian Mounted Police (2008) *Police Internationale*. Ottawa: Gendarmerie Royale du Canada.

Running the World (2009) *The Economist*. 390, 8618, p. 52.

Ruyver, B. de and Surmont, S. (2007) *Grensoverschrijdend drugstoerisme. Nieuwe uitdagingen voor de Euregio's*. Antwerpen/Apeldoorn: Maklu.

Sabatier, M. (2001) *La Coopération Policière Européenne*. Paris: L'Harmattan.

Santiago, M. (2000) *Europol and the Police Cooperation in Europe*. Queenston, Lampeter: Edwin Mellen.

Savage, S., Charman, S. and Cope, S. (2000) *Policing and the Power of Persuasion: The Changing Role of the Association of Chief Police Officers*. London: Blackstone.

Schlegel, K. and McGarrell, E.F. (1991) 'An Examination of Arrest Practices in Regions Served by Multijurisdictional Drug Task Forces', *Crime and Delinquency*, 37 (3): 408–426.

Schmidl, E.A. (1998) 'Police Functions in Peace Operations: an historical overview', in Oakley, R., Dziedzic, M. and Goldberg, E. (eds), *Policing the New World Disorder: Peace Operations and Public Security*. Washington, DC: National Defense University Press, pp. 19–40.

Schmimmelfennig, F. (2004) 'Liberal Intergovernmentalism', in Wiener, A. and Diez, T. (eds), *European Integration Theory*. Oxford: Oxford University Press, pp. 75–94.

Schmitter, P.C. (2004) 'Neo-neofunctionalism', in Wiener, A. and Diez, T. (eds), *European Integration Theory*. Oxford: Oxford University Press, pp. 45–74.

Scott, W.R. (1987) *Organizations: Rational, Natural, and Open Systems* (2nd edn). Englewood Cliffs, NJ: Prentice-Hall.

Scott, W.R. (1992) *Organizations: Rational, Natural, and Open Systems* (3rd edn). Englewood Cliffs, NJ: Prentice-Hall.

Serafini, J. (2006) *Reinvigorating the African Standby Force – How to Develop the Envisioned African Solution for African Policing*. http://media.www.harbus.org/media/storage/paper 343/news/2006/10/03/Viewpoints accessed 27 October 2008.

Serafino, N.M. (2004) *Policing in Peacekeeping and Related Stability Operations: Problems and Proposed Solutions*. Washington, DC: Congressional Research Service, Library of Congress.

Shearing, C. (2007) 'Policing Our Future', in Henry, A. and Smith, D. (eds), *Transformations in Policing*. Aldershot: Ashgate, pp. 249–272.

Shearing, C. and Stenning, P. (1981) 'Modern Private Security: its growth and implications', in Tonry, M. and Morris, M. (eds), *Crime and Justice: An Annual Review of Research*. Chicago: Chicago University Press, pp. 193–245.

Shearing, C. and Stenning, P. (1983) 'Private Security: implications for social control', *Social Problems*, 30 (5): 493–506.

Sheptycki, J.W.E. (1995) 'Transnational Policing and the Making of a Postmodern State', *British Journal of Criminology*, 35 (4): 613–635.

Sheptycki, J.W.E. (1996) 'Law Enforcement, Justice and Democracy in the Transnational Arena: reflexion on the war on drugs', *International Journal of the Sociology of Law*, 24: 61–75.

Sheptycki, J.W.E. (1998a) 'Police Co-operation in the English Channel Region 1968–1996', *European Journal of Crime, Criminal Law and Criminal Justice*, 6 (3): 216–235.

Sheptycki, J.W.E. (1998b) 'The Global Cops Cometh: reflections on transnationalization knowledge work and policing subculture', *British Journal of Sociology*, 49 (1): 57–74.

Sheptycki, J.W.E. (2000) *Issues in Transnational Policing*. London: Routledge.

Sheptycki, J.W.E. (2002) 'Accountability Across the Policing Field: towards a general cartography of accountability for post-modern policing', *Policing and Security*, 12 (4): 323–338.

Sheptycki, J.W.E. (2002) *In Search of Transnational Policing: Towards a Sociology of Global Policing*. Aldershot: Ashgate.

Sheptycki, J.W.E. (2004) 'Organizational Pathologies in Police Intelligence: some contributions to the lexicon of intelligence-led policing', *European Journal of Criminology*, 1 (3): 307–332.

Sheptycki, J.W.E. (2005) *En quête de police transnationale: Vers une sociologie de la surveillance à l'ère de la globalisation*. Brussels: De Boeck & Larcier.

Sheptycki, J.W.E. (2007) 'The Constabulary Ethic and the Transnational Condition', in Goldsmith, A. and Sheptycki. J.W.E. (eds), *Crafting Transnational Policing: Police Capacity Building and Global Policing Reform*. Oxford: Hart, pp. 31–71.

Sherman, L.W. (1997) 'Policing for Crime Prevention', in Sherman, L.W. Gottfredson, D., MacKenzie, D., Eck, J., Bushway, P. and Bushway, S. (eds), *Preventing Crime: What Works, What Doesn't, What's Promising* (Chapter 8). Washington, DC: US Department of Justice.

Sherman, L.W. (1998) *Evidence-Based Policing: Second Ideas in American Policing Lecture*. Washington, DC: Police Foundation.

Siew, V.C. (2001) 'A Cross-Straits Common Market – Working Together to Build Prosperity in the Asia-Pacific Region', 17th Annual Joint Conference of the ROC-Australia and Australia-Taiwan Business Councils. Available at http://www.crossstrait.org/version3/subpage4/sp4-3.htm

Singer, P. (2004) *One World: The Ethics of Globalization* (2nd edn). New Haven: Yale University Press.

Sion, L. (2008) 'Dutch Peacekeepers and Host Environments in the Balkans: an ethnographic perspective', *International Peacekeeping*, 15 (2): 201–213.

Sismanidis, R. (1995) *Police Functions in Peace Operations*. Washington, DC: United States Institute of Peace.

Skolnick, J. (1996) 'A Sketch of Police Officers' "Working Personality" ', in Hancock, B. and P.M. Sharp (eds) *Criminal Justice in America*. Upper-Saddle River, NJ: Prentice-Hall, pp. 89–113.

Smith, B.W., Novak, K.J. Frank, J. and Travis, L.F. (2000) 'Multijurisdictional Drug Task Forces: an analysis of impacts', *Journal of Criminal Justice*, 28: 543–556.

Smith, M.G. [with M. Dee] (2003) *Peacekeeping in East Timor: The Path to Independence*. Boulder, CO: Lynne Rienner.

Smith, R. (2005) *The Utility of Force: The Art of War in the Modern World*. London: Allen Lane.

Soeters, J. and Manigart, P. (eds) (2008) *Military Cooperation in Multinational Peace Operations: Managing Cultural Diversity and Crisis Response*. London: Routledge.

Spapens, T. (2002) 'Case report on the Meuse-Rhine Euroregion', in Den Boer, M. and Spapens, T. (eds), *Investigating Organised Crime in European Border Regions*. Tilburg: IVA, pp. 51–72.

Spapens, T. (2008a) 'Policing a European Border Region: the case of the Meuse-Rhine Euroregion', in Guild, E. and Geyer, F. (eds), *Security Versus Justice, Police and Judicial Cooperation in the European Union*. Aldershot: Ashgate, pp. 225–241.

Spapens, T. (2008b) *Georganiseerde misdaad en strafrechtelijke samenwerking in de Nederlandse grensgebieden*. Antwerp/Oxford: Intersentia.

Spapens, T. and Fijnaut, C. (2005) *Criminaliteit en rechtshandhaving in de Euregio Maas-Rijn*. Antwerp/Oxford: Intersentia.

Spearin, C. (2008) 'What Manley Missed: the human security implications of private security in Afghanistan', *Human Security Bulletin*, 6 (3): 8–10.

Steden, R.V. (2007) *Privatizing Policing*. Cullompton: Willan.

Stein, A. (1990) *Why Nations Cooperate: Circumstance and Choice in International Relations*. Ithaca, NY: Cornell University Press.

Stenning, P. (2000) 'Powers and Accountability of Private Police', *European Journal on Criminal Policy and Research*, 8 (3): 325–352.

Stenning, P. (2009) 'Governance and Accountability in a Plural Policing Environment – The Story So Far', *Policing: A Journal of Policy and Practice*, 3 (1): 22–33.

Sterling, C. (1994) *Crime Without Frontiers: The Worldwide Expansion of Organised Crime and Pax Mafiosa*. London: Warner.

Storbeck, J. (1996) 'Europol: Probleme und Regelungsdefizite', in Hailbronner, K. (ed.), *Zusammenarbeit der Polizei- und Justizverwaltungen in Europa: die Situation nach Maastricht – Schengen und SIS*. Heidelberg: Kriminalistik Verlag, pp. 81–94.

Tanguay, D. (2003) *Récits motards: examen d'un conflit en milieu criminel.* Unpublished Master's thesis, École de criminologie, Université de Montréal.

Terrettaz-Zufferey, A.-L., Ratle, F., Ribaux, O., Esseiva, P. and Kanevski, M. (2006) 'Assessment of Data Mining Methods for Forensic Case Data Analysis', *Journal of Criminal Justice and Security* (Varstovoslovje), 3 (4): 350–355.

Toro, M.C. (1999) 'The Internationalization of Police: the DEA in Mexico,' *The Journal of American History*, 86 (2): 623–640.

Training for Peace Programme (2008) *Police Dimension Workshop: Establishing Management Structures, Implementing Training and Fostering Key AU Police Capabilities.* Pretoria: Institute for Security Studies.

Traynor, I. (2008) 'Bush Orders Clampdown on Flights to US', *The Guardian* (London), 11 February.

Tremblay, P. and Cusson, M. (1995) *Marchés criminel nationaux et analyse stratégique.* École de criminologie, Université de Montréal.

Tremblay, P., Morselli, C. and Cusson, M. (1998) 'Market Offences and Limits to Growth', *Crime, Law and Social Change*, 39, 4: 311–330.

Tupman, B. and Tupman, A. (1999) *Policing in Europe: Uniform in Diversity.* Exeter: Intellect.

Turcotte, M. (2003) *La transmission du savoir au sein d'une escouade spécialisée dans la lutte au crime organisé: Le cas de l'escouade Carcajou.* Master's thesis, École de criminologie, Université de Montréal.

UN (1992) *An Agenda for Peace: Preventive Diplomacy, Peacemaking and peacekeeping.* Report of the Secretary-General pursuant to the statement adopted by the Summit Meeting of the Security Council on 31 January 1992. A/47/277 – S/24111, available at http://www.un.org.Docs/SG/agpeace.html (retrieved 3 December, 2008).

UN (1995) *Survey of Crime Trends and Operations of Criminal Justice Systems.* A/Conf. 169/15/Add. 1.

UN (2000) *Report for the Panel on United Peace Operations.* United Nations. Brahimi Report. http://www.un.org/peace/reports/peace_operations Retrieved 3 December, 2008.

UN (2003) *Global Illicit Drug Trends.* New York: Office on Drugs and Crime.

UN (2007) *Capstone Doctrine for United Nations Peace Operations.* United Nations: Department of Peacekeeping Operations.

UN (2008) *United Nations Peacekeeping Operations: Principles and Guidelines.* Available at http://pbpu.unlb.org/pbps/Library/Capstone_Doctrine_ENG.pdf

UNFDC (2004) *Drugs and Crime Trends in Europe and Beyond.* United Nations: UNFDC.

United Nations Development Programme (2007) *Human Development Report 2007/2008.* New York: UNDP.

Van der Spuy, E. (2000) 'Foreign Donor Assistance and Policing Reform in South Africa', *Policing and Society*, 10: 343–366.

Van der Spuy, E. (2007) 'Police Reform in Africa: theory, policy and practice in the making?', *South African Journal of Criminal Justice*, 3: 307–327.

Van der Spuy, E. (2009) 'Police cooperation in the Southern Africa: politics and practicalities region', *Crime, Law and Social Change*, 51: 243–259.

Van Meter, K.M. (2002) 'Terrorists/Liberators: researching and dealing with adversary social networks', *Connections*, 24 (3): 66–78.

Van Outrive, L. (1998) 'Des tâches policières privatisées à une police grise: quatre recherches belges en la matière', *Criminologie*, 31(2): 7–30.

Van Reenen, P. (1989) 'Policing Europe After 1992', *European Affairs*: 45–53.

Vanderborght, J. (1997) *Over de grens: internationale politiesamenwerking getoetst aan de praktijk.* Brussels: Politeia.

Verbeek, J. (2004) *Politie en de nieuwe internationale informatiemarkt: Grensregionale politiële gegevensuitwisseling en digitale expertise.* The Hague: Sdu.

Vries, M.S. de (2000) 'The Rise and Fall of Decentralization: a comparative analysis of arguments and practices in European countries', *European Journal of Political Research*, 38: 193–224.

Waddington, P.A.J. (1991) *The Strong Arm of the Law.* Oxford: Oxford University Press.

Walker, N. (2003) *Sovereignty in Transition.* Oxford: Hart.

Walker, N. (2004) 'In Search of the Area of Freedom, Security and Justice: a constitutional odyssey', in Walker, N. (ed.), *Europe's Area of Freedom, Security and Justice.* Oxford: Oxford University Press, pp. 3–37.

Walsh, J. (2006) 'Intelligence-Sharing in the European Union: institutions are not enough', *Journal of Common Market Studies*, 44 (3): 625–643.

Walsh, S.J., Ribaux, O., Buckelton, J.S., Ross, A. and Roux, C. (2004) 'DNA Profiling and Criminal Justice – A Contribution to a Changing Debate', *The Australian Journal of Forensic Science*, 36 (1): 34–43.

Weisel, D. (1996) *Police Anti-Drug Tactics: New Approaches and Applications.* Washington, DC: Police Executive Research Forum.

Wendt, A. (2001) 'Driving with the Rearview Mirror: on the rational science of institutional design', *International Organization*, 55 (4): 1019–1050.

Wettestad, J. (2001) 'Designing Effective Environmental Regimes: the conditional keys', *Global Governance*, 7 (3): 317–341.

Whalen, P. (2005) *'Civilian Police in Peace Support Operations', The Ploughshares Monitor.* Available at http://www.ploughshares.ca/libraries.monitor. mond05d.htm. (retrieved 14 February, 2009.

Whose Law Must Mercenaries Obey? (2008) *The Economist*, 388, 8594: 45–46.

Wiener, A. (2000) 'The Embedded Acquis Communautaire: transmission belt and prism of new governance', in Neunreither, K. and Wiener, A. (eds), *European Integration After Amsterdam: Institutional Dynamics and Prospects for Democracy.* Oxford: Oxford University Press, pp. 318–341.

Wilber, D.Q. and De Young, K. (2008) 'Justice Dept. Moves Towards Charges Against Contractors in Iraq Shooting', *Washington Post*, 17 August. Retrieved on 17 November 2008 fromhttp://www.washingtonpost.com/wpdyn/content/article/2008/08/16/AR2008081601967.html?hpid=topnews

Williams, P. (1995) 'Transnational Criminal Organizations: strategic alliances', *The Washington Quarterly*, 18 (1): 57–72.

Williams, P. (1998) 'The Nature of Drug-Trafficking Networks', *Current History*, 97: 154–159.

Williams, P. and Savona, E. (1995) 'Transnational Organized Crime', in special issue of *The United Nations and the Transnational Organized Crime*, 1 (3): 65–83.

Wisler, D. (2007) 'The International Civilian Police Mission in Bosnia and Herzegovina: From Democratization to Nation-Building', *Police Practice and Research*, 8 (3) pp. 253–268.

Wood, J. and Shearing, C. (2007) *Imagining Security*. Cullompton: Willan.

Yang, Y.N. (1998) 'Informal Relationship Channels Are Needed in Dealing With the Cross Strait Criminal Cases', *Chinatimes*, 3 August, p. 15.

Yang, Y.N. (1999) *A Study of Police Organization*. Taiwan: Central Police University Press.

Yang, Y.N. (2000) 'Cross Strait Governments Need to Improve Non-Governmental Cooperation in Fighting with Cross Strait Crime', *Chinatimes*. 17 August, p. 15.

Yang, Y.N. (2006) *Organizational Behavior*. Taiwan: Central Police University.

Young, J. (1999) *The Exclusive Society: Social Exclusion, Crime and Difference in Late Modernity*. London: Sage.

Zagaris, B. (2002) 'US Practice in Cross-border Operations Against Transnational Crime', in Ruyver, B., Vermeulen, G. and Vander Beken, T. (eds), *Combating Transnational Organised Crime*. Antwerpen/Apeldoorn: Maklu, pp. 155–187.

Zhang, S. and K. Chin (2002) 'Enter the Dragon: Inside Chinese Human Smuggling Operations', *Criminology*, 40: 737–767.

Index

Added to a page number 'f' denotes a figure 't' denotes a table and 'n' denotes notes.